D0366593

TAX REFORM WITH THE 20/20 TAX

TAX REFORM WITH THE 20/20 TAX

The Quest for a Fair
and Rational Tax System

James C. Tanner

TAX REFORM WITH THE 20/20 TAX
THE QUEST FOR A FAIR AND RATIONAL TAX SYSTEM

iUniverse books may be ordered through booksellers or by contacting:

iUniverse
1663 Liberty Drive
Bloomington, IN 47403
www.iuniverse.com
1-800-Authors (1-800-288-4677)

Because of the dynamic nature of the Internet, any web addresses or links contained in this book may have changed since publication and may no longer be valid. The views expressed in this work are solely those of the author and do not necessarily reflect the views of the publisher, and the publisher hereby disclaims any responsibility for them.

Any people depicted in stock imagery provided by Thinkstock are models, and such images are being used for illustrative purposes only.
Certain stock imagery © Thinkstock.

ISBN: 978-1-4917-7337-6 (sc)
ISBN: 978-1-4917-7338-3 (e)

Library of Congress Control Number: 2015914666

Print information available on the last page.

iUniverse rev. date: 12/02/2015

In memory of my parents.

And to my wife, Cindy,
and our daughters, Megan, Lindsay, and Kirsten.

CONTENTS

PREFACE AND ACKNOWLEDGMENTS

The journey began in the faculty office of Grant Schafer, my first tax professor while I was in graduate school in the 1970s. Occasional visits to his office would often lead to theoretical discussions about our federal tax code with pointed questions for the learned professor about the reasons for such a complex tax system. He would often agree with me on the need to minimize the complexity of our tax laws, but I also remember him once wisely saying, "Tanner, I'm not sure there will ever be such a thing as a simple income tax or a simple tax of any kind, but if there is, I doubt if the majority of taxpayers would like it."

Over the years, my desire for tax reform has grown to adopt those professorial words, and I have gradually concluded that our nation needs to develop an income tax system that, if not simple, is at least generally understandable by most taxpayers. Rather than accepting the indecipherable Internal Revenue Code that we currently live with, the revised system I envision would be largely comprised of basic concepts that could be widely understood by the majority of voting Americans. We all remember that our war of independence was partly driven by the motto of "No taxation without representation," and yet today we live with a tax system that cannot be considered representative since it is unintelligible to almost all taxpayers.

This book is my zealous effort to explain how taxation in our country has evolved to its current dilemma, and why there is hope for a better solution to our nation's process of generating revenue in a more equitable and intelligible manner. Major tax reform will require a bipartisan effort of most members of Congress working together with the White House, and thus this book offers numerous solutions that would appeal to those on both sides of the aisle. Since the outcome of reform legislation should result in a user-friendly process for tax preparation, this book provides an all-new intuitive framework for the individual tax return process. Unlike our current tax system, the 20/20 Tax does not reduce the incentive to work, save, invest, or be married. Furthermore, this book and its new recommended tax system recognize the need for our nation's tax rates to be globally competitive to allow American companies to compete overseas. Finally, this treatise recommends a novel course of action to navigate the political process that has so often denied the passage of meaningful tax reform.

This book might never have been written if it were not for the motivational suggestion of my wife, Cindy. She had heard me talk for decades about the problems of our tax system and why it needed to be changed. I had considered a tax reform book for many years, but within a minute of receiving her spousal encouragement, the project received my green-light commitment, and there was no looking back. I am very grateful that Cindy has so loyally supported what seemed like an endless task of research and writing, which brought late hours and many weekends apart from each other.

Within a few months of starting this project, I had the fortuitous opportunity of meeting Arthur Johann Brudvick in his resident city of Bergen, Norway, where he taught tax law for many years at the Norwegian School of Economics. Arthur has provided me with a wealth of information about the history of tax reform in his country, which has been described in chapters 3 and 9, and which could be very beneficial to the US tax reform movement. He has written several books on the Norwegian income tax, and our frequent exchange of e-mails over the last four years has given me an invaluable perspective of Norway's very successful income tax and reform process. He has been an inspiration to me as well as a great teacher and mentor.

I am deeply indebted to my good friend and legal editor, Robert Severson, who met with me bimonthly for more than three years to read every line of my text and to serve as a constructive critic and guiding light for much of the tax theory comprising the 20/20 Tax. Bob is arguably the best tax attorney I have ever had the privilege to work with, and his insight and judgment have been priceless resources.

I also want to thank my longtime friend David Swan for his many days and nights of editing for English, grammar, and spelling miscues. He was extremely helpful in analyzing the content of my sentence and paragraph structures. Above all, Dave was a source of constant encouragement and truly a coach in every sense of the word.

Through much of the journey, I had the benefit of excellent research from Jonathan Kyte and Sabrina Strand, both graduate students at the University of Denver Tax Program. Sabrina was also extremely helpful in preparing the initial draft of Appendix A.

A deep debt of gratitude is owed to the participating staff members of my office, including Paul Stratmoen and Sylvia Tanner, who spent many days preparing tax calculations to compare the results of the 20/20 Tax to that of our existing tax law. And how can I say thanks enough to Annette Piltz, who word processed the entire manuscript and reprocessed many parts of it ten to twenty times without ever losing her great positive attitude. Annette was also very instrumental in obtaining authorization from the hundreds of reference sources, as was Dorothy Nies.

Many friends have read large parts of the manuscript and provided valuable input to the content of this book. Several other friends have taken great amounts of time to discuss their views on tax reform, including my colleagues of the AutoCPA Group who, for many years, have been a perpetual source of tax information in the area of small- and medium-sized businesses.

Finally, I wish to thank my CPA partner, Dick Heider, for the many tax reform articles and the long discussions we have had on the subject of future and past tax legislation. He has kept our firm's ship afloat in recent years, allowing me to pursue the elusive goal of a better tax system for our country.

Chapter 1

INTRODUCTION

PURPOSE

As this book goes to press (2015), Americans are dealing with a tax system that is so complex that most accountants, attorneys, politicians, and thousands of employees of the US Treasury Department do not understand the basic framework of the Internal Revenue Code, much less the myriad of finer points of our tax laws. American citizens are paying federal taxes based on a tax code that covers more than 73,000 pages for the statute and the regulations promulgated by the Internal Revenue Service (IRS) to explain this complex code.

What makes matters worse is the cost of compliance with the tax laws of our country. By most estimates, Americans paid over $160 billion last year to comply with the federal tax code. This was primarily the cost paid for tax return preparation and software as well as tax planning services to minimize taxes. That's more than $500 for every man, woman, and child in our country. And this cost does not include the price of enforcement by the IRS, one of the largest and most powerful bureaucracies in our nation.

Given the extreme complexity of our federal tax laws and the high cost of compliance, one would think that our Internal Revenue Code would result in a fair assessment of taxes for most Americans. Unfortunately, most of the people in our country do not believe that our tax system is resulting in fair treatment for American taxpayers.

The majority of accountants and tax attorneys, who prepare tax returns, would confirm this opinion.

The main purpose of this book is to propose a new framework and simplified rules for the federal individual income tax code of our country. This new framework would greatly modify our tax system into one that is easier for all US citizens to understand. The proposed changes in this book would apply the law much more fairly to families and individuals than does our current code. In addition, the changes advocated herein should result in the US Treasury collecting at least as much revenue as our current system, and possibly enough additional tax collections to make a measureable difference in the federal budget deficit. As an important side benefit, the cost of tax compliance and filing tax returns for the American public would be significantly reduced from what taxpayers currently experience.

NONPARTISAN APPROACH

One point I wish to make clear is that this book is not being written to further the ambitions of any one political party or political candidate. It is my hope that this book will serve as a valuable resource for concerned citizens of our country as well as members of Congress on both sides of the aisle. I intend for this written document to serve as a helpful explanation of the current basic framework of our federal individual income tax code for the millions of Americans who have never had a course in our income tax law, and for those who wish to be informed participants in the ongoing political debate about our nation's revenue laws and have a vested interest in its outcome.

DEFINING THE BASIC FRAMEWORK

Throughout this book, I will make numerous references to the "basic framework" of our Internal Revenue Code. This terminology is not a technical term for which you can find a definition anywhere in our tax laws. Rather, it is a term that I have borrowed from my first tax professor, Grant Schafer, who was a highly respected educator at the University of Denver. The term, basic framework, as I will use it and as Professor Schafer would have used it, is a reference to our complex system of income exclusions, itemized deductions, standard deductions, personal exemptions, tax credits, filing status, capital gain treatment, and the various tax rates that pervade our tax code and grow with the passage of time and new congressional tax legislation. This basic framework of our individual income tax code has additional complex dimensions to it, such as the alternative minimum tax (AMT), the kiddie tax, and what we call "stealth taxes" or phase-out taxes. Then there is that whole other tax category often referred to as payroll taxes, including the Social Security tax, Medicare tax, and self-employment tax, which together raise almost as much government revenue in some years as our federal individual income tax. In later chapters, I will attempt to describe and explain the roots of each of these tax terms and their pending value to our federal tax code.

It is one key premise of this book that the basic framework of our income tax code, as defined above, can and should be greatly simplified. Until this is done, our lawmakers will continue to add one layer after another on a tax code that is indecipherable to all but a very few individuals in our country. Our politicians can promise all they want about "lower and flatter rates," or even a "flat tax," but until we simplify the basic framework that I refer to above, we will never have a tax system that is understandable to the general public, nor will we see a significant decrease in the cost of tax preparation and compliance.

AUTHOR'S BACKGROUND

It is important to share my background so that the readers of this book will have some insights into the opinions that I express and the potential bias of my conclusions. I am a married sixty-six-year-old father of three daughters, who went to work for a Certified Public Accounting (CPA) firm more than forty years ago after earning an undergraduate degree in business (1970) at Santa Clara University and an MBA degree with an emphasis in accounting (1971-1972) from University of Denver (DU). Upon earning a second master's degree (taxation) at

DU (1975-1976), I started my own CPA firm in 1976, and I have been a practicing tax accountant ever since. During my career as a CPA, I have prepared or reviewed at least five thousand income tax returns and have watched the Internal Revenue Code be significantly amended well over one hundred times. Those who know my political convictions would correctly describe me as a Republican with a strong independent streak, who usually maintains moderate or conservative positions. I have voted for more than one of my resident state's (Colorado's) Democratic governors in the last forty-four years, but in all the presidential races after JFK, I have favored the Republican candidate (although sometimes reluctantly).

Aside from my party affiliation, I happen to have at least three other biases that are worthy of mention. One, I have worked much of my career with the owners of small- and medium-sized businesses. This experience has given me the opportunity to observe the challenges and problems of business owners, a group of people who create the majority of new jobs for Americans. I have a great deal of respect and empathy for the many issues that business owners deal with. Thus, I think our tax laws need to give the utmost consideration to the affordability and compliance issues that business owners must deal with as part of their existence.

Another bias that I should disclose is that I am a two-time cancer survivor who has dealt with the disease itself and the side effects of treatment off and on for the last seventeen years. My health experience has given me an acute awareness of the medical costs and treatments involved with one of the most dreaded life-threatening diseases. This health history, more than anything, has given me a great appreciation for the benefits of good health insurance and the affordable access to excellent doctors and their assistants. Without their care and treatment, I would not be writing this book and quite likely would not be alive today. My medical experiences have left me with a desire to see good healthcare promoted by our tax laws.

A third bias that many readers would be inclined to consider is the fact that I have worked most of my career as an accountant and tax return preparer. One might ask if I am willing to "bite the hand that feeds me" while writing this book. Let me explain why my livelihood should not be a deterrent to objectively stating the case for true tax reform in our country. Contrary to popular belief, the majority of CPAs do not generate most of their earnings from the preparation of individual income tax returns. To be specific, in my accounting practice, we prepare about 80% of our individual tax returns during four months of the year (March, April, September, and October). The other eight months of the year, we spend most of our time providing tax, accounting, and consulting services primarily to our business clients and not on the tax compliance work of individual tax returns (which is the main subject and focus of this book). For our firm, and this is true of many CPA firms, the preparation of individual income tax returns is a service that we provide to our clients to complement the rest of our work. Many of our individual tax returns are billed at a lower rate than our business clients are charged. To summarize my thoughts on the personal monetary impact of the tax reform advocated in this book, I feel it would have a downward effect on the earnings of my practice during the final years of my career. However, the benefit to my clients and to most Americans would far overshadow the negative impact on the profitability of my firm.

AVOID THE DRY SPOTS

The words "dry" and "tax" are synonymous for most people, as I expect will be the case for many of the readers of this book. You will undoubtedly hit some dry spots while reading the following text. When that occurs or you don't understand certain concepts, I encourage you to mark the spot and move on to the next chapter or subchapter of the book. Most of the chapters can be understood even if you miss something earlier in the book. Also, don't hesitate to use the glossary at the back to understand various technical terms of the dry tax world.

Chapter 2

BRIEF HISTORY OF OUR FEDERAL TAXES

Render to Caesar the things that are Caesar's
and to God the things that are God's.
—Jesus of Nazareth (Mark 12:17)

Ever since the early years of Western civilization, the issue of taxation has been a subject of constant debate. Our country was settled by immigrants who hoped, among other things, to escape from what they considered unfair taxes, only to find that the problem had followed them from the old world to the new.

From pre-revolution colonial days through the early 1900s, most American tax collections were a result of import tariffs and excise taxes. Colonists and early US citizens became accustomed to "indirect taxes" or consumption taxes on salt, tea, tobacco, wine, whiskey, and other commodities. Later, as the industrial age gained traction, the tariff laws were expanded to apply to machinery, equipment, and other manufactured goods.

The income tax is a relatively new concept in the quest for nations to raise revenue. France had attempted a "regressive" income tax in 1355 to finance the Hundred Years War. The rates were set at 10% for the poor, 5% the middle class, and 4% on the rich.[1] The regressivity of the tax was widely questioned and eventually was a contributing factor to its repeal.

The idea of taxing income did not really gain momentum until 1799 when Great Britain adopted a relatively successful wartime income tax, which was later repealed in 1816 after the conclusion of the Napoleonic Wars.[2] One generation later, the British Parliament resumed their income tax in 1842, and it has been continued and modified for the UK ever since.[3] Other European countries, including France, Austria, and Prussia (Germany), enacted their income tax laws in the early to mid-1800s as well.

THE U.S. INCOME TAX

The United States largely avoided an income tax code during the eighteenth and nineteenth centuries, with the exception of the Civil War income tax, which was started in 1862. The 1862 income tax assessed 3% on annual income above $600, plus an additional 2% levy on taxable income above $10,000 (approximately $200,000 in today's dollars). Heated debate over the complexity of the income tax began even before the new tax was signed into law. After the Civil War debt was repaid, there was a prolonged political battle to abolish the income tax, and it was repealed in 1872.[4]

The concept of taxing Americans on their incomes almost became a reality again in 1894 when William Jennings Bryan led the debate on the House floor in favor of reinstating the income tax. His populist bill proposed a 2% tax rate with a $4,000 exemption, so that the tax would affect only 85,000 citizens out of a population of 65 million.[5] The bill passed and became law without the signature of President Grover Cleveland. However, it was soon to be challenged, and in May 1895, the Supreme Court voted 5–4 against taxing "income from personal property" (including stocks, bonds, and rents). The income tax was deemed unconstitutional by the Court, and the entire bill was voided.[6]

The continued push for an income tax received little attention until 1906 when President Theodore Roosevelt proposed an income tax and an inheritance tax to finance many of his spending initiatives. However, it was not until 1909 that the House passed a functional income tax law.[7] Despite opposition by then President William Howard Taft to an income tax, the Senate hearings eventually led to the Sixteenth Amendment, and the required thirty-six states ratified the amendment allowing the income tax by February 25, 1913.[8] The recently elected President Woodrow Wilson called for tariff reductions to be replaced by a flat 4% income tax, but this proposal gave way to House members calling for a graduated tax of 1% to 7% on all income above $3,000 ($4,000 if married). Representative John Nance Garner (D-TX), of the powerful House Ways and Means Committee, argued successfully for "capacity-to-pay," and he won the day despite stiff opposition.[9] Our country has had a graduated or "progressive" income tax system ever since.

What started out to be a modest income tax system with low rates of 1% to 7%, [10] grew very quickly when the United States entered World War I. In 1918, John Nance Garner successfully championed a maximum tax rate of 77%, after telling one of his fellow House Democrats, ". . . we have got to confiscate wealth."[11]

After paying off most of our country's debts of World War I, the top tax rate was lowered to 25% for the years 1925 through 1931. This would have happened earlier (as proposed by Treasury Secretary Andrew Mellon in 1921); however, the lower rates were successfully opposed by Mr. Garner until the beginning of the full term in office of Calvin Coolidge (1925).[12]

In 1932, with the Depression years resulting in lower income tax collections, the Hoover administration desperately proposed a national sales tax of 2.25% on everything except food and inexpensive clothing. The then House Speaker John Nance Garner (1931–1933) reluctantly provided his endorsement for the measure, and it was widely supported by most congressional leaders on both sides of the aisle.[13] However, due to the regressive nature of a sales tax and its impact on manufacturers (resulting in higher consumer prices), it was widely opposed by farmers, retailers, wholesalers, and even the American Federation of Labor. One prominent politician who opposed the national sales tax was Franklin D. Roosevelt, who went on to defeat John Nance Garner as the Democrats' nominee for president in 1932. The sales tax position was one of the major issues that gave Roosevelt an edge over Garner, who became Roosevelt's vice-president from 1933 to 1941. Roosevelt maintained that federal and state governments should not levy taxes on each other's taxable base and that a general sales tax should be the exclusive tax revenue source of the states.[14] That policy decision, to oppose a national sales tax, has stood the test of time for more than eighty years despite many consumption tax proposals by various politicians and political groups over the years.

Up until World War II, the income tax mainly affected the upper class. However, in 1942, Congress passed a "temporary" income tax on individuals, often promoted as a "Victory Tax." The 1942 Revenue Act expanded the income tax from the upper class to a tax on the large majority of income earners. This Act of 1942 introduced the concept of tax withholding on all wage earners. Without this measure, most of the lower and middle class taxpayers would not have adequate funds to pay their taxes on the filing due date in the following years.

During World War II, the maximum tax rate went up to 94%, then dropped shortly after the War to 91% and it stayed there to pay off our war debts until the early 1960s when John Kennedy and Lyndon Johnson advocated a reduced maximum tax rate, which became 77%.[15] In 1969, Richard Nixon persuaded Congress to lower the tax rate on personal service income to a maximum 50% rate, and the highest rate on all other income was lowered to 70%.[16] Ronald Reagan took office in 1981 and in his first term managed to lower the maximum rate on most forms of taxable income to 50% (long-term capital gains on investments held more than one year were taxed at half of the ordinary rates).[17] The decline in tax rates continued in Reagan's second term with the passage of the 1986 Tax Reform Act, which lowered the maximum tax rate to 28% for all forms of income, including capital gains. The 1986 Act resulted in the lowest US income tax rates since 1931 (at 25%), and in the following years, the trend in maximum tax rates has been up and down as follows:

	Maximum	
Years	Rate	President
1990–1992	31.0%	George H. W. Bush
1993–2000	39.6%	William J. Clinton
2001	39.1%	George W. Bush
2002	38.6%	George W. Bush
2003–2008	35.0%	George W. Bush
2009–2012	35.0%	Barack H. Obama
2013–	39.6% *	Barack H. Obama

*The top rate is further increased by 3.8% on most forms of investment income beginning in 2013 as a result of the 2010 Patient Protection and Affordable Care Act.

SOCIAL SECURITY AND MEDICARE TAXES

Any discussion of our nation's income tax laws would be incomplete without addressing the taxpayer funding of Social Security and Medicare. In 1935, Franklin Roosevelt's social security system was adopted with a tax rate of 1% on the first $3,000 of salaries and wages.[18] (Note that this $3,000 of income was essentially untaxed by the individual income tax in the 1930s due to the personal exemption in place at that time.) In 1951, Social Security was expanded to include agricultural and self-employed workers.[19] Over the years, both the tax rates and the taxable wage base have gone up, so that by the year 2014, both the employer and employee were obligated to pay 6.2% of a worker's first $117,000 of earned income (primarily wages, salaries, and self-employment income).

In 1965, Lyndon Johnson signed Medicare into law at a rate of 0.35% of the FICA wage base ($4,200 in 1966).[20] Again, employers were expected to match the amount contributed by the employees up to the FICA wage base. The tax rate on the Medicare wage base was increased eight times between 1966 and 1986 to its current 1.45% rate, which is matched by employers' contributions of 1.45%. The self-employed are obligated to pay twice that rate, or 2.90%. In 1993, the

Clinton administration passed legislation to raise the Medicare taxable base to an unlimited amount of taxpayers' W-2 income.[21]

By 2009, federal revenue from FICA (Social Security tax and Medicare tax) had risen to about 42% of total federal tax receipts, but then it declined to approximately 34% of total federal receipts by fiscal year 2014 as corporate and individual income taxes increased. For the same years (2009 and 2014), federal individual income tax receipts were about 44% and 46% respectively of all federal tax collections.[22]

For discussion purposes, it is safe to say that the major revenue sources of FICA and the federal individual income tax account for approximately 80% of all revenues collected by the US government in recent years. It is with this tax magnitude in mind that most of this book's discussion is focused on the federal individual income tax with ample coverage of the two FICA components of Social Security tax and the Medicare tax.

Chapter 3

THE NORWEGIAN EXPERIENCE

In August 2011, my wife and I had the opportunity to visit the country of Norway. Before leaving the States, I was able to make an e-mail acquaintance with a Norwegian gentleman by the name of Arthur J. Brudvik. My purpose for contacting Mr. Brudvik was to learn what I could about the tax laws of Norway. I could not have found a better person. At that time, Arthur was winding down his career as an associate professor in tax law at the Norwegian School of Economics, located in the city of Bergen, Norway's second largest city. During his career, he has written several books on the subject of Norwegian income taxes. Having asked Arthur for an hour of his time, I was the very welcome recipient one morning of almost three hours of his explanations regarding Norwegian taxes, answers to my many questions, and a thoughtful discussion of the differences between our two countries' tax systems.

One of the first things I learned about Norway's taxes is that their tax system used to be much more complicated than it is today. Arthur explained to me that in 1991, his country's parliament adopted a new income tax system that greatly simplified their tax laws at the national level as well as the county and municipality levels. This new tax law went into effect in 1992. Their tax code of the last twenty-three years provides a much broader taxable base with fewer deductions, income exclusions, or other loopholes as compared to the years prior to 1992.

Arthur pointed out that under their old tax rules, they had several income tax rates, from 20% all the way up to about 70%. Today, the general tax rate in Norway on net income is 27% on almost all sources of income earned by its citizens and by its companies. For individuals, the first 48,800 Norwegian Kroner (NOK) (approximately $6,500) of net income is not taxed. On wages and salaries, individuals have to also pay a "top tax" of 9% on gross income between 550,550 NOK (approximately $73,000) and 885,600 NOK (approximately $118,000), and for salaries above 885,600 NOK the "top tax" is 12%. Thus, the marginal income tax rate for wages and salaries above 885,600 NOK will then be 39% (27 + 12).

When asked about Norway's capital gains rates, Arthur responded that all net income from capital, including capital gains, is taxed at 27% regardless of the total income of the taxpayer. For individuals, dividends are taxed at 27% but the income from dividends is reduced by a risk-free return on capital calculated yearly on the cost of the investments. Dividends paid are not deductible for companies, and dividends received are also not taxable income for companies.

We discussed the depreciation methods of our two countries, and Arthur described what they call the "Saldo method" of depreciation. Norway's approach to depreciation is infinitely simpler than the multiple US code sections and regulations found in our US system for depreciation. Try asking your tax preparer for an estimate of how many hours he or she spent last year computing the depreciation on business assets, or even just on business vehicles alone. The amount of time may astound you, especially if you multiply the preparer's annual hours (while computing depreciation) times their hourly rates (probably $100–$350 per hour). The Norwegians decided a long time ago that depreciation does not have to be as complicated as the United States and some other countries have made it out to be. I would strongly agree with this position.

Arthur went on to explain to me that one section of Norway's income tax code is actually quite generous. He provided the example of deductible interest expense. This deduction, which has become extremely complex and limited under US law, is actually very simple for the Norwegians. Arthur said that all interest paid is deductible under their law at the 27% rate, even interest paid on their credit cards for taking a vacation (a policy he does not actually agree with). Keep in mind that Norwegians are more frugal about taking on consumer debt than are Americans, and most of the Norse debt is incurred on their primary residences and vacation homes, where ownership is strongly encouraged by their policy makers. Arthur stated that regrettably the broad interest deduction has had an inflationary effect on housing prices. The main purpose of the introduction of the "top tax" on gross income of salaries and wages in 1992 was to reduce the benefit of the interest deduction. Nevertheless, can you remember the good old days prior to the 1986 Tax Reform Act, when all interest was deductible on Schedule A of your tax return? Yes, those were the days, my friends … (when life and taxes were much simpler).

When asked about Norway's equivalent to Social Security and Medicare taxes, Arthur informed me that his country has combined their tax for these government entitlements. Norway's tax rate for this is 8.2% paid by employees on the sum of all wages and salaries (of which 5.2% is for pension benefits). The top marginal tax rate for wages and salaries will then be 47.2% (39 + 8.2%). Norwegian employers pay an additional 14.1% on the same employee compensation for these entitlement benefits (the rate is lower for certain areas and certain industries). The self-employed individuals (those owning their own business) in Norway pay 11.4% as compared to their US counterparts paying 15.3% for Social Security and Medicare taxes (less a deduction for half the amount paid).

Note that pension benefits are subject to the 5.2% Norwegian Social Security tax while such benefits are not subject to tax in the United States for our Social Security and Medicare taxes. Also, note that all wages and salaries incur the 8.2% assessment, and not just the first $117,000 of compensation, which we experienced for the 2014 Social Security wage base in the United States. However, our Medicare tax does apply to unlimited wages, salaries, and self-employment income.

Please don't get me wrong. I am not advocating that the United

States adopt most of the provisions of the Norwegian tax code. All of us recognize that Norway is quite different in many respects from the United States, including the size of its population (about 5 million versus 320 million) as well as the social goals and public priorities of Norway's governing body and voting populace. On the other hand, Norway has an economy that is the envy of much of the world, with one of the highest gross domestic product (GDP) per person, abundant natural resources, a strong defense system (they are a highly respected member of NATO), and Norway has a budget *surplus* unmatched in the Western world. The point I'm trying to make is that here is a country with a complex and extremely successful economy that discovered over twenty years ago that it could greatly simplify its tax system and go into the twenty-first century as one of the world's economic bright spots. If Norway could remove the shackles of an overly complex tax system, is there not hope that the United States can do the same?

About halfway through my pleasant exchange with Arthur, I could not help asking him how his country was able to make such a major change to minimize the complexity of their tax system. He explained that it was largely due to the decision to delegate their tax reform and future writing of tax laws to an appointed committee of nonelected officials who were all tax experts. As Arthur explained it, the members of their appointed committee for Norwegian tax policy are much less likely to be swayed by political issues and special interest groups. There were no politicians on the committee. The committee that prepared the proposal for the new tax rules consisted of ten persons; the leader was a highly respected tax professor at the University of Oslo. On the committee was also a professor in economics from the Norwegian School of Economics. All the members were tax specialists or economists, some lawyers and some civil servants from the Ministry of Finance. In addition to the committee, there was a reference group of seventeen persons who also were tax specialists, accounting specialists, and representatives from industry and trade unions (the representatives from industry and trade unions were also tax specialists).

The proposal from the committee went to the Ministry of Finance, which made a law proposal to the parliament, and the law was decided in the parliament. The politicians were involved only in the latter stages, namely on the political level in the Ministry of Finance and in the parliament. The political level in the Ministry of Finance consists only of the Minister of Finance and a few state secretaries. The rest of the staff in the ministry consists of civil servants that are not politically appointed. The citizen committee for tax reform was appointed in 1988 and delivered its proposal in October 1989, and the ministry had the proposal for the new rules ready in 1990. The new rules were decided in the parliament in 1991 and put into effect in 1992.

The main consideration behind the changes of the tax law in 1992 was that the rules should be neutral in a way that it should not influence the use of resources of the country. When a company would choose between several investment projects, the ranking of the most profitable projects should be the same before and after tax. The tax should also be approximately the same regardless of which kind of legal entity was utilized for the project. The business should concentrate on earning a profit and not worry about reducing the taxes. The tax on the profit should be approximately the same if you organize the business as a corporation, a partnership, or as a sole proprietorship. One aim of the new rules was also to widen the tax base and reduce the tax rates. Finally, there should not be any loopholes.

According to Arthur, the Norwegian income tax law, including its regulations, is only about two hundred pages long. Note that the regulations are more detailed rules produced by the finance ministry or the tax collection agency to interpret and supplement the tax code. The law providing assessment of the tax is about one hundred pages (including the regulations). And the law that regulates the payment of tax is about seventy pages. Add it up, and there are less than four hundred pages of official Norwegian print dedicated to the corporate and individual income tax. Of course there are other Norwegian taxes, including the property tax, the value-added tax, and the wealth tax (on net worth), but Arthur informed me that the rules necessary for every type of Norwegian tax at the federal, county, and municipality level can all be found in one book of about 1,900 pages. By comparison, our US federal tax code and regulations currently exceed 73,000 pages, and this does not include the tax laws and regulations of our fifty states and thousands of counties and home-rule cities.

Norway's employers and business entities have to report tax data digitally to the Norwegian tax office much like the US employers and business entities provide to the IRS. Given their system's level of simplicity, every Norwegian taxpayer receives a preliminary tax return prepared by Norway's tax office. The taxpayers only have to correct what is wrong or missing on their government-prepared forms. Most taxpayers accept their government's original computations.

Chapter 4

CONSIDER THE ALTERNATIVES

In 1941, when London was under siege by the Germans in the Battle of Britain, one of the members of the English Parliament asked Prime Minister Winston Churchill if the United States was ever going to enter the War. Churchill is said to have responded with his famous words, "The Americans will do the right thing, but only after they have considered the other alternatives."

Today, our country stands at a crossroads with respect to its complicated system of federal taxes. Almost every year, we get a new tax reform proposal put forth by our politicians, political think tanks, or presidential panels, offering major reform to our tax system. Let's take a look at some of the tax reform proposals that have gained sizeable attention over the last forty years.

VALUE-ADDED TAX

Possibly the most talked about alternative tax system for the United States over the last four decades is the value-added tax (VAT). The VAT is a tax on consumption rather than income. All thirty-four members of the Organisation for Economic Co-operation and Development (OECD) use a VAT, except for the United States. Unlike sales taxes, which are paid only by the end consumer, the VAT is assessed at each level of production. Thus, all forms of business are subjected to the VAT in the same way. The VAT may distort economic decisions less than an income tax, due to the latter having numerous credits, deductions, exclusions and rates.

One noted author, Columbia law professor Michael J. Graetz, described the process of the VAT as follows:

> To illustrate how this works, consider a farmer who sells barley and other supplies to a brewer for $20. The brewer brews the beer and sells it to a retailer for $60. The retailer, in turn, sells the beer to customers for $100. The tax liability of the farmer under a 20 percent VAT is $4 (20 percent of his sales price to the brewer, assuming he hasn't made any purchases that have been subject to a VAT). The brewer's tax liability is $12 (20 percent of $60), less the credit he receives for the tax paid by the farmer ($4), for a net tax liability of $8. Similarly, the retailer's tax liability is $20, less the taxes previously paid on his purchases ($4 by the farmer, and $8 by the brewer), for a net tax liability of $8. Across the three levels of production, there has been a total tax liability (net of credits) of $20, or 20 percent of the final retail sales price, exactly what a retail sales tax at the same rate would collect entirely from the retailer. [1]

> This widely used "credit-method", which requires invoices for sales and purchases, decreases the opportunities for noncompliance under a VAT since the records from one firm can be used to check other firms' sales and purchases. A VAT therefore works essentially like a system of withholding for sales taxes. [2]

The VAT advantages, however, may be overstated by its proponents. Noncompliance for VATs range from 4% to 17.5% of tax owed, according to the OECD, somewhat comparable to the 14% noncompliance rate estimated for America's income tax.[3] Furthermore, certain categories, such as groceries and basic clothing, are often exempted or taxed at lower rates, thus diluting the VAT's efficiency.

Possibly the biggest disadvantage of the VAT is the fact that it is a regressive tax that hits the middle class much harder than the wealthy. To justify the complexity of its existence, most countries adopt a VAT rate of at least 10%, and at these double-digit rates, the tax definitely has a harsh impact on those who spend most of their earnings on consumption subject to the VAT.

In America, a federal VAT could be imposed on top of the retail sales taxes charged by forty-five states. However, the existence of both consumption taxes simultaneously would be a problematic combination. Thus, it seems that a US VAT tax would force most states to adopt a "piggyback" VAT system.

Selling a VAT to the American taxpayer would be extremely difficult. Americans would be asked to pay a brand-new tax on top of existing income taxes and state and local sales taxes. The best possibility may involve the replacement of the income tax or part of the payroll tax obligations for a large share of the middle class.

Liberals in the United States oppose a value-added tax because it falls more heavily on the middle class—that is, it's a regressive tax. Conservatives oppose it because it has the potential to raise taxes substantially. However, several liberals and some conservatives see it as the least of many evils to raise revenue and reduce the budget deficit.

As shown in table 4.1,[4] VATs are collected by governments of the world's major economies, with the notable exception of the United States.

Table 4.1

VATs of the OECD and China

Country	Year VAT First Implemented	VAT Rate In 2014
Australia	2000	10.0
Austria	1973	20.0
Belgium	1971	21.0
Canada	1991	5.0
Chile	1975	19.0
China	1994	17.0
Czech Republic	1993	21.0
Denmark	1967	25.0
Estonia	1991	20.0
Finland	1994	24.0
France	1968	20.0
Germany	1968	19.0
Greece	1987	23.0
Hungary	1988	27.0
Iceland	1990	25.5.
Ireland	1972	23.0
Israel	1976	18.0
Italy	1973	22.0
Japan	1989	5.0
Korea	1977	10.0
Luxembourg	1970	15.0
Mexico	1980	16.0
Netherlands	1969	21.0
New Zealand	1986	15.0
Norway	1970	25.0
Poland	1993	23.0
Portugal	1986	23.0
Slovak Republic	1993	20.0
Slovenia	1999	22.0
Spain	1986	21.0
Sweden	1969	25.0
Switzerland	1995	8.0
Turkey	1985	18.0
United Kingdom	1973	20.0
United States	--	None

Source: Organisation for Economic Co-operation and Development, Revenue Statistics, Table 2.1

As can be seen from table 4.1, the VAT became the "tax of choice" for all of the major European countries in the last one-third of the twentieth century. The movement that started in Western Europe in the late 1960s eventually spread to the Eastern European countries in the 1980s and 1990s upon the unraveling of the Soviet Union. The adoption of the VAT was well-suited to the growth of European social programs and welfare benefits, which required vast amounts of revenue to finance such government entitlements. Not only is the VAT a prolific revenue generator, but its regressive nature is acceptable to most voters when broad-based social programs are the reward for such higher taxes. If the United States continues to avoid the European model of extensive government-provided benefits to all citizens, then it is hard to surmise that American voters would accept a value-added tax. On the other hand, if our country were to adopt a more liberal agenda, then the VAT may gather increased interest.

Most politicians on both sides of the aisle are skeptical about the VAT for three other major reasons. One, it is a relatively complex tax that, when layered on top of our existing bevy of taxes, leads to much more complexity for businesses than what we already have. Second, as with all new tax systems, the resulting procedural changes are rarely popular with the voting public. And finally, as FDR successfully convinced our country in the 1930s, a national sales tax (similar to a VAT since it is a tax on consumption) would infringe on the taxable base of most states, which use the sales tax as a major revenue source.

FLAT TAX

A very popular option considered for US tax reform is the Flat Tax. This tax was well described by one of the more prolific writers about US tax policy, Martin A. Sullivan, an economist who taught at Rutgers University and later served on the Congressional Joint Committee on Taxation. In his recent book, *Corporate Tax Reform*, he provided the following informative explanation:

> The Flat Tax would replace the corporate and individual income taxes with a single-rate tax on individuals and businesses. The tax would be so simple that most taxpayers would only need to file a postcard-size return. The most prominent advocates of the Flat Tax are Steve Forbes, millionaire publisher and former

candidate for the Republican presidential nomination, and Dick Armey, Republican from Texas and former Majority Leader of the House of Representatives. [5]

Mr. Sullivan, while not endorsing this tax, goes on to further describe the Flat Tax as explained in the following paragraphs:

A Flat Tax takes some of the VAT business burden and imposes it on individuals. If you recall, a VAT does not allow a deduction for wages. In contrast, the Flat Tax does allow businesses to deduct wages. So, instead of wages being taxed at the business level, as under a VAT, wages are taxed at the individual level under a Flat Tax. To alleviate the burden on low-income families, the Flat Tax grants a large standard deduction—something like $20,000 each year for a family.[6] (Note that Steve Forbes, promoting his Flat Tax, recently recommended a standard deduction to eliminate the Flat Tax for a family of four on their first $46,000 of income).

A pure Flat Tax would eliminate all credits and special deductions. But there have been Flat Tax proposals that have allowed the deductions for mortgage interest and charitable contributions to remain. In the real world, any Flat Tax that had a chance of becoming law would probably retain many tax breaks that exist under current law. Even still, the exemption of capital gains, interest, and dividends from individual income tax—eliminating so many hundreds of special tax rules on saving and investment income—would make the new tax system much simpler relative to current law.[7]

Because of the generous standard deduction, the Flat Tax imposes less burden on the poor than a plain-vanilla VAT. But wealthy families still would significantly benefit relative to current law because corporate profits would no longer be double-taxed, the estate and gift taxes would be eliminated, and the progressive rate structure would be flattened ...[8]

Another strong proponent of the Flat Tax is Grover Norquist, the president of Americans for Tax Reform and probably the most effective tax-reduction advocate in Washington, if not the entire country. Mr. Norquist maintains that a single tax rate for all Americans is necessary to comply with the Constitution's mandate that taxes be "uniform." Possibly his most convincing argument for a Flat Tax is that it makes it very difficult for politicians to raise taxes due to the potential impact on most taxpayers and not just the wealthy.

After multiple studies and many years of political debate on the merits of the Flat Tax, it has failed to gain traction in our country as a politically acceptable tax system. Alternative versions of the Flat Tax have been used in Russia and some other Eastern Bloc countries with relatively good success. It continues to be favored by many conservatives, but there has been mostly staunch opposition by liberals and moderates in our country who argue that it would greatly increase taxes on the middle class and especially the upper-middle class while lowering taxes for the wealthy.

FAIR TAX

Another tax that has gained considerable attention in recent years is the Fair Tax, a national retail sales tax that would conceivably replace most federal taxes, including the corporate and individual income taxes, Social Security and Medicare taxes, and estate and gift taxes. This proposal was initially presented by Congressman John Linder in 1999, and during his final year in Congress (2010), his last version of the fair tax had some sixty co-sponsors.

The way that Linder's fair tax was to work is that all goods and services would carve out 23% of each dollar spent on a retail transaction, and that amount would go to the federal government. According to

Linder, this was the equivalent of a 23% sales tax. However, critics of the plan were quick to point out that if a widget cost the consumer $100 and this price included tax of $23 (as it would under Linder's fair tax), then the net value of the product was really $77, and the effective tax rate was approximately 30% and not 23%. [9]

John Linder and radio host Neal Boortz, co-authored a book in 2005 called *The Fair Tax Book: Saying Goodbye to the Income Tax and the IRS*. It actually became the first tax-reform book to make the *New York Times* best-seller list, assisted by several months of promotion by Boortz on his daily radio talk show.[10]

Despite the widespread sales of *The Fair Tax Book*, this tax concept has attracted many notable critics. Tax Analysts awarded it the 2005 "Prize for Worst Idea in a Serious Public Policy Debate."[11] The President's Advisory Panel on Federal Tax Reform (2005) concluded that the fair tax would require a federal sales tax rate of at least 34% to collect the equivalent amount of tax as our current federal system that it's meant to replace.[12] The 2005 President's Panel also reported that the added tax burden on most of the middle class would rise by 29%–36%, and not surprisingly, our country would still require a strong tax collection bureaucracy similar to the IRS.[13]

GRADUATED INCOME TAX PROPOSALS

From the previous descriptions of the VAT, the flat tax, and the fair tax, one can see that there is a recurring theme that keeps coming up. In the pursuit of more simple tax laws, our national leaders find themselves confronting regressive tax proposals that subject the middle class to higher tax burdens while lowering the effective tax rates on the wealthy. When you consider the various tax systems that have been implemented by the United States and other advanced countries, the graduated income tax approach is arguably the only major tax collection system that escapes the label of being regressive. In our country, the major government revenue sources are the individual income taxes (federal, state, and city), the Social Security and Medicare (payroll) taxes, state and city sales taxes, and the property taxes of state, city, and local governments. (Note that the corporate income tax and the federal estate tax are not included among these major government revenue sources due to their low percentages of revenue collected.) Of these major tax sources, only the individual income tax can truly be called a progressive tax. The others would properly be described as regressive taxes. In the last twenty years, the federal individual income tax raised approximately 30% of all federal, state, and local taxes in our country, and close to 45% of all federal revenues. As much as US citizens and taxpayers resent the complexity of our individual income tax code, most informed Americans are reluctant to give up one of the two truly progressive tax systems that we have (the other being the estate tax). Most of us would like to see the income tax be fair, more understandable, and easier to comply with. With these goals in mind, let's look at two recent proposals for tax reform of our graduated income tax.

SIMPSON-BOWLES TAX REFORM PLAN

One of the most publicized and enticing proposals for the reform of our tax system is that put forth in December 2010 by the National Commission on Fiscal Responsibility and Reform. This bipartisan commission (formed at the request of President Obama) was co-chaired by Erskine Bowles (D-NC), former White House Chief of Staff under Bill Clinton, and Alan Simpson (R-WY), former US Senator. The commission was comprised of nineteen total members, including six sitting US Senators and six sitting US Representatives, with an equal number of congressional Democrats and Republicans. The overall count tallied ten Democrats, eight Republicans, and one independent.

Following are direct passages from chapter II of the Report of the National Commission on Fiscal Responsibility and Reform:

> America's tax code is broken and must be reformed. In the quarter century since the last comprehensive tax reform, Washington has riddled the system with countless tax expenditures, which are simply spending by another name. These tax earmarks—amounting

to $1.1 trillion a year of spending in the tax code—not only increase the deficit, but cause tax rates to be too high. Instead of promoting economic growth and competitiveness, our current code drives up healthcare costs and provides special treatment to special interests. The code presents individuals and businesses with perverse economic incentives instead of a level playing field.[14]

The current individual income tax system is hopelessly confusing and complicated. Many taxpayers are required to make multiple computations to see if they qualify for a number of benefits and penalties, and many dole out large sums of money to tax preparers. Meanwhile, other taxpayers underreport their income and taxes, hoping to avoid the audit lottery. In short, the Commission has concluded what most taxpayers already know—the current income tax is fundamentally unfair, far too complex, and long overdue for sweeping reform.[15]

Tax reform should lower tax rates, reduce the deficit, simplify the tax code, reduce the tax gap, and make America the best place to start a business and create jobs. Rather than tinker around the edges of the existing tax code, the Commission proposes fundamental and comprehensive tax reform that achieves these basic goals: [16]

(1) **Lower rates, broaden the base, and cut spending in the tax code** ... Simplifying the code will dramatically reduce the cost and burden of tax preparation and compliance for individuals and corporations.

(2) **Reduce the deficit** … Under our plan, revenue reaches 21% of GDP by 2022 and is then capped at that level.

(3) **Maintain or increase progressivity of the tax code** … Tax reform must continue to protect those who are most vulnerable, and eliminate tax loopholes favoring those who need help the least.

(4) **Make America the best place to start a business and create jobs** … [17]

The plan below (Table 4.2) is an illustrative attempt to reflect the priorities of Commission members, but Congress could choose different options. We developed this illustrative plan to demonstrate that it is possible both to reduce rates dramatically and to achieve significant deficit reduction if tax expenditures are eliminated or scaled back and better targeted.[18]

Table 4.2:
Illustrative Individual Tax Reform Plan [19]

	Current Law	Illustrative Proposal (Fully Phased In)
Tax rates for Individuals	In 2010, six brackets: 10%, 15%, 25%, 28%, 33%, 35%. In 2011, five brackets: 15%, 28%, 31%, 36%, 39.6% [1]	Three brackets: 12%, 22%, 28%
Alternative Minimum Tax	Scheduled to hit middle-income individuals, but "patched" annually [2]	Permanently repealed
PEP and Pease [3]	Repealed for 2010, resumes in 2011	Permanently repealed
EIC and Child Tax Credit	Partially refundable child tax credit of $1,000 per child. Refundable EIC of between $457 and $5,666	Maintain current law or an equivalent alternative
Standard Deduction and Exemptions	Standard deduction of $5,700 ($11,400 for couple) for non-itemizers; personal and dependent exemptions of $3,650	Maintain current law; itemized deductions eliminated; so all individuals take standard deductions
Capital Gains and Dividends	In 2010, top rate of 15% for capital gains and dividends. In 2011, top rate of 20% for capital gains, and dividends taxed as ordinary income. [4]	All capital gains and dividends taxed at ordinary income rates. [5]
Mortgage interest	Deductible for itemizers; Mortgage capped at $1 million for principal and second residences, plus an additional $100,000 for home equity	12% non-refundable tax credit available to all taxpayers; Mortgage capped at $500,000; No credit for interest from second residence and equity
Employer Provided Health Care Insurance	Excluded from income. 40% excise tax on high cost plans (generally $27,500 for families) begins in 2018; threshold indexed to inflation.	Exclusion capped at 75th percentile of premium levels in 2014, with cap frozen in nominal terms through 2018 and phased out by 2038; Excise tax reduced to 12%
Charitable Giving	Deductible for itemizers	12% non-refundable tax credit available to all taxpayers; available above 2% of Adjusted Gross Income (AGI) floor
State and Municipal Bonds	Interest exempt from income	Interest taxable as income for newly-issued bonds
Retirement	Multiple retirement account options with different contribution limits; saver's credit of up to $1,000	Consolidate retirement accounts; cap tax-preferred contributions to lower of $20,000 or 20% of income, expand saver's credit
Other Tax Expenditures	Over 150 additional tax expenditures	Nearly all other income tax expenditures are eliminated [6]

1 Note: The 2011 rate changes above were delayed by Congress until at least 2013.

2 The Alternative Minimum Tax has been "patched" or softened by Congress for the years 199?–2011 (and expected for 2012).

3 PEP is the Personal Exemption Phase-Out. Pease is the phase-out of itemized deductions. PEP and Pease have phase-outs at different levels and are viewed as stealth taxes.

4 Collectibles (e.g., coin, art, antiques) are taxed at 28% and unrecaptured gain on real estate is taxed at 25%.

5 An alternative could be to exclude a portion of capital gains and dividends from income (e.g., 20%), reducing the effective top rate on investment income. To offset this while maintaining progressivity in the code, the top rate on ordinary income would need to be increased.

6 Under this plan, a few tax expenditures remain, for instance no changes are made to the tax treatment of employer pensions and tax provisions under PPACA largely remain in place. Note that the *payroll* tax base would remain the same as under current law, though there will be secondary revenue effects on the payroll tax side.

WHAT MAKES THE SIMPSON-BOWLES TAX PLAN SO WORTHY OF CONSIDERATION?

The National Commission, co-chaired by Bowles and Simpson, has fired a giant shot across the bow of our national tax reform debate. The commission's approach is monumental in that it challenges many of the concepts of our existing Internal Revenue Code, and at the same time, it offers major changes to the basic framework of our federal income tax. These changes help to provide a platform to simplify our tax laws, preserve the progressivity of our system, provide more fairness in our tax system, and quite possibly raise more revenue from a taxpayer population with a better understanding of and respect for our tax laws. The proposed changes, if enacted, should result in a more efficient enforcement by government taxing authorities and much less time for taxpayers to prepare and file their returns.

Some of the major provisions recommended by the commission can be summarized as follows:

(1) There should be only three rates (12%, 22%, and 28%) in their Illustrative Proposal for a revised federal income tax system (to replace the six rates for 2010 of 10%, 15%, 25%, 28%, 33%, and 35%). (Note that beginning in 2013, we have incurred a seventh rate of 39.6%.)

(2) The dreaded alternative minimum tax (AMT) would be permanently repealed, as would other so-called Stealth Taxes like the Personal Exemption Phase-Out (PEP) and Pease (the phase-out of itemized deductions). The AMT, PEP, and Pease add considerable complexity to the existing tax system.

(3) The time-honored approach of having itemized deductions (i.e., contributions and home interest), which benefit high-bracket taxpayers at a much larger tax savings than low-bracket taxpayers, would come to an end. Our system of itemized deductions would be replaced with a 12% credit on a reduced list of deductions.

(4) Employer-provided health insurance would no longer be 100% excludable. The exclusion would be capped at the seventy-fifth percentile of premium levels in 2014.

(5) The interest income received from newly issued state and local municipal bonds would not be tax-exempt but rather taxed as ordinary interest.

(6) Tax-deferred amounts paid to qualified retirement plans would be limited to the lower of $20,000 or 20% of earned income.

These and other changes proposed by the Simpson-Bowles Commission will be analyzed in depth in later chapters of this book.

DOMENICI-RIVLIN BIPARTISAN POLICY CENTER TAX REFORM PLAN

Former Senator Pete Domenici (R-NM) and former Budget Director (Clinton Administration) Alice Rivlin served as the Co-Chairs of the significant 2010 effort often known as the Debt Reduction Task Force. This nineteen-member panel was started on January 25, 2010 by the Bipartisan Policy Center, which was founded in 2007 by former US Senators Howard Baker (R-TN), Tom Daschle (D-SD), Bob Dole (R-KS), and George Mitchell (D-ME). The purpose of the task force was to develop a long-term plan to reduce our national debt and place our country on a sustainable fiscal path.

An important outcome of the task force was the formulation of the Bipartisan Policy Center (BPC) Tax Reform Plan, which proposes a major overhaul and simplification of the current tax code. While similar in many ways to the Simpson-Bowles Tax Reform Plan, the BPC Tax Reform Plan is even more innovative in some of its proposals. Following are most of the core elements of the BPC Plan issued on November 17, 2010:

(1) A two-bracket income tax with rates of 15% and 27%. Because there is no standard deduction or personal exemptions, the 15% rate applies to the first dollar of income. The 27% rate applies

approximately to income above $51,000 for single filers and $102,000 for married couples.

(2) The corporate tax rate will be set at 27%, instead of the current 35% level.

(3) Capital gains and dividends will be taxed as ordinary income (with a top rate of 27%), excluding the first $1,000 of realized net capital gains (or losses) for couples, and the first $500 for singles and heads of household.

(4) Introduce a 6.5% broad-based debt-reduction sales tax (DRST), phased in over two years during 2012 and 2013.

(5) To replace the overly complex earned income tax credit (EITC) and to help offset the effects of the DRST and elimination of personal exemptions, the standard deduction and the child credit, the BPC Plan will establish:

- a flat per child tax credit of $1,600 (higher than current law); and

- a refundable earnings credit (similar to the old Making Work Pay credit) but substantially higher at 21.3% of the first $20,300 of earnings.[20]

(6) Instead of the current system of itemized deductions, which disproportionately subsidizes the housing consumption and charitable giving of upper-income taxpayers, the BPC Plan will:

- Provide a flat 15% refundable tax credit for charitable contributions and for up to $25,000 per year mortgage interest on a primary residence.

- Eliminate the deduction for state and local taxes.

(7) Provide a flat, 15% refundable tax credit or a deduction for those in the higher bracket for contributions to retirement saving accounts up to 20% of earnings or a maximum of $20,000.[21]

(8) Include 100% of Social Security benefits in taxable income, but:

- create a nonrefundable credit for Social Security beneficiaries equal to 15% of the current standard deduction; and

- create a nonrefundable credit equal to 15% of an individual's Social Security benefits.

(9) Allow deduction of medical expenses in excess of 10% of Adjusted Gross Income (AGI) (as in current law).

(10) Allow deductions of miscellaneous itemized deductions in excess of 5% of AGI.

(11) Align the top individual capital gains and dividend tax rates (under the same rate of 15% or 27%).

(12) Eliminate the alternative minimum tax (AMT).

(13) Eliminate the need to file returns for most individuals. According to Tax Policy Center projections, only 50% of tax (family) units would be required to file tax returns, as opposed to 88% under the current tax system.[22]

DOMENICI-RIVLIN DEBT REDUCTION TASK FORCE PLAN 2.0

In 2012, the Bipartisan Policy Center (BPC) issued an updated tax reform plan known as Task Force Plan 2.0. The updated plan was similar in many ways to the November 2010 plan, but the following describes some of the major modifications:[23]

(1) The two-bracket income tax would have rates of 15% and 28% (rather than 15% and 27%).
(2) The corporate tax rate will be a flat 28% (rather than 27%).
(3) The child and dependent care credit would be retained from the current tax law.
(4) The refundable earnings credit would be only 17.5% of the first $20,000 of earnings (rather than 21.3% of the first $21,300 as originally proposed).
(5) The flat refundable tax credits for charitable contributions and home mortgage interest would begin at 20% in 2014, and then phase down to 15% over five years (the original plan would compute the credit at just 15% for all years).
(6) Effective in 2015, cap and then phase out over ten years the tax exclusion for employer-sponsored health insurance benefits.
(7) The original plan proposal for a 6.5% debt-reduction sales tax (DRST) presumably would be eliminated, as there was no reference to the DRST in Task Force Plan 2.0.

Chapter 5

A NEW BASIC FRAMEWORK

A major premise of this book is that our Internal Revenue Code is far more complicated than it needs to be and that this excessive complexity is costing Americans over $160 billion every year in professional fees as well as an endless amount of taxpayers' time. It has been almost thirty years (the Tax Reform Act of 1986) since Congress has made a serious attempt to simplify our nation's income tax laws. However, most tax attorneys and tax accountants would tell you that the 1986 Act, although it may have simplified certain sections of the Internal Revenue Code (like the number of tax brackets), for the most part left our country with a more complicated tax code than we had before the 1986 Act.

In order to explain how the basic framework of our current US income tax system works, let me format and define the general structure of an individual's annual tax calculation. Most taxpayers are required to navigate through a series of steps as summarized on the following three pages.

Tax Terminology and Definitions

Gross income is all income from whatever source except as otherwise excluded by the code.

An *exclusion* is an amount not included in a taxpayer's gross income.

A *deduction* is a subtraction from gross income to arrive at taxable income.

A *credit* is an amount subtracted from the tax computed on taxable income.

> ## * * Warning to the Faint of Heart * *
>
> The following three pages may include information that is hazardous to your health, leading to headaches, nausea, or extreme indigestion. If you are like most normal Americans who find the subject of taxation to be extremely mundane, then please feel excused from reading the next three pages, for fear that your confidence in our lawmakers will be shaken to the core, and such indecipherable content may cause you to refrain from reading any further pages in this book. If you are a tax professional, you may not want to read these obtrusive pages due to prior exposure to the material and the resulting cumulative effect of over-exposure. If you do not fit one of the above two classifications, then you must be a courageous reader who deserves the chance to be introduced to the inexplicable organism of the US Internal Revenue Code. Please proceed at your own risk.

FORMAT OF THE 2014 FEDERAL INDIVIDUAL INCOME TAX RETURN

Gross Income	This includes all sources of income, including wages, interest, dividends, business net income, rents, investment gains, pensions, etc.
Less: Exclusions	These are items included in the term "Income" but which are not considered income for tax purposes (i.e., scholarships, municipal-bond interest, employer-provided health insurance, gain on the sale of a residence, etc.).

Result: Total Gross Income

Less: Deductions for AGI:	These deductions *for* adjusted gross income include moving expenses, alimony paid, IRA deductions, student loan interest, self-employed health insurance, and certain other deductions.

Result: Adjusted Gross Income

Less: Deductions from AGI	These deductions *from* adjusted gross income are either the standard deduction (for 2014, $12,400 if married filing jointly) or one's itemized deductions (if greater), which are primarily medical expenses, taxes, interest paid, and charitable gifts.
Less: Exemptions	Most taxpayers are allowed to deduct a stated amount ($3,950 in 2014) for each spouse (if married) and the same amount for each of their dependents (mostly their children).
Result: Taxable Income	This is the amount to which various tax rates are applied and on which a preliminary tax is computed.
Regular Income Tax	This tax is calculated at each rate bracket. For 2014, there were seven "ordinary income" rates (10%, 15%, 25%, 28%, 33%, 35% and 39.6%), [1] three capital gain rates (0.0%, 15% and 20%), and three rates for unrecaptured Section 1250 gain (10%, 15%, and 25%).
Add: Alternative Minimum Tax	Often referred to as the AMT, this add-on tax primarily hits those who have a large amount of capital gains, exemptions, and/or state and local taxes. See chapter 5.4 for more information.

Result: Combined Regular and AMT Tax (Before Credits)

If you thought this part was *not* so bad, wait until you get to the next part where the computation gets more difficult.

Less: Nonrefundable Credits

There are many "nonrefundable" credits, including the foreign tax credit, the child care credit, three different education credits, the retirement savings contribution credit, the child tax credit (partly refundable), various residential energy credits, the mortgage interest credit, the adoption credit (partly refundable), the AMT credit, and dozens of other credits.[2] These nonrefundable credits may be claimed to the extent of the taxpayer's combined regular and AMT tax before credits[3] (prior page).

Result: Tax Less Nonrefundable Credits

Add: Other Taxes

These include self-employment tax (the equivalent of FICA and Medicare tax for business owners), additional tax on IRAs and retirement plans (usually for early distributions), household employment taxes (for W-2s issued to nannies, etc.), and a variety of other less common taxes.

Result: Total Tax

Less: Refundable Credits

There are several refundable credits[4] with the most common being the earned income credit, [5] the additional child tax credit, and the net premium tax credit (ACA). These refundable credits may be claimed even though they exceed the "total tax" calculation as arrived at above. In fact, refundable credits often result in "taxpayers" becoming "taxpayees" who pay no taxes and get refunds that exceed all of their tax withholding.

Less: Payments

Payments by taxpayers normally consist of federal income tax withheld (from wages and retirement benefits) and/or estimated quarterly tax payments. On a smaller scale, we sometimes see excess Social Security withheld when W-2s are issued to the taxpayer by two or more employers.

Result: Refund or Tax Due

> Congratulations on getting through the last three pages, especially if you understand what you just read.

IS THIS THE BASIC FRAMEWORK THAT WE WANT? IF NOT, THEN WHAT?

At this point, given that this three-page format summarizes the current basic framework of our tax system, you have to be asking the question, is this what Americans really want? Is this the best that we can come up with to raise almost half of our country's federal tax revenues? And is this the most fair and understandable approach that we can utilize for our income tax system? I suspect that most readers might respond by saying not only no, but *hell no*. If this is similar to your response, then please read further for an in-depth analysis of what we can do to greatly improve our nation's tax system.

If I were the benevolent king of the Noble (United) States of America (NSA), one of the first things I would set out to accomplish would be the codification of a new tax system that I would call the 20/20 Tax. The goal of this tax system would be to raise taxes in a way that is fair, understandable to all, and conducive to the economic growth of our country. The reason I would call it the 20/20 Tax is because most taxpayers would pay a marginal income tax rate of no more than 20% on their highest dollars earned, while almost all deductions and tax credits would benefit taxpayers at a consistent rate of 20%. For the more financially successful members of our society, there would be a higher income tax rate (30%), with most tax-saving provisions still calculated at a 20% rate. The lower income earners in our country would be taxed at a maximum income tax rate of 10% on earnings while still allowing a 20% rate on almost all tax-saving expenditures (credits and deductions).

In the following chapters of this book, I will explain how and why the 20/20 Tax proposal could replace our current individual income tax system, resulting in a system that is much fairer, much more understandable to all, and certainly much more conducive to economic growth than our present tax system.

The examples I will use in the following chapters will all be based on 2014 tax law since 2015 tax law and 2015 tax forms have not been finalized as of the printing of this book. It is unlikely that we will see significant changes from the amounts in the 2014 examples for either 2015 or 2016 due to the current low rate of inflation and election-year gridlock.

Americans spend 6.1 billion hours a year complying with it (the federal tax code)—enough work to keep over 3,000,000 people employed full-time without producing anything.

—*The Economist*, May 25, 2013, p. 29

Chapter 5.1

RETHINK ALL INCOME EXCLUSIONS

The Internal Revenue Code is filled with income exclusions, which are types of income deemed by Congress to be worthy of tax-free status. In addition, there are many exclusions resulting from the logic of case law, from relevant statutes, or from the US Constitution. These numerous exclusions have resulted in a vast reduction of taxable income for US taxpayers. Most current proposals for tax reform call for the elimination of certain exclusions in order to broaden the tax base for the purpose(s) of lowering tax rates and/or raising more tax revenue. Let's take a look at some of the more common exclusions that should be considered in an effort to broaden the tax base.

MUNICIPAL BOND INTEREST

In its December 2010 report, the National Commission on Fiscal Responsibility and Reform advocated the denial of tax-exempt status for newly issued municipal bonds.[6] This proposal has been pushed by tax reformers for many years and was called for by Randolph E. Paul in his classic 1947 book, *Taxation for Prosperity*, where he wrote "… this loophole, by which wealth finds a hiding place and which makes a mockery of the principle of taxation according to ability to pay, will remain wide open unless Congress takes steps to close it."[7] For several years, the taxation of state and local bond interest was thought to be unconstitutional. However, this issue was put to rest in the 1988 Supreme Court case of *South Carolina v. Baker*, 485 US 505 (1988), which rejected the argument that tax exemption for state and local bonds is constitutionally protected.[8] There is no question that ending the exclusion of municipal bond interest would raise the cost of borrowing for states and municipalities, but reformers argue that much of this additional cost would be offset by the states responding with legislation to tax federal Treasury bonds, which pay interest that is currently exempt in all fifty states.[9]

By one estimate, the 2014 annual cost to the Treasury of tax-exempt municipal bond interest was $42.7 billion,[10] meaning that approximately $130 billion of municipal bond interest income is tax-exempt. Ending this exclusion would have a large impact on our country's effort to broaden the taxable base and eliminate some of the complexity in our income tax code. I fully support the effort to end the tax-free status of new municipal bonds, as proposed by the National Commission on Fiscal Responsibility.

TAXING 0-85 PERCENT OF SOCIAL SECURITY BENEFITS

The taxation of Social Security benefits is one of the most complex and least talked about issues in our tax code, yet it affects the majority of retirees in a very illogical way. Most recipients of Social Security (including many high-net-worth individuals) pay no income taxes on these retirement benefits, while others pay full ordinary tax rates on 85% of their Social Security receipts. As you might guess, there are many taxpayers who fall in between and are taxed on 1% to 84% of their Social Security benefits received. Why the big disparity? It can be explained in just one word: politics. Let's look at the history of this issue.

Following a pair of 1938 Treasury Department tax rulings, Social Security benefits were totally excluded from federal income taxation. This changed, however, with the passage of the 1983 Amendments to the Social Security Act, often hailed as one of the proudest accomplishments of the bipartisan efforts of Ronald Reagan and Tip O'Neill. In the search for revenue to support the 1983 Act, Congress deemed it necessary to tax some retirees on their Social Security. Relying on the 1979 Advisory Council and estimates by the Social Security Administration, it was stated that "workers now entering covered employment in aggregate will make payroll tax payments totaling no more than 17% of the benefits that they can expect to receive. The self-employed will pay no more than 26% on average. Rough justice would be done, however, if half the benefit (the part commonly if somewhat inaccurately attributed to the employer contribution) were made taxable."[11] So with the infinite wisdom of Congress, it was decided in 1983 to tax one half (50%) of Social Security benefits received. However, in an effort to make the increased tax more acceptable, it was decided to provide a generous exclusion so that beneficiaries of low to moderate incomes would not be taxed. Thus, Congress decided to totally exclude Social Security benefits for those single retirees with less than $25,000 of gross income and those married couples with less than $32,000 of gross income. This effectively allowed almost 90% of Social Security recipients to go untaxed on their Social Security benefits in the 1980s.

Ten years later, the 1993 Omnibus Budget Reconciliation Act went one step further and established a secondary set of exclusion thresholds ($34,000 for an individual and $44,000 for married couples filing a joint return). Taxpayers above these modified adjusted gross income (MAGI) levels were then taxed on 85% of their Social Security benefits.

To describe how complicated this provision of the tax code is, let me give you the most understandable (although incomplete) explanation I have been able to find, written by Theodore J. Sarenski, CPA:

> An individual or married couple adds one-half of the Social Security benefits received during a tax year to their modified adjusted gross income (MAGI). MAGI is adjusted gross income (AGI) further adjusted by any of a number of items, including the addition of any tax-exempt interest income that was excluded from AGI. If the total exceeds $25,000 for a single or head-of-household filer or $32,000 for a married couple

filing jointly (base amount), 50% of the Social Security benefit usually is taxable. If the total exceeds a base amount of $34,000 for a single or head-of-household filer or $44,000 for a married couple filing jointly, 85% of the benefit is usually taxable. Social Security benefits are 85% taxable, with no base amount, for taxpayers who are married filing separately …[12]

Did you understand all of that? If there is a part of the tax code that could be simplified and should be, this is it. If we are serious about simplifying the Code and broadening the taxable base, we must draw the line right here and make 50% of all Social Security benefits includable in the adjusted gross income and the taxable income of all recipients, regardless of their income levels. Most taxpayers should be able to understand that this significant change is only taxing the matching portion of FICA (50%) that was paid for by their employers and never previously taxed to the employees. Since the employer pays a matching amount to the Social Security Administration, the amount paid by the employer and later included in the Social Security benefits received by an individual has not been subject to income tax. It is this one half of a retiree's benefits that should be included in taxable income for every US taxpayer.

EMPLOYER-SPONSORED HEALTH INSURANCE

Any serious attempt to broaden the taxable base must give ample consideration to the taxation of employer-sponsored healthcare benefits. This tax-free benefit dates back to World War II when employers found a way to compensate their employees without increasing their taxable wages, which was prohibited during the war effort. For 2011, this tax-free benefit cost the US Treasury approximately $294 billion, including almost $114 billion in FICA taxes.[13] This cost is more than any other exclusion or deduction in the Internal Revenue Code.

Let's take a look at why this tax expenditure is so monumental. First, the majority of Americans are covered by employers' health insurance plans. This coverage often includes dental insurance and a host of other medical-related costs paid for by employers, and sometimes even medical reimbursement for those healthcare items not covered by their employer-provided insurance. These benefits are typically 100% excluded from the employees' W-2 wage statement. Not only are they tax-free for income tax purposes at today's 10–39.6% federal income tax rates, but they are also free of any Social Security and Medicare tax, which saves another 7.65% tax for most employees as well as a matching 7.65% for their employers. Furthermore, most states have their own income tax systems that also exclude employer-sponsored healthcare benefits, saving the employee another 3–13% depending on their state's tax rates. So it's not unusual for some high-income couples to save taxes of fifty cents for every dollar of employer healthcare benefits received. On the other hand, many lower-paid workers who are provided health insurance may only see the savings of the 7.65% FICA tax.

One way or the other, the employees who receive employer-sponsored health benefits have a definite tax advantage over their fellow citizens who must pay for their health insurance out of their own pockets. Those self-paying insured employees (of which there are about 15 million in our country) on individual self-paid medical plans[14] usually get no tax benefit at all, unless their income is low enough to qualify for the new ACA premium assistance tax credit. In order for those paying their own medical insurance to get any tax benefit, they must be one of the 30% of taxpayers who itemize their deductions, and even then their medical expenses, including insurance, are only deductible to the extent that they exceed 10.0% of their adjusted gross income (AGI). Thus, most taxpayers rarely qualify for medical deductions, leaving most of those who buy their own health insurance with little or no tax savings to pay their insurance premiums. (For years after 2012, the medical itemized deduction threshold was increased from 7.5% to 10.0% of AGI for those under the age of sixty-five.[15] The threshold is still 7.5% of AGI for those over sixty-five.)

The question becomes how do we correct this gross inequity in our tax law? Do we really want a system in which the highly compensated potentially get 50% or more of their healthcare premiums paid by government tax dollars while millions of Americans get no tax benefit at all when they pay their own medical insurance? I don't believe so. A simple solution to this issue of apparent injustice would be to do away with the tax benefits completely and essentially tax all employer-provided healthcare benefits at their full cost for each employee who receives such benefits. This draconian approach, by itself, would certainly raise huge sums of money for our federal government (probably more than $3 trillion over the next ten years). And it would substantially improve our Social Security and Medicare trust funds. However, there are at least two major disadvantages to consider in this approach. The first problem is that far fewer employers would offer healthcare benefits if there were no tax savings for employees, and it would increase the employers' Social Security and Medicare matching amount due to the employee taxation of the premium paid by the employer. This by itself would be a deal breaker for the voting public as well as many of our politicians. The second major concern is that most American taxpayers have come to expect and feel entitled to tax-free employer-sponsored health insurance. The thought of having more taxable income with no tax savings at all on healthcare benefits is probably just plain unacceptable to most Americans. In other words, that train left the station a long time ago.

It is my belief that the majority of Americans need government assistance or a "tax break" if they are to maintain health insurance coverage that is either self-paid or employer-provided. Knowing that some taxpayers receive tax benefits exceeding 50% of the cost of employer-provided coverage, and substantially more taxpayers receive zero tax savings on their self-paid coverage, I think the right thing to do is to provide a fixed-percentage refundable tax credit to every American who receives employer-paid coverage that is reported as income on one's W-2, and provide the same credit to those who self-pay their own health insurance. How much should this credit be? It is my opinion that it would take a federal credit of 20% to "politically replace" our current taxpayer subsidy of employer-provided healthcare. At the same time, I believe that most states should and would provide their residents with an additional 4%–6% credit, which would mostly be paid for by the states' higher revenues generated by the newly taxable employer-provided healthcare benefits. Would the 20% federal credit be revenue neutral? It probably would actually increase tax revenues, at least with respect to replacing the tax-free insurance benefits provided by employers. As for the 20% credit going to the self-paying insured, this may be revenue neutral provided the 20% credit is not designated for those who receive similar or greater subsidies under the 2010 Affordable Care Act or other subsidized healthcare programs. This proposed 20% health insurance credit is described henceforth as the Uniform Health Insurance Credit (UHIC).

To minimize the cost to the US Treasury, Congress may consider putting a ceiling on the insurance coverage eligible for the 20% UHIC credit, but I do not feel this is necessary or beneficial.

One might ask, how does the above healthcare tax proposal help to accomplish the stated goals of this book, namely to simplify the tax law and provide a more fair and equitable tax system? With respect to simplicity, it does little except to take away employers' motivation to offer complicated "cafeteria plans" and/or medical reimbursement plans that would no longer be excluded from employees' income. These "tax-advantaged" employer plans would mostly go away if the tax benefits of such plans were repealed. As for the additional reporting of employer-sponsored health insurance by employers, this requirement has already been written into the law by the 2010 Affordable Care Act. It went into effect in 2013 for employers with more than 250 employees, and it will eventually apply to all employers with fifty or more employees. As much as I would like to avoid this healthcare benefit reporting, it would be a necessary obligation of all employers in order for their employees to receive the benefit of a 20% federal tax credit.

Concerning the tax equity issue, it's hard to deny that a 20% federal credit for all citizens' healthcare insurance is considerably more equitable than the tax-free employer benefit system we have experienced for the last seventy years. If we consider two family households who each have adjusted gross incomes of $100,000, but only one of the couples has

$15,000 of additional tax-free employer provided health coverage, is it fair that both couples pay the same amount of income tax and FICA tax? I think most of us would answer that this is not fair.

The 20% federal credit would solve this inequity by allowing the uninsured couple the same tax benefit upon buying their own self-paid coverage. One further consideration in the adoption of a credit-based healthcare tax system is whether all employers offering healthcare should be provided a tax benefit to replace the payroll tax savings they currently experience by compensating their employees with healthcare benefits that are not subject to FICA. There are also modest adjustments to consider for such things as unemployment insurance and workers' compensation insurance that would increase somewhat if healthcare benefits were all reported as employee taxable wages. In order to encourage employers' continued healthcare coverage for their employees, an employer tax credit could be adopted at little or no cost to the US Treasury since it would merely replace employers' current payroll tax savings resulting from the exclusion of employer-provided health insurance. A comparable alternative would be a FICA exemption for employers who would not be required to pay the matching 7.65% on employee income attributable to employer-sponsored health insurance. However, if the employer is not obligated to pay FICA tax on employee health insurance, should the FICA tax be waived for employees as well? For a further explanation and conclusion of the payroll tax issue, this will be covered in Chapter 6.10.

GAIN ON THE SALE OF A PRIMARY RESIDENCE

For many years, a gain upon the sale of a taxpayer's primary residence was taxed only to the extent that the adjusted sales price of the old residence exceeded the total cost incurred in buying a replacement residence. Under prior law, the home replacement had to occur within one year before or after the sale date of the old residence. This section of the tax law resulted in significant taxes on many families who traded down upon selling their home, as well as those families who could not meet the one-year replacement rule. There were also significant complexities in determining the gain on one's third or fourth primary residence due to a complicated formula for carrying forward the lower cost basis of earlier home(s) and the adjustment for the "deferred gain" on each prior residence.

In 1997, Congress decided to simplify the treatment of gain upon the sale of a primary residence. No longer is there any concern about the replacement of a prior home by one of equal or higher price. An individual may exclude from gross income up to $250,000 of gain ($500,000 on a joint return) realized on the sale or exchange of a principal residence.[16] This exclusion may not be used more frequently than once every two years, although a partial or reduced exclusion may be available even if a taxpayer does not meet the "ownership and use" requirements or has already used the exclusion within the two-year period.[17]

The problem with the current tax treatment of excluding gain on one's primary residence is that the exclusion of as much as $500,000 has proved to be an overly generous provision in the tax law, especially during the years of the housing boom. In fact, for many years it encouraged a large amount of housing speculation that was a significant contributing factor to the housing bubble that our country went through in the early years of this century. In 2010, the total cost of this exclusion to the Treasury was estimated to be roughly $15 billion.[18] However, just five years earlier, in 2005 at the peak of the housing boom, the $250,000/$500,000 exclusion on the sale of principal residences cost the Treasury approximately $23 billion.[19]

If Congress has the political will to increase the taxation of high profits upon the sale of one's principal residence, it should consider one of two alternatives. First, the code could be changed to allow the exclusion of only $250,000 rather than $500,000 for a married couple filing jointly, and at the same time limit a single person to only $125,000 of gain upon the sale of a residence. In most parts of the country, this would still avoid taxable gain upon the sale of a large majority of personal residences. However, in certain states with high priced real estate like California and Massachusetts, this would result in many homeowners reporting large taxable gains upon the sale of their homes, thus requiring better recordkeeping of one's home improvements in order to minimize the eventual taxable gain to be reported upon sale.

An alternative solution that could be more politically acceptable would be the concept of allowing the exclusion of as much as $25,000 (single) or $50,000 (married) for each full year of ownership and occupancy up to a maximum of $250,000 (single) and $500,000 (married) after more than ten years of ownership. So, a married couple that owned and lived in a home for just over two years could exclude the first $100,000 of gain upon the sale of their home. Likewise, a married couple who owned and occupied their home for more than ten years could exclude as much as $500,000, the same ceiling as provided under current law, only it would require home occupancy of ten years rather than just two years. I would opt for this second alternative. It may not do anything to simplify the law, but at least it is not a difficult concept to grasp. And it provides a greater sense of fairness to the taxpaying public who would no longer have to listen to the bragging stories of the quick-flip developers who find it tax-appealing to move every two to three years while avoiding any taxable gain upon the sales of their residences.

How much would the US Treasury save by a change in the law that only excludes $25,000–$50,000 per year for years one to ten of home ownership? Available research does not seem to give us an answer, but my best guess is that it would result in additional taxes of $1–$2 billion per year. And, if we can broaden the taxable base in enough ways, a billion dollars here and a billion dollars there will help to significantly lower the tax rates for all Americans.

RETIREMENT PLAN EXCLUSIONS

The US tax law contains numerous provisions to encourage retirement savings. The ones that come to mind for most of us are the traditional Individual Retirement Account (IRA) for individuals and the company-sponsored 401(k) plan to benefit employees. In addition, there are numerous other tax-deferred retirement plans including but not limited to Roth IRAs, SEP-IRA plans, SIMPLE IRA plans, 403(b) plans, 457 plans, profit-sharing plans, defined contribution pension plans, and defined benefit pension plans. These government-sanctioned retirement plans result in billions of dollars of taxpayer savings every year, most of which are on a tax-deferred basis where no tax is paid until money is drawn out of the respective plan to provide for taxpayer consumption.

The Simpson-Bowles Commission put forth a controversial position that would modify retirement plans by putting a cap on the annual tax-deferred contributions "to the lower of $20,000 or 20% of income."[20] A similar concept with the same limits was proposed by the Domenici-Rivlin Debt Reduction Task Force.[21] These proposals from the commission and the task force are often referred to as the "20/20 cap" (not to be confused with the author's "20/20 Tax"). It is not clear if such proposals are intended to apply to traditional defined benefit (DB) plans, which guarantee employees a defined level of monthly benefits upon reaching retirement. If so, this would present difficult challenges to the actuaries involved in making their present value calculations, which are necessary to determine the annual employer contributions for DB plans.

I am left to assume that the 20/20 cap is meant solely for defined contribution (DC) plans for employers that are obligated to contribute to the employees' individual accounts with no employer guarantee of the investment return on such employee accounts. For 2014, the combination of employer and employee tax-deferred contributions was the lesser of $52,000 per year (plus $5,500 for employees over the age of fifty) and a percentage limit of 100% of an employee's compensation.[22] Thus, the thought of lowering the current $52,000 or $57,500 limits down to $20,000 would seem rather Draconian to those who are used to funding their retirements at or near today's higher limits. I am especially concerned about the unintended consequences of the 20/20 cap limits since I know that many small businesses can only justify the time and expense of qualified retirement plans if there are significant benefits going to the highly compensated and the owners of such businesses.

If the current limits are to be reduced for all DC plans, I would advocate a combined limit of $40,000 and eliminate the "catch-up" provision of $5,500 for those over age fifty. Taking this one step further, I believe that the most common form of DC plan, the 401(k) plan, should have a limit of $20,000 for all employee annual contributions rather than today's $17,500 (plus $5,500 for those over age fifty). Likewise, the employers who sponsor 401(k) plans should have the ability to contribute up to a matching $20,000 for each of their participants. As for the proposed 20% limit on employees' compensation, there are very few employers or employees who would feel constricted by this limit, and I think this part of the 20/20 cap should probably prevail, if only to prevent low-paid family members of business owners from taking undue advantage of the qualified plan rules if allowed to use the 100% limit. If 401(k) participants and their employers each have the limit of $20,000 for a combined total of $40,000, it seems logical that 403(b) plans, 457 plans, other profit-sharing plans, and defined contribution pension plans should all have a combined $40,000 limit per employee as well as the 20% of compensation limit for both the employer and the employee contributions.

Obviously, the government will not realize as much revenue with a $40,000 contribution limit as it would using a $20,000 limit (per Simpson-Bowles and the task force), but as a matter of public policy, I find the $40,000 limit to be a more prudent choice for all DC plans except those of an IRA nature which have historically had lower contribution limits to discourage employers from dropping their qualified retirement plans in favor of the less costly and more simplistic IRAs.

LIFE INSURANCE POLICIES

One of the most often discussed exclusions of income is that provided for life insurance settlements. Most life policies are sold with the understanding that upon the death of the insured the policy will pay the named beneficiaries in tax-free dollars. This tax-free payment applies even when the death benefits far exceed the premiums paid on such policy. On the other hand, if the policy is cashed in before the insured is deceased or is terminally ill, there is often a taxable gain resulting in taxes due from the owner and/or beneficiary of the policy.

It is hard to question the tax-free concept of death benefits coming from life insurance, especially when the payments of life insurance premiums are almost never deductible by the party who pays the premium. However, there is at least one large exception to the nondeduction rule of life insurance premiums, and that is the case of group-term life insurance for as much as $50,000 of death benefit per employee. Ever since 1964, there has been an income exclusion for the first $50,000 of group-term life insurance provided on a nondiscriminatory basis to full-time employees of any organization. This provision of the law has been around for so long that most employees take it for granted. There are approximately seventy million people in our country who have as much as $50,000 of group-term life insurance free of cost and free of tax. According to Table 1 issued by the Internal Revenue Service to determine the value of group-term life insurance coverage, the value of $50,000 of annual coverage is only $30 for an employee at the age of twenty-one.[23] However, at the age of sixty-five, that value skyrockets to $762.[24] Clearly, this has been a significant tax-free benefit to older employees. The weighted average tax-free benefit of all insured employees is roughly $200 per employee, and if you figure that the income tax and payroll taxes add up to roughly $60 per employee, then the US Treasury loses approximately $4 billion per year from the exclusion of group-term life insurance. The Treasury could definitely use this money to reduce rates for all taxpayers.

PERCENTAGE DEPLETION ALLOWANCE

The discussion of income exclusions would not be complete without considering the percentage depletion allowance, which can arguably be considered a deduction or an exclusion. If ever there was a divisive issue among politicians, this is it. Many (if not most) Republicans defend percentage depletion as a necessary incentive for the oil and gas industry. At the same time, most Democrats argue that percentage depletion is an unnecessary tax break for the wealthy.

"Depletion" is an accounting term that applies to the diminishing nature of assets such as oil, gas, timber, and mineral deposits. Depletion is intended to reflect the declining value of an asset due to the extraction of the resource. It is often compared to depreciation deductions that permit a direct cost recovery of hard assets (i.e., machinery and equipment), but percentage depletion is actually more of an income exclusion since it allows the taxpayer to deduct a percentage of the gross income derived from the extraction of natural resources, with no relationship to the actual cost of the resource.

An early history of percentage depletion can be found in the book *Taxation for Prosperity by Randolph E. Paul*:

> The original theory was that mineral properties were exhausted in the process of producing financial return, and that part of every dollar received was not taxable because it was not profit, but only a return of capital invested. World War I carried this theory to new outposts. The geologic experts of the day bemoaned our scant supply of oil which, they predicted, would hardly last ten years. The incentive tax experts of 1918 took up the chorus. They proposed that something should be done to stimulate production and protect the prospector or wildcatter who risked drilling in unknown territory.[25]
>
> Congress responded in 1919 with a provision for "extraordinary" treatment of taxpayers discovering oil and mineral properties, giving them the right to base their depletion not on original cost, as previously, but on the fair market value of the property at the time of discovery. The extraordinary became ordinary, and this provision remained in the statute with some modifications for many years, notwithstanding the fact that our oil reserves appeared to be increasing rather than diminishing.[26]

The 1918 Act extended a benefit to the owners of mines and oil and gas wells which other property owners did not have. Insofar as oil was concerned this provision had a good deal of sense to it in the light of its premise – scarcity of oil. It may have been a desirable subsidy at the time, but the provision required the valuation of every discovered well and every newly discovered mine in the United States, which turned out to be a great administrative burden. When the administrative job was largely done, the labor it involved was used as an exchange for changing the statute. Beginning in 1925 depletion of oil and gas wells was to be computed on a percentage basis. Whether he made a discovery or not, the owner of an oil or gas well was to be allowed to deduct 27½% of the gross, or 50% of the net, income from his property, whichever was less. In 1932, similar treatment in varying percentages was accorded to the owners of iron, coal, sulfur, and metal mines ...[27]

The tax law's solicitude for oil and gas producers does not stop when the property has paid for itself, as with depreciation allowances on plants and machines, but goes on as long as production continues. On the average the allowance for oil has consistently run about six times the actual depletion sustained on actual cost. Comparable treatment of taxpayers engaged in manufacturing activities would permit charging the cost of part of physical plant to expense and the continued deduction of depreciation until the amounts charged off aggregated six times the original cost of the plant.[28]

In 1933, the Treasury recommended the elimination of percentage depletion on mines and oil wells on the ground that it was a "subsidy" to a special class of taxpayers. President Roosevelt and the Treasury followed with a similar recommendation in 1937. In 1942 (Treasury) Secretary Morgenthau cited percentage depletion as an "example of special privilege." ... The ill-fated attempts to plug up this loophole were not renewed in 1943.[29]

Fear of interference with the war effort was a large factor in dissuading Congress from accepting the Treasury's 1942 recommendations. That fear need no longer haunt us, and the problem of eliminating a discriminatory subsidy in favor of an established industry must be faced sometime in the future. Whatever may be the situation regarding some minerals, it may be faced without fear of an oil shortage; indeed, if there is danger of a shortage in the future, the wise policy may be to conserve the oil we have rather than to encourage production. Subsidies are sometimes justifiable; at other times they are perilous ventures.[30]

As a separate issue, there is the favorable tax treatment of intangible drilling and development costs (IDCs). Operators of domestic oil, gas, or geothermal wells may elect currently to deduct IDCs rather than charge such costs to capital, to be expensed later over many years through depletion or depreciation.[31] IDCs include labor, fuel, materials, supplies, truck rent, and costs of drilling equipment. The beneficial first-year deductions of these IDCs leave many tax experts hard pressed to justify the additional tax benefit of percentage depletion.

As a result of many years of congressional efforts to eliminate the percentage depletion allowance, the huge tax breaks for large oil companies are a thing of the past. The Tax Reform Act of 1969 reduced the depletion percentage to 22% for oil and gas producers. Then in 1974, with soaring oil profits and high prices at the pump, percentage depletion was completely repealed for large oil companies. According to Martin Sullivan in his book *Corporate Tax Reform*, "Under current law, percentage depletion, is only available to independent producers, and the allowable deduction (exclusion) varies from 5 to 22% of gross income from a producing property (actual percent depending upon the natural resource) …"[32]

Today, percentage depletion only costs the Treasury about $1 billion per year.[33] However, the issue still creates a great amount of political rhetoric, with most Democrats wanting to do away with it completely, and many Republicans holding onto this political baton in favor of the smaller (but still very influential) players in the extractive industries.

It is my belief that our Congress should let this historic legislative battle of the last ninety-seven years come to a close in order to promote overall tax reform (although I realize that this will not happen easily). By itself, the benefit to the Treasury of terminating percentage depletion is hardly enough to lower our tax rates, but the elimination of complexity and political friction would go a long way to promote bipartisan cooperation in the overall effort of tax reform.

Chapter 5.2

THE ISSUES OF CAPITAL GAINS AND DIVIDENDS

> The tax on capital gains directly affects investment decisions,
> the mobility and flow of risk capital ... the ease or difficulty
> experienced by new ventures in obtaining capital, and thereby
> the strength and potential for growth in the economy.
> —President John F. Kennedy, 1963

Another major tax issue that has led to widespread debate among economists, politicians, and taxpayers is the question of how to tax capital gains and losses. A capital gain or loss occurs when there is a sale or exchange of a capital asset. The most common forms of capital assets are stocks and bonds, personal residences, and rental real estate. However, many other types of assets held for investment qualify as capital assets. By definition, capital assets do *not* include inventories or other assets held for sale in the ordinary course of business. Nor does this term include certain other assets such as business accounts receivable or copyrights held by a taxpayer whose personal efforts created the work of a literary or artistic composition.

As a general rule, the gain in value of a capital asset is not recognized for tax purposes until such asset is sold or exchanged. Once the sale or exchange occurs, any gain is normally taxed in that year. A capital gain or loss is considered long-term if the capital asset is held by the taxpayer for more than one year.[34] Long-term capital gains are generally taxed at rates lower than those applicable to ordinary income or short-term gains.

When our nation's income tax was revived in 1913, most tax advisors assumed that capital gains should not be taxed. Their authority for this position was the 1872 Supreme Court case of *Gray v. Darlington* in which the court ruled that because capital gains may be the result of income (or value) earned over several years, taxing such gains as if all of the income had been earned in the year of sale was unconstitutional.[35] This decision was handed down the same year that the initial income tax of the Civil War was repealed.

Despite the 1872 Supreme Court case in favor of the tax-free treatment of capital gains, the Internal Revenue Service ignored this ruling when the income tax was resurrected in 1913.[36] The government's position led to numerous conflicting court decisions. It was not until 1921, in the case of *Merchants Loan and Trust Co. v. Smietanka*, that the Supreme Court overruled itself and decided that capital gains were indeed taxable if Congress were to approve this position.[37]

With the court having decided the issue of constitutionality, it was left up to Congress to decide how capital gains should be taxed. Keep in mind that for the years of 1913–1921, capital gains were taxed as ordinary income, but at the same time capital losses were fully deductible against ordinary income.[38] Because taxpayers had more capital losses than gains, the net result to the Treasury was a loss of revenue[39] from the combination of capital gains and losses being treated as ordinary gains and losses.

In 1921, Congress provided the first legislative relief for capital gains, taxing such gains at a rate of just 12.5% when ordinary income was being taxed as high as 73% in the aftermath of World War I.[40] That same year (1921), Treasury Secretary Andrew Mellon proposed that ordinary rates be lowered to 25% and his proposal was eventually adopted in 1925 after much of the war debt had been repaid.

Over the last ninety-five years, there have been continuous changes in the capital gain rates as determined by Congress. Table 5.2-1 on the next page tells the story of such constant change. As you will note from the table, the first maximum capital gain rate of 12.5% (1922–1933) was replaced with a large tax increase during the depth of the Depression (1934–1937) when capital gains took on a complicated structure that resulted in maximum capital gain rates of 50.4% and 63.2% given an asset holding period of one to five years. If capital assets were held for more than five years, the maximum capital gain rates in 1934–1937 were lower (25.2% and 31.6%). The higher tax rates of the mid-1930s have been considered an economic mistake by many historians and economists alike.

Table 5.2-1 Tax Treatment of Long-Term Capital Gains of Individuals 1913–2012[41]

Year	Holding Period	Percentage of Long-term Capital Gains Includible in Income	Maximum Capital Gain Rate	Highest Ordinary Income Rate
1913-1921	n/a	n/a	n/a	7 -77%
1922-1933	Over 2 years	50	12.5%	24-73%
1934-1937	Over 1 year to 2 years	80	50.4% in 1934-35; 63.2% in 1936-37	63%, 79%
	Over 2 years to 5 years	60	50.4% in 1934-35; 63.2% in 1936-37	63%, 79%
	Over 5 years to 10 years	40	25.2% in 1934-35; 31.6% in 1936-37	63%, 79%
	Over 10 years	30	25.2% in 1936-37; 31.6% in 1936-37	63%, 79%
1938-1941	Over 18 months to 2 years	66.67	30% of included gain, equivalent to a 20% rate	79 – 81.1%
	Over 2 years	50	30% of included gain, equivalent to a 15% rate	79 – 81.1%
1942-1969	Over 6 months	50	25% (26% in 1952-53)	70-94%
1970-1971	Over 6 months	50	29.5% in 1970; 32.5% in 1971	70%
1972-1976	Over 6 months	50	35%	70%
1977	Over 9 months	50	35%	70%
1978	Over 1 year	50 for gains before 11/1/78, 40 after 10/31/78	35% before 11/1/78	70%
			28% after 10/31/78	70%
1979-1980	Over 1 year	40	28%	70%
1981	Over 1 year	40	28% for gains before 6/10/81	69.1%
			20% for gains after 6/9/81	
1982-1986	Over 1 year (6 months for assets acquired after 6/22/84	40	20%	50%
1987	Over 6 months	100	28%	38.5%
1988-1990	Over 1 year	100	28-33%	28-33%
1991-1992	Over 1 year	n/a	28%	31%
1993-5/7/97	Over 1 year	n/a	28%	39.6%

Year	Holding Period	Percentage of Long-term Capital Gains Includible in Income	Maximum Capital Gain Rate	Highest Ordinary Income Rate
5/8/97-1998	Over 1 year	n/a	20% for gains after 5/7/97 (10% for gains otherwise taxed in the 15% bracket) Maximum 28% for collectibles Recapture Sec. 1250 depreciation at 25% Certain small business stock at 14%	39.6%
1999-2000	Over 1 year	n/a	20% (10% for gains otherwise taxed in the 15% bracket) Maximum 28% for collectibles Recapture Sec. 1250 depreciation at 25% Certain small business stock at 14%	39.6%
2001	Over 1 year	n/a	20% (10% for gains otherwise taxed in the 15% bracket) Maximum 28% for collectibles Recapture Sec. 1250 depreciation at 25% Certain small business stock at 14%	39.1%
	Over 5 years	n/a	8% for gain if otherwise taxed at 10%	
2002	Over 1 year	n/a	20%, (10% for gains otherwise taxed in the 15% bracket) Maximum 28% for collectibles Recapture Sec. 1250 depreciation at 25%	38.6%
	Over 5 years	n/a	Certain small business stock at 14%	15%
2003-2007	Over 1 year	n/a	15% (5% for gains otherwise taxed in the 15% bracket) Maximum 28% for collectibles Recapture Sec. 1250 depreciation at 25%	35%
			Certain small business stock at 14%	15%
2008-2012	Over 1 year	n/a	15% (0% for gains otherwise taxed in the 15% bracket) Maximum 28% for collectibles Recapture Sec. 1250 depreciation at 25% Certain small business stock at 14%	35%

Source: Present Law and Background Information Related to the Taxation of Capital Gains
Prepared by the Staff of the Joint Committee on Taxation, September 14, 2012

As you can see from the preceding table 5.2-1, there have been numerous changes to our nation's taxation of long-term capital gains. We have seen only two periods during the first hundred years of the federal income tax where our tax code had a stretch of ten or more years with little or no change in the capital gain rate structure (1922–1933 and 1942–1969). Coincidentally, the twenty-eight-year period of 1942–1969 is considered by many to be the golden years of our economic history and one of the best periods for the US stock market. Back then, it was quite simple for a tax accountant to explain to his or her clients that long-term capital gains were taxed at half of the ordinary rates with a maximum rate of 25 percent.

Unfortunately, in 1969 our Congress started to mess with success or tinker with what seemed to be a good thing. In an effort to raise revenue, the Tax Reform Act of 1969 increased the maximum capital gains rate to 29.5% effective for 1970 and to 32.5% effective for 1971 (or 50% of ordinary rates if less). For each of the following years of 1972–1977, the highest effective rate was raised to 35%. Given these higher rates, one would expect a revenue increase for the Treasury. In fact there was a revenue decrease for capital gains collections for the five year period of 1970–1974 ($32.3 billion)[42] as compared to the previous five years of 1965–1969 ($37.9 billion) when adjusted for inflation. A similar experience occurred after the 1986 Tax Reform Act ushered in a 28% maximum capital gain rate (up from 20%) for the future years of 1987–1996. During the five year period of 1987–1991, the Treasury's capital gain collections totaled $182.2 billion[43] as compared to the previous five-year period of 1982–1986 when the Treasury collected $191.2 billion at the lower maximum rate of 20% (these collections for the earlier years are again adjusted for inflation).

The major reason for lower tax collections at higher tax rates is a factor known as the "lock-in-effect." This widely accepted theory maintains that taxpayers will defer their investment sales in times of high tax rates and that they are much more likely to sell capital assets when the capital gain tax rates are relatively low. In most cases, owners of capital assets have the option of holding their assets for many years, even until death, at which time most assets escape taxation entirely due to the long-standing tax policy of stepped-up basis, which allows the heirs of a decedent a new adjusted tax basis for inherited assets at a value equivalent to fair market value at the date of death. Just as with many economic issues, our economists do not all agree on the impact of the lock-in-effect or at what rate it becomes an influencing factor. However, it is difficult to dismiss totally this concept based on the evidence presented.

ARGUMENTS FOR AND AGAINST LOWER CAPITAL GAIN RATES

In a 1995 policy analysis done by the Cato Institute, a conservative think tank, different positions regarding future capital gain tax cuts were presented.

The following arguments are made for a reduction in the capital gains tax:

1. A cut (rate decrease) would increase investment, output, and real wages. If the tax on the return from capital investments—such as stock purchases, new business start-ups, and new plant and equipment for existing firms—is reduced, more of those types of investments will be made. Those risk-taking activities and investments are the key to generating productivity improvements, real capital formation, increased national output, and higher living standards.

2. A cut would liberate locked-up capital for new investment. For those already holding investment capital, a capital gains tax reduction might create an "unlocking effect": individuals would sell assets that have accumulated in value and shift their portfolio holdings to assets with higher long-run earning potential. The unlocking effect might have strong positive economic benefits as well: the tax cut would prompt investors to shift their funds to activities and assets—such as new firms in the rapid-growth, high technology industry—offering the highest rate of return.

3. A cut would produce more tax revenue for the government. If a capital gains tax cut increases economic growth and spurs an unlocking of unrealized capital gains, then a lower capital gains rate will actually increase tax collections.

4. A cut would eliminate the unfairness of taxing capital gains due to inflation. A large share of the capital gains that are taxed is not real gains but inflationary gains. The government should not tax inflation.[44]

Opponents of a capital gains tax cut question those advantages. They argue that a capital gains cut will do the following:

1. Provide a large tax cut for the wealthiest Americans. Most capital gains taxes are paid by Americans with incomes above $200,000.

2. Have very little positive impact on the U.S. economy. Many argue that taxes do not influence investment decisions and that even if there were an unlocking effect, investors might simply consume the proceeds or shift investment from U.S. assets to foreign assets that may hold greater earnings potential.

3. Increase the budget deficit. If a capital gains tax cut reduces revenues and increases the federal budget deficit, then savings and investment in the United States might actually fall after the tax cut. This would only worsen America's reported capital shortage. Senator Bill Bradley (D-NJ), for instance, has been highly skeptical of the economic dividend from a capital gains tax cut and has argued that eliminating the federal budget deficit should be a higher policy priority.[45]

There is at least one other reason put forth by the opponents of low (or no) capital gains tax. They argue that a low capital gains rate has increased the wealth gap between the very wealthy and the middle class in our country. There may be some evidence for this position, but is this argument and other negative positions sufficient to offset the above listed reasons in favor of preferential treatment for capital gains?

Regardless of one's political affiliation, it is hard to ignore completely the persuasive positions of either side. However, I find the most compelling argument for low capital gain rates to be the issue of inflationary gains and the unjust taxation of such illusory income. The inflation penalty of capital gains taxation is a valid reason to avoid ordinary income rates when taxing the sale of capital investments. A former member of the Federal Reserve Board, Alan Blinder, stated in 1980 that "most capital gains were not gains of real purchasing power at all, but simply represented the maintenance of principal in an inflationary world."[46]

It is not uncommon for taxpayers to pay capital gains taxes on gains that are attributed solely to inflation. In 1993, Wayne Angell, who was then a governor of the Federal Reserve Board, stated the following:

> ... The average real tax rate (after adjusting for inflation) on investments in NASDAQ stocks from 1972 to 1992 had been 68%. The real tax rate on investments in the Standard & Poor's Composite Index over the same time period was 101%. The average real tax on a portfolio of New York Stock Exchange stocks was 123%. And the average real tax on the Dow Jones Industrial Average over that 20-year period was an astounding 233%. In other words, according to three of the four indexes, investors paid capital gains taxes on investments that actually lost money after adjusting for inflation—and thus the tax simply diminished the principal.[47]

One possible solution to the unfairness of taxing capital gains resulting from inflation would be the concept of indexing. The purpose of indexing would be to increase the original cost of capital assets by the percentage of inflation from the time of purchase to the time of sale. This concept has been proposed many times over the years by politicians in both parties, but it has always failed to win approval primarily due to its added complexity as well as the loss of revenue to the Treasury. President George H. W. Bush made a capital gains tax cut the centerpiece of his economic agenda,[48] and his administration argued long and hard for the fairness of indexing. The Democratic Congress, short on revenue, would not buy it. It is interesting to note that Australia is one of the few countries to adopt the indexing concept for taxing capital gains (see table 5.2-2). Apparently, the Australians have found the complexity involved to be worth the benefit of fairness to the taxpayer.

WHY NOT TAX CAPITAL GAIN INCOME AT ORDINARY INCOME RATES?

After sixty-five years of lower rates on capital gains (1922–1986), Congress took a bold step when writing the 1986 Tax Reform Act. As a very controversial piece of this legislation, the lower capital-gain rates were eliminated in favor of taxing almost all types of income at the same rates. This departure from the past was considered a necessary evil in order to dramatically lower ordinary rates, achieve simplicity, and reach agreement with both sides of the aisle. A member of the Reagan administration, which initiated the Act, later called the increase in capital gains tax "the one detrimental fallout from tax reform."[49] Before the ink was dry on the 1986 Act, those in favor of lower capital gain rates were lined up to offer their adverse opinions. By 1991, preferential capital gains treatment had managed to get its nose under the tent with a maximum 28% rate (vs. 31% for ordinary income). This beneficial top rate of 28% became even more significant in 1993 when the highest ordinary rate grew to 39.6% under President Clinton. A few years later, there was the Republicans' famous "Contract with America," which helped to persuade the Clinton administration to drop the highest capital gain rate to just 20% beginning in 1997, roughly half of the ordinary income rate of 39.6%. So, in a period of just over ten years, we essentially came almost full-circle from a 20% maximum rate at the end of 1986 to a new 20% ceiling rate for transactions after May 8, 1997 (although ordinary rates in this timeframe had dropped from 50% in 1986 to 39.6% in 1997).

Now fast-forward to 2010 when President Obama appointed the Simpson-Bowles Deficit Commission. In December 2010, the commission issued its report, titled the *Moment of Truth*, in which the commission proposed a substantial lowering of ordinary rates (maximum 35% dropped to 28% in its Illustrated Plan). This rate reduction would be accomplished by eliminating or at least minimizing many of the deductions, credits, exclusions, and loopholes that are imbedded in the tax code. One proposal by the Deficit Commission that was assumed to have a revenue-raising impact is the taxation of long-term capital gains at the same rates as ordinary income.

Less than a month before the report by the Deficit Commission, there was a similar tax reform plan issued by the Bipartisan Policy Center's Debt Reduction Task Force. Among other proposals, the task force advocated that capital gains be taxed at the same rates as ordinary income.[50]

Since both the Deficit Commission and the task force have come to the same conclusion about their desire to tax capital gains at the same rates as ordinary income, one might conclude that this is the right approach to take. However, in reading the full text of both reports, I could find very little meaningful discussion of the capital gains issue in either report. Both groups must have believed that taxing capital gains at full ordinary rates results in significantly higher revenue for the Treasury, and yet our nation's experience following the Tax Reform Acts of 1969 and 1986 (discussed earlier in this chapter) raises serious doubts about the likelihood of raising much more tax revenue by increasing the capital gain rates. Furthermore, the thought of taxing illusory gains that are largely attributable to inflation should not be considered an option. We should also consider that not only the United States but almost all other developed countries are taxing capital gains at substantially lower rates than they do ordinary income. (See table 5.2-2 for the foreign tax rates on the sale of corporate equities.) Fifteen out of thirty-seven other major economies have a zero capital gain rate, and ten of the remaining countries are taxing capital gains at 20% or less. Only France and Italy utilize capital gain rates of more than 30%.

It seems that the most compelling reason to tax capital gains at ordinary rates is to achieve simplicity. In reality, it would be almost as simple to go back to the method we used for fifty-two of the last 102 years, and that is to exclude from income 50% of all long-term capital gains and then subject the remaining one-half of such gains to the ordinary income tax rates. By doing this, the effective capital gains rate for taxpayers having a 35% ordinary rate would go up from 15% to 17.5%. Those in the 10% and 15% ordinary rate brackets would go up from zero percent in 2012 to 5% and 7.5% respectively. And those in the 25% and 28% brackets would actually go down from the current 15% rate to 12.5% and 14% respectively. There can be no question that this simplistic approach of excluding from income 50% of all long-term capital gains is a pragmatic form of rough justice, but I find its best support in the following quote from the late Randolph E. Paul:

> The impossibility of absolute justice is not a valid reason for failing to do justice that can be done. A perfectionist is a dangerous man in the tax world, which is full of things that need to be done only as well as they can be done.[51]

Please take the time to carefully analyze the upcoming table that compares the capital gains rates on corporate equities in various countries. This table 5.2-2 shows not only the long-term capital gains tax rates upon the sale of corporate equities but also the top corporate tax rates paid on a company's earnings prior to the distribution of earnings. The final column shows the "integrated capital gain tax rate," which aggregates the two tax rates after first applying the top corporate tax rate. As you will see from the table, the United States in 2011 had the fourth highest integrated corporate rates in the world, after Denmark, France, and Italy.

If a similar table were available for 2015, it would show that some countries have dropped their tax rates in recent years while the United States has maintained its top corporate tax rate and actually increased its capital gain rate (in 2013). Thus, table 5.2-2 understates the current US tax gap on corporate equities as compared to other major countries.

Table 5.2-2 [52, 53]

Integrated Long-Term Capital Gains Tax Rates on Corporate Equities			
	Top Corporate Tax Rate (2011)	Top Long-Term Capital Gains Tax Rate (2011)	Integrated Capital Gains Tax Rate (2011)
Australia	30.0%	22.5%	45.8%
Austria	25.0	00.0	25.0
Belgium	34.0	00.0	34.0
Canada	27.6	22.54	43.9
Chile	17.0	20.0	33.6
Czech Republic	19.0	00.0	19.0
Denmark	25.0	42.0	56.5
Estonia	21.0	21.0	37.6
Finland	26.0	28.0	46.7
France	34.4	31.3	54.9
Germany	30.2	25.0	47.7
Greece	20.0	00.0	20.0
Hungary	19.0	16.0	32.0
Iceland	20.0	20.0	36.0
Ireland	12.5	25.0	34.4
Israel	24.0	20.0	39.2
Italy	27.5	44.5	59.8
Japan	39.5	10.0	45.6
Korea	24.2	00.0	24.2
Luxembourg	28.6	00.0	28.6
Mexico	30.0	00.0	30.0
Netherlands	25.0	00.0	25.0
New Zealand	28.0	00.0	28.0
Norway	28.0	28.0	48.2
Poland	19.0	19.0	34.4
Portugal	26.5	00.0	26.5
Slovak Republic	19.0	19.0	34.4
Slovenia	20.0	00.0	20.0
Spain	30.0	21.0	44.7
Sweden	26.3	30.0	48.4
Switzerland	21.2	00.0	21.2
Turkey	20.0.	0.00	20.0
United Kingdom	26.0	28.0	46.7
United States	**39.2**	**19.1**	**50.8**
OECD Avg. (non-US)	29.1	17.8	41.7
Brazil (non-OECD)	34.0	15.0	43.9
Russia (non-OECD	20.0	13.0	30.4
India (non-OECD)	33.2	00.0	33.2
China (non-OECD)	25.0	00.0	25.0

Note: Includes both central government and subnational (e.g., state) tax rates.

Credible sources have estimated that the net effect of excluding 50% of all long-term capital gains in 2012 would have resulted in an annual increase of approximately $38 billion to the Treasury.[54] At the same time, it is expected to have had very little of the lock-in effect that is discussed earlier in this chapter, mainly due to the minor increase in capital gain rates at each level (except the 25% and 28% taxpayers who would see a small decrease in rates). Keep in mind that my 50% exclusion concept does reverse the tax break started in 2008 whereby taxpayers in less than a 25% ordinary tax bracket experience a 0.0% tax rate on long-term capital gains and qualified dividends. This policy of taxing capital gains at a 0.0% rate was intended to give the middle class an additional tax benefit and incentive for investing. In reality, much of this tax benefit has gone to those people who may have less than $75,000 of annual taxable income at ordinary rates but also have thousands of dollars in tax-free municipal bond interest and qualified dividends as well as millions of dollars invested in the stock market. This indeed is another case of well-intended legislation leading to unintended consequences.

The strange result of the 0.0% capital gain and qualified dividend rate for 2008 and later years is that many relatively wealthy people have been paying zero federal income tax ever since 2008. They are among "the 47% who pay no income tax" in our country (as was highly publicized in our 2012 national elections). In fact, many of these Americans are retired, and so they not only avoid all income taxes, but they also have zero payroll taxes, thus no Social Security or Medicare tax. I am serious when I say that our country has thousands, and possibly hundreds of thousands of "former taxpayers" who have a net worth of at least $1 million and yet pay zero federal income tax. It is difficult to find hard data to quantify this point due to the fact that the 0.0% capital gain rate just went into effect in 2008. However, the IRS Statistics of Income for 2009 shows that there were 697,273 income tax returns filed for 2009 with the highest marginal tax rate being 0.0% (for capital gains and qualified dividends),[55] and yet zero income tax was generated on all of these returns that averaged $29,967 of adjusted gross income per return.

I see some of these zero-income tax returns for my clients who used to pay a sizeable amount of income tax before 2008. If our tax system were to go back to the concept of excluding 50% of all capital gains and qualified dividends, it would greatly reduce the occurrence of reporting zero income tax amounts for many relatively wealthy citizens who clearly have the ability to pay taxes to our country.

QUALIFIED DIVIDENDS TAXED AT CAPITAL GAIN RATES

For most of the last hundred years, dividends paid by corporations were subject to ordinary income tax rates. However, beginning in 2003, "qualified dividends" were given the same maximum tax rate as long-term capital gains (15%). "Qualified" dividend income is defined as dividends received during the tax year from a domestic corporation or a qualifying foreign corporation.[56] This action by Congress was long overdue, but if history is any indication, it is entirely possible that a higher dividend tax rate could return in the future.[57] Most people, including many of our politicians, do not understand the reasons for giving dividends the same tax treatment as capital gains. There are at least three good reasons: First, the corporations that pay dividends are already subject to corporate income tax (mostly at 35%), so any tax on shareholders' dividends is essentially a second tax on corporate earnings. Second, if dividends are not paid out, the shareholders later realize a larger selling price for their stock, resulting in capital gain taxes paid at a later date. Finally, if corporations do not pay dividends during the lifetimes of their shareholders, the earnings retained in these companies will often go free of any capital gain or dividend tax upon the death of such shareholders. For these three reasons, our Treasury is better off providing an exclusion of 50% of qualified dividends similar to the 50% exclusion of capital gains to encourage more dividend distributions and the resulting taxes paid much earlier.

SHOULD CARRIED INTEREST BE TAXED AS CAPITAL GAINS?

One of the least understood concepts in the discussion of capital gains is that of "carried interest." Most tax accountants have never prepared a tax return that reports carried interest income, and most attorneys and business people don't even know what this term means. This term is not an accounting term, nor is it a tax term, but rather it has emerged in the last twenty-five years as an industry term used by those in the investment world to describe a type of profit or gain that is earned by managers and organizers of hedge funds, private-equity funds, energy investments, and other investment entities usually organized as limited partnerships or limited liability companies (LLCs). There are currently thousands of these investment vehicles that pay carried interest to the general partners or managing members who make all the investment decisions for such financial entities. It is hard to provide a concise definition of carried interest without giving an example.

Let me try to explain how carried interest is often created. Suppose that Joe and Sam organize a private-equity fund for a group of wealthy investors. This fund is organized as a limited partnership for which Joe and Sam serve as the general partners who are responsible for managing the fund. Most if not all the investors are limited partners who have no risk beyond their invested cash (capital). Because of the partnership status, there are no corporate taxes, so any taxable profits (and losses) flow through to the personal tax returns of all the partners. It's very common for the organizers of such funds (Joe and Sam) to charge a combined fee known as "two and twenty." [58] This is essentially a 2% guaranteed annual fee of the fund's total assets plus 20% of its net gains and profits. Quite often most of the net gains allocated to the investors (80%) are eligible for long-term capital gain treatment subject to the maximum 23.8% federal tax rate for 2014. The other 20% of the gains that goes to the organizers can also be treated as capital gains and taxed at a 23.8% rate under the carried interest theory. This occurs even though the organizers and managers of such funds rarely have any invested capital in these investments other than their own time. You might ask how are the 2% annual fees taxed, those which are based on the total assets being managed? Those 2% guaranteed fees are normally considered ordinary income subject to our highest tax rates and to all applicable payroll taxes.

The proponents of carried interest argue that only the 2% guaranteed fees should be subject to full taxation, as this amount represents the management fees for all the services that are rendered. On the other hand, the opponents of the carried interest theory will argue that the entire "two and twenty" should be considered compensation to the general partners and organizers in return for their investment management services. More precisely, the opponents contend that carried interest is not an investment. Since the best reason for capital gain treatment is to avoid taxing inflationary gains on investments, and these elements of inflation and investment simply do not exist in the context of carried interest, one should conclude that the 20% carried interest compensation should be taxed as ordinary income.

You would think that Congress would have long ago addressed this growing loss of Treasury revenue coming from carried interest. Indeed the issue has been debated many times in both the House and the Senate. In fact, four times in the years 2007–2010, the Democratic House passed legislation to end the capital gain treatment of carried interest.[59] All four times, the measure failed to get approval in the Senate where members from both parties voted the House bills down.[60] Keep in mind that Wall Street is a major source of both Democratic and Republican campaign contributions, which quite likely has influenced the Senate decisions to allow carried interest to continue receiving the lower capital gain tax treatment.

An interesting side note to consider is the 2012 presidential campaign when Governor Mitt Romney received multiple requests for his tax returns. The governor's 2010 tax return reported $21.6 million of total income of which $7.4 million (approximately 35%) was traced to carried interest.[61] Much of the rest of his income came from long-term capital gains and qualified dividends. The fact that Mr. Romney paid an effective rate of 13.9% of his 2010 income for federal taxes was used repeatedly by Democrats in their ads and speeches to vilify a candidate who had no evidence of any improprieties or illegal reporting. This political attack on the Republican candidate appeared to be very effective, and it resulted in millions of dollars of campaign commercials. We can only ponder the question of which way the election would have turned out without this lightning rod issue brought about partially due to the preferential treatment of carried interest.

One might ask just how much tax revenue is this concept of carried interest costing the Treasury. The IRS cannot tell us because there are no specific lines on the federal tax forms that identify carried interest. This income gets buried in those high-end tax returns that report long-term capital gains flowing through limited partnerships and other investment entities. One article from 2011 states that carried interest is being generated by more than 1,000 private equity funds, 8,000–9,000 hedge funds, and 1.2 million real estate limited partnerships.[62] According to the article, "the sum of the carried interest earned annually by just these categories amounts to more than $50 billion—and $50 billion times the 20% (rate) differential between the ordinary rate (35%) and the capital gains rate (of 15%) (for years 2003–2012) is $10 billion per year."[63] The actual number may be more or less than $10 billion, but we are talking about the avoidance of a considerable amount of tax revenue. If we are serious about broadening the tax base, most applications of carried interest should be treated as ordinary income.

SUMMARY OF THE 20/20 TAX TREATMENT OF CAPITAL GAINS AND DIVIDENDS

For the reasons stated in earlier pages, the 20/20 Tax adopts the approach of excluding 50% of most long-term capital gains and qualified dividends from the calculation of taxable income. The strongest argument for this approach is the effect of inflation on capital gain income as explained earlier in this chapter. Furthermore, as part of the capital gain formula, it is important that Congress scrutinize certain concepts like carried interest, which should be more appropriately treated as ordinary income subject to full ordinary tax rates. Finally, it will be explained in chapter 6.2 why the upper 1% of income earners (those who realize the majority of all capital gains and dividends) should be subject to indexing of capital gains. This approach of indexing would result in a more accurate calculation of the effects of inflation and a more equitable computation of the tax obligation for the very wealthy citizens of our country.

Chapter 5.3

EXEMPTIONS AND ITEMIZED DEDUCTIONS REPLACED BY TAX CREDITS

The 1970s and 1980s are considered by some to be the Age of Enlightenment for tax reform in much of the Western world. During this period there was considerable discussion about replacing deductible dependent exemptions and itemized deductions with a combination of tax credits.

As described earlier in this book, most taxpayers are allowed to deduct a personal exemption ($3,950 in 2014) of their own and of their spouse (if married) and the same amount for each of their dependents (usually their children). Exemptions are reductions of a taxpayer's taxable income. In our country's graduated tax rate structure, the tax savings of an exemption is determined by the highest marginal tax rate of the taxpayer taking the deduction. Thus an exemption claimed by a taxpayer in the 33% bracket for 2014 derived a tax savings of $1,304 ($3,950 x 0.33). Comparatively, a taxpayer in the 15% bracket only received a tax savings of $593 ($3,950 x 0.15).

Itemized deductions, also described in chapter 5 (primarily medical expenses, taxes, interest paid, and charitable donations), have a similar impact as exemptions on a taxpayer's return when the combined total of all itemized deductions exceeds the standard deduction ($12,400 for 2014 if married filing jointly). Thus, a taxpayer who itemizes deductions and is in the 33% tax bracket will usually save $330 upon making a charitable donation of $1,000. The same donation for a taxpayer who itemizes and has a 15% marginal tax rate will only save $150 of federal tax ($1,000 x 0.15). Because of this advantage favoring the wealthy, itemized deductions are often called "upside-down" subsidies.

At the same time that federal tax rates started coming down in the 1970s, critics of our tax law began to question the fairness of personal exemptions and itemized deductions due to the higher tax benefits going to the wealthy. One economist, Thomas F. Pogue, wrote in 1974 that "dependency exemptions are a mechanism by which the community shares or subsidizes the subsistence cost of children."[64] Based on this rationale, he took the position that credits should replace deductions to give all taxpayers a fixed amount credit for each of their dependent exemptions.[65] Doing this would usually result in the same tax benefit for the exemptions of all taxpayers. Following this approach, the 20/20 Tax adopts the concept of replacing personal exemptions and dependent exemptions with a new provision for "personal credits," to be explained in chapter 5.6.

Definition of Tax Credit

An item that reduces the amount of actual tax owed by a taxpayer as opposed to a tax deduction that merely reduces a taxpayer's taxable income. Since a credit does not depend on the taxpayer's tax rate, the amount of the credit is of equal value to all taxpayers regardless of income level.

The Bradley-Gephardt Fair Tax Act of 1983 provided that itemized deductions be replaced with a tax credit, and that credit would reduce one's tax liability at the lowest marginal tax rate[66] (14% in 1983). This proposed legislation was primarily authored by Senator Bill Bradley (D-NJ), considered by some to be the godfather of tax reform.[67] The bill received very good press, but it stalled in Congress, and it was soon followed by the Kemp-Kasten tax simplification proposal (1985). Both legislative proposals were popular bipartisan bills that reduced tax rates while repealing various deductions, exclusions, and credits, but notably calling for credits or deductions at the lowest marginal rates on the more popular deductions,[68] such as charitable deductions and home mortgage interest. These two bills provided some of the basic principles that were later codified in the Tax Reform Act of 1986, but the concept of tax credits to replace the deductibility of personal exemptions and itemized deductions was not included in the 1986 Act.

It is interesting to note that in 1987 Canada adopted a major reform of its income tax system whereby previous deductions for dependents, medical expenses, and charitable contributions were all changed to tax credits, generally at a rate of 17% which is Canada's lowest marginal rate.[69] The stated goals of Canada's 1987 tax reform were "to ensure that the tax system is made less complex wherever possible and is structured so that the burdens are shared in an equitable manner."[70]

Another example to look to is Norway where their comparable itemized deductions are all deductible at Norway's lowest marginal tax rate of 27%. By doing this, the Norwegians all obtain a tax benefit of 27% of their interest paid (as discussed in Chapter 3) and 27% of other deductions. This concept has been a part of their tax law ever since Norway's major tax reform of the 1990s.

As described in the previous pages, the possibility of replacing today's personal exemptions and itemized deductions with a credit-type approach had great momentum in the 1980s. Notably this concept resurfaced in 2010 when the Simpson-Bowles Commission issued their report. As stated in chapter 4 of this book, under Simpson-Bowles the deductions for home mortgage interest and charitable contributions would be replaced by 12% nonrefundable tax credits.[71] The 12% rate comes from the *lowest* marginal tax rate in the commission's *Illustrative Proposal*.

At almost the same time (November 2010), the Domenici-Rivlin Debt Reduction Task Force independently came to a similar conclusion about replacing the current exemption and itemized deduction system with a 15% refundable credit for all taxpayers.[72] How did they come up with 15%? That just happens to be the *lowest* marginal tax rate in their proposed tax rate structure. Does this sound familiar?

For over thirty years now, we have been seeing basically the same proposal come forth from some of our most respected politicians on both sides of the aisle (Bill Bradley, Dick Gephardt, Jack Kemp, and others). The same theme has been echoed by "Blue Ribbon" commissions like the Simpson-Bowles Commission and the Domenici-Rivlin Debt Reduction Task Force. Why doesn't Congress approve comparable legislation? I believe the answer lies with the "lowest marginal tax rate" being proposed as the credit rate. In other words, a credit rate of 12–15% may not yield high enough tax benefits for American taxpayers and the special interest groups to allow our politicians to go forward with such legislation. This is especially true given the fact that most itemized deductions are currently yielding federal tax savings of 25–39.6% on each dollar spent. Thus, if the tax savings from proposed credits for home mortgage interest and charitable contributions are reduced by more than half for millions of Americans, is it any surprise that our politicians are not gaining adequate support for their proposals? It may be time to raise the ante (a higher credit percentage) if Congress expects to get widespread acceptance of tax credits to replace some or all of our itemized deductions and personal exemptions.

It is my opinion that it will take a federal tax credit rate between 18% and 22% along with a lowering of all tax rates in order to gain acceptance of new tax credits that replace itemized deductions. Let me give you an example. The *Illustrative Proposal* of the Simpson-Bowles (S-B) report calls for just three rate brackets of 12%, 22%, and 28%.[73] Suppose that Congress chose these three rates for the future, and further suppose that Congress was to replace certain itemized deductions (medical expenses, home mortgage interest, and charitable contributions) with a 22% tax credit (the middle rate of the S-B *Illustrative Proposal*). What would be the results of this action, and would Congress gain widespread acceptance of this major change? The results I see happening if a 22% tax credit is substituted for the deduction of itemized deductions are as follows:

1. *Increased tax collections* - The amount of income taxes collected by the Treasury should increase if we adopted the 22% tax credit. Note that almost 70% of all taxpayers take the standard deduction instead of itemizing deductions.[74] These taxpayers taking the standard deduction are usually in the 10% or 15% rate brackets. Currently, most taxpayers who itemize deductions are those in the 25–39.6% tax brackets. Since these upper tax brackets are larger than the 22% credit in my example, the difference in percentages should result in additional taxes collected by the Treasury. IRS statistics show that approximately 13% of tax returns reporting income under $50,000 are itemizing.[75] For households with income levels above $75,000, approximately 76% itemize,[76] and more than 94% of taxpayers with income above $200,000 claimed itemized deductions.[77] These are the taxpayers who are mostly in the 25–39.6% tax brackets. Those in the 35% and 39.6% tax brackets have by far the highest amount of itemized deductions and would realize far fewer tax benefits if we adopted the 22% tax credit across the board.

2. *Easier tax planning* -Taxpayers would find it much easier to do tax planning and make tax-related decisions if they knew they could rely on an almost certain tax credit of 22% for future years regardless of the level of their income. This would be particularly helpful for the homebuyers who find it hard to predict future earnings when about to make the long-term decision to purchase a home.

3. *Home mortgage interest incentives* - Most taxpayers would consider a 22% tax credit (of their mortgage interest) to be sufficient incentive to proceed with the purchase of a home and the related financing, provided the home is within their means. In my example with S-B tax rates of 12 to 28%, those taxpayers in the 12% tax bracket would be more likely to purchase a home than today's comparable taxpayers in a 15% bracket, merely because of the higher tax subsidy of 22% as compared to 15%. Those taxpayers in the new 22% tax bracket would be unlikely to change their buying behavior as compared to today's 25% taxpayers since the small difference in the tax subsidy compared to the previous benefit (22 vs. 25%) is hardly

significant to most people. Taxpayers currently in the 28–39.6% tax brackets would presumably be in the revised 28% bracket. Would they be as likely to buy a new home or as expensive a home with a 22% tax subsidy as they would have purchased with a 28–39.6% subsidy? The answer is possibly no. The choice for some would be not to buy, or at least to buy a home that required less financing. However, this is not necessarily a bad consequence, since most people at these higher income brackets are still going to choose to own nice homes.

To some extent, the proposed home mortgage tax credit would shift some of the home interest government tax subsidy from the wealthier to the lower income families, but at least most home-buyers who finance their acquisitions would obtain the same percentage tax subsidy of 22% in my example. Thus, lower income families will receive much larger tax subsidies than under current law, while high-income families who can afford home ownership without government assistance will receive somewhat lower tax benefits. The net result should be an overall increase in the rate of home ownership in our country.

4. *Charitable contributions.* When it comes to charitable contributions, the possibility of instituting a 22% credit has considerable merit as a replacement of today's itemized deduction for charitable giving. The Congressional Budget Office (CBO) has estimated this current deduction's ten-year cost to the Treasury for 2014–2023 should be approximately $568 billion.[78] Thus it will cost the Treasury roughly $56 billion per year for the coming decade. It is not unreasonable to anticipate that by replacing today's deduction with a 22% credit, our government would see an annual increase in revenue of $10 billion or more. This is due to the fact that charitable contributions, like other itemized deductions, are mostly being deducted by taxpayers in the 25–39.6% brackets. One might ask what impact this would have on charitable organizations if all itemizing taxpayers were to obtain only a 22% tax benefit for gifting. Interestingly, the economists who have studied this issue do not agree on the extent

that charitable giving responds to tax incentives.[79] We do know that when tax rates dropped substantially with the 1986 Tax Reform Act, there was almost no change in our nation's overall charitable donations.[80] Recent studies have shown that, historically, Americans have donated on average, approximately 2% of GDP to charitable and other tax-exempt organizations regardless of the highest marginal tax rates.[81]

This percentage of giving has changed very little over the last forty years (ranging from 1.7% to 2.3% for each year from 1971 to 2011)[82] despite the dramatic decrease in our marginal tax rates of the last four decades (from the highest rate of 70% in 1971 to as low as 28% in 1988). Charitable giving has been a distinguishing quality of American society that sets our country apart from other nations. The tradition of giving is unlikely to decline by a substantial amount if a tax credit of 18–22% were to replace our current charitable deduction at today's tax rates of 10–39.6%.

NOTE: *A specific tax credit rate of 20% has been adopted as a consistent standard of the 20/20 Tax (not the 22% as used in the above examples).*

Chapter 5.4

REPEAL OF THE ALTERNATIVE MINIMUM TAX AND STEALTH TAXES

It was an early autumn day in 1969 when as a college senior I was preparing for an afternoon of coaching the St. Clare's sixth- and seventh-grade football team. As I reached for my clipboard and practice agenda, I noticed an interesting article on the front page of that day's *Wall Street Journal*. When I was in college, I rarely looked at this publication, but my roommate, Doug, was an economics major who was a regular subscriber and reader of the *Journal*. The title that caught my eye had to do with the passage of new tax legislation with a provision known as the minimum tax on tax preference items, later to be known as the alternative minimum tax (AMT). According to the article, Congress enacted the minimum tax in response to testimony by the secretary of the Treasury that 155 taxpayers with adjusted gross income above $200,000 had paid no income tax on their 1967 tax returns. With great interest, I read the article from beginning to end, knowing that I might be late for practice with the kids. Fortunately, I had a dedicated assistant, John Ahern, who I expected would be at the park by 3:00 p.m. to start the team drills.

Upon finishing the tax article, I started the five-minute walk to the practice field, all along thinking about the new minimum tax legislation that would supposedly put an end to the economic injustice of high-end taxpayers paying zero federal income tax. At the time, this new code section appealed to me, considering I had never yet taken an income tax class and had only completed a handful of accounting courses. As I arrived at the park, I first noticed our quarterback, Tom, throwing a long pass that was being chased by the two shortest but fastest receivers on the team, Ed and Fred. At that moment, I forgot about taxes and did not revisit the theory of the minimum tax until more than two years later when taking my first full course of Individual Income Taxes in graduate school.

HISTORY OF THE ALTERNATIVE MINIMUM TAX

Originally, the alternative minimum tax (AMT) was legislated to compensate for a flawed IRS tax code that allowed some wealthy people to avoid payment of any federal income taxes. Today it creates much more unfairness than what existed before its enactment. In its early years, the AMT was intended to collect taxes from all those making more than $200,000 per year (the equivalent of more than $1,200,000 of annual income in today's dollars). However, during recent years, most of the AMT tax has been paid by the middle class and upper-middle class, those making $100,000–$500,000 per year. Rarely does it impact those taxpayers with annual incomes in excess of $1 million.

Following is a brief summary of the evolution of the AMT as described succinctly in a 2007 report from the Journal of Business and Economics Research:

> The original minimum tax was an add-on tax of 10% on (certain) tax preferences. The tax was amended in 1976 when a Treasury study found that 244 taxpayers with adjusted gross income above $200,000 were still paying no income tax. Under this amendment the tax base was broadened and the rate was raised to 15%. The tax was amended again in 1978, 1986, 1990 and finally to its present incarnation in 1993.[83]

Before the 1986 Tax Reform Act, about 85% of AMT preferences were related to capital gains and tax shelters.[84] In the first sixteen years of the AMT, tax shelters were quite popular, and these shelters helped to reduce or eliminate taxes for many high-income taxpayers. The typical tax shelter succeeded by investing in assets that generated capital gains (at lower tax rates) while utilizing investment interest, depreciation, and other expenses that were deductible at high ordinary tax rates. This combination often resulted in little or no taxes being paid by taxpayers in the shelters' early years and sometimes huge after-tax profits at capital gain rates.

For the last twenty-nine years, the AMT has been a totally different animal. It no longer attacks exotic tax shelters or some of the more egregious loopholes in the tax code. Rather, its main focus is primarily on some everyday deductions of middle-class taxpayers. According to Leonard Burman and Joel Slemrod who wrote an excellent book, *Taxes in America* :

> Ironically, the bulk of the AMT's taxable income adjustments have nothing to do with anybody's notion of a loophole. The largest is the deduction for state and local income and property taxes, which accounted for 68% of all AMT adjustments in 2008. Personal exemptions—the $3,700 deduction (in 2011) for each family member and dependent—account for another 19% of AMT add-backs, and so-called miscellaneous itemized deductions, such as employee business expenses, make up 12% of the total.[85]

The authors of the same book go on to describe how the AMT actually works today.

> Here's how it works. First you calculate your regular taxable income and income tax liability. Then you start over, and add back a bunch of tax breaks to

taxable income, deduct a flat AMT exemption amount ($74,450 for couples and $48,450 for singles in 2011) and calculate the tax at rates of 26% or 28%. If the tax under this alternative calculation is more than tax owed under the regular income tax rules, you must add the difference to your tax bill; this is equivalent to owing the higher of the two tax liability calculations. Hence, the logic behind the name "alternative minimum" tax.[86]

As you might guess, the households most likely to be hit by the AMT are large families who live in high-tax states.[87] This is because the AMT calculation adds back personal exemptions for taxpayers and their dependents as well as deductions for state and local taxes. Since the AMT "exemption" for couples is less than double that for singles, and the AMT tax brackets do not recognize marital status, the AMT often results in sizeable marriage penalties. Due to the AMT factors working against marriage and children, couples were more than twenty times as likely as singles to face the AMT in 2010.[88]

As a basic example of how the AMT can affect a family, consider a couple earning $180,000 in 2014 with six children and taking the standard deduction. Under the regular tax, their taxable income would equal $180,000 minus $31,600 in personal exemptions (8 X $3,950) minus a standard deduction of $12,400, resulting in taxable income of $136,000 and regular tax of $25,713 (before the child tax credit). For AMT purposes, the personal exemptions ($31,600) and even the standard deduction ($12,400) would be added back to the regular taxable income to get AMT income of $180,000. This AMT income of $180,000 would be reduced by the 2014 AMT exemption of $76,225, resulting in $103,775 of net AMT income after the exemption. This amount is then multiplied times the lower AMT rate of 26% which results in an AMT of $26,982. Since the AMT is higher than the regular tax of $25,713, this family would incur an additional AMT tax liability of $1,269. The family's total tax including the AMT would be $24,482, after subtracting the child tax credit of $2,500.

Now let's compare the tax picture of our hypothetical family to that of a single parent earning $180,000 in 2014 after having gone through a divorce. Let's assume that the single parent pays child support and $90,000 of alimony to his former spouse while being entitled to claim the exemptions for three of their six children. Let's further assume that the single taxpayer will take the standard deduction and does not qualify for head of household filing status because the children reside with the former spouse. Under the regular tax, the taxable income would be $68,000 after deduction of the four exemptions (4 x $3,950 = $15,800) and the standard deduction ($6,200). The single parent's regular tax would be $12,857 (before the child tax credit). To calculate the AMT, one would have to add back the personal exemptions ($15,800) and the standard deduction ($6,200) to arrive at AMT income of $90,000. This AMT income of $90,000 would be reduced by the 2014 AMT exemption of $52,800, resulting in $37,200 of net AMT income after the exemption. This amount is then multiplied times the lower AMT rate of 26% which results in an AMT of $9,672. Note that the AMT of $9,672 is lower than the regular tax of $12,857; therefore, the AMT does not apply.

For those of us who comprehend numbers and tables better than words, let us analyze these two examples side by side to get an understanding of the marriage (and child) penalties of the AMT.

Taxation Under the Regular Income Tax—2014

	Married Couple	Single Parent
Wages and salaries	$180,000	$ 180,000
Other income	0	0
Total income	180,000	180,000
Deductions for AGI (Alimony)	0	-90,000
Adjusted Gross Income (AGI)	180,000	90,000
Less: Standard Deduction	-12,400	-6,200
Equals: AGI less deductions	167,600	83,800
Less: Personal Exemptions	-31,600	-15,800
Equals: Taxable Income (Regular)	$ 136,000	$ 68,000

Regular Income Tax Before Credits		
Taxed at 10% ($18,150) ($9,075)	$ 1,815	$ 908
Taxed at 15% ($55,650) ($27,825)	8,348	4,174
Taxed at 25% ($62,200) ($31,100)	15,550	7,775
Regular Income Tax Before Credits and AMT	25,713	12,857
Child Tax Credit (note the disparity)	2,500	2,250
Regular Income Tax After Credits	$ 23,213	$ 10,607

Taxation Under the Alternative Minimum Tax

	Married Couple	Single Parent
Adjusted Gross Income	$180,000	$ 90,000
Ignore: Standard Deduction	N/A	N/A
Plus: Taxes and Misc. Itemized Deductions	0	0
Plus: Other Tax Preferences	0	0
Equals: AMT Income	180,000	90,000
Less: AMT Exemption ($82,100 – [25% X 23,500])	76,225	52,800
Equals: AMT Income Less AMT exemption	$ 103,775	$ 37,200
Alternative Minimum Tax at 26%	$ 26,982	$ 9,673
Regular Income Tax Before Credits and AMT	25,713	12,857
AMT (added tax) Liability ($26,982 - 25,713)	1,269	
($10,244 - 13,243 = 0)	0	0
Total Regular and AMT Tax Before Credits	26,982	12,857
Less Child Tax Credit	-2,500	-2,250
Total Tax After Credits	$24,482	$10,607

As you can see from the above comparison, the married couple is paying far more than twice as much federal income tax as the single parent. To get the full picture, we must complete the story by showing the tax for the former spouse who receives $90,000 of alimony, which must be reported on her tax return. Assuming the alimony is the former spouse's only source of income and that she can claim the personal exemptions for three of their six children, she will have the same regular taxable income ($68,000) as her former spouse, the same potential AMT tax ($9,672), and the same child tax credit ($2,250). However, she can realize additional tax savings by claiming the filing status of head of household since she has custody of the children. This will result in her having total federal income tax of only $8,444. The divorced couple will thus have total combined federal income tax of $19,051, or $5,431 less than the married couple who has the same income as the divorced couple and the same deductions, exemptions, and credits. The only factual difference is that the second couple decided to formally terminate their marriage. We might call this tax savings a "divorce bonus."

After reading the above, you may think divorce is a popular tax-planning device for couples facing the AMT. Actually, I have never seen a couple file for divorce just to avoid the AMT, but I am sure that it has happened. At the very least, the above examples portray some of the many injustices (namely the marriage and child penalties) that have been created by the AMT monster.

In our previous examples, we have seen how even the standard deduction and personal exemptions are denied for those entrapped by the AMT. However, the marriage and child penalties of the AMT (as revealed) are usually not nearly as costly for taxpayers as the loss of state and local tax deductions for those taxpayers who itemize. Millions of Americans lose their state income tax and property tax deductions partially or totally due to the AMT. The "tax preferences" of state and local tax deductions are a greater source of government revenue than all other AMT preferences combined. It is hard to justify why a large majority of taxpayers who itemize can fully deduct their state and local taxes, while AMT taxpayers lose much of their tax benefit when paying state and local taxes merely as a result of being ensnared by an arbitrary formula. This raises the question: should Congress allow *any* taxpayers to deduct state and local taxes? This deduction, dating back to the 1930s, has been challenged in almost every tax-reform movement of the last sixty years. It was almost completely terminated as part of the 1986 Tax Reform Act, but Congress succumbed to the lobbying of high-tax states by only denying these valuable deductions for those unfortunate taxpayers who fall into the unfair trap of the AMT. As a country, we need to ask ourselves if this injustice that hits the upper middle-class the hardest should be allowed to continue.

Another issue that makes the AMT so onerous is the concept of hidden tax brackets. Many taxpayers (and some tax advisers) are under the impression that the AMT imposes tax rates of "only" 26% or 28%. However, the AMT "exemption" phases out at the rate of 25% for each dollar of AMT income over $150,000 for married couples ($112,500 for singles). Thus, if a couple's AMT income increases from $150,000 to $180,000 (see our earlier example), the AMT exemption will drop by $5,875 to an amount of only $76,225 rather than $82,100. This can have the result of raising the "effective" AMT bracket from 26% up to 32.5%. For those higher earners in the 28% AMT bracket, the true effective AMT rate can go as high as 35%. Does this make you wonder what kind of deceptive minds crafted this legislation? This concept of hidden tax brackets (sometimes known as a "stealth tax") is one more reason the AMT is one of our most hated taxes. The AMT is merely a revenue generator that serves no beneficial public policy and is rife with injustice from beginning to end for an unfortunate minority of taxpayers who just happen to have the wrong combination of income, deductions, and exemptions.

By now you are probably asking, why do our elected officials allow the AMT to continue? Every person in Congress will agree that this tax is not fair. Over the last forty years, the AMT has been amended and patched too many times to count, resulting in tax code sections and regulations that are practically undecipherable. Today it is hard to find an economist, accountant, or tax attorney who will defend the AMT or advocate its continued existence. There is only one reason to keep it, and that reason is revenue. By many estimates, the AMT is expected to raise at least a trillion dollars of revenue over the next ten years. However, it should be noted that these ten-year estimates usually do not factor in the likely congressional patches of the AMT as we have seen in every year of this century (2001–2014). By raising the AMT exemption amount every year, Congress has avoided the creation of millions of new AMT taxpayers. This process of temporarily fixing the AMT has been referred to as the "AMT patch." If the AMT continues to be a part of our tax code, we can probably count on these annual patches to continue. For this reason, it is unlikely that the real ten-year loss of revenue to the Treasury would be upwards of a trillion dollars upon the abolishment of the AMT. Considering the survival instincts of congressional members, if the AMT continues as is, its future revenue stream is likely to increase at a similar rate as seen in recent years. According to the statistics of the Urban-Brookings Tax Policy Center, for the recent ten-year period of 2003–2012, the AMT is estimated to have generated the following revenue:[89]

AMT Receipts

Year	(Billions, by Fiscal Year)	Year	(Billions, by Fiscal Year)
2003	$11.2	2008	$33.2
2004	19.5	2009	29.5
2005	24.4	2010	33.4
2006	29.1	2011	33.2
2007	32.3	2012	33.9

The same source projects future AMT revenues as follows, assuming the AMT fix under current policy uses the AMT exemption levels specified in Senate Bill S.3413 for 2012 and 2013, indexes the 2013 levels in later years, and allows nonrefundable personal credits.

AMT Receipts[90]

Year	(Billions, by Fiscal Year)	Year	(Billions, by Fiscal Year)
2013	$32.6	2018	$51.5
2014	36.9	2019	55.7
2015	40.7	2020	58.3
2016	44.3	2021	61.3
2017	48.0	2022	65.0

As projected above, the repeal of the AMT would undoubtedly be far less than a trillion dollars over the next ten years. The projected amount shown above adds up to $494.3 billion, still a large amount of revenue to replace. Let's look at some of the options for replacing any potential revenue lost upon repeal of the AMT.

REPLACEMENT OF AMT REVENUE UPON REPEAL

There are many options to consider to produce the revenue needed if Congress were to repeal the AMT. Some of the suggested possibilities are as follows:

1. *Eliminate the deduction for state and local taxes.* This option is very appropriate for many reasons. One, it is the major generator of AMT "tax revenue," usually accounting for over 60% of all annual AMT "preferences." A simultaneous repeal of the AMT along with state and local taxes would be a legislative gesture putting all taxpayers in the same boat. If AMT taxpayers cannot benefit from the state and local taxes they pay, then why should any taxpayers benefit from such deductions? A second reason to eliminate the state and local tax deduction is the magnitude of this tax expenditure. For the next ten years, the itemized deduction for state and local taxes has been estimated to cost the Treasury $1.1 trillion,[91] much greater than the ten-year cost of AMT revenues projected earlier in this chapter. A third and possibly the most compelling reason to end the state and local tax deduction is that it's hard to justify a deduction that favors high-tax states over low-tax states, and most economists show little favor for this deduction in the context of good tax policy.

2. *Eliminate or lower the tax benefit of personal exemptions for all high income individuals.* This tax benefit has been the second highest generator of AMT tax. Again, why are most taxpayers entitled to this tax benefit when it's being denied for AMT taxpayers? It would be much more equitable to give all taxpayers the same benefit from personal exemptions, as opposed to our current system providing federal tax savings between $0 and $1,304 per exemption (in 2014).

3. *Eliminate or minimize miscellaneous itemized deductions.* This assortment of deductions (i.e., financial advice, tax preparation fees, unreimbursed business expenses, etc.) was almost totally

repealed by the 1986 Tax Reform Act. After much debate, Congress established the 2% rule, which allows taxpayers to only deduct certain miscellaneous expenses that exceed 2% of one's adjusted gross income. This category of itemized deductions is beneficial to only a small percentage of taxpayers (largely due to the AMT), but it is often a very time-consuming part of tax return preparation even for those who receive no tax benefit. Miscellaneous itemized deductions often test the gray area of the tax code and have led to infinite challenges by the IRS. The elimination of most, if not all, miscellaneous itemized deductions would make a significant down payment toward replacing revenues lost upon AMT repeal. And it would provide a sizeable step in the direction of tax simplification.

4. *Eliminate the lower tax rates on capital gains and dividends.* Some would argue that part of the process of repealing the AMT should involve the taxation of capital gains at ordinary rates. Keep in mind that the original minimum tax on tax preference items (1969) was largely an assault on the lower capital gains rates of the 1960s and 1970s. However, the 1986 Tax Reform Act eliminated this AMT adjustment because capital gains were determined in the '86 Act to be taxed at the same rate(s) as ordinary income.

   For most of the recent ten-year period when there was a 15% maximum capital gain rate (2003–2012), the amount of AMT generated by capital gains was second or third after that generated by the state and local tax deduction. This is largely due to the fact that capital gains often absorb the AMT exemption amount, causing an indirect increase in the AMT. Some might reason that if the AMT is repealed, there would be a windfall benefit to those taxpayers who realize capital gain income. Thus, they conclude we should consider asking taxpayers with capital gains to partially pay for the repeal of the AMT by paying higher (ordinary) rates on capital gain income.

5. *Impose higher marginal tax rates at all levels to raise comparable revenue without the AMT.* The deceptive simplicity of this approach makes it sound like the natural choice until one considers the possible

effects on ordinary tax rates. A study was done in 2003 to predict the future (2010) rates needed to allow for the repeal of the AMT without changing the average tax burden for any level of income earners. The outcome was reported as follows:

> It would be possible to mimic the distribution of average tax burdens under current law even with AMT repeal. If taxpayers in each bracket were to make the same aggregate tax payment in 2010 after the elimination of the alternative minimum tax as they would under current law, the 10 percent tax rate would have to be raised to 10.7 percent, the 15 percent tax rate to 16.3 percent, the 25 percent tax rate to 29.2 percent, the 28 percent tax rate to 33.8 percent, the 33 percent rate to 43.0 percent and the 35 percent tax rate would be *lowered* to 33.2 percent. That is, the statutory regular income tax rate would have to rise for those in the bottom five brackets and fall in the highest income group.[92]

Once equivalent rate changes are considered, it becomes evident that this fifth option is not all that appealing. In fact, both the fourth and fifth options, involving large rate increases across the board, would quite likely be political suicide for a number of members of Congress. Thus, it is my opinion that the first three above described options should be judiciously utilized to replace the revenue that would be lost upon the ultimate repeal of the AMT. Each of these three revenue replacements will be further described in later chapters.

CONCLUSION FOR AMT

Over the last ten years, almost every comprehensive tax reform plan has proposed the complete elimination of the AMT. This list includes the following highly recognized plans:

- President's Advisory Panel on Federal Tax Reform, chaired by Connie Mack, III (2005)
- Bipartisan Tax Fairness and Simplification Act of 2011, introduced by Senator Ron Wyden (D-OR) and Senator Dan Coats (R-IN)
- The National Commission on Fiscal Responsibility and Reform, co-chaired by Erskine Bowles (D-NC), former Clinton White House Chief of Staff, and Alan Simpson (R-WY), former US Senator (2010)
- Bipartisan Policy Center "Debt Reduction Task Force," co-chaired by former US Senator Pete Domenici (R-NM) and former Clinton Administration Budget Director, Alice Rivlin (2010)
- Bipartisan Policy Center, Domenici-Rivlin Debt Reduction Task Force Plan 2.0 (2012)
- Roadmap for America's Future, US Representative Paul Ryan, (R-WI) (2012)

It is time to put the nail in the coffin of the AMT. During the last forty-five years, it has created much more harm than good for American taxpayers and the integrity of our US tax system. There should be no further attempts to amend or patch this monstrosity. Full repeal of the AMT is needed as soon as possible.

> "If income were taxed comprehensively by the regular tax code, there would be no way of legally avoiding taxation, and not one taxpayer would have to file the AMT form even if the law were still on the books."
>
> —Patrick W. Fleenor, Chief Economist, Tax Foundation
> Special Report, May 2007, No. 155

ELIMINATION OF STEALTH TAXES AND PHASE-OUTS

One of the many proposals to come out of the Simpson-Bowles Tax Reform Plan was the permanent repeal of two of the major stealth taxes that were temporarily allowed to lapse from 2010 through 2012. The first of these is the Personal Exemption Phase-out (PEP), which gradually eliminates the tax benefit of one's personal exemptions ($3,950 per family member in 2014) as income increases. For married couples, the PEP starts once their adjusted gross income (AGI) exceeds $305,050 (in 2014). Joint taxpayers must reduce their exemptions by 2% for each $2,500 or fraction thereof that their AGI exceeds $305,050. When the couple's 2014 AGI reaches $427,550, they will have totally lost the tax benefit of all their personal exemptions. For singles, the 2014 PEP phase-out threshold starts at $254,200 and concludes at $376,700. This stealth tax is one that you don't hear or see much about. It just silently operates to raise taxes on high-income taxpayers. Essentially, the PEP has the same effect as raising marginal tax rates on taxpayers at certain income levels. Your politicians don't want this stealth tax to look like higher tax rates, but that is what it really is, just in a hidden form. Similar to the AMT, it hits the upper-middle class the hardest (most of whom fall in the phase-out ranges.)

The other stealth tax targeted for elimination by the Simpson-Bowles Tax Reform Plan is a provision commonly known as "Pease," named after the late congressman who authored this legislation. Under Pease, the tax benefit of up to 80% of itemized deductions is gradually phased out. For 2014, the Pease threshold also starts at $305,050 of AGI for married couples and $254,200 for single filers. When income exceeds those levels, the total amount of itemized deductions allowed is reduced by three cents for each dollar of AGI over the threshold. However, the Pease provision has a limit so that no taxpayers can lose more than 80% of their entire itemized deductions.

The Simpson-Bowles Plan proposes the elimination of these stealth taxes in order to minimize the complexity of our tax code. The truth be known, there are dozens of other phase-in and phase-out provisions embedded in the tax code that limit various credits, deductions, and exemptions.

In 2001, the Joint Committee on Taxation listed twenty different personal income tax provisions involving phase-ins or phase-outs, estimating that taxpayers made over thirty million worksheet calculations (per year) as a result of such provisions.[93]

For the reasons of simplicity and systemic integrity, the 20/20 Tax will almost totally avoid the implementation of stealth taxes, phase-ins and phase-outs. The PEP and Pease limitations will be repealed and not replaced. The 20/20 Tax includes many features that limit credits, deductions and exclusions for all taxpayers and not just the wealthy. In most cases, the wealthy will experience a 20% tax benefit from statutory credits, which is the same percentage benefit that will be realized by our lower and middle income taxpayers. The 20/20 Tax will allow very few deductions as compared to our current system, since deductions inevitably lead to the high income taxpayer receiving a higher percentage benefit from each dollar deducted. Because of the composition of the 20/20 Tax system, there is much less revenue benefit or political temptation to load up the system with stealth taxes or other deceptive mechanisms to soak certain classes of taxpayers the way our current tax law does. Our country deserves a transparent tax system, and it is about time that we get one.

Chapter 5.5

NEW INDIVIDUAL TAX RATE BRACKETS AND FILING STATUS AMOUNTS

You have made it this far, and you're still reading this treatise. That's either a credit to your intellectual stamina or it's an indication of your morbid curiosity. Either way, I admire your persistence, and I encourage you to forge ahead in pursuit of a better tax policy for our country.

The focus of this chapter is on the tax rate structure of the 20/20 Tax. As many a politician has learned, countless elections have been won or lost over tax rates and what segment of our population incurs the highest or lowest rates. Despite the great political emphasis on tax rates, most of us have come to know and understand that various income tax rates can be quite deceptive, and that really the devil is in the details.

In order to understand the 20/20 Tax and grasp its rate structure, it is important to recognize that we are dealing with a totally new framework as compared to our current tax system. With the 20/20 Tax there is no longer the fixation with adjusted gross income (AGI), a term that most taxpayers never really understood, and which is about to go away under the new tax system. Other terms that will be abandoned by the 20/20 Tax are personal exemptions, itemized deductions, and even the standard deduction. The framework of the 20/20 Tax will be much more streamlined and easy to navigate. The 20/20 Tax rates (there are only three) will be applied to "taxable income."

The 20/20 taxable income is derived by adding up total income and subtracting applicable exclusions (all of which are 50% exclusions) and then subtracting three uncommon deductions. It's that simple.

Let's take a look at the next page to see how page one of the 20/20 tax return is expected to be drafted. It is important to note that this first page of the tax return results in the bad news of the 20/20 Tax. In other words, it only tells you the total income tax *before* credits. Later in the book, you will read about the good news, which is the list of carefully designed credits to reduce your income tax liability in an understandable manner.

FORM 1040   **2020**   **PAGE ONE**

M D Y

Taxpayer Name _____	Date of Birth __/__/__	SSN _____
Spouse Name _____	Date of Birth __/__/__	SSN _____
Address _____		
City, State, Zip _____		

Filing Status   1 ___ Single   4 ___ Head of household (SSN of qualifying person) _____
                2 ___ Married filing jointly   5 ___ Qualifying widow(er) with dependent child
                3 ___ Married filing separately
                Enter separate-filing spouse's SSN above and full name here _____

Personal Credits: 6a _____ Yourself. 6b _____ Spouse
6c Dependents – Names (First)   (Last)   Birth Date M/D/Y   SSN   Relationship
_____
_____
_____

6d Total eligible for Personal Credit between the ages of 18 and 65 (include taxpayer and spouse under 65)   _____
6e Total eligible for Personal Credit age 65 and over (include taxpayer and spouse if over 65)
NOTE: Dependent children under the age of 18 are only eligible for the Child Tax Credit on Line 62 of taxpayer's return.
        All children under 18 filing their own tax returns may claim the Personal Tax Credit but not the Child Tax Credit.

Ordinary	7	Wages, salaries, etc. Attach W-2(s) (To include employer-provided health insurance)	7 _____
Income	8	Alimony received 8b Payor's SSN _____	8 _____
	9	Business income or (loss). Attach Schedule C	9 _____
	10	Short-term and other gains or (losses). Attach Form 4797	10 _____
	11	IRA, 401(k), 403(b) and 457 distributions 11a _____ Taxable amount	11b _____
	12	Pensions and annuities 12a _____ Taxable amount	12b _____
	13	Rental real estate, royalties, partnerships, S Corporations, trusts, etc. Attach Schedule E	13 _____
	14	Partnership self-employment income (Should not be included in line 13)	14 _____
	15	Farm income or (loss). Attach Schedule F	15 _____
	16	Unemployment compensation	16 _____
	17	Other income. List type 17a (SE Income)_____ 17b (Non SE) _____	17 _____
	18	Total Ordinary Income—Combine the amounts on lines 7 through 17.	18 _____

Exclusionary	19	Interest - Attach Schedule B	19 _____
Income	20	Dividends - Attach Schedule B	20 _____
	21	Long-term capital gains - Attach Schedule D	21 _____
	22	Social Security benefits	22 _____
	23	Disability benefits	23 _____
	24	Workers' compensation	24 _____
	25	Total Exclusionary Income (Add lines 19 through 24) 25a _____ (X 50%) 25b _____
	26	Total Combined Income (Add lines 18 and 25b) 26 _____

Deductions	27	Moving expenses-Attach Form 3903	27 _____
	28	Self-employed SEP and qualified retirement plans	28 _____
	29	Alimony paid b. Recipients SSN _____ 29a _____
	30	Total deductions (Add lines 27 through 29) 30 _____
	31	Taxable Income (line 26 minus line 30) 31 _____

Tax Calculation:		Single & H of H	Married Filing Jointly	Married Filing Separate	
	32	Tax at 10% rate $0–30,000	$0–50,000	$0–25,000	32 _____
	33	Tax at 20% rate $30,001–120,000	$50,000–200,000	$25,001–100,000	33 _____
	34	Tax at 30% rate $120,001+	$200,001+	$100,001+	34 _____

35a   Income Tax Before Credits (Add lines 32 thru 34)   35a _____
35b   Income Tax Before Credits With Indexing Added (Sch. D) 35b _____   (35a+35b)35c _____
NOTE: Lines 35b and 35c only apply if taxable income exceeds $300,000 (Single); $500,000 (MFJ); and $250,000 (MFS).

TAX RATE SCHEDULES FOR THE 20/20 TAX

Here are the new individual income tax rates proposed for the first fully applicable year of the 20/20 Tax. The tax is computed by applying the rate from the following appropriate schedule to the taxpayer's taxable income (line 31, previous page).

Married Filing Jointly and Qualifying Widows

If Taxable Income Is:	The tax Is:
Not over $50,000	10% of taxable income
Over $50,000 but not over $200,000	$5,000 plus 20% of that over $50,000
Over $200,000	$35,000 plus 30% of that over $200,000

Single Individuals and Heads of Households

If Taxable Income Is:	The tax Is:
Not over $30,000	10% of taxable income
Over $30,000 but not over $120,000	$3,000 plus 20% of that over $30,000
Over $120,000	$21,000 plus 30% of that over $120,000

Married Individuals Filing Separately

If Taxable Income Is:	The tax Is:
Not over $25,000	10% of taxable income
Over $25,000 but not over $100,000	$2,500 plus 20% of that over $25,000
Over $100,000	$17,500 plus 30% of that over $100,000

ORIGINATION OF TAX BRACKETS FOR THE 20/20 TAX

It is important to understand how the proposed tax rates and income brackets were derived and what mathematical results they are expected to lead to. In order to formulate the tax rate schedules of the 20/20 Tax, there are four guiding principles that were followed.

First, the future tax obligations for all taxpayer income levels should fall within the same range as we have experienced during the last five presidential terms (1993–2012). More precisely, the effective tax rates should be no more than the average effective tax rates incurred over the ten-year period of 1996–2005 for various income levels in the US population. This ten-year period was chosen to blend the last five years of the Clinton administration (relatively high taxes) with the first five years of the George W. Bush administration (relatively low taxes).

Second, the degree of progressivity for the new income tax rate structure should approximate the average found in the twenty-five-year period from 1988 to 2012. This progressive tax criteria would avoid the two most progressive tax rate periods of the last thirty years, which occurred during the middle years of President Reagan (1985–1986) and the most recent years of President Obama (2013–2014).

The third guiding principle of the 20/20 Tax rates is the minimization of the marriage penalty and its countertrend known as the marriage bonus. These two phenomena in today's tax code have created gross inequities for married spouses as well as singles and cohabiting couples, sometimes resulting in the wrong reasons for being married or not being married.

The fourth and final guiding principal is that the number of rates should be minimized, and the least complex rate structure should be adopted while still allowing for the first three principles (in the order presented) as higher priorities. Let's examine the adherence to each of these guiding principles as contained in the 20/20 Tax rate schedules.

EFFECTIVE TAX RATES TO BE SIMILAR FOR MOST INCOME LEVELS

As previously stated, it is one of my goals to have our future tax code result in comparable tax amounts for all income levels with effective tax rates clearly lower than the years 1995–2000 but somewhat higher than 2001–2005. These periods were chosen because they represent a relatively stable period in our nation's economic history and because they compare the last five years of the Clinton tax philosophy with the first five years of the George W. Bush tax strategy.

In the world of tax policy, there is no such thing as perfect or ideal tax rates. Selecting rates is a very subjective process in which most people on the left side of the aisle propose to tax the wealthy at much higher rates than the middle class, while those on the right would prefer either a flat tax rate structure or a moderately progressive rate schedule. In reality, the Clinton tax rates were not nearly as progressive as the Bush II rates, but rather they were much higher effective rates across the board, especially for the middle class. In order to illustrate this statement, let's take a look at selected data comparing the effective tax rates for certain income groups from Clinton's fifth year in office (1997) as compared to George W.'s fifth year in office (2005), with both years' results being very representative of each former president's full eight-year tenure.

Table 5.5-1 Total Income Tax as a Percentage of Adjusted Gross Income [94]

Size of AGI (in 2009 $)	1997	2005	% of Effective Rate Decrease
$10,000–$20,000	4.3%	2.2%	48.8%
$30,000–$40,000	9.6	5.6	41.7
$50,000–$60,000	11.3	7.8	31.0
$70,000–$80,000	13.4	8.8	34.3
$90,000–$100,000	15.2	10.1	33.5
$125,000–$150,000	17.7	13.4	24.3
$175,000–$200,000	20.5	16.2	21.0
$300,000–$400,000	26.1	21.6	17.2
$500,000–$1,000,000	29.0	23.8	17.9

From this snapshot you can see that the effective tax rates incurred by all taxpayers were much higher at every level in 1997 than they were in 2005. At the $10,000–$20,000 income level, the effective tax rate dropped almost 50% from 1997 to 2005 (4.3% to 2.2%). However, at the two highest income levels, the Bush tax cuts lowered taxes by only 17.2% and 17.9% respectively. Of course in terms of absolute dollars, the wealthy saw their taxes reduced by several thousand dollars per year after 2000, while the lower middle class often saved just a few hundred dollars. The Bush tax cuts were so dramatic that individual income taxes fell from 10.3% of GDP in 2000 to 7.0% of GDP in 2004.[95] This percentage of GDP rose above 7.0% for most of the next four years (2005–2008) but then actually dropped below 7.0% for the first two years of the Obama presidency (2009–2010). It is my opinion that our individual income tax system must raise revenue of at least 8.5% of GDP in order for our country to have a serious chance at a balanced budget in future years without imposing another major federal tax. I believe that the 20/20 Tax has the potential to collect income taxes between 8% and 9% of our GDP provided our nation follows almost all of the recommendations of this book.

The 20/20 Tax is designed to tax every income level at effective tax rates at least as high as the 2005 percentages displayed in table 5.5-1. For the lower and middle income levels, the effective tax rates should be almost the same as the 2005 percentages. However, for those married taxpayers with over $200,000 of total income, some will see another 1% to 5% of their total income spent for federal income taxes (as compared to 2005). Irrespective of which income level we are talking about, all levels will experience a lower average effective tax rate than seen during the Clinton years when our total federal taxes were among the highest effective tax rates of the last sixty years.

Keep in mind that one of my goals for the 20/20 Tax is to be revenue-neutral with respect to its ability as an individual tax system to raise the same amount of revenue as our 2014 individual tax system. This means that we have to consider the significant income tax revenue raised by the American Taxpayer Relief Act of 2012 (ATRA), passed by our Congress and signed by the president in January 2013. Due to this considerable revenue bill, if we truly want bipartisan comprehensive tax reform that is revenue neutral, then almost every income level should probably see at least a slight increase in the effective tax rate as compared to the years 2003–2012. The ATRA legislation, which mostly went into effect January 1, 2013, has targeted the wealthy (those with incomes above $200,000 single, and $250,000 married, but primarily those above $400,000) for all of the new tax increases. The 20/20 Tax concept was mostly formulated long before ATRA and it has been based largely on the concepts of the Simpson-Bowles Commission and the Domenici-Rivlin Bipartisan Policy Center reports of 2010. Those two very distinguished commissions did not recommend anything close to the new ATRA tax law we received in January 2013, which was driven by partisan politics in the shadow of "the fiscal cliff." Thus, I am not at all inclined to tailor the 20/20 Tax after the ATRA legislation with its steep progressive curve (at the upper income levels) that may well prove to be an aberration and not a trend in our nation's tax history.

On the following two pages, you will see the effective tax rates of most of the last thirty years. These rates are the Treasury's calculations arrived at by taking the total income tax paid as a percentage of taxpayers' adjusted gross income. The following table 5.5-2 is the source document used to create the previous table 5.5-1.

Table 5.5-2[96]

Total Income Tax as a Percentage of Adjusted Gross Income, 1986-1998

Size of 2011 AGI	1986	1987	1988	1989	1990	1991	1992	1993	1994	1995	1996	1997	1998
	(1)	(2)	(3)	(4)	(5)	(6)	(7)	(8)	(9)	(10)	(11)	(12)	(13)
All Returns Total	**14.8**	**13.3**	**13.4**	**13.3**	**13.1**	**12.9**	**13.1**	**13.5**	**13.7**	**14.0**	**14.5**	**14.7**	**14.6**
$1–$10,000	3.0	2.9	2.9	2.7	2.5	2.3	2.0	1.9	1.8	1.8	1.8	1.8	1.7
$10,000 under $20,000	7.8	6.8	6.5	6.4	6.1	5.5	5.1	4.9	4.8	4.7	4.6	4.3	4.3
$20,000 under $30,000	10.6	9.4	9.3	9.3	9.1	8.7	8.4	8.2	8.1	7.9	7.7	7.6	6.8
$30,000 under $40,000	12.2	10.6	10.9	10.9	10.6	10.5	10.2	10.1	10.0	9.8	9.7	9.6	8.8
$40,000 under $50,000	13.8	11.8	11.6	11.5	11.4	11.0	10.8	10.7	10.8	10.7	10.8	10.7	10.0
$50,000 under $60,000	15.5	13.5	13.2	12.9	12.4	12.1	11.6	11.5	11.4	11.4	11.3	11.3	10.7
$60,000 under $70,000	16.9	15.1	14.5	14.2	13.8	13.2	12.9	12.7	12.6	12.5	12.3	12.1	11.4
$70,000 under $80,000	18.7	16.5	15.6	15.3	14.9	14.4	14.0	13.9	13.8	13.6	13.6	13.4	12.6
$80,000 under $90,000	19.9	17.8	16.6	16.2	15.8	15.4	15.0	15.1	14.9	14.6	14.6	14.4	13.5
$90,000 under $100,000	20.8	18.8	17.4	17.3	16.6	16.0	15.9	15.7	15.9	15.8	15.4	15.2	14.8
$100,000 under $125,000	23.1	20.1	18.8	18.4	17.5	17.3	16.9	17.0	17.0	16.9	16.7	16.5	16.0
$125,000 under $150,000	25.2	21.8	20.3	19.8	19.2	18.6	18.7	18.6	18.6	18.3	18.4	17.7	17.7
$150,000 under $175,000	28.0	23.0	21.6	21.1	20.4	19.8	19.6	19.7	19.9	19.9	19.8	19.3	18.8
$175,000 under $200,000	29.3	23.9	22.5	21.8	21.1	21.0	20.7	21.2	21.4	20.9	20.9	20.5	20.0
$200,000 under $300,000	31.1	25.8	23.7	22.8	22.6	22.7	22.9	23.8	23.9	23.8	23.4	22.9	22.4
$300,000 under $400,000	33.7	27.0	24.0	23.6	23.7	24.3	24.4	26.9	26.9	26.8	26.6	26.1	25.4
$400,000 under $500,000	36.2	28.2	24.1	23.9	23.6	24.9	25.3	28.4	28.6	28.7	28.2	27.4	26.9
$500,000 under $1,000,000	38.4	29.0	24.6	24.0	24.0	25.7	26.0	30.0	30.2	30.2	30.1	29.0	28.2
$1,000,000 or more	40.2	28.6	25.0	24.2	24.1	26.2	26.8	31.2	31.1	31.4	30.8	28.8	27.5

Table 5.5-2[97]

Total Income Tax as a Percentage of Adjusted Gross Income, 1999-2011

Size of 2011 AGI	1999	2000	2001	2002	2003	2004	2005	2006	2007	2008	2009	2010	2011
	(14)	(15)	(16)	(17)	(18)	(19)	(20)	(21)	(22)	(23)	(24)	(25)	(26)
All Returns Total	**15.0**	**15.4**	**14.4**	**13.2**	**12.1**	**12.3**	**12.6**	**12.7**	**12.8**	**12.5**	**11.4**	**11.8**	**12.5**
$1 under $10,000	1.7	1.7	1.0	0.7	0.7	0.6	0.6	0.6	0.6	0.5	0.4	0.4	0.4
$10,000 under $20,000	4.1	4.1	3.4	2.6	2.4	2.3	2.2	2.1	2.0	1.5	0.9	0.9	1.5
$20,000 under $30,000	6.7	6.5	5.9	4.7	4.2	4.1	4.0	3.9	3.7	3.3	2.5	2.5	3.2
$30,000 under $40,000	8.6	8.5	8.0	6.7	6.1	5.8	5.6	5.5	5.4	5.0	4.0	4.2	4.9
$40,000 under $50,000	9.8	9.8	9.4	8.1	7.4	7.2	6.9	6.8	6.7	6.3	5.3	5.4	6.2
$50,000 under $60,000	10.6	10.6	10.2	9.2	8.5	8.1	7.8	7.7	7.6	7.4	6.3	6.5	7.5
$60,000 under $70,000	11.2	11.2	10.8	9.6	9.0	8.5	8.4	8.4	8.3	8.1	6.9	7.3	8.2
$70,000 under $80,000	12.4	12.1	11.6	10.6	9.4	9.0	8.8	8.7	8.8	8.6	7.5	7.8	8.8
$80,000 under $90,000	13.5	13.5	12.9	11.6	10.1	9.5	9.4	9.2	9.1	8.9	8.0	8.3	9.2
$90,000 under $100,000	14.5	14.4	13.7	12.7	11.0	10.5	10.1	9.9	9.7	9.5	8.6	8.9	9.7
$100,000 under $125,000	15.8	15.8	15.2	14.2	12.4	12.0	11.5	11.3	11.1	10.9	9.9	10.1	10.8
$125,000 under $150,000	17.6	17.4	16.8	16.0	14.2	13.7	13.4	13.3	13.0	12.7	11.7	12.0	12.6
$150,000 under $175,000	19.0	18.6	18.2	17.3	15.4	15.1	14.8	14.5	14.2	14.1	13.4	13.7	14.0
$175,000 under $200,000	20.0	19.9	19.1	18.4	16.8	16.4	16.2	15.8	15.3	15.2	14.9	15.1	15.3
$200,000 under $300,000	22.4	22.4	21.6	21.0	19.2	18.9	18.6	18.1	17.7	17.7	17.5	17.7	17.7
$300,000 under $400,000	25.4	25.0	24.7	24.2	22.4	22.1	21.6	21.3	21.0	21.1	21.3	21.3	21.4
$400,000 under $500,000	26.7	26.6	26.1	25.7	23.8	23.2	22.9	22.8	22.7	22.9	23.2	23.1	23.3
$500,000 under $1,000,000	28.4	28.3	28.1	27.9	24.9	24.3	23.8	23.6	23.4	23.9	24.2	24.1	24.2
$1,000,000 or more	27.9	27.7	28.3	28.5	24.8	23.4	23.0	22.5	22.1	23.1	24.4	23.2	23.3

HOW PROGRESSIVE SHOULD OUR TAX LAW BE?

Before we answer this question, it may be helpful to define the term "progressive tax system." One of the better attempts at defining this term can be found in a well-written working paper by Thomas Piketty and Emmanual Saez, which reads as follows:

> The definition of a progressive tax system usually starts with the idea of a proportional tax, in which everyone pays the same share (percentage) of income in taxes. From that baseline, a progressive tax is when the share of income paid in taxes rises with income, and a regressive tax is when the share of income paid in taxes falls with income. Of course, real-world tax codes are complex and full of rules that have different effects across the income distribution. Thus, a more general definition is that a tax system can be defined as progressive if after-tax income is more equally distributed than before-tax income, and regressive if after-tax income is less equally distributed than before-tax income.[98]

Most people in our country have supported the concept of a progressive tax system. This acceptance often stems from the belief that those who are well off should not only pay higher taxes but they also should pay a higher percentage of their incomes toward the common good than does the middle class. This principal was built into our original individual income tax over one hundred years ago when Congress adopted a 1% tax rate on all those with incomes above a personal exemption of $3,000 (about $66,000 today) and a maximum rate of 7% on individuals with incomes above $500,000 (roughly $11 million today).[99] Thus, almost nobody owed any substantial amount of tax under this very progressive initial tax.

By 1960, our income tax rates had evolved to a minimum rate of 20% and a top income tax rate of 91% while the exemption had declined to only $600. In the 1960s, Presidents Kennedy, Johnson, and Nixon all successfully advocated the lowering of tax rates at the upper and lower levels of income. In 1981, Ronald Reagan supported the Kemp-Roth tax bill, which lowered the top tax rate from 70% to 50% as well as the lowest tax rate from 14% to 11%. Although these 1981 rates were much lower than the previous fifty years, they were still quite progressive since the top rate was almost five times as great as the bottom rate.

While the US Congress was reducing our tax rates to their lowest levels in half a century (11–50%), Margaret Thatcher and her Conservative Party of Great Britain managed to leapfrog America by lowering their top income tax rates to an astoundingly low 40% (phased in from 1980 to 1988) from a previous maximum level of 98%. This bold action caught the developed world by surprise. When reducing the top rates, the Brits managed to maintain their lower income rates at similar levels to prior years, thus in effect producing a "flatter" income tax for the British taxpayers. Mrs. Thatcher and the English Parliament had come to realize that their many years of high tax rates had driven off thousands of their country's entrepreneurs and high earners, while taking millions of additional jobs with them.

Following the lead of the British, over the next twenty years almost every major country lowered its top tax rates, flattened its rate schedules, and reduced the degree of progressivity in its income tax systems. Of course, the United States was one of the first countries to follow suit with its infamous 1986 Tax Reform Act, lowering our top tax rates to 28–33% while adopting one lower rate of 15% for the middle class. There is no question that we still had a fairly progressive income tax after the 1986 Tax Act. It was just not nearly as progressive as it had been in the 1970s or early to mid-1980s. For the sake of comparison, please refer to table 5.5-2 earlier in this chapter to see how the effective tax rates of 1986 (the last year the highest marginal rate was 50%) compare to those effective rates for 1988 when the 1986 Tax Reform Act was fully phased in with the top rates of 28–33%.

The "tax revolution" of the 1980s and 1990s can be largely attributed to at least two major factors other than just entrepreneurs leaving their homelands. One, the world had come into the age of globalization where national boundaries provided fewer barriers to manufacturers' choice of location for their production. The cost of the end product was usually the deciding factor, and each nation's tax system was one of the biggest elements in the overall cost of production. Most developed countries found little choice but to participate in this "race to the bottom" with respect to tax rates. Failure to lower a nation's tax rates meant the loss of many good jobs for the upper class as well as the middle class. Thus, the progressive tax systems that dominated most of the developed countries for the first eighty years of the twentieth century have been greatly scaled back to less progressive and flatter tax systems over the last thirty years.

The other major issue that factored into many nations' decisions to go less progressive was the preponderance of tax sheltering and downright wasteful spending that was taking place to avoid tax rates of 70–90%. Economists came to realize that many of the wealthy could find legal ways to get around high tax rates by playing the tax shelter game. This often led to the gross misallocation of resources, causing countries like ours to have too many office buildings, railroad cars, and other costly assets that provided tax deductions to the rich. If it wasn't tax shelters the wealthy were buying, it might be opulent homes, airplanes, or "business yachts" where at least the interest and property taxes were deductible, if not a whole lot more. After all, if the "government was going to pay for most" of these type of expenditures at 70% or more, why not acquire them? This kind of thinking and resulting actions led to additional inflation in many countries, including our own. After years of public debate, many of these prodigal deductions were repealed, but only with the political trade-off of lower tax rates.

In order to illustrate the evolution of our progressive US tax system over the last half century, please see table 5.5-3 on the next page. It is very important to note that this table reflects the average *effective* federal tax rates for the combination of individual income taxes, corporate income taxes, payroll taxes, and estate taxes. It does not include any state or local taxes. Also, it is important to note that the column for the year 2004 is a fairly good reflection of the years 2005–2008. However, the years 2009–2012, if they were available, would show somewhat lower percentages, due largely to the Great Recession and the resulting stimulus tax cuts, including the 2% Social Security reduction of 2011–2012. The main purpose of the following table is to show the large decrease in tax progressivity since 1960. Similar trends would be found for most other developed countries if comparable tables were provided.

Table 5.5-3

Effective Tax Rates by Income Groups from 1960 to 2004[100]

Average Federal Tax Rates (percent)

Income Groups	Average Income (pre-tax)	1960	1970	1980	1990	2000	2004
(1)	(2)	(3)	(4)	(5)	(6)	(7)	(8)
Full Population	$52,110	21.4	23.3	26.6	25.8	27.4	23.4
P20–40	15,897	13.9	18.5	16.3	16.2	13.1	9.4
P40–60	29,870	15.9	20.2	21.4	21.0	20.0	16.1
P60–80	52,137	16.7	20.7	24.5	24.3	23.9	20.5
P80–90	83,012	17.4	20.5	26.7	26.2	26.4	22.7
P90–95	117,709	18.7	21.4	27.9	27.9	28.7	24.9
P95–99	199,033	23.5	25.6	31.0	28.6	31.1	27.2
P99–99.5	428,690	34.0	36.1	37.6	31.5	35.7	31.3
P99.5–99.9	863,607	41.4	44.6	43.0	33.0	38.4	33.0
P99.9–99.99	3,158,720	55.3	59.1	51.0	34.3	40.2	34.1
P99.99–100	18,113,612	71.4	74.6	59.3	35.4	40.8	34.7

Notes: Computations are based on income tax return statistics and NBER TAXSIM calculator. P20–40 denotes families between percentile 20th and percentile 40th of the income distribution (second quintile), etc. Average income includes realized capital gains and imputed payroll and corporate taxes. Tax rates are estimated relative to income including realized capital gains and imputed payroll and corporate taxes. Payroll tax includes employee and employer Social Security and Medicare taxes (excludes payroll taxes for unemployment and workers compensation). The table displays the average federal tax rate (including individual, corporate, payroll, and estate) for various groups of the income distribution, for various years. 2004 figures are based on 2004 tax law applied to 2000 incomes adjusted for economic growth.

The concept of a progressive tax system may suggest the appearance of being the right thing to do on moral or political grounds. However, like all good theories, it has its limitations, and too much of a good thing can have harmful, unintended consequences. In order to compete in a world that has embraced globalization, we must be able to compete in the arena of tax rates. This is one reason why the 20/20 Tax has been designed to be somewhat less progressive than our tax system of 2014, yet still more progressive in most respects than that of the 1990s.

MINIMIZING THE MARRIAGE PENALTY AND THE MARRIAGE BONUS

One of the more difficult issues in choosing tax rates is the issue of the marriage penalty or its countertrend, the marriage bonus. The marriage penalty can be defined as the additional tax that some couples pay after marriage because they must file as married rather than as single taxpayers. On the other hand, the marriage bonus can be defined as the reduction in tax liability that certain married couples experience as a result of filing as married taxpayers rather than as single.

Many couples are surprised to find out how much their federal income tax increases upon getting married. For example, a married couple in 2014 with two children and $150,000 of income, earned equally by both spouses, can pay about $6,300 more in federal taxes than if they had stayed single with the same income, deductions, and exemptions, while filing as head of household.

On the other hand, the same couple with all $150,000 of income earned by just one spouse would see a tax decrease of almost $5,700 as compared to their days of filing as single taxpayers. This is the classical marriage bonus.

Believe it or not, the marriage penalty could exceed $18,000 in 2014 for those couples with combined earnings in excess of $500,000 where each spouse had one previous child and earned over $200,000 of the total. Wouldn't it be nice to put that difference toward a couple's honeymoon, or better yet, set it aside for the future college tuitions of the family's children?

One might ask just how prevalent is the marriage penalty or the marriage bonus? There is not an abundance of research on this issue, but one recent paper published in the *National Tax Journal (December 2012)* analyzed the relationship between marriage and taxes by examining tax returns filed by cohabiting couples. The writers, Emily Lin and Patricia Tong, published the following results:

> If cohabiting couples in our sample had filed joint returns, 38% would have a tax decrease (bonus) of an average amount of $914; 48% would have a tax increase (penalty) of an average amount of $1,657; and 15% would experience no change in federal income tax liability.[101]

Much of the marriage penalty is brought about because the tax brackets for married taxpayers are not twice as much as the brackets for singles. Under 2013–2014 tax law, this "twice as much" formula only occurs for taxpayers in the 10% and 15% brackets. A good case in point is that for 2014, the 35% tax rate starts at the same income level of $405,100 for both singles and married couples filing jointly. By filing a joint return, a wife's income is being stacked on top of her husband's, often resulting in a higher tax bracket and much higher taxes than two singles with the same combined income.

Another contributing factor to the marriage penalty is the wide array of phase-outs in the tax code that are almost never fixed at twice the amount for married filers as for singles. Then we run into further marriage penalties with the alternative minimum tax, the earned income credit, and a host of other provisions in the tax law.

The primary culprits that led to the marriage penalty in our recent 2013 tax law were as follows:

Tax Rates on Taxable Income (If Above)	Single	Married
28%	$87,850	$146,400
33%	183,250	223,050
35%	398,350	398,350
39.6%	400,000	450,000

Capital Gains Rates (If Taxable Income Above)

20%	$400,000	$450,000

Phase-outs (Based on AGI)

Personal exemptions	$250,000	$300,000
Itemized deductions	250,000	300,000
Earned-income credit	17,530	17,530
Child tax credit	75,000	110,000
Adoption credit	194,580	194,580

Other (Based on AGI)

Social Security benefits taxable	$25,000	$32,000
0.9% Additional Medicare tax	200,000	250,000
3.8% Net investment income tax	200,000	250,000
Alternative minimum tax (Exemption)	51,900	80,800
Head-of-household tax rates	Var.	Var.

HOW THE 20/20 TAX ALLEVIATES THE MARRIAGE PENALTY AND MARRIAGE BONUS ISSUE

It is impossible to completely eliminate marriage penalties in a tax system of graduated rates without exacerbating the occurrence of marriage bonuses. In other words, if all rate brackets of married couples were twice as much as that of singles, then the magnitude and number of marriage bonuses would go up dramatically. The 20/20 Tax reaches a middle ground on this issue by using a 5:3 ratio for all married vs. single tax bracket income levels. Thus, the 10% income tax rate applies to the first $50,000 for married couples and the first $30,000 of taxable income for singles. The 20% rate bracket applies up to $200,000 of taxable income for married filers and only $120,000 for singles. By choosing this middle-ground approach, the marriage penalties and bonuses will be much more moderate than if our tax code uses a 2:1 ratio. It is important to note that for many years prior to the Revenue Reconciliation Act of 1993, our tax code pegged most single tax bracket levels at approximately 60% of the married levels, the same approach as used for the 20/20 Tax.

The 20/20 Tax has the added advantage of having almost no phase-outs that would result in marriage penalties. One of the few phase-out provisions, found in the earned income credit of the 20/20 Tax, is designed to have less than half of the marriage penalty potential as in our current tax law (see chapter 5.6). Also, most marriage penalties will be largely avoidable by using married filing separate status of the 20/20 Tax.

Although the marriage penalty and bonus will still be a common occurrence in the 20/20 Tax, the amounts will most often be in the hundreds of dollars rather than in the thousands.

HEAD OF HOUSEHOLD RATES ARE ELIMINATED

For longer than I have been a practicing CPA (over forty years), our tax code has always provided a separate tax rate table for those who qualify as head of household. This rate table has typically been gauged to assess taxes for the head of household taxpayer at about half the difference between the married filing jointly status and the single individual status.

If the 20/20 Tax were to provide a separate tax rate table for heads of households, it would consist of the following amounts in order to split the difference between marrieds and singles:

Head of Household

If Taxable Income Is:	The Tax Is:
Not over $40,000	10% of taxable income
Over $40,000 but not over $160,000	$4,000 plus 20% of the excess over $40,000
Over $160,000	$28,000 plus 30% of the excess over $160,000

Using this tax rate schedule and the ones found at the beginning of this chapter for married as well as single taxpayers, one would arrive at the following amounts of total income tax (before credits) under the 20/20 Tax:

Taxable Income	$50,000	$200,000
Married Filing Jointly	$5,000	$35,000
Single Individuals	7,000	45,000
Heads of Households	6,000	40,000

As you can see, the head of household taxpayer earning $50,000 per year would incur $1,000 more income tax than a married couple filing jointly, but the same person's taxes would be $1,000 lower than the single taxpayer. Now compare the three taxpayers if their earnings are all at the $200,000 level. At this higher income level, the head of household pays $5,000 more income tax than the married couple, but his or her tax would be $5,000 less than the single taxpayer.

What are we seeing here? Is this not another prime example of the upside-down subsidy that is so pervasive in our current tax code? In other words, the higher-income taxpayers benefit much more from this tax break in the code than do the less fortunate in our society. In my example, the $200,000 earner would receive five times as much tax benefit ($5,000) as would the $50,000 earner who would receive only $1,000 of tax benefit by qualifying as head of household.

There is another major concern to consider, which is the high occurrence of the marriage penalty for those formerly claiming head of household status. It turns out that those individuals who have head of household status are the ones who are most likely to experience the marriage penalty upon getting married. As evidence for this concern, I refer to the same paper that studied the tax results of cohabiting couples and their potential for marriage penalties.

> … For dual single-filer couples, 43% would have a marriage penalty, 37% would have a marriage bonus, and 20% would have no tax change. These couples would have a higher likelihood of having no tax change and a lower likelihood of having a marriage penalty than average. When at least one person claims the head of household filing status, the likelihood of having a marriage penalty is much higher than average. A marriage penalty would result for 82% of couples with one head of household filer and 92% of couples with two head of household filers.[102]

After studying this issue long and hard, I have come to the conclusion that the fairest and simplest solution available is to replace the head of household rates with a nonrefundable head of household credit in the amount of $1,000. Thus, all head of household taxpayers would be eligible for the same tax benefit ($1,000) for providing a home for one or more dependent relatives. This amount was chosen because it is the amount that is calculated in my earlier example showing a head of household taxpayer earning $50,000 who incurs a tax liability $1,000 lower than the single person who does not qualify for head of household status. It is important to note that this tax difference would be the same at all taxable income levels between $50,000 and $120,000, a range that encompasses nearly half of middle class taxpayers. Thus, if the head of household rates, using the traditional split-the-difference formula, would result in a $1,000 tax savings for nearly half of middle class tax returns, then it seems right (or at least rough justice) to give all head of household taxpayers a tax credit of $1,000. This solution is way less complex (and conceptually more fair) than our current tax law that rewards anywhere from $0 to more than $7,400 for being head of household, with the higher earners being the biggest winners.

There is no question that the demise of the head of household rate schedule, as part of the 20/20 Tax reform package, will have numerous detractors. However, the arguments in favor of retaining this separate rate schedule are mostly emotional. A large majority of the single parents who provide a home for their loved ones will be better off with a nonrefundable $1,000 tax credit as compared to our current complicated rate schedules that give so many parents little or nothing for being a head of household.

THE SIMPLICITY OF THE 20/20 TAX RATES

The fourth and final guiding principle in my formulation of the 20/20 Tax rate structure is that the number of rates should be minimized, and the least complex rate structure should be adopted while still allowing for the first three principles (described earlier) as higher priorities.

There have been many valid tax reform proposals that have put forth the concept of just one or two tax rates. Presumably, those proposals with one single rate would result in a much less progressive income tax system than our nation has ever seen. It is my opinion that any single-rate income tax system would have no chance of political acceptance at our national level.

The tax reform proposals that advocate only two rates have gained considerable attention. Journalists often refer to the 1986 Tax Reform Act as a dual rate system of 15% and 28%. In reality, it was really a three-rate system due to the 33% "bubble rate" that was essentially a stealth tax that haunted the upper middle class as it phased out the benefit of the lower 15% bracket.

There have been some very good dual-rate tax systems proposed in recent years, possibly the most notable being the Domenici-Rivlin Plan originally put forth in 2010 as explained in chapter 4. Most of these dual-rate proposals have top rates of less than 30%, but rarely do they advocate preferential treatment for long-term capital gains (one exception being Paul Ryan's *Roadmap for America's Future*, which was proposed in 2012). Not surprisingly, most dual-rate tax proposals tend to be less progressive than tax systems that have three or more rates.

Probably half or more of the comprehensive tax reform proposals of the last thirty years have incorporated three different rates. An income tax system with three rates allows for a modest tax rate on low-income earners, a stronger tax rate for much of the middle class, and of course the highest tax rate for the upper income taxpayers. I have chosen to make the 20/20 Tax a three-rate system that in many ways is patterned after the Simpson-Bowles illustrative proposal as described in chapter 4 of this book. Although the Simpson-Bowles Plan does not provide an abundance of detail, it does lay the groundwork for a profound change in our nation's tax laws. In many ways, it has provided the headwaters for this book and the 20/20 Tax.

For many years, I have yearned for an income tax system that has a simple rate structure like 10-20-30. That's the way football fields are laid out, and it makes the game understandable for most fans. Can you imagine the level of gridiron comprehension if the line markers were drawn at 10-15-25-28-33-35-39.6? How and why did we ever choose these seven percentages to put on our 2014 federal tax rate schedules? Do our lawmakers not understand that we could have accomplished approximately the same tax results with 10-20-30-40 applied to modified income bracket levels?

Hopefully, most Americans will agree that the 20/20 Tax rate structure of 10%, 20%, and 30% is very simple. It's almost as easy as 1-2-3, and it allows many of us to do the math in our heads. That simplicity has a lot to do with the choice of the 20/20 Tax rate structure.

Chapter 5.6

REFUNDABLE AND NONREFUNDABLE CREDITS

For most of its existence, the Internal Revenue Code has encouraged socially beneficial activities, such as charitable contributions, home ownership, and retirement savings. In more recent years, tax incentives have been added to subsidize and promote education, adoption, energy conservation, and many other causes. During its first half-century, our federal income tax law relied primarily on exclusions, exemptions, and itemized deductions to encourage taxpayers to make the "right choices."

By way of definition, an exclusion is an amount not included in a taxpayer's gross income (i.e., muni-bond interest). Exemptions apply in various ways, with the most common one being the exemption for each dependent child, which in 2014 reduced a family's taxable income by $3,950 for each dependent. Then we have the infamous itemized deductions, which include medical expenses, state and local taxes, interest paid, charitable donations, and a host of other deductions. Itemized deductions are amounts subtracted from gross income to arrive at taxable income.

The above described exclusions, exemptions, and itemized deductions all have one common denominator: the higher your tax bracket, the more tax you will save from these incentives. For this reason, they are sometimes referred to as "upside-down subsidies."

In chapter 5.3, I explained and proposed the use of tax credits to replace exemptions and itemized deductions. The resulting attribute of this approach is that most taxpayers would receive the same proportional benefit from each dollar spent on government-encouraged activities. Under the credit concept, a taxpayer in the 39.6% bracket would no longer see tax savings of 39.6% of each dollar deducted or excluded while the taxpayer in the 15% bracket realizes only a 15% savings on such deductions, exclusions, or exemptions. If Congress decided on a 20% credit rate, then all taxpayers who qualify for various tax credits would save twenty cents on each "do-good" dollar spent.

The History of US Tax Credits

For many years, there was nothing in the Internal Revenue Code comparable to what we have come to know as tax credits. Then in 1960, as a young presidential candidate, John F. Kennedy, made a campaign pledge to promote an investment tax credit (ITC) to get business in America moving again. As history unfolded, Kennedy won the election, and by 1962 Congress enacted the tax credit he had promised. Under this new provision, business taxpayers were entitled to a credit of 7% of the cost of depreciable personal property acquired and placed in service. Thus, in a year when a $10,000 business machine was purchased and first utilized, the business was able to reduce its taxes by $700 (in addition to the tax benefit of depreciation). If the business had no taxes for that year, the credit could be carried back to earlier years or forward to later years when there was a tax liability to absorb the credit.

Ten years later, in 1972, another future president, Ronald Reagan, proposed an altogether different type of tax credit for his state when he was governor of California.[103] This proposed credit was similar to the earned income credit (EIC) adopted in 1975 during the Gerald Ford administration. The main congressional reason for enacting the EIC was to encourage more work participation among low-income parents by reducing some of the work disincentives caused by government transfer programs (i.e., food stamps). The EIC had the distinction of becoming the first fully refundable tax credit on the books. The refundable nature of this credit meant that a taxpayer could have no tax obligation and still get a full refund of the credit amount.

After the introduction of the EIC, we started to see a proliferation of numerous nonrefundable credits that sprung up, such as the child care credit, the residential energy credit, and the new jobs credit. With nonrefundable credits, a taxpayer can only use the credit savings to reduce his or her tax obligation (dollar for dollar) for the current year. If there's no tax liability, then the credit is usually lost. However, there are some exceptions (like the foreign tax credit) where the unused credit can be carried forward to later tax obligation years.

Today there are more than one hundred nonrefundable tax credits in the Internal Revenue Code. Most of the nonrefundable credits, due to their limited application and unusual nature, have never been used for the benefit of clients by the majority of CPAs.

For twenty-two years, the EIC was the only refundable tax credit. In 1997, a second refundable credit, the child tax credit (CTC), was added to the Internal Revenue Code.[104] Initially, the CTC allowed a $400 credit per dependent child and was partially refundable to the extent that a family's FICA taxes exceeded their EIC.[105] The CTC amount and its refundability have been expanded multiple times over the last fifteen years, resulting in today's version that provides a maximum credit of $1,000 per dependent child under the age of seventeen. The CTC is now fully refundable for the majority of families who qualify for this credit.

In recent years, more refundable credits have crept into the code, such as the first-time homebuyer credit and the making work pay credit, both of which have expired. By the beginning of 2013, five of the eleven refundable tax credits available in 2010 had expired,[106] and by the beginning of 2014, there were only five refundable credits remaining as shown in the following chart:

ESTIMATED COSTS OF REFUNDABLE TAX CREDITS IN CALENDAR YEAR 2014 AND 2021 [107]

(BILLIONS OF 2013 DOLLARS)

Credit	2014	2021
Earned Income Tax Credit (EIC)	$68	$61
Child Tax Credit (CTC)	57	40
American Opportunity Tax Credit (expires 12/31/17)	21	0
Small Employer Health Insurance Credit (PPACA)	3	2
Premium Assistance Tax Credit (PPACA)	35	110
Total	184	213

CAUTION: DRY ZONE AHEAD BUT EXTREMELY IMPORTANT TO READ.

TAX RESULTS OF REFUNDABLE OR NONREFUNDABLE CREDITS

By now, you are probably asking why our lawmakers choose refundable or nonrefundable credits rather than using the traditional approach of deductions and exclusions? It is important to note that the traditional approach is currently yielding the largest tax benefits to higher-bracket taxpayers despite the abundance of tax credits available. See the following illustrative examples of three couples who each have two young children, each paid $10,000 for health insurance, and each had home mortgage interest of $20,000. All of the computations use my proposed tax rates from chapter 5.5 as well as the personal tax credits ($1,000) as described in chapter 5.7 together with a credit rate of 20% on the health insurance (refundable) and home interest(nonrefundable). The earned income credit (later explained in chapter 5.7) will be $4,800 for all three couples.

Annual Income = $40,000

	If Deductions of $30,000	Tax Credits of 20% X $30,000 20/20 Tax	All Refundable
Taxable Income:			
Before deductions	$40,000	$40,000	$40,000
Minus deductions	-30,000	n/a	n/a
After deductions	10,000	40,000	40,000
Tax Rate (Percent)	10	10	10
($0–50,000 @ 10%, $50,001–200,000 @ 20%)			
Tax Liability:Before credits	1,000	4,000	4,000
Minus nonrefundable credits	n/a	-5,000	n/a
Before refundable credits	1,000	0	4,000
Minus refundable credits *	-7,800	-8,800	-13,800
After all credits	0	0	0
Refundable Credits Exceeding Tax Liability	$ 6,800	$ 8,800	$ 9,800
*Summary of Refundable Credits:			
Earned Income Credit (EIC 20/20)	$ 4,800	$ 4,800	$ 4,800
Personal Tax Credit (PTC 20/20)	1,000	n/a	1,000
Child Tax Credit (CTC 20/20)	2,000	2,000	2,000
Health Insurance Credit (20/20)	n/a	2,000	2,000
Home Mortgage Interest Credit (20/20)	n/a	n/a	4,000
Totals	$ 7,800	$ 8,800	$13,800

Annual Income = $200,000

	If Deductions of $30,000	Tax Credits of 20% X $30,000	
		20/20 Tax	All Refundable
Taxable Income:			
Before deductions	$200,000	$200,000	$200,000
Minus deductions	-30,000	n/a	n/a
After deductions	170,000	200,000	200,000
Tax Rate (Percent)	10/20	10/20	10/20
($0–50,000 @ 10%, $50,001–200,000 @ 20%)			
Tax Liability: Before credits	29,000	35,000	35,000
Minus nonrefundable credits	n/a	-5,000	n/a
Before refundable credits	29,000	30,000	35,000
Minus refundable credits	-7,800	-8,800	-13,800
After all credits	$ 21,200	$ 21,200	$ 21,200
Refundable Credits Exceeding Tax Liability	$ 0	$ 0	$ 0

Annual Income = $300,000

	If Deductions of $30,000	Tax Credits of 20% X $30,000	
		20/20 Tax	All Refundable
Taxable Income:			
Before deductions	$300,000	$300,000	$300,000
Minus deductions	-30,000	n/a	n/a
After deductions	270,000	300,000	300,000
Tax Rate (Percent)	10/20/30	10/20/30	10/20/30
($0–50,000 @ 10%, $50,001–200,000 @ 20%, 30% on $200,001+)			
Tax Liability: Before credits	56,000	65,000	65,000
Minus nonrefundable credits	n/a	-5,000	n/a
Before refundable credits	56,000	60,000	65,000
Minus refundable credits	-7,800	-8,800	-13,800
After all credits	$ 48,200	$ 51,200	$ 51,200
Refundable Credits Exceeding Tax Liability	$ 0	$ 0	$ 0

If you analyze the first example, you will see that the couple with $40,000 of annual income shows no tax liability using any of the three approaches (frameworks). In fact, this couple is entitled to refunds under all three approaches even assuming no withholding. You should note that the greatest refund ($9,800) occurs using the framework with all refundable tax credits. The second-best refund ($8,800) was $1,000 lower because the nonrefundable credits, ($5,000) for personal tax credits and home interest, were $1,000 higher than the tax liability before the credits ($4,000). This is a common disadvantage of nonrefundable credits, often causing lower-income taxpayers to lose the benefit of their credits. Finally, the smallest refund occurred using the traditional approach of deductions and exclusions (rather than credits) to yield tax savings for the couple's health insurance and home interest. This lowest credit refund ($6,800) was $3,000 less than the refund of the fully refundable credit framework ($9,800) simply because the couple's tax bracket of 10% was lower than the credit rate of 20%. With $30,000 of health insurance and home interest, the 20% refundable credit saves $6,000 of tax. Using the deduction approach, the 10% tax bracket multiplied times $30,000 results in just $3,000 of tax savings. Thus, we see additional tax benefits of $3,000 from the refundable credit framework.

Now let's take a look at the next example of the second couple with annual income of $200,000. It should be noted that all three of the approaches yield the same tax result with $21,200 of final tax liability after all credits. There are two main reasons for this occurrence. First, the couple's highest marginal tax rate is 20% which is the same as the credit percentage of 20% being applied in our examples. Given this equal level of tax bracket and credit percentage, the resulting tax savings will usually be identical. The second reason is based on the fact the couple's income is high enough that no credits (or deductions) are wasted. As we saw in the first ($40,000 income) example, a nonrefundable credit can go unused (wasted) when the preliminary tax before credits is lower than the nonrefundable credit itself. That is the nature of the beast and the reason these credits are called nonrefundable. Lower-income taxpayers often lose the benefit of these tax credits merely because they do not have sufficient income and the preliminary tax to absorb the benefit of their nonrefundable credits.

Finally, let's look at our highest income couple with annual income of $300,000. You will observe that both of the credit frameworks result in a higher tax result ($51,200) than if our couple was able to use the deduction approach which results in only $48,200 of total tax. The reason for this is rather simple. The couple's highest marginal tax rate is 30% which when multiplied times $30,000 of deductions will provide tax savings of $9,000. However, when our tax credit framework only allows 20% credits, the tax savings on $30,000 of tax preferences is only $6,000, resulting in $3,000 of higher tax liability than the deduction approach.

Please excuse the meticulous detail of the last three pages. You have been extremely persistent to get this far, and if you have been able to absorb the concept of refundable and nonrefundable tax credits, then you are well on your way to understanding the inherent characteristics of the 20/20 Tax. The pages you just read should be used for future reference to refresh your understanding of a basic tax credit framework.

THE CHOICE BETWEEN REFUNDABLE AND NON-REFUNDABLE CREDITS

Based on the forgoing explanations, you may be asking, why do we have a vast constellation of nonrefundable credits and only a handful of refundable credits? Much of the answer is found primarily in the budget constraints of Congress. Simply put, the cost to the Treasury of refundable credits is always higher than nonrefundable credits. Many taxpayers do not always have sufficient income or the pre-credit tax to take advantage of all nonrefundable credits for which they may qualify. For this reason, the multitude of nonrefundable credits are not costing our government nearly as much as the refundable credits, which are much fewer in number.

Despite the budgetary issues involved, there are compelling reasons to adopt refundable credits for certain purposes that Congress wishes to promote. One article from the *Stanford Law Review* makes a strong case for refundable credits, declaring them to be "the most efficient type of tax incentive"[108] among the choices available. Thus, if policymakers want the general public to devote financial resources to certain causes, the refundable credit may be our most effective tool in the tax code. The *Law Review* article further maintains that "refundable credits represent the only simple individual income tax incentive that can apply uniformly across different annual and lifetime income groups and, within a given lifetime income group, across different earning patterns."[109] This article opines that "tax incentives should provide the same price adjustment to all households" [110] unless there is strong evidence that more good is accomplished by targeting certain income groups.

On the other hand, the opponents of refundable tax credits often point out the effects that such credits have on the simplicity of the tax system. Inevitably, refundable credits lead to more effort and higher costs for taxpayers to prepare their returns. For most of these credits, taxpayers and their preparers are forced to read more instructions, complete additional tax schedules, assemble further data, and store copious records to defend themselves in the event of an audit.

There is also the issue of governmental complexity in dealing with refundable tax credits, which has been described as follows in a recent report by the Congressional Budget Office:

> Administering refundable tax credits also strains the limited resources the IRS has to provide services to taxpayers and to enforce the tax code. The number of tax returns increases as people who do not have to file returns do so in order to claim benefits. Complicated rules for refundable tax credits increase the number of telephone calls to the IRS from confused taxpayers and contribute to the tax gap (the difference between the amount of taxes that should be paid in a timely fashion and the amount that is actually paid). Some taxpayers probably make errors because they do not understand

the tax law, whereas others—perhaps sensing that complexity makes the tax code more difficult to enforce—intentionally misreport their income, family characteristics, and other information on their tax returns.[111]

Having seen refundable tax credits come and go in recent years, it is my conclusion that there have been good ones, and there have been some very bad ones. I believe the cash for clunkers credit and the first-time homebuyer credit have been two of the most misguided pieces of tax legislation in recent memory. It is my opinion that in the future, Congress should only adopt refundable credits that at least meet all of the following criteria:

A. The availability of the credit should be to a broad base of taxpayers and not have a narrow focus on any particular industry or special interest group.

B. The credit should be established to replace an already existing government subsidy or tax benefit, and there should be sufficient evidence to support that the refundable credit would be a more efficient tool than any existing subsidy, tax benefit, or other government incentive(s) available.

C. It must be shown that our government enforcement agencies (i.e., IRS, DOL, etc.) can efficiently enforce the parameters and inherent rules of such credits without experiencing widespread fraud and erroneous taxpayer claims. This will often entail the government's ability to implement an effective "matching program" requiring the issuance of 1098 Forms to verify taxpayer expenditures.

Upon thoughtful study of the five refundable credits under our current 2014 tax law, I have come to the following conclusions regarding the merits of each credit:

1. *Earned Income Credit (EIC).* This long-standing provision of the law has been successful by most standards and meets the first two

criteria spelled out above. However, it has battled the ongoing stigma of massive fraud and erroneous claims, and the time has come for a major overhaul of this program. It is my opinion that the revised EIC that is later described in chapter 5.7 would go a long way toward reducing the fraud and error rate that currently exists, if for no other reason than the inherent simplicity of this revised EIC. The eligibility standards of the 20/20 EIC are much easier to understand than our existing EIC, and the IRS would not have to spend millions of hours educating the public on the qualification rules and the complex calculations that are necessary. The 20/20 EIC can be reported on one understandable page without the use of software and without a rocket-scientist mentality.

2. *Child Tax Credit (CTC)*. Here again, this credit has been successful in providing support for lower- and middle-income families. However, its rules are far too complex for the average American taxpayer, resulting in a constant challenge for the IRS to enforce. The 20/20 Tax proposes a new child tax credit and a revised EIC (see chapter 5.7) to replace dependent exemptions as well as the current child tax credit. This new child tax credit would be a major improvement over our current CTC and the existing system of dependent exemptions. There would be no complex phase-outs of the new child tax credit the way we have with today's child tax credit and dependent exemptions. There would simply be a refundable $1,000 child tax credit for the parent(s) of every American child.

3. *American Opportunity Tax Credit (AOTC)*. Following is a technical description of this partially refundable credit that has been in effect since January 1, 2009:

> The credit amount is the sum of 100% of the first $2,000 of qualified tuition and related expenses plus 25% of the next $2,000 of qualified tuition and related expenses, for a total maximum credit of $2,500 per eligible student per year. The credit is available for the first four years of a student's post-secondary education.

Up to 40% of the credit amount is refundable should the taxpayer's tax liability be insufficient to offset the nonrefundable credit amount. The credit amount phases out ratably for taxpayers with modified AGI between $80,000 and $90,000 ($160,000 and $180,000 for joint filers) (Code Sec. 25A(i)(4)). Modified AGI is the taxpayer's AGI with any amounts excluded under the provisions for foreign or U.S. possessions earned income and foreign housing expenses (¶ 2402). The American opportunity credit may not be taken by married taxpayers who file separate returns (Code Sec. 25A(g))."[112]

Is it any wonder that half of the above six sentences have managed to confuse many of our best and brightest college-bound students and their families? Actually, the first sentence is easy to understand, and that's the part that basically says if you spend at least $2,000 on qualified tuition, then you get a dollar-for-dollar credit of $2,000 from the government. This is where I have a big problem with the American opportunity credit. It is one of the few tax credits our country has ever enacted that potentially reimburses some taxpayers for 100% of their do-good expenditures.

It is my opinion that none of our tax incentives should be dollar-for-dollar, and I believe the highest percentage tax credit that I could ever endorse would be a 50% credit. In my mind, the purpose of tax credits is to *encourage* certain beneficial action and/or spending by our citizens. Credits should never be used to pay all of a person's qualified expenditures, or even the first $2,000 per year for such expenditures. There are many college students whose total spending is $2,000 or less per year on qualified tuition, especially those who receive scholarships. It does not seem right that the government and its taxpayers should totally reimburse all of the first $2,000 per year of qualified tuition and related expenses. Thus, I believe that at least this part of the education credit should be substantially modified.

I have other problems with the American opportunity credit including its *partial* refundability (40%) which means that most of the married families with incomes of $60,000–$160,000 will usually receive a full credit of $2,500 while those joint filers who happen to be much below $60,000 of income will often only receive the refundable credit of $1,000 (40%).

In recent years, there have been three education-related credits: the Hope scholarship credit (unavailable after 2011), the American opportunity tax credit, and the lifetime learning credit.[113] All have different credit amounts, AGI limits, and percentage applications. None are refundable except the AOTC, which is partially refundable. There is also a tuition deduction of as much as $4,000 for those married couples with adjusted gross incomes of less than $160,000 ($80,000 for singles) provided they do not claim any of the education credits for the same student. Then there is a maximum deduction of $2,500 per year for interest paid on any "qualified education loan"[114] for taxpayers below certain AGI limits. Altogether there are at least fourteen tax incentives to encourage saving for and spending on education.[115]

The 20/20 Tax would replace all three credits and both of the above deductions with one fully refundable credit called the higher education credit (HEC). It would be equal to 20% of the first $10,000 of qualified tuition and fees paid per calendar year. Each individual student would be eligible for as many as ten calendar years and would have to pay for the equivalent of at least ten completed semester hours for each calendar year in order to qualify for the credit. The maximum credit available over ten years would be $20,000 per student. The HEC credit would be available for post-secondary education, including graduate-level and professional degree courses as well as qualified trade schools. And the parent or student who pays the highest amount of tuition and fees for the calendar year would be entitled to claim the credit.

The higher education credit would have no phase-outs for high-income taxpayers as is the case with the AOTC, which phases out for married taxpayers with modified AGI between $160,000 and $180,000. We should recognize that married taxpayers who have an AGI above $180,000 represent less than 10% of all married filers, and I simply don't believe it is right to discriminate against these taxpayers who usually pay the greatest amount of tax as well as the highest percentage of their income in federal taxes. If our Congress has to resort to the phase-out of credits for higher-income earners in order to minimize the drain on the Treasury, then I suggest the tax benefit of such credits should be lowered for everybody rather than taking the entire benefit away from a small percentage of taxpayers at the top of the income scale.

Finally, the elimination of the deduction for student loan interest is easy to justify when you consider that most college loans have low interest rates that are heavily subsidized by the government or the academic institutions involved. Many of these education loans also have generous forgiveness provisions sometimes allowing waiver of much of the principal. The actual tax benefit that goes to college graduates who deduct interest is usually minimal relative to the lure of tax savings when students are applying for these loans, knowing that they potentially have ten to fifteen years after graduation to repay such loans.

Most college students would be much better off knowing that their only educational tax savings would be one simple refundable tax credit of 20% of their college tuition up to $10,000 per year for a total annual credit of $2,000 for as many as ten years. The higher education credit as proposed in the 20/20 Tax would provide this simple result and avoid a maze of tax laws, complex rules, erroneous refunds, and unnecessary return preparer fees.

4. *Small Employer Health Insurance Credit.* As one may see from the chart earlier in this chapter, this credit has a relatively low cost to the Treasury, which is expected to be $2–$3 billion per year for the next eight years. That's the good news. The bad news is that the formula

and limitations of this credit are so tight that it precludes all but the smallest of businesses with very low wage scales from obtaining any tax benefits. Although our CPA firm works with a larger number of small businesses, I have seen only two of our business clients able to utilize this credit in the first five years that the credit has been available (2010–2014). In both cases, our accounting fees (less discounts) were almost as high as the tax benefits obtained by our clients. I am sure that there are some businesses that find this credit to be quite beneficial, but this has not been our firm's experience. I will stop short of calling for the elimination of this credit, but I suggest that it be carefully scrutinized in future congressional tax decisions.

5. *Premium Assistance Credit (also known as the net premium tax credit).* As of this writing, the full regulations have yet to be released on this significant refundable tax credit. This credit went into effect January 1, 2014 with a first-year cost estimated at $35 billion.[116] That cost is projected to more than triple by 2021 to an estimated cost of $110 billion.[117] At this time, it is far too early for me to provide an educated assessment of the premium assistance credit. It is a cornerstone of the Affordable Care Act, which is currently the law of the land. We will have to wait and see how it works out.

In addition to the five refundable tax credits described above, the 20/20 Tax would initially adopt two more refundable tax credits. The first of these new credits would be the uniform health insurance credit (UHIC) as described in chapter 5.1. This provision replaces the current exclusion for employer-provided health insurance with a 20% refundable tax credit. The same credit would be available to those who self-pay their own healthcare insurance. The UHIC credit will be further described in chapter 6.1 of this book.

The second all-new refundable credit of the 20/20 Tax would be the new Credit IRA. This credit of 20% would apply to as much as $5,000 per year contributed to one's IRA account, resulting in a tax savings of as much as $1,000 per year. Chapter 6.3 will explain how this new credit will go a long way toward simplifying the decision-making involved with IRA savings.

In addition to the refundable tax credits described above, the current law has a whole myriad of nonrefundable tax credits. Later, chapter 6 has been organized to describe how the 20/20 Tax will reduce this myriad of tax credits and deductions to a pragmatic number of credits that can be largely understood by most taxpayers. Please read on.

Chapter 5.7

SIMPLIFY THE EARNED INCOME CREDIT AND CHILD TAX CREDIT WHILE REPLACING EXEMPTIONS

The impact of tax reform on low-income families is a critical concept not to be ignored. According to economist, Jason Furman, "The two most important facets of the tax system for low-income families are payroll taxes and the earned income tax credit (EIC), the former of which levies a tax on earned income, and the latter (which) (sic) provides a tax credit (and refunds) for earned income."[118]

With the persistence of wage stagnation at lower levels and the growth of income inequality, low-income families are struggling to survive in today's world, not just in our country but in most developed nations. There has been much debate about the causes of depressed wages and the wealth gap, but these issues do not seem to have feasible legislative solutions. One of the few options that Congress has found to ameliorate the economic problems of low-income families is the EIC, which was first established in 1975 during the Gerald Ford administration and later expanded in 1986, 1990, 1993, 2006, 2009, and recently with the 2012 Taxpayer Relief Act. Over the years, this tax credit has served to cushion the financial hardship for families at the bottom of the economic scale.

President Ronald Reagan once called the EIC "the best anti-poverty, the best pro-family, the best job creation measure to come out of Congress."[119] Despite criticism by some conservatives, the EIC attracts a substantial amount of bipartisan support as well as requests for its expansion. Presidents Reagan and George H. W. Bush both favored raising the EIC as a better way of helping the working poor than increasing the minimum wage.[120]

"Almost all economists praise the EIC as an effective program for aiding the working poor."[121] Research studies have consistently shown that the EIC has improved the labor force rate considerably among single mothers. "From 1984 to 1996, the employment rate for single mothers with children jumped nine percentage points at the same time that the employment rate for single women without children fell slightly."[122] Much of this improvement has been attributed to the expansion of the EIC in 1986, 1990, and 1993.

By now you are probably asking just what is the earned income credit (EIC) and why do we have it? Part of the answer is that several years ago our country moved from a system that rewarded welfare to a system that supports personal labor and meaningful work. This policy shift led to a large allocation of government resources to encourage and to reward low-income workers to seek employment. A key element in the effort to minimize welfare is the EIC, which has become the main driving stimulus of our nation's work-support program. This tax credit has provided over $50 billion per year[123] in recent years for low-income workers, mostly single mothers.

How does the EIC work? "The basic idea of the EIC is to subsidize earnings from work by offering a credit for every dollar earned up to a certain level; to limit the benefits to low-income households, it phases out after a certain income threshold is reached … the EIC is refundable, meaning that if it is larger than your total tax bill, you get a check for the difference."[124] This explanation sounds rather straightforward. Unfortunately, the process gets quite complicated as can be seen in the following technical explanation of *some* of the EIC's finer points (this explanation below and on the following page is optional reading for those who wish to maintain their sanity):

Amount of Credit. The credit amount is determined by multiplying an applicable credit percentage by the individual's earned income that does not exceed a maximum amount (called the earned income amount). In 2014, the maximum earned income amount for taxpayers with one qualifying child is $9,720, with two or more qualifying children is $13,650, and with no qualifying child is $6,480 (Rev. Proc. 2013-35). The credit amount is then reduced by a limitation amount determined by multiplying the applicable phaseout percentage by the excess of the amount of the individual's AGI (or earned income, if greater) over a phase-out amount (discussed below). The earned income amount and the phaseout amount are adjusted yearly for inflation. The amount of allowable credit is determined through the use of the tables that appear at ¶ 87 (not included).

The credit percentages and phaseout percentages limit the maximum amount of credit that may be claimed (Code Sec. 32(b)(1)). For 2014, the maximum earned income credit for taxpayers with one qualifying child is $3,305, with two qualifying children is $5,460, with three or more qualifying children is $6,143, and with no qualifying children is $496 (Rev. Proc. 2013-35).[125]

Credit Limitations. In 2014, the credit begins to phase out when taxpayers with a filing status of single, surviving spouse, or head of household and with one or more qualifying children have an AGI of $17,830, and with no qualifying children have an AGI of $8,110. Phase-out of the credit is complete when taxpayers with a filing status of single, surviving spouse, or head of household with one qualifying child have an AGI of $38,511; with two qualifying children have an AGI of

$43,756; with three or more qualifying children have an AGI of $46,997; and with no qualifying children have an AGI of $14,590. The credit amount begins to phase out when taxpayers with a filing status of married filing jointly and with one or more qualifying children have an AGI of $23,260, and with no qualifying children have an AGI of $13,540. Phase-out of the credit is complete when taxpayers with a filing status of married filing jointly with one qualifying child have an AGI of $43,941; with two qualifying children have an AGI of $49,186; with three or more qualifying children have an AGI of $52,427; and with no qualifying children have an AGI of $20,020 (Rev. Proc. 2013-35).[126]

Earned Income. The credit is based on earned income, which includes all wages, salaries, tips, and other employee compensation (including union strike benefits), plus the amount of the taxpayer's net earnings from self-employment (determined with regard to the deduction for one-half of self-employment taxes (¶ 923). Earned income is determined without regard to community property laws (Code Sec. 32(c)(2)). Earned income does not include: (1) interest and dividends; (2) welfare benefits (including AFDC payments); (3) veterans' benefits; (4) pensions or annuities; (5) alimony; (6) Social Security benefits; (7) workers' compensation; (8) unemployment compensation; (9) taxable scholarships or fellowships that are not reported on Form W-2; (10) fixed or determinable periodic income of a nonresident alien not connected with a U.S. business (¶ 2431); (11) amounts received for services performed by prison inmates while in prison; or (12) payments received from work activities (including work associated with the refurbishing of public housing) if sufficient private sector employment is not available and from community service programs (Section 407(d)(4) and (7) of the Social Security Act). The earned income credit calculation is based on the taxpayer's adjusted gross income (Code Sec. 2(a)(2)(B) and (c)(2)).[127]

As you can see, the EIC Section 32 of the tax code is barely understandable. The combination of extreme complexity together with a refundable credit has resulted in rampant fraud and mistakes by tax preparers and taxpayers. "In early 2011 the Treasury Department's inspector general for tax administration reported that in 2009, $11 billion to $13 billion of EIC payments had been claimed improperly."[128] This is almost 25% of all EIC benefits for that year, which far exceeds the error and fraud rates for the Food Stamp program or Medicare (each thought to be under 6% in recent years).[129]

As the economy gradually emerged from the Great Recession, the amount of EIC benefits grew with more new jobs paying low wages. "In the tax year 2011, over 27 million eligible workers and families received nearly $62 billion total in EIC."[130] As the amount of EIC has grown, the occurrence of fraud and tax-preparer mistakes has increased.

Congress and the IRS have taken bold steps to try to curb the abuse and errors in claiming the EIC, including heavy penalties for preparers and taxpayers. As a result, one of the nation's leading tax seminar instructors has recommended that all CPA preparers give serious consideration to turning away clients who may be entitled to the EIC. His reason is the high exposure to mistakes and penalties due to misinterpretation of the law.

In recent years, many proposals have been put forth to simplify the earned income credit. In November 2005, the President's Advisory Panel on Federal Tax Reform made a serious attempt at simplification when they proposed a "work credit" to replace the EIC. The work credit would be coordinated with another creation of the panel called the "family credit," which was intended to replace the personal exemption, the standard deduction, the head-of-household filing status, and the child tax credit under current law. The work credit would approximate the EIC under current law, and taxpayers would determine the amount of their work credit based on a lengthy form and two applicable tax schedules.[131]

The Panel's approach to replacing the EIC with a work credit would be somewhat less complex than our current law but would still not be clearly understandable to most taxpayers. In fact, the panel must have been concerned about the inherent complexity of their proposed credit when it was decided under their plan that taxpayers would have the option of allowing the IRS to compute the work credit based on information provided on the tax return and family credit schedule, thus eliminating the need for taxpayers or their tax preparers to compute the work credit.

One very novel approach to reducing the complexity of the EIC was put forth by the Debt Reduction Task Force. In their initial report of November 2010, they proposed an "earnings credit of 21.3% of the first $20,300 of earnings for each worker in the tax unit (family), with the threshold amount indexed to the CPI."[132] The task force went on to state, "There will also be no phase-outs creating marriage penalties and work disincentives."[133] Essentially, the task force proposed giving a refundable earnings credit (as much as $4,324 indexed for inflation) to *all* wage earners and self-employed under age sixty-five earning at least $20,300, provided they cannot be claimed as a dependent on another's tax return.[134] Presumably a married couple with each spouse earning at least $20,300 would receive a combined tax credit of $8,648 in the first year of the task force's earnings credit (even if they have no children). The primary way to pay for this proposed credit for some 160 million Americans was to apply the 15% basic tax rate to the first dollar of income with no standard deductions or personal exemptions.

There is no question that the substitute-EIC proposal of the task force would simplify the process of determining who is eligible for the EIC and how much the credit should be. On the other hand, it would increase the number of taxpayers claiming the EIC by at least tenfold. It is likely that this proposal would create some unintended consequences and may lead to more errors and fraud than our current EIC, if for no other reason than the additional volume of taxpayers claiming the credit. Nevertheless, I must give the task force an A for effort in trying to simplify the current EIC. Their proposal is a practical solution that merits strong consideration when seeking comprehensive tax reform. Among other things, it totally eliminates the EIC marriage penalty and major disincentives to attain higher wages, two of the primary criticisms of our existing EIC. Currently, a taxpayer's marriage to another low-wage earner can result in an effective marginal tax bracket of more than 50%, and an EIC recipient who marries another employee or self-employed person with above-average earnings will usually lose all tax benefits from the EIC. This would no longer be the case with the earnings credit proposed by the task force, which includes no phase-out as earnings increase or singles get married.

As explained in chapter 4, the task force issued an updated 2012 report (Task Force Plan 2.0) in which they lowered their proposed credit computation to a refundable earnings credit equal to 17.5% of the first $20,000 of earnings[135] for a maximum of $3,500 per individual or $7,000 per couple filing jointly. As in their original report, the Task Force Plan 2.0 would have no phase-out of the credit, but the maximum $3,500 credit would apply to most American wage earners and self-employed persons under the age of sixty-five with annual earned income of $20,000 or more (except those being claimed as a dependent on the tax return of another taxpayer).

In its December 2010 report, the National Commission on Fiscal Responsibility and Reform (Simpson-Bowles Commission) proposed that the EIC and the child tax credit should "maintain current law or an equivalent alternative."[136] The Commission's report pointed out that under current law (2010) the refundable EIC is between $457 and $5,666 while the *partially* refundable child tax credit is $1,000 per child. However, the Commission went no further in its recommendations to propose any change in the structure of these valuable credits. By dodging this complex policy issue, the commission avoided multiple hours of debate and internal study for an issue that has challenged Congress for over thirty-five years.

It is my conclusion that the revised EIC concept, as put forth in the Task Force Plan 2.0, is the least complex and most understandable approach to the EIC conundrum that I have been able to find. It accomplishes basically the same purpose as our current law EIC, which is to raise the earnings power and give further incentive to the low-income workers in our society. At the same time, it provides an enhanced substitute for the standard deduction since it produces a generous shelter from taxes (income and payroll) for the wage earner and self-employed. The downside of this credit concept is its extremely high cost to the Treasury in lost revenues. By giving most employed individuals a refundable $3,500 credit along with a universal refundable $1,600 child tax credit for every dependent child, this combined credit proposal leaves the task force with the duty of raising vast sums of substitute revenue through other large tax assessments (new taxes, higher rates, or lower credits and deductions).

While I respect the Plan 2.0 concept, the actual formula and amount of EIC that I propose is quite different from that of the task force. My proposal starts with a 4.0% credit of the first $20,000 (single) and $30,000 (married couple) of earned income, for an initial savings of up to $800 or $1,200 for taxpayers ages eighteen and over (no upper-age limit). This amount is then increased as much as $1,800 per child of the taxpayer for two children (if single) or three children (if married). Then it gradually phases out above taxable income of $200,000 or $300,000 (for single or married as described later). In addition to budgetary concerns, the reason my EIC starts at a lower rate is to direct much of the benefit to families with children and to adjust for the lowest tax rate in my 20/20 Tax proposal, which is 10.0% as compared to the task force's lowest rate of 15.0%. Let me demonstrate in the following table how single low-income taxpayers without children would receive comparable results (as recommended by Simpson-Bowles) from the 20/20 Tax proposal when compared to the 2014 current law.

Single Taxpayer No Dependents

	Current 2014 Law		20/20 Tax Proposal	
Total wages	$10,000	$20,000	$10,000	$20,000
Standard deduction & exemption	(10,150)	(10,150)	N/A	N/A
Other deductions (assume none)	0	0	0	0
Taxable income	0	9,850	10,000	20,000
Tax at 10% bracket	0	908	1,000	2,000
Tax at 15% bracket	0	120	0	0
Tax before credits	0	1,028	1,000	2,000
Earned Income Credit	(349)	0 *	(400)	(800)
Personal Credit (explained later)	N/A	N/A	(500)	(500)
Tax Due (Refund)	$ (349)	$ 1,028	$ 100 **	$ 700

*Under the 2014 current law, the EIC is totally phased out for single taxpayers with adjusted gross income above $14,590 and no qualifying child.
** The 20/20 Tax will often result in lower taxes than shown above due to the common occurrence of additional credits (i.e., charitable contributions).

REVISE OR REPLACE THE CHILD TAX CREDITS, EXEMPTIONS, AND THE STANDARD DEDUCTION

The 20/20 Tax proposal makes tax returns much simpler for those currently utilizing the EIC, the child tax credit, the additional child tax credit, the standard deduction, personal exemptions, and dependent exemptions. These six elements have become integral parts of millions of middle-class families' tax returns. In the following pages, I will explain how these six complicated tax-saving provisions can all be replaced by three understandable credits known in the 20/20 Tax as the revised earned income credit, the revised child tax credit, and the new personal tax credit.

The federal tax law of 2014 provided a deductible personal exemption of $3,950 for each taxpayer, and it allowed taxpayers to claim another $3,950 for each eligible dependent. The resulting tax savings per exemption ranged from $0 for many low-income persons to $1,304 for those in the 33% bracket ($3,950 X 33%) while being phased out for rate brackets above 33%. By definition, exemptions are one of those upside-down subsidies of the code that benefit the wealthy much more than the lower or middle class. The tax benefit of exemptions is never "refundable," so it's basically "use it or lose it," and many low-income citizens often do not have sufficient income to use their exemption(s). To make matters worse, the rules to decipher the eligibility of dependents are quite complex and often lead to taxpayer disputes with the government, former spouses, and sometimes even with one's own children.

In response to the regressive nature of dependent exemptions, the child tax credit was enacted in 1997. By adding this credit, Congress addressed concerns that our tax law did not sufficiently reflect a family's ability to pay their taxes as one's family added children. The amount of the child tax credit was initially $400 per child, and it has grown to $1,000 where it has been since 2003. Multiple changes in the law have gradually made it refundable[137] for most but not all taxpayers.

Just as we saw with the earned income credit (EIC), the child tax credit involves a mind-numbing maze of rules to determine eligibility, as can be seen in the following technical explanations (once again optional reading for those who do not delight in masochistic mental exercises):

> *Qualifying Child.* The definition of a qualifying child for purposes of the child tax credit is the same as that for claiming a dependency exemption (¶ 137A) except that the child must not have attained the age of 17 by the end of the year. In addition, the qualifying child must be either a U.S. citizen, national, or resident of the United States (Code Sec. 24(c)).[138]

> *Limitation of Child Tax Credit Based on Modified AGI.* The child tax credit begins to phaseout when the taxpayer's modified adjusted gross income (AGI) reaches

$110,000 for joint filers, $55,000 for married taxpayers filing separately, and $75,000 for single taxpayers. The credit is reduced by $50 for each $1,000, or fraction thereof, of modified AGI above the threshold amount (Code Sec. 24(b)). Modified AGI is defined as AGI determined without regard to the exclusions for foreign or U.S. possessions earned income and foreign housing expenses (¶ 2402).[139]

Nonrefundable Portion of Child Tax Credit. In general, the child tax credit is a nonrefundable personal credit. For tax years after 2011 all refundable tax credits are allowed to the full extent of the taxpayer's regular tax and alternate minimum tax liability. Code Sec. 26(a).[140]

Refundable Amount of Child Tax Credit. For tax years beginning in 2009 through 2017, a portion of the child tax credit is refundable for all taxpayers (referred to as the additional child tax credit), regardless of the amount of the taxpayer's regular tax or AMT liability. The credit is refundable in an amount equal to the lesser of the unclaimed portion of the nonrefundable credit amount or 15% of the taxpayer's earned income in excess of $3,000 (Code Sec. 24(d)). Military families may elect to include otherwise excludable combat zone pay in their earned income when calculating the refundable portion of the credit. Taxpayers with three or more children may use an alternative method to calculate their refundable child tax credit. Under this method, the refundable credit is the excess of the taxpayer's share of Social Security taxes (including one-half of any self-employment taxes) over his or her earned income credit for the tax year. The additional child tax credit is claimed on Form 8812.[141]

While it is not as complex as the earned income credit (EIC), most people find the child tax credit to be very confusing. In order to eliminate most of the confusion brought about by our current version of the EIC and the child tax credit, please study the following explanations of my revised EIC and new personal tax credit as proposed in the 20/20 Tax.

THE REVISED EARNED INCOME CREDIT

The 20/20 Tax would substantially revise the earned income credit (EIC) to fit the following parameters:

1. Every compensated employee and self-employed individual ages eighteen and over who is a US citizen, and who claims his or her own personal tax credit, and provides more than half of his or her own support, shall be entitled to the EIC.
2. The EIC is initially calculated at 4% of the first $20,000 per year of earned income for a single taxpayer and head of household, and 4% of the first $30,000 per year for a married couple filing jointly. For married individuals filing separately, the taxpayer's credit amount would be 4% of the first $15,000 per year.
3. The definition of "earned income" is basically the same as under current law, essentially all income reported in Box 1 of an individual's W-2 statement as well as net self-employment income subject to SE tax. This would also include taxable health insurance benefits.
4. The EIC would be further increased for any taxpayer entitled to claim the child tax credit for natural children or adopted children under the age of eighteen. The amount of the EIC would be determined as follows:

Single/Head of Household (X $20,000)			Married Taxpayers (X $30,000)*		
	Rates	Maximum		Rates	Maximum
Parent	4.0%	$ 800	Parents (2)	4.0%	$1,200
Child 1	9.0%	1,800	Child 1	6.0%	1,800
Child 2	9.0%	1,800	Child 2	6.0%	1,800
Child 3	N/A	0	Child 3	6.0%	1,800
Child 4	N/A	0	Child 4	N/A	0
Total Limit	22.0%	$4,400	Total Limit	22.0%	$6,600

* For married filing separately, the same 4.0% rate applies to the taxpayer, and as many as two children can be claimed at a rate of 9% each based on maximum income of $15,000 for a total EIC of 22% X $15,000 = $3,300.

5. The tax benefits of the EIC would be phased out as follows:

	Single & H of H	Married Joint	Married Separate
2.0% of *taxable* income exceeding:	$200,000	$300,000	$150,000
The highest income level for the EIC credit phase-out would be:	$420,000	$630,000	$315,000

THE NEW PERSONAL TAX CREDIT (PTC) AND REVISED CHILD TAX CREDIT

The 20/20 Tax would completely eliminate personal exemptions and dependent exemptions as we know them. Taking the place of personal and dependent exemptions would be the all new personal tax credit, which would provide a nonrefundable $500 tax credit for every taxpayer. An additional $500 nonrefundable personal tax credit would be provided for those US citizens over the age of sixty-five. Following are the core attributes of the new personal tax credit:

1. Every legal citizen would be entitled to claim the $500 nonrefundable PTC credit on his or her federal tax return. There would be no phase-out of the personal tax credit as found with exemptions under current law.

2. For those minors under the age of eighteen, a $1,000 refundable child tax credit would go to their birth parent(s), adoptive parent(s), grandparent(s), or legal guardian(s) who provides the most support,

unless it could be shown that the minor provided more than half of his or her own support, in which case nobody would be entitled to the child tax credit.

3. For dependent children and lineal relatives age eighteen and over, the PTC credit of $500 would go to the taxpayer providing more than half the support for the dependent. If the lineal relative is age sixty-five or over, the PTC credit would be $1,000.

4. The new personal tax credit would be nonrefundable, allowing one to use the credit to offset income tax but not self-employment tax, FICA, or the new Healthcare tax described later. If the personal tax credit is greater than one's income tax liability, the difference would not be refunded.

5. If a dependent child is claimed on the tax return of a parent providing more than half of the child's support, the child may still claim a personal tax credit of $500 on his or her federal tax return.

6. Parents or guardians would not be entitled to claim the $500 PTC for children under the age of eighteen.

ELIMINATION OF THE STANDARD DEDUCTION AND EXEMPTIONS

The tax savings created by the revised EIC, the revised child tax credit, and the new personal tax credit would totally eliminate the need for the standard deduction, personal exemptions, and dependent exemptions. This would remove three upside-down subsidies from our antiquated tax code, and it would provide a more fair and understandable structure to our tax system.

COMPARING 2014 CURRENT LAW TO THE 20/20 TAX PROPOSAL

Let's take a look at the results of hypothetical taxpayers entitled to the EIC and the child tax credit under 2014 current law as compared to the 20/20 Tax proposal.

	Current 2014 Law	Author's 20/20 Tax
(A) Head of Household with One Child		
Total wages	$20,000	$20,000
Standard deduction and exemptions	(17,000)	N/A
Other deductions (assume none)	0	0
Taxable income	3,000	20,000
Tax at 10% bracket	300	2,000
Other taxes (assume none)	0	0
Tax before credits	300	2,000
Personal Credit	N/A	(500)
Head of Household Credit	N/A	(1,000)
Child Tax Credit	(1,000)	(1,000)
Earned Income Credit	(2,954)	(2,600)
Other credits (assume none)	0	0
Tax Due (Refund)	$ (3,654)	$ (3,100)
(B) Head of Household with Two Children		
Total wages	$20,000	$ 20,000
Standard deduction and exemptions	(20,950)	N/A
Other deductions (assume none)	0	0
Taxable income (cannot be below zero)	0	20,000
Tax at 10% bracket	0	2,000
Other taxes (assume none)	0	0
Tax before credits	0	2,000
Personal Credit	N/A	(500)
Head of Household Credit	N/A	(1,000)
Child Tax Credit	(2,000)	(2,000)
Earned Income Credit	(4,998)	(4,400)
Other credits (assume none)	0	0
Tax Due (Refund)	$ (6,998)	$ (5,900)

(C) Married Joint Filers with Three Children

Total wages	$40,000	$ 40,000
Standard deduction and exemptions	(32,150)	N/A
Other deductions (assume none)	0	0
Taxable income	7,850	40,000
Tax at 10% bracket	785	4,000
Other taxes (assume none)	0	0
Tax before credits	785	4,000
Personal Credit	N/A	(1,000)
Child Tax Credit	(3,000)	(3,000)
Earned Income Credit	(2,612)	(6,600)
Other credits (assume none)	0	0
Tax Due (Refund)	$ (4,827)	$ (6,600)

If you noticed that the head-of-household taxpayers receive larger refunds under current 2014 law, please do not consider this a standard outcome. For the sake of simplicity, I have omitted other credits, which will typically be much larger under the 20/20 Tax than current 2014 tax law, thus resulting in more comparable refunds for low-income taxpayers using either current 2014 law or the new 20/20 Tax.

As you can see from the preceding examples, the EIC under current 2014 law often results in a large marriage penalty. In other words, if Head-of-Household Taxpayer (A) gets a refund of $3,654 under current 2014 law, and Head-of-Household Taxpayer (B) gets a refund of $6,998, you would think they should be able to get married and combine their incomes, as we show for Married Taxpayers (C), to obtain a perceived joint refund of roughly $10,652. However, our Married Taxpayers example shows an actual refund of only $4,827, resulting in a marriage penalty of $5,825. For a couple with combined earnings of only $40,000, this marriage penalty is a very strong reason not to get married. In comparison, the 20/20 Tax examples with identical income amounts and the same number of dependent children (three) results in a marriage penalty of only $2,400. You can calculate many comparative examples of the current tax system compared to the 20/20

Tax proposal and get similar results with the current law EIC marriage penalty usually being $3,300 to $6,100. This will leave you asking, "Why would low-income wage earners with dependent children ever get married given the current tax law?" On the other hand, the 20/20 Tax should rarely result in an EIC marriage penalty of more than $2,400, and it will frequently provide a marriage bonus.

Another compelling reason to change the current law EIC can be found in the earnings disincentives when the EIC is phased out for a taxpayer. The effective tax rates for an unmarried parent earning $17,000 to $50,000 can be in the range of 40–50%. This could result in a taxpayer with two jobs, who is earning the federal minimum wage of $7.25 per hour, getting to the point of taking home less than $4.00 per hour for the last several thousand dollars of annual earnings. This is all as a result of the phase-out of the current EIC.

The 20/20 Tax minimizes the marriage penalty, and it effectively eliminates the phase-out penalty, which low-income taxpayers have come to abhor as they pay their tax-return preparers several hundred dollars to find out that "they just earned too much" to get an EIC refund.

Chapter 6

REFORM THE MYRIAD OF TAX EXPENDITURES

For the sake of clarity, it is appropriate that we start this chapter with a definition of terms. Economists, tax reformers, and financial journalists often refer to the "myriad of tax expenditures" within the tax code. According to *Webster's Dictionary*, the word "myriad" is a Greek word that when used as a noun can mean ten thousand, or it can mean an immense number. It is safe to say that there are not exactly ten thousand tax expenditures in our tax code, so let's just say there is an immense number. As an adjective, *Webster's Dictionary* defines the term, myriad, as innumerable or multitudinous. Whether using the word, myriad, as a noun or an adjective, it succinctly describes the magnitude of the tax expenditure issue.

The more important question to ask is how do we define "tax expenditures"? According to the Congressional Budget and Impoundment Control Act of 1974, tax expenditures are "those revenue losses attributable to provisions of the federal tax laws which allow a special exclusion, exemption, or deduction from gross income or which provide a special credit, a preferential rate of tax, or a deferral of tax liability."[1] In other words, tax expenditures are those legislative provisions that our lawmakers have allowed to permeate the tax code in order to reduce taxpayers' income taxes for certain types of income, expense, activity, family status, industry sector, business acquisition, or various other financial transactions.

Tax expenditures, per se, are not a bad thing. Every country that has an income tax code also has codified tax expenditures to avoid unjust taxation and to encourage social or economic goals of that country's government. On the flipside, there are at least three problems with the tax expenditures in our Internal Revenue Code. One, they have multiplied over the last hundred years, causing our tax laws to be much more complicated than they should be, and once imbedded in the tax code, those tax breaks are difficult to eliminate even when outdated or no longer justified. Second, tax expenditures are often just spending programs in disguise, and they are not always the most efficient way for our government to allocate funds to worthy causes. Third, and most importantly, tax expenditures cause tax rates to go up for all of us because they substantially narrow the base of taxable income, leaving our politicians with no alternative but to maintain high marginal tax rates to raise sufficient revenue.

According to most estimates and government statistics, the amount of tax expenditures for each of the last three years has totaled at least $1.1 trillion per year. Following is a table that estimates ten of our largest such expenditures.

Table 6-1[2]
Largest Tax Expenditures in Fiscal Years 2013–2023, in Billions of Dollars

Provision	2013	2014–2023
1. Exclusion for employer-sponsored health insurance[a]	$248	$3,360
2. Lower tax rates on capital gains and dividends[b]	161	1,340
3. Net retirement contributions and earnings[a]	137	1,999
4. State and local tax deduction	77	1,098
5. Mortgage interest deduction	70	1,011
6. Earned Income Credit	61	661
7. Child Tax Credit	57	549
8. Capital gains on assets transferred at death	43	644
9. Charity deduction (other than education, health)[c]	39	568
10. Excluded Social Security and R.R. benefits	33	414
Memorandum:		
Credits for Premiums in Health Insurance Exchanges	0	920

    a.   Includes effect on payroll taxes.

    b.   Congressional Budget Office (CBO) and Joint Committee on Taxation (JCT) estimate that a significant amount of capital gains realizations and dividend payouts were accelerated into calendar year 2012 in anticipation of the tax rate increases that were scheduled to take effect in 2013. Because the taxes owed on those capital gains would probably be paid mostly in calendar year 2013, that shifting boosts the estimated amount of the fiscal year 2013 tax expenditure.

    c.   Charitable deductions for education and health are estimated to be another $37 billion in 2013.

Observation: The above table does not include one of the most costly of all tax expenditures, the standard deduction, which is estimated to have cost the Treasury roughly $120 billion for 2013.

Most of chapter 6 (and its subchapters 6.1 to 6.11) is focused on minimizing and simplifying the myriad of tax expenditures in our tax code. Obviously, I will not be able to address all or even most tax expenditures because that would require a book longer than Tolstoy's *War and Peace*. Thus, much of this chapter will concentrate on the ten tax expenditures listed in table 6-1, all very significant tax breaks. According to the CBO, "In fiscal year 2013, those 10 major tax expenditures, taken together, will equal about one-third of total federal revenues and will exceed spending on Social Security, Defense, or (net) Medicare (expenditures)."[3]

It almost goes without saying that our tax code has far too many tax expenditures, and most of the ones we have are much too complicated to understand and to enforce. The 20/20 Tax takes a giant step in the direction of eliminating unnecessary tax expenditures and in reducing the complexity of those that are retained. It is a major premise of this book that almost all tax-saving provisions that occur on an everyday basis can be reduced to a comprehensible level that should be understood by the majority of college graduates and quite likely by the majority of high school graduates. This could be accomplished by minimizing the barriers to qualify for various tax breaks and by eliminating most of the phase-in and phase-out rules that arbitrarily take many taxpayers out of the running for certain tax benefits.

It is also a major premise of this book that almost all nonbusiness tax deductions that survive the cut of the 20/20 Tax proposal should be changed from deductions (that reduce taxable income) to tax credits that reduce the amount of actual tax owed by a taxpayer. Since a tax credit does not depend on the taxpayer's tax rate, the amount of the credit is of equal value to all taxpayers regardless of income level.

As explained in chapter 5.3, it is my opinion that it will take a federal tax credit rate between 18% and 22% in order to gain political acceptance of new tax credits to replace most itemized and other nonbusiness deductions. The 20/20 Tax actually adopts a 20% tax credit rate for all of its proposed credits. The reasons for the 20% rate are many. First, this rate is high enough to provide adequate incentive for most taxpayers to do the "right thing," which might be a donation to their favorite charity, the financing of a couple's first home, or the decision to attend a student's top choice of colleges. A second reason to adopt the 20% credit rate is that it's low enough to keep taxpayers from making unwise or silly decisions, which will often occur when the government is subsidizing 40–100% of a taxpayer's donations, home mortgage interest, tuition, or even health insurance. Still another justification of the 20% credit rate is that the majority of taxpayers who actually pay federal income taxes under the 20/20 Tax will probably have a top marginal tax rate of 20%, and thus the 20% tax credit rate appears to be numerically justified. Finally, a crowning advantage of the 20% tax credit rate is that it's just plain simple, easy to remember, and it lends itself to doing the math in your head if you're so inclined. What more can I say?

Now let's move on to more specific examples of our effort to reform the myriad of tax expenditures.

Chapter 6.1

HEALTH INSURANCE AND MEDICAL COSTS

Clearly the largest federal tax expenditure of the US Treasury is for employer-sponsored health insurance (ESHI). By the time this book goes to press, the ESHI exclusion from taxable income will cost our federal government approximately $300 billion per year of foregone tax revenue. As explained in chapter 5.1, our current American healthcare system largely revolves around health insurance provided by employers. More than half of all Americans obtain health insurance from their employers or the employers of their family members. This system of employer-based health insurance has served our country well, but it has some serious shortcomings. Some of these are as follows:

1. Our tax policy of excluding all ESHI benefits from the taxable income of employees has been very favorable to the wealthy and not nearly as beneficial to the poor and lower-middle class. In other words, this tax expenditure is highly regressive (see chapter 5.1 for a partial explanation).

2. There is strong evidence that the abundance of generous health insurance policies, provided by employers for little or no cost to employees, has led to much higher pricing of services throughout the healthcare industry.

3. The ESHI exclusion often influences employees to choose additional insurance options because they are paying with after-tax dollars. These more inclusive policies tend to fuel higher healthcare prices.

4. A large amount of research on this issue documents the distortions to the labor market resulting from our current healthcare system, including limited job transfer mobility.

5. The extreme tax advantages of ESHI policies have been a contributing factor to their domination of the private health-insurance market where in recent years almost 90% of non-Medicare policies are employer-provided and only about 10% of policies are individually purchased. This imbalance has been somewhat ameliorated by the Affordable Care Act, but the numbers are still heavily skewed toward ESHI policies. Due to this insurance market distortion, most economists argue that there is a fundamental failure of insurance pooling in the private individual market.[4] The inevitable result is higher pricing for those lower volume policies. As long as individual self-paid policies have little or no tax advantages under our tax code, the extreme deficiencies of the private individual market are practically guaranteed.

It is my sincere belief that all of the above deficiencies can be greatly reduced, if not totally eliminated, by replacing the current ESHI income exclusion (IRC Sec. 106) with the 20 percent Uniform Health-Insurance Credit (UHIC) as described in chapter 5.1. This major policy change would result in the inclusion of all future employer-sponsored insurance premiums as taxable income while allowing a 20% refundable tax credit based on the taxable premium amount included in an employee's W-2 income as well as the premium dollars expended by an individual for unsubsidized health insurance coverage.

To explain the redemptive factors of the UHIC tax credit, let's start by considering the first shortcoming cited above, which is the regressive nature of the ESHI income exclusion. Many of the highest earners in our country receive ESHI coverage that is fully excludable from their taxable income on which they would have paid 33% to 39.6% federal tax rates. In most states, these high-income taxpayers avoid paying state income taxes of 5% to 13% because of the ESHI income exclusion from taxable income. By the time you add in the avoidance of paying combined Medicare tax of 2.9% and the new 0.9% additional Medicare tax because of the ESHI exclusion, the federal and state governments are often subsidizing between 41% and 56% of healthcare insurance costs for the very wealthy. At the same time, most rank-and-file employees in our country are in the 10% or 15% federal tax brackets, and all of their income is subject to the 7.65% FICA tax. Thus, most middle-class workers currently avoid federal taxes of 17.65% or 22.65% upon receiving ESHI coverage. They also avoid state income tax, which usually ranges from 2.5% to 7.5% for the middle class in most states. Add this all up, and the middle class worker is normally receiving tax savings of 20% to 30% on their ESHI coverage, roughly half as much tax benefit as the very wealthy. It is easy to see why our current system is very regressive with respect to employer-provided healthcare benefits.

This regressive aspect of ESHI coverage can be totally eliminated by the 20% UHIC tax credit as proposed earlier in this chapter and in chapter 5.1. In addition to receiving a federal income tax savings of 20% of all employer-paid health insurance, many states with income taxes would very likely provide their residents with a state tax credit of 4% to 6% paid for by additional taxable income generated upon eliminating the current ESHI exclusion.

One other very large consideration is that by subjecting all employer-provided health insurance benefits (currently more than $1.1 trillion per year) to the 7.65% employee FICA tax, a significant part of the Social Security underfunding problem would be solved. This should increase the collection of FICA taxes by approximately $80 billion per year with more than $60 billion of the additional revenue going to the Social Security Trust Fund.

Given the above reasons, it is my conclusion that our country should make the choice to subject ESHI benefits to the federal income tax rates of each taxpayer as well as the employee FICA taxes, while providing a tax-savings with the 20% UHIC tax credit. Most states should then be encouraged to provide their own versions of the uniform health insurance credit at their politically chosen rates of 4% to 6%. The issue of FICA taxes for employers and employees will be further addressed in chapter 6.10.

HOW TO STOP FEEDING THE RISING COSTS OF HEALTHCARE

Now let's address the second and third shortcomings I have described with the current employer-based healthcare system. Those are the abundance of generous health-insurance policies that is fueling the rise in healthcare costs in our country along with additional optional policies purchased by employees. For many years, American employers have provided very opulent healthcare benefits to the majority of employees. The typical large and mid-size employer benefit packages have usually provided low-deductible comprehensive health insurance plans on a tax-free basis, and these plans are often supplemented with further insurance options (dental, eye care, etc.), which can be purchased with before-tax dollars through employers' Section 125 cafeteria plans. As if this is not enough, many employers also provide medical reimbursement plans (under Section 105) that reimburse employees with tax-free dollars for co-pays, children's braces, and prescription sunglasses among a multitude of other medical-related expenses not covered by insurance. All of this makes for a very nice benefit package for those who have it. However, the problem that most economists will point out is that this abundance of generous insurance policies has largely contributed to the United States having the most expensive healthcare system in the world.

This is not to say that most Americans are over-insured when it comes to health insurance. It could be said that about 30% of Americans have very generous insurance benefits through their employers while approximately 15% of our country has very ample coverage through Medicare. It is these two groups representing about 140 million Americans that create over 80% of the demand for healthcare in our country. Most of these people think of their healthcare as almost free, or at least consider it relatively low cost, and they won't hesitate to utilize their medical benefits regardless of the fees charged to their insurers by healthcare providers. It is for this reason that there was much debate about "Cadillac insurance" plans during the legislative process of the 2010 Affordable Care Act. The conclusion of that debate was to put a legal cap on the ESHI exclusion of high cost insurance plans. This cap will supposedly be enforced by a "Cadillac tax," a 40% excise tax levied on insurance companies for high cost policies with premiums that exceed $10,200 for singles and $27,500 for families, beginning in 2018. This 40% excise tax is projected to provide much of the funding for the Affordable Care Act, but critics have raised serious doubts about this revenue source.

Needless to say, the Cadillac tax has created many opponents and arguments against its justification. Some will maintain that putting one set of caps on all US health insurance policies cannot be rationalized, since the real cost of insuring a sixty-year-old is several times that of insuring a thirty-year-old. And the cost of healthcare for the insured living in New York City will be considerably more than that for the insured person in Payson, Arizona or other parts of the country.

Here's where the 20% uniform health insurance credit comes into the picture as a potential solution. No longer will employees be unaware of the cost of "free" health insurance being provided by their employers. The full cost will show up every pay period with their pay stubs, and the value of this benefit will be included in their taxable compensation. Yes, they will be entitled to the 20% UHIC tax credit, but because most taxpayers will experience a top marginal tax rate of either 20% or 30% with the new 20/20 Tax, there will be a net tax to be paid of at least the FICA rate by most employees.

Now the table has turned toward insurance that has a tax cost that should help to make employees more responsible buyers of healthcare policies. Suddenly, the high-deductible policies, which have been widely rejected by employees, should become much more acceptable. Costly dental plans and eye-care policies will not be as appealing to employees if they only get the 20% UHIC credit rather than today's 33%–56% tax subsidy for higher earners. The end result should be less comprehensive insurance coverage and more shopping for reasonably priced healthcare services. This change in public policy should help to moderate the prices of our healthcare industry. It may even eliminate the need for a Cadillac tax on high-cost policies, removing a great administrative burden from our government and pleasing many people on both sides of the aisle who have questioned the concept of an insurance cap tied to an excise tax. For the first time in many years, we will start to see more natural market forces enter into consumer decisions when it comes to healthcare choices.

LIMITED JOB MOBILITY AND INSURANCE CHOICES

The last two issues on the list of current-law health insurance shortcomings is that of job mobility and the dominating tax advantages of employer group insurance over individual health coverage. These two issues clearly go hand-in-hand. Our nation's employees have lived for years under the pall of restricted job mobility due to our long-standing bias toward employer-provided health insurance. Once an employee's family is connected to an employer's insurance company, it can be very difficult to make a change to another employer who may not provide coverage with access to the same doctors or healthcare facilities. This issue becomes even more difficult for the employee who wants to become self-employed and start his or her own business. This problem can be exacerbated when preexisting conditions are a factor, despite the positive steps put forth on this issue in the Affordable Care Act.

One of the main contributing elements to the job mobility issue is the extreme tax advantage of ESHI coverage. This tax advantage has relegated individual coverage to such a small portion of the private health insurance market that employee job transfers are often problematic to say the least. It is my contention that the 20/20 Tax with its 20% UHIC tax credit will put individual health insurance almost on an even playing field with employer coverage, at least with respect to the tax advantages. This should be a giant step forward in opening up the availability and the affordability of individual coverage.

A final health insurance point to make is that the 20/20 Tax would not provide the 20% UHIC tax credit for those health policies already subsidized by the government by programs such as Medicare or the Affordable Care Act. Where ACA tax credits are available on health insurance policies, taxpayers would have to choose between the ACA tax credit and the UHIC tax credit, so there would be no double dipping.

HEALTH SAVINGS ACCOUNTS

Health Savings Accounts (HSAs) are a tax-advantaged means for building a savings account to pay for current and future healthcare expenses incurred by individuals. The earnings on these special accounts are tax-free along with any withdrawals as long as they are utilized to pay for eligible medical expenses. Contributions to HSAs are deductible if made by an eligible individual who has a high-deductible health plan. Employers can make contributions to their employees' HSAs, and the amounts contributed are excluded from the employees' W-2 wages for income and FICA taxes.

For 2014, the dollar limits for HSA deductions and exclusions were $3,300 (for self-only coverage) and $6,550 for family coverage (IRS Revenue Procedure 2013-25). Individuals over the age of fifty-five can increase their annual deductions by $1,000. The future limits are indexed for inflation and destined to go up accordingly in later years. As with employer-sponsored health insurance, the high-bracket taxpayers stand to gain the most tax benefits from HSAs.

The 20/20 Tax would continue the HSA concept but would no longer allow taxpayers a deduction or exclusion for the annual contributions, and any amounts contributed by employers would be subject to both income and payroll taxes. Employer and employee contributions to HSAs would be entitled to the 20% UHIC tax credit. The HSA annual dollar limits would be slightly lowered to $3,000 for individual coverage and $6,000 for married or family coverage. There would be no additional dollar limit for those over the age of fifty-five.

OTHER MEDICAL AND HEALTHCARE COSTS

The application of the refundable UHIC tax credit would not apply to other medical and healthcare costs under the 20/20 Tax. This would be far too costly and difficult for the IRS to enforce. Instead there would be a 20% nonrefundable healthcare credit that would apply to those medical and healthcare costs that exceed 10% of one's taxable income (similar to current law itemized medical deductions). This 10% threshold would apply to all taxpayers, including those over the age of sixty-five who currently must exceed only 7.5% of their adjusted gross income in order to deduct medical expenses. Due to the 10% threshold, this nonrefundable credit would apply to a small percentage of taxpayers, mostly those with lower taxable income and those without adequate health insurance.

Chapter 6.2

TAX RATES ON CAPITAL GAINS AND DIVIDENDS

For 2013, the preferential treatment (lower rates) for capital gains resulted in the second largest tax expenditure on the CBO list (see table 6.1). The ranking of this tax expenditure is expected to drop to third place for 2014 and later years, primarily due to the 2013 rate increases for capital gains, which will not reach their full revenue potential until fiscal year 2014.

It is important to note that many tax experts (including myself) consider the preferential rates on capital gains and dividend income to be a matter of economic justice to offset the effects of inflation that result in "phantom" gains. Please see chapter 5.2 for my detailed explanation of the preferential treatment of capital gains. That chapter concludes by stating that the 20/20 Tax adopts the approach of excluding 50% of most long-term capital gains and qualified dividends from the calculation of taxable income. This would result in the lowest-bracket taxpayers paying a 5% capital gains tax (half of the lowest ordinary income rate of 10%). Likewise, those taxpayers in the 20% and 30% brackets would experience capital gain rates of 10% and 15% respectively. As pointed out in chapter 5.2, the exclusion of 50% of long-term capital gains is a much more expedient process than our current rate structure of 0%, 15%, 20%, and 23.8% for capital gains, which adds additional pages to millions of tax returns. The overwhelming majority of taxpayers will find the 20/20 Tax approach for capital gains to be much more understandable and less complex to calculate.

I have promoted simplicity throughout this book, but the time has come to reveal a rather complex concept that the 20/20 Tax would impose on some very wealthy taxpayers. This is the concept of inflation-indexing capital gains to determine the actual amount subject to taxation. The concept of indexing has been proposed in many forms ever since the legislative proceedings of the 1986 Tax Reform Act. In theory, indexing to adjust for inflation makes ultimate sense to avoid taxing capital gains attributable solely to inflation. Few will argue that such inflationary gains should be taxed. For instance, a farm bought in 1970 for $100,000 and sold in 2014 for $400,000 actually yields no economic gain to the seller, since the sales price of $400,000 in 2014 dollars is worth much less than its original cost of $100,000 in 1970 dollars at the time of acquisition. The value of the dollar has dropped more than 80% from 1970 to 2014, and thus our hypothetical farmer would actually be selling his farm for less than $80,000 if measured in 1970 US dollars. Most would agree that the "gain" in this example should not be taxed, and that possibly the farmer should be entitled to a deductible loss.

The other side of indexing could be seen if an investor bought a property in 2009 at a recession-low price of $100,000 and then sold the property five years later in 2014 for $400,000. Since the total US inflation for this five-year period was approximately 10%, the resulting index-adjusted cost basis of the property would be $110,000. Thus, the indexed capital gain would be $290,000, which the 20/20 Tax would subject to the taxpayer's ordinary tax rate, most likely 30%. The net effective tax rate on this transaction (ignoring inflation) would be 29%, and not 15% as we would typically see with the 20/20 Tax general rule of excluding 50% of all long-term capital gains.

At this time, I would only propose the application of the indexing concept for the upper 1% of income earners, defined as those married couples with at least $500,000 of taxable income and single taxpayers with at least $300,000 of taxable income. It is important to note that the

Congressional Budget Office has estimated that 68% of the tax savings from preferential tax rates on capital gains and dividends went to the upper 1% of taxpayers for the year 2013.[5] It should not be a large burden for this segment of society to adjust its preferential rates on capital gains by subjecting such gains to inflation-indexing.

If this approach strikes you as being a fair way of taxing capital gains, you may be asking why it should apply only to the very wealthy. The answer lies in the additional complexity and added preparation time and cost of doing tax returns. For the tax reporting of exchange-traded stocks, it may not be that much more difficult to index capital gains. This is especially true given the reporting requirements imposed on brokerage firms in recent years. However, with the sales of family businesses, vacation homes, limited partnerships, and a variety of other investments, the indexing concept can get very complex.

For those required to index, the 20/20 Tax would provide for an applicable tax rate of 20% on qualified dividends and all other capital transactions for which inflation cannot be measured (i.e., unknown acquisition dates). These transactions subject to a 20% rate would then be calculated with all inflation-indexed capital transactions to determine the actual effective capital gains rate. This aggregate capital gains rate would have a floor of 15% and a ceiling of 30%. By establishing a 15% floor rate, the indexing for inflation would never provide a tax advantage greater than that provided to those taxpayers who are not eligible for indexing (the lower 99% of income earners).

Let's take a look at two examples of how inflation-indexing would work. Our first example is that of the farmer described above whose wife happens to be a successful doctor who had 2014 earnings of $400,000. The farmer decided the first of the year to sell his farm and retire, thus realizing a price of $400,000 after forty-four years of owning a farm that cost $100,000. The couple sold one stock (costing $100,000 in 2009) for a price of $300,000 while also realizing $60,000 of annual dividends. The front page of this couple's tax return could be summarized as follows:

Income Description	Unadjusted Gross Income	Standard 20/20 Taxable Income	Inflation-Indexed Taxable Income
Medical income	$ 400,000	$400,000	$400,000
Farm income	100,000	100,000	100,000
Gain on farm	300,000	150,000	-0-[a]
Gain on stock	200,000	100,000	190,000[b]
Dividends	60,000	30,000	40,000[c]
Total income	$1,060,000	$780,000	$730,000
Tax on first $500,000	n/a	$125,000	$125,000
Tax on gains and dividends	n/a	84,000	69,000[d]
Total tax before credits	n/a	$209,000	n/a[d]

a. The inflation-indexed basis of the farm would be over $500,000, creating an inflation-adjusted loss that cannot be deducted. Thus -0- income should be recognized.

b. The stock cost of $100,000 should be inflated by 10% after a five-year holding period, resulting in stock basis of $110,000 and an inflation-indexed gain of $190,000.

c. The inflation adjustment for dividends requires an effective 20% rate. This is the equivalent of 33.33% exclusion rather than a 50% exclusion under the standard 20/20 Tax.

d. The inflation-indexed tax on capital gains and dividends cannot be less than that calculated for the standard 20/20 taxable income. Thus the calculation of ($190,000 + $40,000) X 30% = $69,000 should be ignored since it is lower than $84,000 (the standard 20/20 Tax amount).

Now let's look at a second example that involves all of the same facts, except that it replaces the farmer (who owned his farm forty-four years) with the investor who owned his farm property for only five years. The front page of our second couple's tax return could be summarized as follows:

Income Description	Unadjusted Gross Income	Standard 20/20 Taxable Income	Inflation-Indexed Taxable Income
Medical income	$ 400,000	$400,000	$ 400,000
Farm Income	100,000	100,000	100,000
Gain on farm	300,000	150,000	290,000[a]
Gain on stock (see prior page)	200,000	100,000	190,000
Dividends (see prior page)	60,000	30,000	40,000
Total income	$1,060,000	$780,000	$1,020,000
Tax on first $500,000	n/a	$125,000	$125,000
Tax on gains and dividends	n/a	84,000	156,000[b]
Total tax before credits	n/a	n/a[c]	$281,000[c]

a. The inflation-indexed basis of the property would be 110% of the original cost of $100,000 after five years, resulting in the property's adjusted basis of $110,000 and an inflation-indexed gain of $290,000.

b. The inflation-indexed tax on capital gains and dividends would be ($290,000 + 190,000 + 40,000) X 30% = $156,000.

c. The total tax before credits would be that based on inflation-indexed income ($281,000) since it is higher than the standard 20/20 Tax ($125,000 + $84,000).

d. Note that only 20/20 taxable income in excess of $500,000 is subject to indexing with the earliest gains counted first.

As you can see, the 20/20 Tax concept of inflation indexing is not simple. This is the main reason that I do not propose it for more than the upper 1% during the early years of the 20/20 Tax, and possibly forever.

Is the benefit of inflation-indexing worth the complexity? The two above examples reveal the potential fairness of this approach, as it is a way to avoid taxing inflationary gains while saving the Treasury billions of dollars in preferential treatment for those gains less affected by inflation. I believe that a prudent use of inflation-indexing for capital gains is a necessary step in the equitable taxation of capital gains. The 20/20 Tax for capital gains and dividends should raise several billion dollars more in revenue than our current system for taxation of capital gains and dividends.

Chapter 6.3

RETIREMENT PLAN DEDUCTIONS, CREDITS, AND INCOME

Most Americans hope to retire someday and to have a comfortable amount of income to get through their golden years. Our tax laws have numerous provisions that help make this happen for many, although arguably not for a preponderance of our retiring citizens. According to one noted author, Bruce Bartlett, who wrote *The Benefit and the Burden (2012),* our federal tax code annually "spends $67 billion encouraging people to save for retirement through 401(k) plans, $45 billion for defined benefit pensions provided by employers, $17 billion for Keogh plans for the self-employed, and $16 billion for individual retirement accounts."[7] There is no denying that these tax-deferred retirement plans have greatly benefited millions of Americans, but like many provisions in our tax code, the lion's share of tax benefits have gone to households with annual incomes over $100,000. In recent years, Congress has been very generous in its advancement of retirement plans, often raising the contributions limits faster than the rate of inflation. This has had a very positive effect on the tax-deferred savings of the wealthy and upper-middle class, but the overall benefit to the majority of Americans is questionable.

Let's define the major types of retirement plans referred to above and discuss their allowable contribution levels and the modifications proposed by the new 20/20 Tax.

401(k) plans are the most common of all tax-advantaged retirement plans. They allow an employee the option of receiving a certain amount of his or her compensation in cash that is taxable or having it contributed pretax to one's retirement plan. These plans are classified as one of many defined contribution plans that by law provide each participant an individual account but no guaranteed amount of benefits. An employee's deferrals to all 401(k) plans (and 403(b) plans for employees of tax-exempt organizations) were subject to a limit of $17,500 for the year 2014. This amount was increased (for 2014) by an additional $5,500 for those employees over the age of fifty, to a total of $23,000. As much as 100% of an employee's salary and wages could be deferred with a 401(k) plan up to the $17,500 or $23,000 limit. Employers often match their employees' contributions with as much as a 100% matching contribution, and these matching contributions are not subject to the annual $17,500 limit on deferrals. As a practical matter, employer matching contributions usually only apply to the first 2% to 6% of an employee's total compensation. Under current law, the annual limit for combined employee and employer contributions to 401(k) plans and other defined contribution plans is $52,000 for 2014. In technical jargon, this is known as the Section 415(c) limit.

The magnitude of the Section 415(c) limit ($52,000) has been questioned by Congress and led to a proposal put forth by the Simpson-Bowles Commission in their December 2010 report that would limit the sum of employer and workers' combined annual contributions to the lower of $20,000 or 20% of an employee's compensation. This so-called "20/20 cap" has at least one clear shortcoming in that plans with a match provided by the employer would result in the lowering of an employee's ability to voluntarily contribute to his or her tax-deferred retirement account. This could have the unintended effect of encouraging employers to reduce their matching incentive, thus contributing less to employees' retirement plans due to the $20,000 overall limit.

It is the author's opinion that public policy would be better served by allowing all employees (including those over the age of fifty) to contribute the lesser of $20,000 or 20% of one's W-2 income to their 401(k) plans. At the same time, an employer would be entitled to contribute as much as $20,000 or 20% of W-2 income to each employees account as a matching contribution when combined with any employer deposits to other defined contribution retirement plans for the participant. This combination of $20,000 (employer) and $20,000 (employee) limits would be considerably less than the current overall limit of $52,000 allowed for year 2014, and yet it would still allow the accumulation of a comfortable nest-egg for workers who participate in these plans for several years. For the technical reader, this change would effectively roll back the Section 415(c) limit to its original 2001 base-period amount of $40,000.

The other significant part of the Simpson-Bowles "20/20 cap" is the deferral limitation of only 20% of one's total compensation rather than 100% as found in current law. The author fully concurs with the commission on this revision of the law, which is intended to encourage retirement savings but not provide an added tax break to those who can live on other income while tax-deferring as much as 100% of their compensation. Thus, the 20/20 Tax would impose a "20/20/20 cap" on 401(k) plans (combined with other defined contribution plan(s)), which would limit both the employee and all employer contributions to $20,000 each but never more than 20% of the participant's annual compensation for each.

Defined benefit plans are those retirement plans often utilized by government entities and large, stable companies. "A defined benefit plan generally is a traditional pension plan which provides specific benefits to participants based on a formula reflecting compensation and years of service."[8] The employer will make contributions to a defined-benefit common fund for the entire organization, and such pooled funds are invested for the purpose of yielding the future benefits promised to participants.

As with 401(k) plans and other tax-deferred retirement plans, Congress has allowed the limits on annual employee pension payments of defined benefit plans to escalate with inflation. Starting at a generous base-period limit of $160,000 in 2001,[9] the Section 415(b) limit has gradually grown to an amount of $210,000 in 2014.[10] This limit essentially allows an employer to fund its retirement plan with enough deductible dollars to provide a lifetime pension of $210,000 per year for some of the highly compensated employees of an organization. In the situation where a company hires a new CEO at the age of fifty-five and has just ten years to fund the executive's retirement pay (assuming normal retirement age of sixty-five), the company may be obligated to fund its defined benefit plan at an average rate of close to $400,000 per year. It is important to note that all of this $400,000 per year is deductible by the company, and that is for just one person. Defined benefit plans often cover the majority of a company's or government entity's employees, and so it is easy to see why this type of qualified plan is so costly to the US Treasury and very expensive for the employers providing these plans.

The new 20/20 Tax would roll back the Section 415(b) limit to its original 2001 base-period amount of $160,000. This would mostly affect the retirement pay of those employees who have average annual compensation in their three highest-paid years of more than $160,000. Given this modification, companies and government entities could no longer deduct their contributions to fund annual pensions in excess of $160,000. This measure would save the US Treasury billions of dollars each year, or it could be used to reduce tax rates across the board.

Keogh plan is a term used in the past to distinguish a retirement plan established by a self-employed individual or partnership, as opposed to a plan established by a corporation. Self-employed and partnership retirement plans are now generally referred to by the name that is used for the particular type of plan (e.g., simplified employee pension-individual retirement account (SEP-IRA), self-employed 401(k), etc.).[11]

There is general parity between retirement plans established by a partnership or self-employed proprietor and those plans established by other business entities (corporations). Current law applies the same Section 415 (c) limit of $52,000 to some (but not all) retirement plans of partnerships and the self-employed. The new 20/20 Tax would lower the $52,000 employer contribution limit (wherever applicable) for partnerships and those who are self-employed to $40,000 (once again the original 2001 Section 415(b) limit).

Given the new 20/20 Tax, all partners, those who are self-employed, and their common-law employees would see their retirement contributions limited to 20% of compensation (or earnings) similar to the corporate rules described earlier.

Another concept that is imperative to recognize with all qualified retirement plans is that of compensation limits. "An employer-provided retirement plan will not qualify (for tax deferral) unless the annual compensation of each employee taken into account under the plan for any year does not exceed a specific dollar amount (Code Sec. 401(a) (17))."[12] The maximum compensation limit for 2014 is $260,000.[13] The new 20/20 Tax would lower this limit to $200,000, which is the original 2001 base-period limit. The lowering of this limit would have the net effect of allocating more retirement dollars to the rank-and-file employees and somewhat lower benefits to the highly compensated. This maximum compensation limit should apply to all defined contribution plans, including 401(k) plans and the various self-employed retirement plans.

Traditional IRAs have been a part of the tax landscape since 1974 when adopted by the Employee Retirement Income Security Act (ERISA). These original IRAs have come to be known as traditional IRAs and are still the primary type of IRA held by taxpayers. They allow taxes to be deferred on both the IRA contributions and the accumulated earnings until the assets are withdrawn at retirement. Withdrawals before the beneficiary reaches age fifty-nine and a half are penalized at a rate of 10% as well as taxed at the highest marginal rate of the beneficiary. Contributions to traditional IRAs can only be made by individuals who receive compensation for services (e.g., wages, salaries, self-employment income).

The early IRAs of 1974–1981 only allowed a taxpayer to deduct 15% of one's compensation up to a maximum contribution of $1,500, and any participants in an employer-sponsored retirement plan could not contribute to an IRA. However, the Economic Recovery Tax Act of 1981 (ERTA) expanded IRA eligibility to almost all working taxpayers by extending IRAs to workers who participated in their employers' retirement plans.[14] The 1981 Act further enabled an individual to contribute as much as 100% of one's compensation up to $2,000 per year to an IRA.[15] Not surprisingly, IRA contributions jumped dramatically in 1982 and continued at a high rate through 1986, only to be slowed by the Tax Reform Act of 1986, which put renewed curbs on upper income workers who were covered by employer retirement plans.

Having gone through many more legislative changes over the last twenty years, the traditional IRA rules of 2014 allow a maximum yearly contribution of $5,500, which is increased to $6,500 for taxpayers over the age of fifty. These amounts are limited to 100% of taxable compensation, but the deduction is reduced or eliminated for active participants in an employer's retirement plan for those married couples with modified AGI (defined next paragraph) between $96,000 and $116,000.[16] The phase-out reduction for singles and head of households is between $60,000 and $70,000 for 2014.[17]

For the purpose of IRA eligibility rules, the term "modified adjusted gross income" is defined as "adjusted gross income figured without taking into account any IRA deduction or foreign-earned income exclusion or foreign housing exclusion (deduction), any deduction for student loan interest, any qualified bond interest exclusion, and exclusions for certain tax-exempt interest amounts."[18] Also, one must add back the exclusion of employer-paid adoption assistance and any deductions for tuition and related expenses as well as for domestic production activities.

There are two main advantages of a traditional IRA. First, the taxpayer's marginal tax rate during one's working years when funding the IRA is usually higher than when the retirement benefits are distributed. The taxpayer thus receives an incremental savings based on the difference between the two tax rates. A second and often larger advantage of an IRA is that the invested funds grow tax-free over an extended period of time. One thousand dollars invested in an IRA at an 8% yield grows to $4,660 in twenty years. If the total is eventually taxed at a 25% rate, the IRA beneficiary receives net proceeds of $3,495 after tax. However, if $1,000 is invested in a taxable account yielding 8% with taxes paid on the initial contribution and on each year's earnings (at a 25% tax rate), the taxpayer would be left with only $2,405 (31% less) after tax.

Despite the distinct financial advantages of traditional IRAs, this tax benefit has its critics. Some economic research indicates that the effect of IRAs on our overall national savings rate is actually quite small. This reasoning maintains that assets are merely being moved from taxable accounts to tax-deferred IRA accounts, primarily by high-income taxpayers, and that little new savings is being generated other than from the tax benefits. The greater concern of critics is that most of the tax savings and wealth accumulation of traditional IRAs is going to the wealthy and upper-middle class, and not to the middle class and lower income taxpayers where it is needed the most. Evidence of this can be found in a recent Statistics of Income Bulletin by two economists of the IRS who concluded the following:

> For 2010 … those making between $100,000 and $200,000 per year were more than twice as likely to contribute to an IRA as those making $30,000 to $40,000 annually. Taxpayers reporting no AGI had high participation rates and average contributions, which were most likely due to the inclusion of many wealthy individuals who experienced temporary losses. Along with the percentage of taxpayers contributing, average contributions also rose with higher income levels for those with an AGI greater than zero.[19]

The 20/20 Tax would make six major changes to recast the traditional IRA rules in order to skew the benefits more in the direction of the middle class as opposed to upper-income taxpayers. These changes are as follows:

1. In lieu of deductible IRA contributions, which have given the largest tax savings to higher bracket taxpayers, there would be a new "Credit IRA" that would give taxpayers a 20% refundable credit for contributions made. Thus, a $5,000 contribution to a Credit IRA account would result in a sure $1,000 tax savings regardless of the taxpayer's income level or tax bracket. This would provide an element of certainty that does not exist in today's law where most taxpayers do not know their IRA tax savings (if any) until their tax returns are prepared. The Credit IRA would totally replace today's traditional IRA for future IRA contributions.

2. To partially pay for the cost of the refundable attribute of the Credit IRA, the maximum annual limit for IRA contributions would be $5,000 rather than today's $5,500 limit. Also, the additional $1,000 catch-up contributions for taxpayers over age fifty would no longer be allowed.

3. Taxpayers would no longer be able to contribute 100% of their compensation up to the IRA maximum limit ($5,000). They would be limited to 20% of their compensation similar to the 401(k) limitations. This would result in a higher degree of real savings and a lower probability of merely having transfers from taxable accounts to tax-deferred IRA accounts.

4. Under current law, many taxpayers are prevented from contributing to IRAs because they are considered an active participant in an employer-sponsored retirement plan. Only one dollar allocated to a taxpayer's individual account by an employer is considered active participation. This active-participant disqualifier would be eliminated for all IRAs.

5. Traditional IRAs and their replacement, the Credit IRAs, could no longer be converted to a Roth IRA. The current Roth conversion policy, liberalized in 2010, is expected to cost the US Treasury at least $15 billion in the next ten years if not reversed. The law change, which allows the rollover of traditional IRA funds into a Roth IRA, has been a significant tax planning tool for wealthy taxpayers over the last five years. It is not unusual to see high-net-worth individuals

experience very low tax brackets in some of their later years. This tax planning opportunity has been extremely generous to a large percentage of taxpayers, and it really should be eliminated.

6. The Credit IRA and Roth IRA would adopt identical standards with respect to contribution limits (as explained later under Roth IRAs).

7. The Credit IRA would be subject to most of the same rules and tax treatments as current traditional IRAs.

Roth IRAs were introduced as part of the Taxpayer Relief Act of 1997. The Roth IRA account differs from traditional IRAs in many important ways, including the following:

1. The most significant difference is that contributions to Roth IRAs are not tax-deductible. Consequently, Roth retirement distributions, unlike traditional IRAs, are generally tax-free.

2. There is currently no requirement for a taxpayer to start distributions from a Roth IRA beginning at age seventy and a half as is required with a traditional IRA. The 20/20 Tax would change this to require all IRAs (including Roths) to start distributing in the year the original IRA owner turns age seventy and a half.

3. Individuals who receive taxable compensation and who are under age seventy and a half throughout the tax year are generally entitled to make contributions to a traditional IRA. Current law has no such age restriction for eligible Roth IRA contributions. The 20/20 Tax would add a measure of consistency by disallowing Roth IRA contributions for those over the age of seventy and a half.

4. For 2014, the allowable Roth IRA contribution is phased out when modified AGI is between $114,000 and $129,000 for single filers, and between $181,000 and $191,000 for joint filers.[20] Participation in an employer-sponsored retirement plan is not a factor for Roth IRAs. For traditional IRAs, the rules are more complicated and provide various phase-out amounts depending on whether the taxpayer and/or a spouse are participants in an employer-sponsored

plan. The 20/20 Tax would set a common standard for Roth IRAs and Credit IRAs, which would both be phased out for single filers when modified taxable income (not modified AGI) is between $110,000 and $120,000, and joint filers would be phased out between $180,000 and $200,000. Participation in an employer-sponsored plan would be irrelevant for Roth and Credit IRA eligibility rules. "Modified taxable income" would simply be defined as taxable income after adding back the taxpayer's personal share of the deduction for self-employed SEP and qualified retirement plans (line 28 on Form 1040).

With the above changes to Roth and traditional IRA plans, the comprehension level of IRAs and the incentives for tax-deferred savings would be greatly enhanced. As a result, there should be considerably more utilization by the middle class taxpayers who have largely ignored this important tax incentive ever since the Tax Reform Act of 1986.

Chapter 6.4

STATE AND LOCAL TAX DEDUCTIONS

A famous quote from the French statesman Jean-Baptiste Colbert, the minister of finances under King Louis XIV, had this to say about raising taxes: "The art of taxation consists in so plucking the goose as to obtain the largest possible amount of feathers with the smallest possible amount of hissing."

Similar quotes have been attributed to some American politicians, including the late Wilbur Mills who ruled the House Ways and Means Committee as chairman for seventeen years (1958–1974). This famous quotation is no more meaningful than when considering the deduction for state and local taxes. At the 1913 inception of the federal income tax, the tax code was made more palatable by having *all* taxes deductible against taxable income, including *federal*, state, and local taxes not directly tied to a personal benefit[21] (i.e., neighborhood improvements, etc.).

Over the next fifty years (1914–1964), the list of deductible taxes declined. In 1964, federal legislation created a list of specifically deductible taxes, including state and local taxes on income, real and personal property, general sales, and the sale of gasoline and other motor fuels.[22] Several years later, the Revenue Act of 1978 repealed the deduction for nonbusiness gasoline taxes, partly because the tax was considered a "user charge" for the use of our highways.

Ever since the 1980s, the entire deduction for state and local taxes has come under fire. The Bradley Gephardt bill of 1983 proposed that this deduction (along with others) be limited to a 14% credit rate, down from a maximum deduction rate of 50%. The Kemp-Kasten bill of 1985 took a larger step forward by proposing that only property taxes be deductible, and not income or sales taxes. In the early stages of the 1986 Tax Reform proceedings, both the Treasury and the Reagan administration backed the total elimination of *all* state and local tax deductions. The repeal of such deductions was meant to help pave the way for lower rates as part of the tax reform movement.

This issue became a lightning rod in the 1986 Tax Reform discussions with the House (controlled by Democrats) favoring the continued deduction of state and local income, property, and sales taxes. At the same time, the Senate, with a slight Republican majority, fought a bitter internal battle over state tax deductions with stalwarts like Patrick Moynihan (D-NY) and Bob Dole (R-KS) in favor of retaining not only the deductions for income and property taxes, as supported by most other senators, but also the deduction for sales taxes.[23] Despite pressure from the Reagan White House to repeal the deduction for all state and local taxes, the Senate voted in 1986 to retain the deduction for income and property taxes but to eliminate the deduction for sales taxes. This position was codified in the 1986 Tax Reform Act, and it continued unchanged until 2004.

In recent years, the battle over deducting state and local taxes has been reignited. The sales tax deduction was renewed as an alternative to claiming the deduction for state and local income taxes. This was mainly a concession to those states that had no income tax and relied heavily on the sales tax for government revenue. This provision was written into the law for a ten-year period of 2004–2013. It was extended for 2014, but its renewal for 2015 and later years is questionable.

In 2005, President Bush's tax reform panel called for the total elimination of the deduction for state and local taxes, maintaining that such taxpayer expenditures "should be treated like any other non-deductible personal expense, such as food or clothing, and that the cost of these (public) services should be borne by those who want them—not by every taxpayer in the country."[24]

In 2010, and again in 2012, the Domenici-Rivlin Bipartisan Task Force proposed the elimination of all state and local tax deductions.[25] It was unclear what position the Simpson-Bowles Fiscal Commission was taking on such tax deductions in their original 2010 report. However, in their later report of April 2013, the fiscal commission very clearly advocated the repeal of all state and local tax deductions.[26] This deduction, which has no comparable equivalent in most other countries, has been similarly targeted for elimination by many other tax reform groups.

ANALYZING THE COST OF THIS DEDUCTION

If one looks at the cost to the Treasury of state and local tax deductions, it is easy to see why it has become one of the cornerstones of many tax reform plans. According to the Congressional Budget Office, the federal government stands to lose $77 billion in 2013 and $1.1 trillion over the next ten years from all state and local tax deductions.[27] This amount would be considerably greater if the alternative minimum tax was repealed (part of most tax reform proposals), since the AMT derived 68% of its revenue in 2008 from the adjustment for state and local taxes,[28] and comparable amounts in later years.

Currently about 60% of the deductible portion of state and local taxes is coming from income taxes.[29] In recent years, the property tax deduction has accounted for approximately 38% of all state and local tax deductions, while the sales tax has been roughly 2% of such deductions.[30]

To understand the political dynamics of the deduction for state and local taxes, one needs to consider which states' residents are benefiting the most from this deduction. A study was done by the Internal Revenue Service for tax year 2002 showing the allocation of tax benefits derived from state and local tax deductions. The results found that 60.6% of such tax savings went to the taxpayers of just ten states (California,

New York, New Jersey, Illinois, Ohio, Pennsylvania, Massachusetts, Michigan, Maryland, and Virginia).[31]

As a matter of political history, all ten of these states voted Democratic for president in 2008 and again in 2012. Thus, it is easy to see why the deductibility of state and local taxes has become an issue of red states vs. blue states. The "reds" want to eliminate this deduction in order to lower tax rates, while the "blues" want to soften the impact of high state taxes and avoid paying more federal income tax by continuing this long-standing deduction.

Those in favor of preserving the deduction say it's unfair to have to pay federal taxes on income that is already absorbed by state and local taxes. They argue that only disposable income (after state and local taxes) should be taxed, and to repeal this deduction would result in double taxation. Proponents of existing law maintain that state and local tax deductibility is needed to compensate high income taxpayers for supporting government programs that primarily benefit the lower and middle class. They reason that the amount of state and local taxes paid are often not equivalent to the public benefits received by taxpayers, and that altruistic motives of higher taxes should be subsidized.

The people who are opposed to the deduction of state and local taxes maintain that it is a subsidy primarily benefiting high-tax states and their residents, especially those with very progressive income taxes. Opponents point out that the 65–70% of taxpayers who do not itemize get no benefit from this deduction and that the deduction is very regressive while primarily benefiting the rich. Also, the residents of states relying mostly on sales tax revenues derive little benefit from the state tax deduction since sales taxes take a higher percentage of income from the middle class, who is much less likely to itemize. Possibly the strongest argument against the state and local tax deduction is that its existence has perpetuated the alternative minimum tax, which would be unnecessary and almost useless if Congress were to repeal the deduction for state and local taxes. The AMT has become a huge burden of complexity and unfair treatment for millions of taxpayers, and its best chance for repeal hinges on the elimination or major reduction of the state and local tax deduction.

It is probably safe to say that a large majority of American taxpayers would favor the demise of both the state and local tax deduction along with the alternative minimum tax, if presented with all the facts. It would not be surprising to find that even the majority of most blue-state residents would be happy to see these sections of the Internal Revenue Code go away if it meant the overall lowering of tax rates. Assuming a large majority of our country favors the repeal of these two provisions, then why wouldn't Congress just make them go away? The answer lies in four words: politics and special interests.

Our tax code is much like other areas of American legislation; once a law is on the books, it doesn't go away easily. All we have to do is look back to the 1850s when most people in our country wanted slavery to go away. Even the majority of white southerners were opposed to slavery, with only 6% of the free South being slave-owners. When our legislative process did not work, Americans found themselves going to war to change the law in order to abolish slavery.

Obviously, I'm not suggesting that our country go to war to eliminate the state and local tax deduction, the alternative minimum tax, or any other tax code provision. Fortunately, I believe there is a political solution to these legislative tax issues that have plagued our lawmakers for the last thirty years. Keep in mind that the single issue of state and local tax deductions almost completely derailed the 1986 Tax Reform Act and could have prevented it from becoming law. Instead of eliminating this contentious deduction, Congress severely modified the alternative minimum tax as part of the 1986 Tax Reform Act, which left us with two complex devils as a curse rather than just the single issue of state and local taxes.

In order to solve the dilemma of state and local taxes, the 20/20 Tax proposes a new approach that tries to recognize the concerns of both sides. This proposed concept is somewhat similar to that used for medical deductions, which has a percentage floor that disallows deductions beneath the floor. Thus, today's tax law only allows taxpayers under age sixty-five to deduct medical expenses that exceed 10% of one's adjusted gross income. This approach recognizes the obligation of most taxpayers to pay for a certain amount of basic medical costs without assistance from our tax law. For those who pay an exceptionally high amount of medical costs (more than 10% of their income), the tax law subsidizes those higher costs.

Using this same concept, the 20/20 Tax would provide a 20% nonrefundable credit for state and local taxes that exceed a threshold floor of 10% of one's 20/20 taxable income (same as the medical floor). The state and local taxes eligible for this credit would include income taxes, property taxes, and sales taxes. A large majority of taxpayers would not exceed the 10% floor and thus would not benefit from this new tax credit. That outcome is the intended result of a tax benefit designed mainly for those who pay an above-average percentage of income for state and local taxes. Since the credit threshold (10% floor) is based on income, and because it provides a flat 20% credit rate, the resulting tax benefits would be less regressive than our current state and local tax deduction. Undoubtedly, a higher percentage of the tax subsidy would go to the residents of high-tax states as compared to today's deduction, but the overall cost to the Treasury would be considerably less.

You might be asking, why was the floor of 10% of taxable income chosen? The answer can mostly be found by analyzing table 6.4 in this chapter. It shows the percentage of state and local tax paid by the residents of various states for 2011. The percentages range from a high of 12.6% for New York residents to a low of 6.9% in Wyoming. The average for all fifty states was 9.8% [32] according to the article from which the table was derived. It is important to note that the percentage of taxes paid by individual state residents includes corporate income taxes and excise taxes (alcohol, gasoline, etc.) totaling 1–2% for most states, and these taxes are not deductible for individuals under current law or in the proposed 20/20 Tax. Thus, if the average percentage of income paid for state and local income tax, property tax, and sales tax is somewhere between 8% and 9%, it is my opinion that 10% represents the most acceptable floor for a credit for state and local taxes.

Table 6.4[33]

<u>States with the Highest and Lowest Taxes - 2011</u>

(Taxes paid by residents as percentage of income)

<u>Rank</u>	<u>State</u>	<u>Percentage</u>
1.	New York	12.6%
2.	New Jersey	12.3%
3.	Connecticut	11.9%
4.	California	11.4%
5.	Wisconsin	11.0%
6.	Minnesota	10.7%
7.	Maryland	10.6%
8.	Rhode Island	10.5%
9.	Vermont	10.5%
10.	Pennsylvania	10.3%
41.	Alabama	8.3%
42.	South Carolina	8.3%
43.	Nevada	8.1%
44.	New Hampshire	8.0%
45.	Tennessee	7.6%
46.	Louisiana	7.6%
47.	Texas	7.5%
48.	South Dakota	7.1%
49.	Alaska	7.0%
50.	Wyoming	6.9%

If we can theorize that the 20/20 Tax proposal becomes new law with respect to state and local taxes and there is repeal of the alternative minimum tax, then let us speculate about the net revenue impact on the US Treasury. Although there's not a simplistic answer, we can start with the estimate that today's state and local tax deduction will cost the Treasury approximately $1.1 trillion over the next ten years if left unchanged.[34] Then we have to subtract the revenue that would be lost due to the AMT repeal, which has been estimated at $494.3 billion for the ten years of 2013–2022[35] (let's round that to $500 billion). My best estimate of the revenue forgone due to the new 20% credit for state and local taxes is $150 billion over the next ten years. Given this combination of changes, the net resulting savings to the Treasury would be approximately $450 billion, give or take $50 billion for other collateral effects. This impact on our nation's tax revenue would be a large contributing factor to the lowering of tax rates in the process of tax reform.

Chapter 6.5

HOME MORTGAGE AND OTHER INTEREST DEDUCTIONS

The home mortgage interest deduction (MID) has been a part of our American tax tradition for over one hundred years. Some economists have suggested that the deduction is so ingrained in the American lifestyle that it will never be repealed. Simply put, it is considered by many to be an untouchable section of our tax code.

Starting with the original income tax code of 1913, all personal and business interest could be deducted. It was not until the Tax Reform Act of 1986 that limits were imposed on the deduction of personal interest. The 1986 TRA disallowed most personal interest deductions with the notable exception of interest resulting from debt used to purchase, construct, or improve a taxpayer's primary residence and one other residence. The technical term for such debt came to be known as "acquisition indebtedness."

At first there was no limit on the amount of home acquisition indebtedness that could be used to result in deductible mortgage interest. However, at the end of 1987, Congress passed the Omnibus Budget Reconciliation Act of 1987, which limited the MID to interest on the first $1 million of acquisition indebtedness.[36] The Act of 1987 went one step further to allow the deduction of interest on the first $100,000 of "home equity indebtedness," which is debt (other than acquisition indebtedness) that is secured by the taxpayer's primary or second residence,[37] more commonly known as home equity loans. According to the House Report (p. 1033), interest on qualifying home equity indebtedness is deductible even though the proceeds of the debt are used for various nonresidential expenditures, such as education or medical expenditures.[38] This has been liberally interpreted over the years to include interest on debt incurred for the purchase of automobiles, boats, and any other consumer expenditures. Taxpayers borrowing for the acquisition of a new car or SUV may be the most frequent users of the interest deduction on home equity indebtedness.

It is important to note that the limit of $1 million for acquisition indebtedness is only $500,000 for a married individual who files a separate return. Likewise, the $100,000 limit for home equity indebtedness is only $50,000 for a married taxpayer who files separately. An interesting part of the 1987 legislation is that the limits of $1 million and $100,000 are the same for a married couple as they are for a single taxpayer. In most areas of our tax code, Congress has bestowed higher limits on a married couple filing jointly than those provided for a single taxpayer. However, the 1987 law was not written to provide better home mortgage limits for married couples than for singles. Some tax commentators believe this was a congressional oversight. This has created one more example of the "marriage penalty" at work since two engaged singles who wish to retain each of their homes having $1 million mortgages would forfeit much of their interest deduction upon marriage. A more glaring concern is the fact that married couples usually require larger homes than single people, and one would think that our tax laws would recognize this difference with higher MID limits for married couples.

The home mortgage deduction has been criticized in recent years by many economists and think tanks. In a recent paper by the Brookings Institution, the following arguments against the MID are stated (as paraphrased by the author):[39]

1. Over the next five years (2013–2017), the US Treasury is projected to forgo over $606 billion of income tax revenue as the impact of the MID grows from $101 billion (FY 2013) to $144 billion (FY 2017).

2. The mortgage interest deduction only benefits a small share of US taxpayers. In 2009, just 26% of the 140.5 million taxpayers claimed the mortgage interest deduction.

3. Research indicates that the mortgage interest deduction largely fails to fulfill its stated purpose of increasing home ownership. The home ownership rate in the United States has fluctuated in a limited range between 63% and 68% since 1950, and several countries without mortgage subsidies have comparable rates of home ownership.

4. The current $1 million cap on the total mortgage debt on which interest payments can be deducted ensures that upper-income households primarily benefit from the subsidy. Many taxpayers in the upper tax brackets would most likely own homes regardless of whether or not they receive a tax subsidy from the mortgage interest deduction, so the generous mortgage value cap on the MID simply allows a relatively small number of upper income households to, in many cases, purchase larger and more expensive homes.

5. States on the East and West Coasts receive the largest share of the value of the mortgage interest deduction. In California, the average value of the MID was $15,755, well above the national average of $10,640, while in Wisconsin, the average mortgage interest deduction was $7,793.

6. As with states, the benefits of the mortgage interest deduction are concentrated in a few regions and metropolitan areas.

7. The MID also impacts home prices within a metropolitan area. In metropolitan real estate markets with a limited supply of housing, the mortgage interest deduction often has the effect of driving up real estate prices.

It is no surprise that the National Association of Home Builders (NAHB) has challenged most of the above assertions specified by the Brookings Institution. In a 2013 memo prepared for the House Ways and Means Committee, the NAHB provided a rebuttal to many of the positions put forth by those opposing the current MID provisions in our tax code. A total of ten positions were presented in the NAHB memo, of which I have chosen to quote the six points of view that appear to best present the case for the current MID tax provisions.[40]

Claim #1—*The wealthy get most of the benefit from the mortgage interest deduction.*

Fact: The majority of the tax benefits from the MID go to middle-class households. Data from the Congressional Joint Committee on Taxation shows that 86% of households who benefit from the mortgage interest deduction have incomes of less than $200,000. It is also useful to keep in mind that the majority of home-owning households are married couples, so the household income measures will often include two incomes.

Claim #2—*Repealing the mortgage interest deduction would not damage the economy or individual households.*

Fact: Almost all studies examining the elimination of the mortgage interest deduction find that it would reduce demand for housing by raising taxes on prospective home buyers. This reduction in housing demand would also lower home values for existing home owners who would experience a significant loss in wealth.

A 1% decline in home prices would result in a loss of $185 billion to American households. Just a 6% decline would eliminate $1 trillion in household net worth. If repealing the deduction lowered prices by 10% or more, Americans would lose trillions of dollars in household net worth. If home values fall, then more families will find themselves under water, in default and in foreclosure. Eliminating the mortgage interest deduction would reduce the financial resources families can draw on for education, entrepreneurship and retirement. And if home values fall, then state and local tax revenues fall, making it harder to fund schools, infrastructure, public safety and other important government functions. Repealing the MID would have serious economic consequences.

Claim #3—*Only a small percentage of homeowners claim the mortgage interest deduction.*

Fact: The mortgage interest deduction is broadly claimed. Seventy percent of home owners with a mortgage claim the MID in a given year, and almost all home owners benefit from the deduction at some point during their homeownership lifecycle. The argument that only an estimated "quarter of taxpayers" claim the deduction is misleading because it ignores the lifecycle element of homeownership. Of the two-thirds of households who are home owners, one-third own free-and-clear with no mortgage. And of those with a mortgage who claim the standard deduction in lieu of the MID, many are in the final years of a mortgage and are paying small amounts of interest and greater amounts of principal. In the early years of their mortgage when much greater amounts went to interest, those home owners very likely claimed the mortgage interest deduction.

Claim #7—*Because mortgages on second homes also qualify for the mortgage interest deduction, taxpayers are subsidizing vacation homes for the wealthy.*

Fact: The rules relating to second homes are complicated, and often apply to situations that do not involve a vacation home. The rule allows owners who sell their home and buy another—those who own more than one primary residence in a tax year—to claim the MID for both homes on their annual tax return. The rules also allow home owners who are building a new home to claim construction loan interest as a deduction.

And, the rules support investment in seasonal residences that provide an economic foundation for many parts of the country. In fact, 49 states in the U.S. have at least one county where more than 10% of the housing stock fits the tax definition of a second home. But we are not talking about million-dollar homes on the beach, which are usually paid for in cash or claimed as rental property. According to an analysis of the Consumer Expenditure Survey, the average income of a household with a mortgage on a second home is $71,344.

Claim #8—*While the mortgage interest deduction supports homeownership, federal policy neglects renters.*

Fact: Housing policy support, in dollar terms, is roughly proportional to the total population living in renter and owner-occupied homes. For example, the report of the Housing Commission of the Bipartisan Policy Center, which looked at all of the tax and spending programs for rentership and homeownership, found that about one-third of housing policy spending is attributable to rental housing, which is equal to the share of the population living in that form of housing. Such analysis is important because it shines a spotlight on important housing programs for affordable rental housing, including the low-income housing tax credit (LIHTC).

Claim #9—*Since not all homeowners itemize, a credit would be better for the market.*

Fact: Identifying winners and losers from moving an itemized deduction to a credit depends on a number of factors, most importantly the tax credit rate. For example, the Simpson-Bowles report recommended a 12% tax credit, meaning a tax benefit of 12 cents for every dollar of qualified mortgage interest paid. A revenue-neutral tax credit would be approximately 20%. Thus, such a low rate as 12% would represent a significant tax hike for home owners. Moreover, it is important to remember that under most MID tax credit proposals, the property tax deduction (worth on average about one-third of the value of the MID) would cease to exist, further increasing the tax burden on homeowners.

You will note that in the interest of brevity, I have omitted claims four, five, six, and ten in the NAHB memo to Congress. These omitted claims and their related responses have very little connection to the Brookings paper cited in prior pages and are less important to our overall analysis of the mortgage deduction.

Having studied at length the pros and cons of the mortgage interest deduction, I feel that it is the first four opposing arguments in the Brookings paper that deserve the most attention. Let's look at these one at a time.

First, there is no question that the MID entails a huge tax expenditure on the part of the US Treasury. Will the amount be as great as $606 billion for the five fiscal years of 2013 through 2017? Probably not. Due to the lowering of interest rates and widespread refinancing in recent years, the projected MID expenditures have started to come down from those quoted in the Brookings paper. But even if the MID costs the Treasury close to $500 billion over the years 2013–2017, we must ask ourselves if the taxpayers are getting their money's worth. Clearly, the

25–30% of all taxpayers who are rewarded by the MID subsidy each year are happy to see the benefit of this deduction and don't want it to go away. Then there are another 15–20% of taxpayers (mostly taxpayers over sixty) who used to realize the MID tax benefit and understand its significance in the early years of home ownership. Most of the people in this older group would argue that the deduction is beneficial to our country and thus are in favor of keeping it. But that still leaves at least 50% of the taxpayers in our country who have never experienced the MID tax savings on their income tax returns, and many of them may never do so given their present economic status and our current tax laws.

So how do we explain such large tax expenditures to the other half of taxpayers who have not benefited from the MID subsidy? In response, those who strongly advocate the mortgage deduction will often point out the resulting economic benefits that go to both homeowners and renters alike as a result of the MID. These widespread benefits include increased jobs and higher paying wages for most Americans as a result of a vibrant housing market stimulated by the mortgage deduction.

A recent report by the Tax Foundation, a nonpartisan research institution, published the following findings:[41]

> Eliminating the deduction of mortgage interest for owner-occupied housing would:
> - Increase tax revenues by $101 billion on a static basis; *
> - Reduce GDP by $254 billion;
> - Increase revenues by $39 billion on a dynamic basis; *
> - Reduce employment by the equivalent of approximately 659,000 full-time workers; and
> - Reduce hourly wages by 1.1%.
>
> Trading the static revenue gains solely for individual rate cuts would:
> - Allow for an across-the-board rate cut of 8.7%;
> - Lower GDP by $107 billion per year;

-Reduce federal revenues by $26 billion on a dynamic basis;

-Increase employment by the equivalent of approximately 187,000 full-time workers; and

-Reduce hourly wages by 0.9%.

* The term static basis means that one ignores changes in consumer behavior and other economic consequences despite the revised tax policy. Conversely, the results on a dynamic basis attempt to quantify and consider those behavior modifications and economic consequences that potentially occur with a policy change.

As one can see from the above research, the elimination of the MID tax provision could have severe adverse effects on our nation's economic production. We might raise more tax revenue upon elimination of the MID, but the large contraction in GDP, jobs, and the wage scale would not be an acceptable trade-off.

It is interesting to note the second part of the Tax Foundation's research. This set of projections presupposes that a Treasury revenue gain of $101 billion from the MID elimination would be used to finance an across-the-board federal income tax rate cut of 8.7% of the marginal tax rates on ordinary income. Thus, the 35% rate would be reduced to 32%, while the 25% rate would be reduced to 23%, etc. The research shows this policy change would result in the decline of three out of four economic indicators, including a lower GDP, reduced federal revenues, and reduced hourly wage rates. The only improvement would be in the number of full-time workers. Again, the resulting picture is not a good trade-off.

Based on the research of the Tax Foundation and their Case Study #1 regarding the MID, most economic observers would conclude that the home mortgage deduction is worth the annual tax expenditure of roughly $100 billion per year in forgone revenue to the Treasury. A decision to repeal this valuable deduction could result in serious negative consequences to our economy and specifically the construction jobs in our country.

Now let's take a look at the second argument against the MID as put forth in the 2012 paper by the Brookings Institution. This argument maintains that the mortgage interest deduction only benefits a small share (26%) of US taxpayers. This position has been sufficiently challenged in the 2013 memo prepared by the NAHB in their rebuttal to claim number three (only a small percentage of homeowners claim the mortgage interest deduction). As pointed out by the NAHB memo, "Seventy percent of homeowners with a mortgage claim the MID in a given year, and almost all homeowners benefit from the deduction at some point during their home ownership lifecycle."[42]

Another point to recognize is that it's somewhat misleading when the Brookings paper states that "In 2009, just 26% of the 140.5 million taxpayers claimed the mortgage interest deduction."[43] A large majority of taxpayers who take the MID deduction are married filing jointly. These couples filing joint returns are each counted as just one taxpayer in the total of 140.5 million taxpayers. Also, there are millions of sons and daughters living at home who indirectly benefit from the MID deduction. When these factors are considered, the home mortgage deduction, benefits close to half of our national population in any given year, a much higher number than the 26% figure would suggest.

Probably the strongest argument to be made by the Brookings paper is point number three that the "mortgage interest deduction largely fails to fulfill its stated purpose of increasing homeownership."[44] Many studies have supported this position although there is not clear evidence to uphold their conclusions. After all, many factors influence the choice of home ownership, and it is hard to determine how many homeowners would have avoided the decision to buy if it were not for the enticing tax benefits. One thing that we do know for sure is that the tax benefits of home ownership have declined significantly for the middle class since the Tax Reform Act of 1986. The reasons for this are twofold.

First, the 1986 Act established a relatively high standard deduction of $5,000 for joint returns and $3,000 for singles. These amounts, having been modified as well as adjusted for inflation, have grown to $12,400 and $6,200 in 2014. Consequently, many of the middle-class couples who have purchased a home in recent years have found that their mortgage deduction and real estate tax do not exceed the standard deduction by much if anything at all. They are entitled to either take the standard deduction, or alternatively, they can itemize their deductions to claim the mortgage interest, property taxes, etc., but the difference is often minimal for most couples with less than $100,000 of joint income and a modest home mortgage. For example, a couple may have mortgage interest of $7,500 along with real estate taxes of $2,500 and additional itemized deductions of $4,000. This results in total itemized deductions of $14,000, which is only $1,600 higher than the standard deduction for 2014. The additional federal tax savings of home ownership would only be $240 if our couple is in the 15% tax bracket, and the added federal tax savings would be just $400 if given a 25% tax bracket. Neither amount of tax benefit is adequate incentive to encourage a couple to purchase their own home. And yet, as a tax accountant, I see this happening to many clients who have chosen home ownership for other reasons than the tax advantages.

There is a second reason why the Tax Reform Act of 1986 reduced the tax benefits of home ownership (especially for the middle class), and that has to do with the lower tax rate structure. The pre-1986 tax rate structure for individuals consisted of as many as fifteen rate brackets capped at a top rate of 50%. [45] A middle-class couple filing jointly in 1985 would have experienced six different tax rates of 25%–45% for taxable income between $25,000 and $100,000. By 1988, these rates had dropped dramatically to either 15% for taxable income under $29,750 or to 28% for taxable income between $29,750 and $71,900.[46] Taxable income between $71,900 and $149,250 was taxed at 33%, with the rate dropping back down to 28% for all taxable income above $149,250.[47] As a result of the tax rates of the 1986 Act, itemized deductions taken at the lower rates of 15%–33% (post-1986) were not nearly as beneficial as the pre-1986 itemized deductions when our middle-class couple was taxed at 25%–45%. A married couple having $25,000 of taxable income and $10,000 of mortgage interest and property taxes might get a federal tax benefit from home ownership of $2,500 in 1985 but not more than $1,500 of tax savings in 1988.

If we fast-forward to 2014, the tax rates for almost all middle-class couples were still in the range of 15%–28%, with well over half of these couples being in just the 15% bracket. Thus, homeowners are not getting nearly the "tax bang" out of their mortgage interest bucks as they did prior to the 1986 Tax Reform Act. This is especially true when you consider the fact that the standard deduction for 2014 has grown to $12,400 for married couples and $6,200 for singles, largely diluting the tax benefit of most itemized deductions, especially those for home ownership.

Point number four of the Brookings paper states that "The current $1 million cap on the total mortgage debt on which interest payments can be deducted, ensures that upper-income households primarily benefit from the subsidy."[48] There is validity to this statement provided that your definition of "upper-income households" includes those taxpayers earning $100,000 to $200,000 of annual income. This economic class of homeowners is often considered to be upper-middle income and is located in the top quintile of American earners. As a group, they are responsible for buying a large percentage of America's new homes and resale homes. Without their participation as homebuyers, our housing market would be a moribund picture. The significant role of these upper-middle class earners has provided the credence to the following pertinent testimony before the US Senate Finance Committee in 2011 by an economist, Dr. Robert Dietz:

> According to the distributional tax expenditure estimates from the Joint Committee on Taxation (JCT), *90% of mortgage interest deduction beneficiaries earn less than $200,000 in economic income.* And 70% of the net tax benefits are collected by homeowners with economic income of less than $200,000.[49] It should be noted that the income classifier used by (JCT)

for these distribution analyses is economic income, a definition that generates income higher than adjusted gross income (AGI) (for example, economic income includes employer-paid health insurance premiums and payroll tax). Accordingly, these estimates understate the benefits collected by the middle class on the more recognized AGI income definition.[50]

This testimony should serve as evidence that the deduction of mortgage interest is not just a rich man's game. Still, it must be acknowledged that approximately 30% of the MID tax benefit is going to a small percentage of households earning over $200,000 per year. It is my opinion that the 20/20 Tax has the potential to strengthen our housing market while allocating at least 80% of the mortgage tax benefit to those households earning less than $200,000 per year, leaving less than 20% of the home interest tax benefits going to those above the $200,000 income level.

HOW WOULD THE 20/20 TAX IMPACT THE MORTGAGE INTEREST DEDUCTION?

Although the MID tax benefit has served us well, the 20/20 Tax proposes a number of changes to replace this dated deduction. These are as follows:

1. *The itemized deduction for mortgage interest and points would be replaced by a 20% nonrefundable mortgage interest credit (NMIC) to possibly become a refundable credit (ReMIC) after five years.* This credit would benefit all home mortgage payers at the same rate (20%) rather than our current MID upside-down subsidy that gives some taxpayers a zero benefit while other high-income taxpayers realize a federal and state subsidy of more than 40% of all their mortgage interest incurred. The refundable attribute would not take effect until at least five years after enactment of the 20/20 Tax, and

only then with the Treasury's assurance of adequate enforcement controls.

2. *The mortgage limit for married couples filing jointly would remain at $1 million, but single taxpayers would see a revised limit of $500,000.* There would be exceptions allowing the full $1 million limit for surviving spouses and certain divorced individuals keeping their house after one's marriage is dissolved.

3. *There would be no deduction or credit for the interest on the $100,000 of home equity indebtedness,* although home equity loans used for home acquisition and improvements would still be eligible for the credit within the $1 million limit.

4. *Mortgage insurance premiums would no longer be deductible or eligible for any tax credit.*

5. *The new home interest tax credit would apply to a primary residence and one secondary residence, as under current law.*

6. *The future refundable credit would only apply to home interest substantiated by a detailed Form 1098 from a qualified lender.* The detail of the Form 1098 would state the percentage of the loan principal resulting from the original home acquisition indebtedness. Taxpayers without a detailed Form 1098 from a qualified lender may still be eligible for a *nonrefundable* 20% credit provided they can trace their borrowed funds to the acquisition or improvement of their homes.

7. *There would be a five-year grandfather provision for interest paid on as much as $100,000 of previously incurred home equity indebtedness and for interest paid on prior acquisition indebtedness between $500,000 and $1 million for a single taxpayer who incurred the debt prior to the date of enactment.*

According to economists for the National Association of Homebuilders, it would take a mortgage interest tax credit of approximately 20% to replace the current MID and still be revenue-neutral.[51] Thus, there should be little gain or loss to the Treasury for this new credit with respect to married couples who have a $1 million limit. However, there would be a larger share of the tax subsidy going to the middle class and a lesser amount going to high-income earners. This should provide similar incentives to what the middle class received back in the 1960s and 1970s when the MID yielded significant tax benefits for home ownership. The refundable aspect of the ReMIC would also provide ongoing tax refunds to homeowners during times of unemployment and disability, as compared to our current MID, which provides very little if any tax benefit to most unemployed or disabled, due to the loss of taxable income that they experience in difficult times. The credit, being refundable, should be a stabilizing factor for many families dealing with hardships, as well as for the housing market and the overall economy in times of recession.

Admittedly, the 20% NMIC or ReMIC is more generous to taxpayers than the proposals put forth by the Simpson-Bowles Commission or the Bipartisan Policy Center Task Force. Both of these highly respected groups also advocated replacing the MID with tax credits. However, the S-B Commission favored a 12% nonrefundable tax credit[52] while the task force 2.0 Plan called for a 20% refundable credit to be gradually phased down to 15% over five years.[53] Keep in mind that the primary focus of the S-B Commission and the task force was to raise tax revenues and to lower the budget deficit, whereas the 20/20 Tax strives to be revenue neutral with respect to the individual income tax system as of 2014. Nevertheless, it is significant to note that mortgage interest tax credits (not deductions) have been proposed by the Fiscal Commission, the task force, and several other reform efforts of the last thirty-two years, going back to the landmark Bradley-Gephardt bill of 1983. The time is here to proceed with this well-studied concept by adopting the NMIC or ReMIC as a fixture of the 20/20 Tax.

It is my opinion that it's very important to retain the current $1 million mortgage limit for couples when the MID is replaced by a 20% credit. This limit was established in 1987, and average housing prices have more than doubled since then. While $1 million may seem like an extravagant level for most parts of the country, in cities like San Francisco and many parts of the East and West Coasts, $750,000 to $1 million is a frequent range of mortgage levels for upper-middle class couples. Simpson-Bowles proposed lowering the mortgage limit to $500,000, which, as I explained earlier, should be a justifiable amount for single taxpayers. However, I believe the values of nicer neighborhoods and the construction of many future homes would be jeopardized if Congress were to lower the $1,000,000 mortgage limit for married couples, which has been a stable number in our tax code for nearly thirty years.

On the other hand, the time has come to completely stop the itemized deduction and subsidy for interest on the additional $100,000 of home equity indebtedness. This provision has allowed the deduction of interest regardless of how the proceeds of the indebtedness are used. According to one industry publication, nearly two million new cars were purchased with home equity loans in 2007.[54] Many astute observers of the 2008–2009 Recession have criticized home equity loans as a contributing factor to the housing meltdown that our country recently experienced, and the tax deductibility of home equity interest was just fuel on the fire for homeowners to become further overextended. In a report prepared by the Joint Committee on Taxation, the following reasons were given to change this part of our tax law:

> The present-law deduction for interest on home equity indebtedness is inconsistent with the goal of encouraging home ownership while limiting significant disincentives to saving. A taxpayer may deduct interest on a loan of up to $100,000 secured by his residence that has no relation to the acquisition or substantial improvement of the residence. This acts as a disincentive to savings and is unrelated to the purpose of encouraging home ownership. Further, the present-law home equity indebtedness rules provide inconsistent treatment by allowing deductible interest for homeowners' consumption spending that is not allowed to similarly situated non-homeowners.[55]

In the same report, the Joint Committee on Taxation estimated the increased annual revenue from the repeal of the home equity interest deduction to be $4.4 billion.[56] The revenue from this source would be quite helpful in the efforts to lower tax rates and simplify the tax code.

With respect to the issue of mortgage tax benefits for a taxpayer's second home, I believe the National Association of Home Builders makes a compelling case in their 2013 memo[57] prepared for the House Ways and Means Committee. In their response to claim #7, it is stated that the interest deduction (for a second home) often does not involve a vacation home. That has been the experience with most of my clients, many of whom have mostly utilized the deduction upon the transition from one home to another, often while waiting for a buyer of the former residence. Furthermore, I have some clients where husband and wife work in different cities and require two different homes to reside in for an extended period of time, and each spouse is rightfully inclined to own rather than rent his or her home. Although I do have many clients with vacation homes, very few of them have large mortgages, if any mortgage, on these properties. Supporting evidence would show that most vacation homes with a mortgage are usually a modest luxury of the middle class and not the high-end dream homes of the rich and famous. I believe our tax code should provide the mortgage interest tax credit for the primary residence and a second home for taxpayers, limited to the combined mortgage balance of $1 million (married filing joint) or $500,000 (single).

INVESTMENT INTEREST DEDUCTION AND CREDIT

One other nonrefundable credit available under the 20/20 Tax would be the 20% credit for one-half of all investment interest expense, as defined under current law. This would replace the current law investment interest deduction. One reason that only half of the interest is eligible for the credit is that such interest expense normally finances assets that yield 50% exclusionary income (interest, dividends, and long-term capital gains). Since only half of this income is taxable, the credit should only apply to half of the interest expense. A second reason for applying the credit to just one-half of investment interest expense is to be consistent with the 20/20 Tax deduction of interest on *business* debt (to be described in Chapter 7.1).

STUDENT LOAN INTEREST NO LONGER DEDUCTIBLE

In our mammoth Internal Revenue Code, there are some deductions that are hardly worth the time to calculate. One of these is the deduction for student loan interest. Like so many deductions provided in our tax laws, this one has multiple limitations and phase-outs that have caused frustration for many of our recent college graduates. If a former student even qualifies for this deduction, the amount of tax benefit is often so low that it's an insult to the intelligence of the young taxpayer. The Joint Committee on Taxation (JCT) prepared a recent report estimating that 7,858,000 tax returns for 2012 claimed the student loan interest deduction, resulting in total tax savings for the taxpayers of $1,305,000,000.[58] That's an average tax savings of $166.07 per tax return. And that average does not include all of the taxpayers who calculated the deduction in their return preparation but did not qualify.

I could write several pages about why the deduction for student loans has not been a productive strategy for our country. However, let me end the discussion by saying that the 20/20 Tax does not endorse the continuance of this deduction, nor does it advocate a similar credit.

Chapter 6.6

CHARITABLE DONATIONS

A bone to the dog is not charity. Charity is a bone shared
with the dog when you are just as hungry as the dog.
—Jack London, American Writer

The deduction for charitable contributions has had a long and illustrious history. This tax provision (Code Section 170) was added to the tax code in 1917 when Congress was concerned that the higher tax rates brought on by World War I could discourage charitable giving. One of the main concerns was that wealthy taxpayers, subject to these higher levels of taxation, would no longer contribute to institutions of higher learning.[59]

The original code section for charitable contributions was only one paragraph long for a total of 109 words. It essentially allowed a decrease of one's taxable income for all donations to qualified charities, but not in excess of 15% of the taxpayer's taxable net income as computed without the charitable deduction.[60] This became a common tax break for most taxpayers for more than twenty-five years. However, the simple one-paragraph deduction gradually became quite complicated, and today our tax code devotes approximately twenty-two full pages of fine print to various types of charitable deductions while the Treasury regulations provide over one hundred pages of additional complex rules.

While it was World War I that led to Section 170 for charitable contributions, World War II brought on the standard deduction (in 1944). This new concept was created for the purpose of simplicity, since wartime had increased the percentage of American income taxpayers from approximately 5% to almost 75%. Congress did not want millions of new taxpayers to have to deal with the complexity of various deductions, and so they introduced the standard deduction as an optional replacement for the tax benefits of nonbusiness (itemized) deductions. Taxpayers who chose the new standard deduction could no longer take itemized deductions, including the popular charitable deduction.

Not surprisingly, charitable organizations considered the new standard deduction as a threat to their fundraising activities. Henceforth, the majority of their contributors would no longer receive a tax benefit for their donations due to the standard deduction being the preferred option of most taxpayers. This issue has continued to be a dilemma for nonprofit groups who have lobbied their elected officials for the last seventy years to provide a better answer. With the exception of the years 1982–1986, their efforts have been futile, and today more than 70% of all individual tax returns report the standard deduction, nullifying any tax benefit of the charitable donation.

WHY THE CHARITABLE DEDUCTION?

As part of this discussion, one must reconcile or justify the purpose of the charitable tax subsidy. Has it outlived its original purpose of 1917, and do we still need it almost one century later? A fitting response can be found in a well-written report from the Urban-Institute stating "the deduction helps support the provision of goods and services that would not be supplied sufficiently by the free market."[61] This report goes on to say:

> One type of such market failure derives from so-called "public goods." Public goods are goods that once purchased by one person can be enjoyed at little or no additional cost by many, such as pollution control, basic scientific research, or parkland. These goods may be undersupplied if people fail to contribute and instead free-ride on the contributions of others. The

government, of course, can provide such goods, but at times it might also want to encourage individuals to do so. For instance, goods whose benefits cross local governmental borders, such as support for delinquent boys or girls, might not be adequately provided by any one government, but some local group might (with federal fiscal support) be willing to tackle the problem. Other gaps might arise because of constitutional or practical restrictions on what government may do. Governments generally must offer their services equally to all, whereas private individuals may target their assistance more easily. And government, of course, cannot directly support religious worship. Charitable organizations can also create an environment or public sphere in which changes to government behavior are discussed and advocated; government is less likely to criticize itself. Also, there are practical limits on tax collection, partly because of its own set of costs such as for enforcement.[62]

The same report further states that "giving is also viewed as a way that a capitalistic society reduces the tensions that arise from the unequal distribution of power and wealth. The power of the wealthy may be less threatening if they adhere to a social norm of eventually sharing a significant part of their gains."[63]

There is much that has been written about the benefits derived by society from charitable deductions. Nevertheless, there are many critics who question the cost-effectiveness of this tax subsidy. They ask to what extent it really affects the desire to donate. Would most taxpayers give almost the same amount if there was no tax deduction? What would happen to overall donations if the percentage of tax subsidy were lowered, especially for the wealthy as proposed by the Obama administration (28% cap to replace a maximum 39.6% rate of deduction)? These are all questions worth asking, especially when the estimated five-year cost to the Treasury for charitable deductions is $246 billion.[64]

Nobody really anticipates that Congress will eliminate the deduction for charitable contributions. However, much can be done to make this tax subsidy fairer and more efficient than under current law. Let's look at some of the various changes that could be made.

CAP THE DOLLAR AMOUNT OR THE PERCENTAGE OF THE DEDUCTION

Today's tax code limits the deduction of cash contributions to 50% of one's adjusted gross income (AGI), a limit that is rarely reached. Some proposals would lower this percentage limit or just have a dollar ceiling of say $25,000. These proposals have gained minimal interest among policy makers and much resistance by the nonprofit world. The one cap proposal that has gained serious attention was put forth in the American Jobs Act (2011) that failed to secure passage. This proposal would have allowed wealthy taxpayers no more than a 28% benefit for each dollar contributed. This concept was viewed by many as just an indirect way to increase tax on wealthy individuals. It had no precedent in our history of taxation, and it would have been one more complicating factor in our tax code. As a result, it gained only moderate support by Democrats and no support among Republicans.

It is my opinion that Congress will find very limited acceptance of any changes in our current cap limits of 50% of AGI for cash contributions and 30% of AGI for most noncash contributions. Also, the concept of lowering the percentage of tax savings for the wealthy to a 28% deduction rate hardly appeals to most citizens' sense of fairness, unless the choice is to go to the same percentage (i.e., 20%) for *all* taxpayers with an across-the-board credit. Thus, it appears inadvisable that Congress should legislate new or revised caps for charitable deductions.

ALLOW ONLY DEDUCTIONS ABOVE A CERTAIN FLOOR

The Simpson-Bowles Fiscal Commission recommended a 12% tax credit for those charitable contributions that exceed a floor of 2% of AGI.[65] Other commissions and tax policy groups have advocated a similar donation floor of either 1% or 2% of AGI. Part of the rationale for this position is that we should only reward those who give higher than average contributions to charitable causes. Probably even more important is the fact that a floor would relieve the IRS of the necessity of auditing millions of taxpayers who make donations of less than 1% or 2% of their income. Similar to the floors for medical deductions and miscellaneous itemized deductions, it would reduce complexity for the majority of taxpayers who do not exceed the floor. Furthermore, a floor on the deduction of contributions would help to eliminate the questionable donations of old clothing and household items, which are often overstated and overvalued by dauntless taxpayers and their preparers.

After careful consideration and much discussion with my legal editor, Robert Severson, we both concluded that the 20/20 Tax should incorporate a pair of 1% floors for charitable deductions or credits. Cash contributions should be subject to a 1% floor, and likewise, noncash contributions should be subject to another 1% floor (both floors based on taxable income of the 20/20 Tax). This way the marginal cash gifts and noncash donations made by the majority of taxpayers could often be eliminated in the return preparation process. This elimination of the deduction for smaller contributions should have a minimal effect on the overall contributions received by charities. At the same time, taxpayers and their preparers would collectively save millions of hours accounting for small donations that have historically yielded little or no tax benefit to most taxpayers.

PROVIDE A DEDUCTION FOR NON-ITEMIZERS

As explained earlier, taxpayers claiming the standard deduction are not able to deduct charitable contributions. Allowing this deduction for non-itemizers would undoubtedly increase charitable giving, but it would also reduce tax collections and increase tax complexity. However, the pair of 1% floors as explained above would help to ameliorate the issues of reduced tax revenue and increased complexity.

A more important fact to consider is that the 20/20 Tax eliminates the standard deduction, making it much easier to accomplish the wishes of charitable organizations that advocate the ability of all taxpayers to claim charitable deductions.

TAXATION OF CAPITAL GAINS ON NONCASH CONTRIBUTIONS

Many noncash or in-kind contributions are made involving appreciated assets, such as stocks, real estate, or artworks. In most cases, the capital gain (difference between the original cost and the appreciated value) goes untaxed. When this occurs, the taxpayer essentially gets two tax benefits; one is the avoidance of capital gain tax on the increase in value of the gifted asset, and the other is the charitable deduction of the full market value (not just the original cost) of the donated property. Some commentators find this to be an unfair tax benefit, which almost always inures to the wealthy, who often are owners of appreciated property. Despite the semblance of inequity, this double tax benefit has been sanctioned by our tax rules for almost as long as the charitable deduction itself. Most nonprofit advocates would argue that many appreciated property donations would never happen if their donors had to pay the capital gains tax as part of the charitable transfer. There is also the assertion that the largest donors would often circumvent any proposed capital gain tax by retaining the appreciated assets until death in order to obtain the stepped-up basis, thus delaying the benefits to worthy charities.

I find the arguments on both sides of this issue to be quite valid. The 20/20 Tax would allow gains on donated property to go untaxed for tangible property related to the purpose of the charitable organization if used by the donee for a period of at least three consecutive years (i.e., artwork to a museum). Also, qualified conservation contributions would be entitled to a 20% credit at fair market value without taxable gain being recognized on appreciated property. Gains on all other noncash contributions would be taxable.

REPLACE THE CHARITABLE DEDUCTION WITH A TAX CREDIT

The Simpson-Bowles Commission recommended a 12% nonrefundable tax credit for charitable donations to replace our current upside-down tax deduction subsidy for donations.[66] The Domenici-Rivlin Bipartisan Task Force advocated a 20% *refundable* tax credit (which would phase down to 15% over five years) to replace charitable deductions.[67] Some other policy centers have come out in favor of a 25% fully refundable tax credit in lieu of the current tax deduction for charitable gifts. All of these groups recognized the perception of fairness in designating the same percentage of tax savings for all income levels regardless of one's marginal tax rate.

The 20/20 Tax would adopt a 20% nonrefundable tax credit for donations to replace the current charitable deduction. I strongly recommend that Congress avoid the selection of a *refundable* charitable credit and allow only those citizens with tax liabilities to benefit from a nonrefundable credit. The potential for abuse and manipulation of a refundable charitable credit is far too great for the IRS to control. In a country with thousands of 501(c)(3) organizations and no reliable "matching program" to verify taxpayer contributions, the fraudulent claims for refundable charitable credits would undoubtedly be in the billions of dollars each year. The government enforcement of a refundable credit for contributions would be a totally different challenge than mortgage interest credits where a limited number of lenders have a long history of issuing the Form 1098 to allow the IRS matching program to trace the actual interest paid by taxpayers. Thus, I agree with Simpson-Bowles in their choice of a *nonrefundable* charitable credit but at the rate of 20% rather than just 12%.

The following table estimates the results of a 12% refundable credit and not the author's proposed 20% nonrefundable credit.

Table 6.6-1
Distribution of Tax Benefits from the Charitable
Deduction – 2008 Tax Returns [68]

AGI	Percent of Total AGI	Percentage Share of Contributions (2008)	Percentage Share of Tax Benefits (2008)	Percentage Share of Contributions 12% Credit	Percentage Share of Tax Savings 12% Credit
1–10,000	0.1	0.4	0.0	0.8	0.8
10–20,000	0.6	1.4	0.0	2.0	2.0
20–30,000	1.3	2.4	0.0	3.2	3.3
30–40,000	2.4	3.4	2.1	3.8	4.0
40–50,000	3.3	4.1	2.5	4.7	4.9
50–75,000	10.8	11.5	7.1	13.0	13.6
75–100,000	12.2	11.5	7.1	12.9	13.6
100–200,000	28.0	23.5	24.1	23.3	23.7
200–500,000	16.5	13.7	16.8	12.6	12.4
500–1,000,000	6.5	5.5	7.9	4.6	4.2
≥ 1,000,000	18.3	22.6	32.4	19.2	17.6

Many critics will oppose the reduction of tax benefits for high income contributors (a credit to replace the deduction), largely based on the theory of reduced contributions going to charities. Although there is a realistic possibility of lower overall donations, we must remember that charitable giving was largely unaffected in the late 1980s after the maximum tax bracket was reduced from 50% to 28% with the 1986 Tax Reform Act.[69] There is the alternate possibility that total donations could increase once all taxpayers are eligible for the new credit.

In summary, I believe our country, our citizens, and our charitable organizations would all be better off if most taxpayers could take a 20% nonrefundable credit for cash donations that exceed 1% of their taxable income, and at the same time take a 20% tax credit for noncash contributions that exceed 1% of their taxable income. This approach would be much more reasonable and equitable than our current system, and it would level the playing field for all charitable taxpayers.

Chapter 6.7

EARNED INCOME CREDIT, CHILD TAX CREDIT, STANDARD DEDUCTION, AND EXEMPTIONS

This chapter will be intentionally brief and is designed to rely on chapter 5.7, which covered the earned-income credit (EIC) and child tax credit (CTC) in explicit detail. As was pointed out in table 6-1, the EIC and CTC are two of our most costly tax expenditures and together are expected to cost the Treasury more than $1.2 trillion over the next ten years.

To save you the anxiety of reading chapter 5.7 over again, let me highlight a few of the key points. First, the EIC is a refundable tax credit designed to subsidize the earnings of low income workers. It has been found to be an effective tool to reduce welfare payments and has been supported by most Democrats, Republicans, and economists. The major downside of the EIC has been its extreme complexity and its propensity to lead to erroneous and fraudulent payments made to undeserving tax filers. As structured under current law, it has another disadvantage of placing a heavy marriage penalty on singles who decide to tie the knot, and it is imbued with strong disincentives against higher earnings for the worker who is in the phase-out wage level of the EIC.

Over the last ten years, two very reputable tax panels have strongly advocated the expansion of the earned-income credit but with the understanding that an expanded EIC be used to replace the age-old standard deduction. This was essentially the recommendation of the 2005 President's Advisory Panel that proposed a "work credit" to simulate the EIC, and when paired with another creation of the panel called the family credit, this combined proposal would replace the existence of our current law's EIC, personal and dependent exemptions, the standard deduction, the child tax credit, and even the head of household filing status.[70] A similar but more expansive EIC proposal was put forth by the Debt Reduction Task Force as explained in chapter 5.7 of this book.[71] The proposal by the task force creates an earnings credit that is never phased out, much like today's standard deduction. This credit, without any phase-out, adds an element of simplicity to the law but only at an extremely high cost to the Treasury and/or taxpayers who must accept higher tax rates as a trade-off.

The 20/20 Tax draws heavily from the EIC positions of both the President's Advisory Panel and the task force. To a large extent, the President's Panel had it right when they proposed a work credit that phased out upon higher earnings similar to our current EIC. However, my main objection to the panel's work credit is its inherent complexity, including the lengthy format of its calculations and the need for two applicable tax schedules to compute the credit. For this reason, the 20/20 Tax proposes its own revised earned-income credit as explained in simple English in chapter 5.7. This revised EIC provides a fully refundable tax credit of 4% to 22% (based on family size) on the first $20,000 of earned income for single and head of household taxpayers, and on the first $30,000 for married taxpayers. The resulting maximum is $4,400 (single) and $6,600 (married). This credit is then phased out as one's taxable income exceeds $200,000 (single) or $300,000 (marrieds). Given this high income phase-out, less than 5% of all taxpayers will experience the phase-out which has the effect of adding 2.0% to the top marginal rate of wealthy taxpayers until the EIC is eliminated. The computations can be easily calculated on a single page without reference to additional tax schedules and without the need for software applications. Most taxpayers should find the process almost as simple as the concept put forth by the Debt Reduction Task Force, which had no phase-out of the EIC.

If we wish to reform the myriad of tax expenditures, there is no better place to start than the interaction of the earned-income credit, the child tax credit, the standard deduction, and the personal and dependent exemptions. These provisions in the law have provided redundant benefits that collectively are no longer necessary to serve their original intended purposes. As explained in chapter 5.7, our tax code would be more concise, more equitable, and more understandable if we adopted the revised EIC and personal tax credits of the 20/20 Tax while bidding farewell to the outdated standard deduction and exemptions that have dominated our tax laws for several decades.

The standard deduction originated in the early days of World War II when Congress wanted to help millions of new middle class taxpayers avoid the complexity of itemizing their deductions at a time when most workers could not afford professional tax preparers and there was no such thing as tax software. The outdated nature of the standard deduction is revealed by its creation at a time when most tax expenditures were listed as itemized deductions, and the standard deduction was established as a substitute for claiming itemized deductions. Today, the large majority of tax-saving provisions are *not* itemized deductions but rather tax credits or above-the-line deductions (i.e., alimony, IRA deductions, etc.). Thus, the original reasons for the standard deduction have largely dissipated over the years.

Long after World War II was over, the standard deduction started taking on a new role of expanding to allow the lower-middle class to pay little or no income tax. However, as the amount of the standard deduction was increased, so was the benefit to some higher-bracket taxpayers, resulting in the perverse effect of propagating relatively high tax brackets. Another unintended consequence of the growing standard deduction is that it has greatly diluted the tax savings for home mortgage interest and charitable contributions, especially for the middle class, who often get as much if not more tax benefit from the standard deduction than they might obtain by itemizing. This occurs even when they are homeowners (with moderate interest expense and property taxes) because of the either/or correlation of itemized deductions and the standard deduction, allowing taxpayers to claim one or the other. The revised EIC of the 20/20 Tax would completely avoid this dilution of tax benefits that many experience from their deductions for home mortgage interest and charitable contributions. With the 20/20 Tax, most taxpayers would be allowed to claim the revised EIC at the same time as claiming tax credits for home interest and/or contributions paid.

As described in chapter 5.7, the revised EIC would also have the positive effect of minimizing the offensive marriage penalty, while at the same time limiting marriage bonuses that lower one's taxes when a higher-income earner marries a person with little or no earnings. One further benefit of the revised EIC is the elimination of the unacceptable earnings disincentives when the EIC is phased out for a taxpayer. The EIC "phase-out" range often extracts tax at an effective rate of 40–50%, and sometimes even higher. With the 20/20 Tax, the effective income tax rate in the phase-out range would increase from 30% to 32% on some high income earners, hardly a disincentive to increase one's earnings.

I explained in chapter 5.7 that the 20/20 Tax completely eliminates personal and dependent exemptions from the tax code. To replace these exemptions, there would be a new, simple, personal tax credit that would provide a nonrefundable $500 tax credit for every taxpayer in the United States and his/her dependents (lineal relatives) who are age eighteen and over. The fully refundable child tax credit of $1,000 would be provided for those dependents under the age of eighteen, and an increased $1,000 nonrefundable personal tax credit would apply to those taxpayers and dependents over the age of sixty-five. Also, those who qualify as head of household would see a nonrefundable $1,000 head of household tax credit in lieu of a dedicated tax-rate table (see chapter 5.5).

Many tax reform proposals have proposed expanded amounts for the standard deduction, the personal and dependent exemptions, and even the child tax credit. Their reasoning invariably centers around the concept of shrinking the tax rolls to make our tax laws simpler and more enforceable. It is my opinion that this approach is misguided and that our nation's budget deficit issues make it problematic to further reduce the number of citizens who pay income tax. The attempt to simplify the law with larger exemptions or an increased child tax credit is counterproductive since it perpetuates the requirement for complicated phase-outs and regulations that channel the benefits to the needy who can ill-afford competent tax preparers to properly interpret the law and calculate the proper tax breaks.

As for making our tax laws more enforceable, it is dangerous to assume that a higher standard deduction to shrink the tax rolls will make the tax code easier to enforce. One great drawback of this approach is that more taxpayers will be annually going in and out of the requirement to file (due to fluctuations of taxpayers' income, deductions, etc.), and this can present a bigger enforcement problem than the processing of millions of simple tax returns on a consistent basis. I believe that the 2005 President's Advisory Panel and the 2010 Debt Reduction Task Force of the Bipartisan Policy Center have made the proper decisions to eliminate the standard deduction as well as all personal and dependent exemptions in favor of a revised earned-income credit (or work credit) combined with concepts similar to the personal tax credit as proposed in the 20/20 Tax.

Oddly enough, the standard deduction as well as personal and dependent exemptions are rarely described or quantified as tax expenditures, and yet when combined they are much more costly to the Treasury than the current EIC and the CTC, and they often provide an unintended duplication of tax benefits. While the 20/20 Tax will not decrease the Treasury's outlay for the EIC, the systemic elimination and replacement of the standard deduction, and all personal and dependent exemptions by the revised EIC, the new personal tax credit and the revised child tax credit will facilitate the lowering of federal tax rates. The 20/20 Tax will send a larger portion of the savings from these tax benefits to the middle class and lower-middle class, and there will be no further need for complicated phase-outs of the child tax credit or taxpayers' exemptions and itemized deductions for higher earners.

Chapter 6.8

CAPITAL GAINS ON ASSETS TRANSFERRED AT DEATH

The taxation of inherited wealth goes back to ancient times of the Romans and even the Egyptians. Our federal government imposed inheritance or death taxes sporadically during the 1800s primarily to finance different wartime efforts, but these taxes were not of a lasting nature. Finally in 1916, Congress passed an estate tax to fund our involvement in World War I, and this tax in various forms has been part of the American tax system ever since.

A tax issue closely related to the estate tax is that of not taxing capital gains on assets transferred upon death, something that Congress has steadfastly adhered to. It has long been said that the only way to avoid the capital gains tax is to die, a morbid but truly effective tax-saving strategy.

HISTORY OF CAPITAL GAINS ON INHERITED PROPERTY

In the Revenue Act of 1921, Congress rejected the Treasury's position of carryover basis,[72] which would have required the heirs of estates to retain the decedents' adjusted basis when reporting gains and losses upon the sale of inherited assets. The 1921 Act provided estate beneficiaries with a more liberal method known as the step-up basis, which meant that heirs of property were to utilize an adjusted basis equal to fair market value at the date of the decedent's death. This more generous basis rule has allowed the recipients of inherited property to completely avoid income tax on any of the gain that occurred during the decedent's lifetime. Members of Congress have historically justified this position based on the fact that inherited wealth is taxed heavily by the estate tax, and it would be unfair to expect another tax on the pre-death gain in value of one's inheritance.

For over forty years, the step-up basis concept went largely unquestioned. Then in 1963, President John Kennedy took exception with this long-standing premise of our inheritance laws. It was his position that the estate tax rates should be lowered (from a top rate of 77%), and that this rate reduction should be paid for by the taxation of all capital gains at death.[73]

A tax on the appreciation of inherited property was debated in Congress over several years, but it was not until the Tax Reform Act of 1976 that we saw passage of the first legislation calling for carryover basis. New Section 1023 of the 1976 Act sanctioned the carryover or retention of a decedent's adjusted basis on assets acquired from decedents dying after December 31, 1976.[74] Thus, a taxpayer who inherited property would also inherit the adjusted basis for such property, and any unrealized gain at the date of death could potentially be subject to tax upon eventual sale of the property. The ink was hardly dry on this landmark legislation when the critics came out in force, including the professional organizations of the American Bar Association and the American Institute of Certified Public Accountants. These organizations argued vociferously that the extreme complexity of carryover basis made this provision all but unenforceable by the IRS while making estate administration prohibitively expensive for attorneys and accountants to provide accurate carryover basis information.

The impetus behind adopting carryover basis was the congressional desire to pay for some of the major changes of the 1976 Act, most significantly the increase of the estate tax personal exemption from $60,000 to $175,000 (essentially a reduction of a decedent's taxable estate). Aside from budgetary concerns, Congress embraced carryover basis as a result of the following two-part logic:

First, step-up is inequitable because it "results in an unwarranted discrimination against those persons who sell their property prior to death as compared with those whose property is not sold until after death."[75] In the former case, gain in the form of appreciation is subject to the income tax, but in the latter that same gain is forever forgiven. Second, Congress believed that step-up creates a "lock-in" effect by inducing people to refrain from selling property during their lifetimes in order to pass property with a stepped-up basis to their heirs.[76] By discouraging pre-death sales, lock-in "distort[s] allocation of capital between competing sources."[77, 78]

The merits of both of these arguments can be debated. The first position regarding the inequity of step-up basis is clearly the stronger of the two positions. While the logic of the lock-in theory has been challenged by some economists, the arguments supporting this position have many followers.

While awaiting the date of full enactment of the Tax Reform Act of 1976, the provision for carryover basis was delayed in 1978 (until 1981) by a bill cosponsored by Senator Byrd (D-WV) and Senator Dole (R-KS). Despite extensive Senate amendments in the 1978 bill to simplify carryover basis, the Ninety-Sixth Congress retroactively repealed this controversial provision by the Crude Oil Windfall Profit Tax Act of 1980.[79] This repeal was largely due to a combination of technical issues and a well-organized opposition.

The occurrence of carryover basis reared its head again with the passage of the Economic Growth and Tax Relief Reconciliation Act of 2001.[80] This bill provided that carryover basis would replace the estate tax upon its one-year lapse in 2010. Although most of the prognosticators predicted that Congress would never allow the federal estate tax to expire in 2010, the political battle raged on in 2009–2010 only to end much as it started, with no required 2010 death tax. For that one year, carryover basis became an elective reality for thousands of estates as a replacement for the estate tax. It is interesting to note that in the year 2010, approximately 25,000 wealthy people died whose estates would have been subject to the estate tax.[81] Among those wealthy decedents were at least five billionaires, including George Steinbrenner, former owner of the New York Yankees.[82] It is probably safe to assume that at least 30% of the 25,000 taxable estates chose to apply the carryover basis rules (which taxed appreciation in excess of $1.3 million at a maximum rate of 15%) rather than paying the new alternative estate tax using the 2011 estate tax rules at a 35% rate for wealth transfers above the $5 million exemption. On a $1 billion taxable estate, it would not be unusual to have saved over $200 million of federal tax by electing the carryover basis option rather than paying the 2010 (2011) estate tax. Given this enormous estate tax savings, 2010 was indeed the "right time to die" for many wealthy people.

NOW IS THE TIME TO RECONSIDER CARRYOVER BASIS

As stated at the beginning of chapter 6, the exclusion of capital gains on assets transferred at death is expected to cost the Treasury $644 billion over the ten-year period of 2014–2023.[83] Obviously, this is a lot of forgone revenue for our government, resulting in higher tax rates for most taxpayers, while the majority of tax experts agree it is an unfair provision in the law. Almost forty years have passed since Congress made a serious attempt at taxing pre-death capital gains on inherited property. Opponents of such taxation have successfully blocked capital gains tax on pre-death appreciation of property with two main arguments. First, the estate tax is already a bitter pill for grieving families to cope with, and any additional tax on the appreciated value of assets may result in double taxation. Second, the concept of carryover basis is too difficult to administer resulting in a huge burden for family heirs and their professional advisers, not to mention the IRS. Let us analyze these two arguments, which in my opinion are outdated and highly overstated positions.

In response to the first argument, that the estate tax is already taking its pound of flesh, we need to recognize that when carryover basis was first decreed in 1976, the exemption for avoiding estate taxes was increased to $175,000. If adjusted for inflation, this is less than

$1 million in today's dollars. As of 2010, Congress had raised this effective exemption amount to $5 million, and we have since seen that level rise to $5,340,000 for 2014 (due to indexing for inflation). The significance of this large increase is that today less than 1% of all estates are now subject to the federal estate tax, and in fact most inherited wealth in our country is not subject to either the estate tax or a capital gain tax on the appreciated value. While I do not fault Congress for exempting the first $5,340,000 of net wealth upon one's death (avoiding a 40% estate tax), I do believe that a huge loophole has been created by ignoring the vast sums of appreciation in value that are going untaxed for those estates of $1 million to $5,340,000. For all such estates, there is certainly no double taxation, and in fact there is a clear avoidance of single taxation since no capital gain tax is assessed on the appreciation of property before death, and then the estate tax exempts those under $5,340,000.

To illustrate how stepped-up basis has become one of our most utilized tax planning concepts, consider the following simplified example. Mary is a widow at the age of eighty-five when she passes away in 2014, more than ten years after her husband died. At the time of her death, she had just two major assets, $1 million of cash (mostly CDs) and a $4 million resort home, rarely used anymore by Mary and her extended family. The resort home (with no mortgage) was built by Mary and her husband approximately thirty years earlier at a cost of $1 million and had always been titled in Mary's name. If she had sold the resort home during the year before her death, the federal tax rate could have been as high as 23.8% resulting in tax of $714,000 on her $3 million capital gain. However, she followed the advice of her accountant and attorney to keep the home for the rest of her life, to be sold by her estate and the proceeds divided amongst her heirs. By retaining the home, Mary and her estate saved as much as $714,000 of income tax on the capital gain. Also, there was zero estate tax because the total net value of the estate was less than $5,340,000 and Mary had made no taxable gifts during her lifetime.

Now let's compare Mary's situation to that of Judy who also died in 2014 several years after her husband. At the time of her death, she also had just two major assets: $1 million of cash and CDs and a $4 million majority interest (80%) in a fix-and-flip business with her son who owned the remaining 20% interest. When Judy's husband died, she used the proceeds of his $1 million life insurance policy to buy the initial properties for her home renovation business. Her son was a good contractor but needed Judy's business expertise to run the business. Together they built a successful business with each taking six-figure salaries and reinvesting their net profits (after salaries) into additional construction projections. By the time of her death, Judy had paid income tax on $3 million of reinvested profits at a federal tax rate of 35% ($3 million X 35% = $1,050,000), thereby increasing the adjusted basis in her business (S-corporation stock) from the initial $1 million to an even $4 million by the time she died. Since Judy's adjusted basis of $4 million was the same as her $4 million business value, she could have sold her business before her death for $4 million without having to pay any additional income tax. Similar to Mary, Judy's estate paid zero estate tax, again because the net value was less than $5,340,000.

Note, however, that the important point to be made is that Judy had no choice but to pay annual taxes during her lifetime on $3 million of profit, while Mary had a choice late in life to sell and pay taxes on $3 million gain or to retain her home until death and have the capital gains tax totally washed away forever. This option is the magic (or the inequity) of our current rules for stepped-up basis.

Some might conclude that our Mary-Judy outcome should be rectified by annually taxing the yearly increase in value of all taxpayer's investments. Thus, when a taxpayer dies, the appreciation of investments would already have been taxed, and the adjusted basis would equal the fair market value at date of death. Very few countries have attempted this concept since the annual calculation of values is a monstrous task, and it creates severe liquidity problems for investors.

A more acceptable approach to consider is that of taxing most unrealized capital gains with the final tax return of the decedent. Often known as constructive realization, under this model, gain or loss would be constructively realized and taxed at death. This approach, as recommended by President Kennedy in 1963, is followed in Canada and calculated as part of the decedent's final income tax return. Because such an untimely tax creates severe liquidity problems (especially for family businesses and farms), the Canadian tax law provides that this tax can be paid on an installment basis over ten years. It is doubtful that this tax would be politically acceptable in our country today due to its unpopular death tax semblance and timing.

The approach generally followed in US tax legislation proposals since 1976 is the concept of giving heirs a carryover basis for inherited property instead of a step-up in basis. Potential capital gains tax liabilities are thus deferred until the time that such assets are actually sold, and the tax is reported on the heir's income tax returns while using the heir's tax rates for the same year(s) that inherited asset sales occur. This approach completely avoids the liquidity problems found in the estate tax and other death transfer taxes discussed above. The further issue of double-taxation can and should be avoided by adding any estate tax assessment to the carryover adjusted basis of the assets transferred at death using the highest marginal rate of the applicable estate tax. This concept is already in practice under current law for transfers subject to the US gift tax.

The other compelling argument against carryover basis and the taxation of pre-death gains is the long-held belief that the administrative burden of tracing the adjusted basis of a decedent's assets is often an overwhelming task. Opponents argue that the time required by family members, their professionals, and the governments' auditors to establish the original cost of certain assets purchased several years before death is not worth the fairness created or the additional tax revenues raised. This argument had as much influence as any single issue that resulted in the demise of the carryover basis provision in the 1976 Act.

There is no doubt that the requirement of carryover basis would add an element of complexity to estate administration. It is important to note, however, that basis record-keeping in the twenty-first century has been vastly improved over what we saw in the 1970s. Some of the reasons for this improvement can be traced to computers and software applications, but also much can be attributed to new tax laws and government regulations for the retention of basis and depreciation records. A good example of this is the requirement for brokerage firms to track the basis of all stocks and securities purchased by their clients and to provide such information to investors at least annually. An even better example is the job of determining the basis of mutual fund shares acquired in different lots under a dividend reinvestment plan. Twenty years ago, the process of this computation was a sheer nightmare even for the living client, not to mention the family of the deceased. However, in recent years this calculation has been part of the mandatory record retention rules for all mutual funds, making it very easy for taxpayers to determine long-term capital gains upon the sale of mutual funds.

This is not to say that there would not be some difficult unknown basis issues to resolve upon the adoption of carryover basis for larger estates. For instance, a family farm may consist of many fences, structures, and other land improvements that have changed during a farmer's long career. In certain cases, estimates or inflation-adjusted amounts would have to be used. But this is really no different from what accountants are currently required to do for many long-held assets of our living clients with sketchy records. Also, very similar situations often arise with gifted property (usually subject to carryover basis) where no gift tax return is available, if even filed.

All things considered, the obligation of tracing carryover basis to determine capital gains on inherited property would not be a formidable task for many estates today, provided our tax laws and regulations on this subject are written in a reasonable manner and only apply to larger estates. If Congress has serious doubts about the degree of difficulty involved in tracing carryover basis, a thorough study should be conducted of the estimated seven thousand estates that elected carryover basis for 2010 decedents. Most of these estates have been settled by now, and the estate executors involved could attest to their time required and the applicable professional costs needed to avoid the pending estate tax in favor of eventually paying capital gains tax on certain inherited assets.

I have yet to read any tax journal articles that have pointed out severe problems for estate administrators who chose to elect the carryover basis treatment for 2010 decedents.

Overall, I think the concept of carryover basis is one of the better recommendations to be endorsed by the Simpson-Bowles Commission as well as the Bipartisan Policy Center Task Force.[84]

CARRYOVER BASIS UNDER THE 20/20 TAX

As an initial legislative step, it is important to establish a floor for the value of estates that would be affected by the new rules for carryover basis. Although the carryover concept can be implemented with a reasonable amount of effort, it is not something that should be imposed on all estates or even the majority of estates. Since most American wealth is owned by people with over $1 million of net worth, and since $1 million has been an often-used threshold in our estate and gift tax laws over the last fifteen years (since 2000), this amount has been chosen as a starting point for those estates that should be required to use carryover basis and file a Carryover Basis Schedule. Estates with less than $1 million of net worth would have no obligation to file this schedule and would transfer most assets to the heirs, using the current rules allowing basis to be stepped-up to fair market value as of the decedent's date of death.

Those estates that exceed $1 million of net worth (less than 5% of all estates in the United States) would need to report information to the IRS on a new form for carryover basis.

OTHER CONSIDERATIONS IN THE ADOPTION OF CARRYOVER BASIS

An important feature for married couples would be the portability attribute of the $1 million basis step-up. Thus, if one spouse dies with only $400,000 of total assets available for step-up, the estate of the surviving spouse would be able to utilize the remaining $600,000 of step-up, in addition to the $1 million already allowed for the second spouse. This would deal a fair hand to those couples who have an unbalanced ownership of assets or experience an early death of one spouse.

It is very important to note that the adoption of carryover basis would not be intended as a replacement of the estate tax in our country. However, it would allow a major revision of our estate tax structure. Today the US estate tax freely exempts the first $5,340,000 of net assets from taxation, but then it extracts 40% of every dollar above the exemption. As a result, most of the wealthy people in our country take extreme measures to avoid having a taxable estate, or they at least minimize the size of their taxable estates by utilizing any number of tax avoidance schemes, often combined with gifting to their children. Some members of Congress have tried for years to close certain loopholes but have met with fierce resistance, partially due to most lawmakers' distaste for the high estate tax rates, which have varied from 35% to 55% over the last thirty years. Many politicians have maintained that if the tax rates were lowered for estates, then most of the loopholes could be closed, but without comprehensive tax reform, neither event is likely to happen.

The 20/20 Tax would use carryover basis as a stepping-stone for restructuring the estate tax. Rather than having a flat 40% tax rate applied to depleted taxable estates calculated after multiple loopholes, there would be graduated rates applied to a much broader base for taxable estates with very few tax-avoidance schemes. The graduated rates would be set at 10%, 20% and 30%, just like the 20/20 income tax rates. No longer would high net worth individuals be able to dodge the estate tax as we see with the current law. If given the lower rates of 10% and 20% on most large estates, we would not experience nearly the disdain for the death tax that we see today. A summary of proposed changes to the estate and gift tax laws will be further explained in chapter 7.2 of this book.

Chapter 6.9

MUNICIPAL BONDS AND
INTEREST INCOME

The world hates change, yet it is the only
thing that has brought progress.
—Charles Kettering, American Inventor

One of the more perplexing issues of our tax system is the concept of
taxing interest income in various ways. The taxation of interest earned
usually occurs when the income is received, but there are exceptions
that make some interest taxable when accrued, even though not yet paid
or received. The earnings on most federal, corporate, and private debt
obligations are eventually fully taxable for federal income tax purposes
at ordinary tax rates. However, all states and US cities allow taxpayers
to exclude their interest earned on almost all federal debt obligations so
that generally, interest paid by our federal government is not taxable on
one's state or city income tax returns.

If you are finished pondering the above paragraph, then let's explore
the taxation of another type of debt commonly known as municipal
bonds. These are debt securities issued by states, cities, counties,
and other municipalities to finance various public expenditures. The
interest income from this type of debt has always been exempt from
federal taxation. The roots of this exemption can be traced to 1894
when Congress voted to reinstate the income tax after its brief tenure

as a revenue source to finance the Civil War. Included in the 1894 income tax was a provision to tax municipal bond interest. The tax was challenged, and in its initial decision of March 1895, the Supreme Court found certain provisions to be unconstitutional, including the tax on municipal bond interest, which was said to infringe on state and local taxing powers.[85] Upon rehearing in May 1895, the entire income tax was found to be unconstitutional,[86] eventually to be reversed by the Sixteenth Amendment in 1913, although it did not address all possible constitutional issues of the income tax. Today, as previously discussed in chapter 5.1, there is no longer a constitutional reason to prohibit the taxation of muni-bond interest.[87] Nevertheless, our tax code has adhered to the precedent established by the Supreme Court in 1895.[88]

To further complicate matters, municipal bond interest, although exempt for federal purposes, is generally taxable by all states having an income tax. The exception to this rule is that bonds issued in any given state or city are typically exempt from taxation in that state where the debt obligation was issued. Thus, if a California resident purchases bonds issued by the state of California, then the interest earned on those bonds will be double-exempt, resulting in no federal or California tax.

Proponents of tax-exempt municipal bonds maintain that the exemption lowers the cost of borrowing for state and local governments because investors are willing to accept lower interest rates if they don't incur taxes on bond yields. It is further held that lower interest rates on muni-bonds are needed to stimulate the development of necessary infrastructure and improvements in our states, cities, and counties.

Several economic reports have challenged the efficiency of tax-exempt bonds by showing that the amount of tax reductions for investors is much greater than the interest rate savings realized by state and local governments. This form of subsidy by the federal government to states and municipalities could arguably be done at a lower cost with direct payments to the states. There is also the inequity created among investors since those in a 39.6% tax bracket will save approximately 60% more in federal tax with muni-bonds as compared to those taxpayers in a 25% bracket. Partly for this reason, the Obama administration has proposed a 28% cap on the effective tax benefit that could be obtained by investors in municipal bonds. Another possible solution to give investors equal tax benefits would be full taxation at ordinary rates combined with a 20–25% tax credit for the interest income received.

After many hours of considering the municipal bond issue, I have come to the conclusion that logically there should be just one method of taxation for all forms of interest income, regardless of whether the source is federal bonds, municipal bonds, corporate bonds, business loans, or even a private loan between two individuals. I find it incongruous that states expect their bonds to yield tax-free interest for federal purposes, and yet forty-one states collect tax on the bond interest paid by other states.

TAXING THE INFLATION FACTOR OF INTEREST INCOME

When taxing interest income, the 20/20 Tax would take into consideration the inflation factor that exists with all bonds and debt obligations. This is an issue that has been ignored in our federal tax code for the entire hundred-plus years of its existence. The concept of indexing interest income for inflation was put forth by the Treasury early in the negotiations of the 1986 Tax Reform Act.[89]

> Under their plan, a lender would be taxed on interest income only to the extent that the interest rate exceeded the inflation rate. Likewise, a borrower would be able to deduct interest payments only to the extent that the interest rate exceeded the inflation rate. Such comprehensive indexing was a bold and ambitious effort, and also a complex and confusing one. It was an essential element in the ideal tax system, but one unlikely to win support among practical politicians.[90]

The concept of inflation indexing for taxpayers' interest income did not survive the elimination process of the 1986 Tax Reform Act. Despite its inherent equity, indexing was deemed to be too complex and very time-consuming for a new law that had simplification as a goal. The Treasury's proposal had been a literal interpretation of indexing, using the actual yearly inflation rates, and the Reagan administration wanted no part of this added complexity. The 20/20 Tax would not make the same mistake. My proposal for "quasi-indexing" of interest income would take a page from our long history of taxing capital gains, which for over fifty years had excluded 50% of all long-term gains from ordinary taxable income. A similar exclusion of 50% of interest income would be very simple to calculate, and its net result should, in most years, approximate the effective rate of inflation when averaged amongst all loans and interest-bearing obligations. The 20/20 interest income proposal would apply to all individuals who collect interest from banks, businesses, corporations, the federal government, state and local governments, foreign governments, financial institutions, and even from other individuals. The 50% interest exclusion would not apply to interest that is collected *by* banks, financial institutions, and businesses in the practice of lending money. For interest rates exceeding 8%, only 4% would be excluded (subject to adjustment for future inflation rates).

In theory, the interest rates for all taxable bonds and loans would be reduced if 50% of the interest received was tax-exempt. However, the interest rates on municipal bonds would not be at the same low level as we currently see with today's tax-exempt municipal bonds. Nevertheless, the forty-one states that currently have a state income tax would see their budget pictures improve for the following reasons. First, most, if not all, states would no longer exclude 100% of interest earned on federal obligations. If federal law under the 20/20 Tax were to exclude 50% of all interest on federal, state, and local debt obligations, this would undoubtedly be the general policy of the states. Thus, if only 50% of interest income paid on federal obligations were tax-exempt, the increased tax collections from the taxable 50% portion would more than offset those lost revenues that states currently collect from fully taxing other states' municipal bonds (which would drop from 100% taxable to only 50% taxable).

The second and more important reason why quasi-indexing would improve states' finances is due to the corollary of the Treasury's interest-indexing proposal. That is "a borrower would be able to deduct interest payments only to the extent that the interest rate exceeded the inflation rate."[91] The 20/20 variant of this concept would simply provide for the deduction of only 50% of interest paid rather than 100% as under current law, once again a very easy calculation. This concept would only apply to business and investment interest paid, and not to home mortgages. It is important to note, however, that most business and investment interest expense is paid to banks and financial institutions that would continue to report 100% of the interest as taxable income. The interest income taxed to individuals, although only 50% taxable, would be considerably less than the interest paid to banks and financial institutions and thus would not have a detrimental impact on states' budgets.

THE EFFECT OF QUASI-INDEXING ON CORPORATE INTEREST PAID

The 20/20 Tax would tax individuals on their interest income in essentially the same manner as they are taxed on most corporate dividends received. In other words, 50% of interest as well as 50% of dividends would be tax-exempt for individuals. While the primary reason that half of interest income should be excluded is the inflation factor, the dividend exclusion is justified for multiple noninflationary reasons as explained in chapter 5.2. By providing equal treatment for interest and dividend income, the 20/20 Tax will minimize the tax favoritism that has existed in recent years by our current law making dividends taxable at rates of 0 to 23.8% while corporate bond interest is fully taxable at federal rates as high as 43.4%.

Possibly, a more important issue to consider is the age-old problem of corporate tax bias that favors debt over equity financing for corporate expansion. The nature of this debate among tax scholars has been well chronicled by one concise paragraph in a timeless book first published in 1947, *Taxation for Prosperity,* by Randolph E. Paul:

Suppose, for example, that a corporation has $200,000 worth of assets, equally divided between "equity capital" from stockholders and "borrowed capital" from bondholders. If the interest paid is 5 percent, the corporation would be allowed a $5,000 interest deduction on the $100,000 of borrowed capital. If the corporation realized a 7-percent return on the total investment of $200,000, it would have a profit before interest of $14,000. With a $5,000 interest deduction, it would be taxed on only $9,000. But if the corporation were entirely financed with equity capital there would be no tax deduction for interest paid. The corporation would be taxed on the entire $14,000. By issuing $100,000 worth of bonds, instead of stock, it would cut its taxes about one-third.[92]

The tax advantages of corporate debt financing have been well documented over the years and thoroughly taught in every MBA program. There is little doubt that it has led to the distortion of the capital position of many corporations, often resulting in corporate financial structures that are too shaky to withstand the problems of hard times. The quasi-indexing of corporate interest deductions would largely reduce the tax incentive of corporate debt financing by allowing only 50% of interest expense as a write-off. It would also provide a more equitable result by only permitting the deduction of interest to the extent that the company's interest rate exceeds an approximate inflation factor.

It is interesting to note that in January 1992, the Treasury Department under George H. W. Bush wanted to eliminate the debt/equity bias by making corporate dividends and interest paid totally tax-free at the individual level, but the interest paid would no longer be deductible at the corporate (business) level. This Treasury proposal faded from view with the 1992 Bush election loss.[93]

THE PHASE-OUT PERIOD FOR TAXING MUNI-BOND INTEREST

There is no question that interest to be paid on previously issued municipal bonds should maintain its current tax-exempt status for the remaining lives of such debt obligations. It would be unfair to investors in these muni-bonds to suddenly lose the tax benefits allowed when the bonds originated. Because of this presumed continuation of tax-exempt interest, the revenue gain to the Treasury from the elimination of exempt bonds would be a lengthy process. The Congressional Research Service did an analysis in March 2012, which pointed out that for fiscal year 2014 the cost to the Treasury of tax-exempt tax-credit bonds would amount to $42.7 billion, 3.6% of all 2014 tax expenditures.[94] However, the Joint Committee on Taxation has estimated that full taxation of new municipal bonds issued in 2013 and later years would result in additional taxes of just under $3 billion for fiscal year 2013, increasing to about $29 billion by fiscal year 2021.[95] Thus, we could be looking at a lead time of eight to nine years to phase out approximately 70% of the current tax law benefits going to the holders of existing muni-bonds.

Chapter 6.10

SOCIAL SECURITY AND MEDICARE TAXATION

We put those payroll taxes there so as to give the contributors
a legal, moral, and political right to collect their pensions and
their unemployment benefits. With those taxes in there, no
damn politician can ever scrap my social security program.
—Franklin Delano Roosevelt

The purpose of this chapter is to define several technical modifications
to the treatment of Social Security and Medicare with respect to their
integration into our federal income tax system. It is no secret that
these two entitlement programs are in dire need of major reform,
both from the revenue side as well as the future spending for benefits.
Although I have strong opinions on some of the solutions needed for
Social Security and Medicare, it could easily take another two hundred
pages to thoroughly explain what those might be. Thus, I consider the
major reform issues of these entitlements as being outside the realm of
this book. Furthermore, I believe that Congress will choose to tackle
comprehensive reform of our income tax system at least a year before it
decides to go to the mat over our nation's largest entitlement programs.
This chapter proposes how to bridge that gap, anticipating eventual
major reform of these programs.

The combination of proposals that are to follow is intended to marginally increase government revenues with respect to the ongoing funding of Social Security and Medicare. I consider an increase preferable to a decrease in revenues given the receding trust funds of both programs. It is also my intent to continue to allocate the burden of payroll taxes among all income classes in a manner similar to that of the last twenty-five years. One major purpose of the following proposals is to simplify the many computations involving both Social Security and Medicare taxes as required in the preparation of individual income tax returns. This multiformity of the tax return process has become far too complex over the years, and its simplification is imperative to comprehensive tax reform.

As a brief warning for most readers, the next ten pages are likely to seem drier than a fall leaf and will probably be of most interest to the accountants and tax preparers of the world. However, this chapter's content is quite important to the practical applications of the 20/20 Tax.

THE TAXATION OF SOCIAL SECURITY BENEFITS

Chapter 5.1 of this book explains how the 20/20 Tax would restructure the income exclusions found in our current tax code. One of the first exclusions covered in that chapter was for Social Security benefits. As you may remember, currently 15–100% of Social Security retirement benefits are excluded from one's taxable income. The applicable percentage of the exclusion is based on the taxpayer's modified adjusted gross income, a complex formula by itself, which is then combined with another complex formula to get the resulting income exclusion as described in chapter 5.1. Since all of this complicated hocus-pocus is the outcome of lengthy political wrangling and congressional job preservation, the 20/20 Tax proposes a much more rational and simple solution. The exclusion for all Social Security benefits (including survivors' income and disability income) should be 50%, pure and simple. The logic for this basic solution, as explained in the next paragraph, will make more sense than all of the legislative research of today's law could ever reveal.

Our Social Security system, starting in 1937, has been financed primarily by employment taxes paid equally by the employee and by one's employer. Social Security has been viewed as a social insurance program, loosely modeled after private insurance systems,[96] with benefits financed by the eventual recipients and their employers. It is an established premise of our tax law that whether disability benefits received by employees are taxable depends on who pays the premiums and whether they are paid on an after-tax basis.[97] If the employee pays the premium with after-tax dollars, then the eventual benefits of the insurance are tax-free. Life insurance receives comparable tax treatment. It seems logical that Social Security's old-age, survivors, and disability insurance (OASDI) should be treated with similar accord. After all, the employees have basically paid for half of the funding (premiums) of Social Security, and they have paid with after-tax dollars subject to federal income taxes. The concept of taxing 50% (at most) of Social Security benefits was in fact adopted by the 1983 Amendments to the Social Security Act, only to be increased ten years later by the 1993 Omnibus Budget Reconciliation Act with the deciding vote cast in the Senate by Vice President Al Gore. Ever since 1993, millions of Americans have been subject to tax on as much as 85% of their Social Security benefits. The 20/20 Tax would tax all Americans on just 50% of such benefits.

EMPLOYER-SPONSORED HEALTH INSURANCE AND THE SOCIAL SECURITY TAX RATES

The tax rate for Social Security started at 1.0% in 1937 based on the first $3,000 of wages, and the rate did not increase until 1950 when it went to 1.5%.[98] After 1950, the tax rate on the Social Security wage base increased every one to four years until it topped out at 6.2% for 1990 and later years.[99] Considering the problems of our Social Security system and the trend of rate increases from 1950 to 1990, most observers would conclude that the system is due for another rate increase. However, keeping in mind this book's overall goal of revenue neutrality, and while awaiting congressional action to tackle the third rail of politics, the 20/20 Tax would actually reduce the current 6.2% Social Security tax rate to 6.0% for all forms of W-2 compensation in order to partially offset the new FICA taxation on health insurance benefits.

As discussed in chapters 5.1 and 6.1, with the 20/20 Tax the current income tax exclusion for employer-sponsored health insurance (ESHI) would go away. The loss of this exclusion would essentially be offset on the average income tax return by the 20% uniform health-insurance credit (UHIC). For income tax purposes, the UHIC would often neutralize the lost exclusion, but it would not be designed to offset most taxpayers' additional Social Security taxes. This is because the taxable Social Security (OASDI) wages would increase by $2,000 to $10,000 for most employees participating in their company's health insurance plan. Thus, the older employee receiving $10,000 of annual medical premiums would pay an additional $600 of Social Security tax at the revised 6.0% OASDI rate. For the younger single employee who might have only $2,000 of annual premium compensation, the additional tax at the revised 6.0% rate would only be $120. Please note that much of this tax increase would be offset by the decrease in the tax rate from 6.2% to 6.0%.

Because the 20/20 Tax no longer excludes ESHI benefits, all employers would be faced with added payroll taxes on healthcare benefits. The 20/20 Tax would assist employers with a tax credit equal to 5 percent of all ESHI benefits provided. This would offset the cost of most additional employer payroll taxes, and the tax deduction of such payroll taxes would usually cover all of the remaining difference.

ADJUST THE MEDICARE TAX RATES

The tax rate for Medicare started at 0.35% in 1966.[100] It was limited to the same 1966 OASDI wage base ($6,600)[101] as the Social Security tax. The Medicare tax rate quickly climbed to 0.5% for 1967, 0.6% for 1968–1972 and to 1.0% for 1973. This tax rate started to increase again in 1979 (1.05%), then took its largest jump in 1981 (to 1.3%), and eventually increased to 1.45% in 1986, which is where it stands today. Thus, the Medicare tax rate more than quadrupled during its first twenty years in existence.

Over the years, the OASDI and Medicare wage bases gradually increased together to $51,300 for 1990. However, beginning in 1991, we saw the elimination of the wage-base ceiling for the Medicare tax. Thus, for the last twenty-five years *all* wages, salaries, and other earned income have been subject to the Medicare tax rate of 1.45% for employees, which is matched with another 1.45% paid by one's employer.

Since the 20/20 Tax will include employer-provided health insurance as taxable wages for Medicare purposes, it is important to determine what rate will be necessary to maintain at least the current level of funding for this important entitlement. Considering the fact that ESHI benefits will no longer be excluded under the 20/20 Tax, our country's taxable Medicare wages should increase at least 3%. An increase in Medicare wages of this magnitude would allow a decrease in the tax rate from today's 1.45% down to a revised 1.40%. However, it's important to introduce another concept to the equation, which is the additional Medicare tax initiated in 2013 as legislated by the Affordable Care Act of 2010. This controversial law imposes a 0.9% "Medicare surtax on the wages, salaries, and self-employment income of higher income individuals. The additional tax rate applies to taxpayers with AGI in excess of $250,000 for married filing joint, $200,000 for single and head of household, and $125,000 for married filing separately.[102] To make matters a little more complicated, this added Medicare tax of 0.9% is imposed only on employees and not required to be matched by employers.

It is important to note that the new additional 0.9% Medicare tax is the first and only progressive payroll tax in our nation's history of tax laws. Not only has it gone against our country's precedent of level payroll tax rates for all income levels, but one would be hard pressed to find another country that has adopted a similar graduated payroll tax system that taxes higher income levels at a greater rate than lower income. This anomaly is largely a result of politicians keeping a presidential campaign pledge of the 2008 and 2012 elections promising no tax increases on married couples making less than $250,000 per year or on singles making less than $200,000. It is egregious that such a small tax increase has created so much additional work for the accountants, seminar speakers, and payroll personnel of America.

Rather than belabor the issue of the ill-conceived 0.9% additional Medicare tax, it is more important to propose a solution to simplify it. The 20/20 Tax would merely allocate this tax increase among all wage-earners and their employers so that rather than having the overall Medicare tax rate decrease from today's 1.45% to a reduced 1.40% (as explained earlier), the rate would actually increase to 1.50% to be paid on all wages and salaries by employees and employers alike. This slight increase in the Medicare tax rate would raise all the revenue intended to be assessed by the 0.9% Medicare surtax of the Affordable Care Act, and it would save hundreds of thousands of hours in processing payrolls, preparing tax returns, and advising clients how to avoid the additional tax or how to cope with its unintended consequences.

THE NEW 3.8% NET INVESTMENT INCOME TAX

Now let's deal with part II of the Affordable Care Act's healthcare tax increases. Since the inception of our country's Medicare system, the Medicare tax has only been imposed on employee wages and salaries and on the self-employment income of the self-employed. However, for tax years beginning after 2012, a new 3.8% (3.8% NIIT) has been imposed on some or all of the investment income of certain individuals, estates, and trusts.

If you want to know why they say the devil is in the details, please try to comprehend the following definition of investment income for purposes of the net investment income tax:

> Net investment income is the excess of the sum of the following items, less any otherwise allowable deductions properly allocable to such income or gain. (Prop. Reg. §1.1411-4):
>
> • gross income from interest, dividends, annuities, royalties, rent and substitute

interest and dividend payments, but not to the extent this income is derived in the ordinary course of an active trade or business;

- other gross income (not described above) from a passive activity under Code Sec. 469 (¶ 2053), or from a trade or business of a trader trading in financial instruments or commodities; and

- net gain included in computing taxable income that is attributable to the disposition of property, but not to the extent the property was held in an active trade or business.[103]

Assuming you can understand the above, here is how the 3.8% NIIT works:

For individuals, the net investment income tax is 3.8 percent of the lesser of (1) the taxpayer's net investment income for the tax year, or (2) the excess of MAGI for the tax year over the threshold amount of $200,000 ($250,000 for married taxpayers filing jointly and surviving spouses, and $125,000 for a married taxpayer filing separately). MAGI is the taxpayer's adjusted gross income (AGI) increased by any foreign income excluded from gross income for the year under Code Sec. 911 less any deductions, exclusions, or credits properly allocable to such foreign income. The tax applies to all individuals subject to U.S. taxation other than nonresident aliens.[104]

These few paragraphs above have resulted in tax attorneys writing entire books on the subject of the 3.8% NIIT and how to best avoid it or at least minimize its impact on clients' tax returns. Once again, the drafting of this tax provision in the Affordable Care Act of 2010 was careful not to violate an election campaign promise about raising taxes on the middle class, but its complexity and absorption of professional hours has created another quagmire for the American taxpayer. It has consumed countless hours of research and interpretation by accountants and tax preparers since it took effect in 2013, and it will undoubtedly result in many tax court adjudications.

Because the 20/20 Tax strives to simplify the tax code in an equitable manner, it would replace the 3.8% NIIT with a much more understandable solution for partially funding the Affordable Care Act. This could be achieved by the adoption of a 2.5% healthcare tax as explained later in this chapter.

THE 2.5% HEALTHCARE TAX FOR SELF-EMPLOYED TAXPAYERS

A major issue to consider is that the 2.5% healthcare tax would replace the Medicare portion of the self-employment tax, which is one of the more questionable funding mechanisms of our entitlement programs. The self-employment tax applies to most unincorporated business owners, farmers, ranchers, and other self-employed individuals who essentially work for themselves. Most employees pay what's known as the FICA tax, named after the legislation that started it (Federal Insurance Contribution Act). However, the self-employed are taxed under the Self-Employment Contributions Act, sometimes called the SECA tax but more commonly known as the SE tax. Whereas the FICA tax collects employee tax of 6.2% for Social Security on the first $117,000 of (2014) wages and 1.45% Medicare tax on all wages, with matching contributions (6.2% + 1.45%) from the employer, the SE tax assesses a combined amount (12.4% + 2.9%) from the self-employed individual. Thus, the self-employed pay SE tax that is exactly double the rate that most employees pay in FICA tax.

If you think the self-employed are treated rather harshly by having to pay twice as much payroll tax as the typical employee, not surprisingly you can find many of the self-employed who will agree with you. Actually, most taxpayers who own their own business can often understand paying twice as much for Social Security as do common-law employees. Without this doubling of the FICA tax, the self-employed would only be providing half as much funding for their Social Security of which the eventual benefits are largely based on the amount of one's contributions to the system. However, the argument for the self-employed to take a double hit on the Medicare tax (2.9% of all net income) is a bit more difficult for many to swallow. After all, the Medicare system does not provide higher benefits to those who contribute more during their working years. And, it's important to consider that the majority of self-employed taxpayers are just one-person operations. They are the barbers, carpenters, painters, gardeners, house cleaners, consultants, security guards, handymen, and numerous other people making an honorable living without a formal employer. It is hard for many of these taxpayers to understand why they should pay twice as much for Medicare tax as their friends who have an employer.

Another point to consider is the history of the Medicare tax. For its first eighteen years (1966–1983), the tax rate for self-employed workers was exactly the same as for common-law employees. By the early 1980s, the rate had increased to 1.3% for employees as well as 1.3% for the self-employed, and its assessment was limited to the Social Security wage base ($35,700 in 1983). However, beginning in 1984, the self-employed were required to double-down on their Medicare portion of the SE tax by paying a doubled rate of 2.6%. This was part of the solution to resolve Social Security-Medicare financing problems as determined by the National Commission on Social Security Reform in January 1983 (often known as the Greenspan Commission). One has to ask if this doubling of the SE Medicare rate was an equitable decision made by the commission, or was it a desperate reach for revenue to partially solve a pending funding crisis? To add insult to injury, seven years later (in 1991), the earnings cap on Medicare wages was removed, and all wages and self-employment income became subject to the Medicare tax, which by then was taxed at today's 2.9% rate for the self-employed.

In all fairness, it is important to point out that for 1990 and later years, the self-employed were given a deduction for half of all self-employment taxes paid. This deduction is intended to put the self-employed on an equal footing with corporate owners and employees who are employed by their companies, which can take a deduction for the employer share of FICA tax. Unfortunately, the calculation is rather complex as can be deciphered from the following description:

> Beginning in 1990, self-employed workers are allowed a deduction, for purposes of computing their net earnings, equal to half of the combined OASDI and HI (Medicare) contributions that would be payable without regard to the contribution and benefit base. The OASDI contribution rate is then applied to net earnings after this deduction, but subject to the OASDI base.[105]

A more thorough explanation could be given on this deduction of half the self-employment tax by providing an example of the Schedule SE and walking you through the mechanics of computing the SE tax while also showing how it affects pages one and two of the Form 1040. But, rather than put you through this mind-numbing experience, let me cut to the chase and show mathematically the effective SE tax rates paid when using four of today's more common tax brackets.

Marginal Income Tax Bracket	Gross SE Rate	Gross SE Rate X 92.35% = Net SE Rate	Decrease in Effective Rate Caused by the 50% Deduction	Effective Rate of SE Tax
0%	15.30%	14.13%	0.00%	14.13% *
15%	15.30	14.13	1.06	13.07
25%	15.30	14.13	1.77	12.36
35%	15.30	14.13	2.47	11.66 **

* It is important to understand that some taxpayers who have a 0.0% marginal *income* tax bracket can still be obligated to pay the 15.3% SE tax, which has a true effective rate of 14.13%.

** Those taxpayers who have a 35% marginal income tax bracket will usually be subject to the 0.9% additional Medicare tax on top of the 11.66% effective rate of SE Tax as shown in the above table (for years after 2012).

Notice how the effective rate of today's SE tax drops lower as the marginal income tax rate of the taxpayer goes up. What you are seeing is another example of the upside-down subsidy at work. In other words, the lower earning taxpayers are paying the highest effective rates of SE tax.

This upside-down outcome along with the above nonsensical calculations would be totally avoided with the 20/20 version of the self-employment tax. There would be just two simple line item calculations to put on the tax return to replace today's nine mysterious lines for the SE tax. The Social Security portion of the SE tax would simply be 10.0% of self-employment income up to the OASDI wage base. And the 2.5% healthcare tax would be applied to all self-employment income. There would be no deductions or arcane calculations, and every self-employed taxpayer would experience the same effective SE tax rate.

WHY SHOULD WE USE THE RATES OF 10.0% AND 2.5% FOR THE 20/20 SE TAX?

In order to explain how I arrived at the 10.0% Social Security portion of the SE tax and the 2.5% healthcare (Medicare) portion, let's take a look at the mathematical model of the 20/20 SE tax when using the old way of calculating the SE tax by allowing a deduction for half of the net SE tax.

Marginal Income tax Bracket	Gross SE Rate	Gross SE Rate X 92.50% = Net SE Rate	Decrease in Effective Rate Caused by the 50% Deduction	Effective Rate of SE Tax
10%	15.00%	13.88%	0.69%	13.19%
20%	15.00	13.88	1.39	12.49
30%	15.00	13.88	2.08	11.80

The calculations that you see above result in three potential effective rates for the 20/20 version of the self-employment tax. Those are 13.19%,

12.49%, and 11.80%. The 20/20 Tax would adopt the median rate of 12.49 (but rounded to 12.5%) as the appropriate combined payroll tax rate to apply to all self-employed taxpayers on their net SE income up to the ceiling of the OASDI wage base. This combined rate of 12.5% is considered the best choice because it correlates with taxpayers in the marginal income tax bracket of 20% which is anticipated to be the most frequent top tax bracket among 20/20 taxpayers. The 12.5% rate is also very close to the average effective rate of SE tax on all taxpayer brackets if the 20/20 SE tax is calculated with a 50% deduction factor. One other consideration is that the new 12.5% rate should raise approximately the same tax or slightly more than the weighted average effective SE tax rate under current law.

Now let's take a look at the decision to allocate the 12.5% rate of the new SE tax between Social Security (10.0%) and Healthcare or Medicare (2.5%) tax. This can most easily be explained by again utilizing the foregoing mathematical model.

Marginal Income Tax Bracket	Gross Soc. Sec. Rate/ Healthcare Rate	Gross SE Rate X 92.50% = Net SE Rate	Decrease in Effective Rate Caused by the 50% Deduction	Effective Rate of Soc. Sec. Tax/ Healthcare Tax
20%	12.00%	11.10%	1.11%	10.00%
20%	3.00%	2.78%	0.28%	2.50%
Combined Rate	15.00%	13.88%	1.38%	12.50%

The above may seem like an exercise in futility, but the whole purpose is to provide a simplified approach to the self-employment tax, which for years has baffled millions of taxpayers and even many accountants. Once the 20/20 version of the self-employment tax is adopted, there will no longer be a need for the Schedule SE, a form that most taxpayers never understood. Also, the calculation of the SE tax would be so basic that most fifth graders could produce the right answer. Finally, all self-employed taxpayers will be subject to just one effective rate for Social Security and one effective tax rate for healthcare (Medicare).

WHY IMPOSE THE 2.5% HEALTHCARE TAX ON MOST OTHER FORMS OF INCOME?

Historically, the only income subject to the Medicare tax was W-2 income and self-employment income. Initially, Congress chose to finance our Medicare program based on the labor of the American worker. When Medicare was enacted in 1965, it was patterned mostly after Social Security, which has always been financed by taxing wages and self-employment income. However, with the passage of the Affordable Care Act of 2010, our lawmakers took a different approach to the financing of national healthcare. Rather than raise payroll taxes, the Democratic Congress chose to adopt the 3.8% Net Investment Income Tax. This 3.8% NIIT was targeted at the upper 3%–5% of income earners, primarily those with large amounts of investment income (interest, dividends, rent, royalties, capital gains, etc.).

Without dwelling on the politics of the new 3.8% NIIT, it is my opinion that Congress could have made a much better decision than taxing a small percentage of wealthy taxpayers on just their investment income in order to subsidize the healthcare for a majority of Americans. I fully understand going beyond the typical payroll tax approach. In fact, I have often asked why does a well-endowed trust-fund child who might pay very little Medicare tax during his or her lifetime end up entitled to the same Medicare benefits as those who pay over $1,000 of Medicare tax during every year of one's career? It is my opinion that assuming our country continues to provide Medicaid, Medicare, Obamacare, and other forms of national healthcare, then there should be a flat-rate healthcare tax that applies to most of our citizens on most taxable income. And that tax rate should be increased to pay for every significant increase in the future healthcare benefits voted in by our lawmakers. With this philosophy in mind, the 20/20 Tax would initiate a healthcare tax as described earlier, which taxes all forms of taxable income at the same 2.5% rate that replaces our self-employment

Medicare tax. There would be the notable exceptions of W-2 income, IRA distributions, 401(k)-type deferred income, and Social Security benefits, since these forms of income are already subject to Medicare tax or were subject to Medicare tax upon initial funding.

One could argue that other sources of income should be considered for exclusion from the healthcare tax, such as interest or annuity income, which often have been at least partially subjected to the Medicare tax prior to the funding of such investment vehicles. There is some validity to this argument, but even if one could trace the Medicare tax paid on interest or annuity income, the percentage of such amounts would invariably pale in comparison to the percentage of Medicare tax paid by an employee and his/her employer on the typical wages or Social Security benefits received.

The amount of tax revenue to be raised by this 2.5% healthcare tax would dwarf the amount currently being raised by the 3.8% NIIT. It may also provide a suitable replacement for the infamous Cadillac tax, which is scheduled to take effect in 2018 at the onerous rate of 40% on all high-premium policies (those over $10,200 per year for singles and over $27,500 for families). Politicians and policy experts alike have been very skeptical of the Cadillac tax, which is one of the primary revenue-raisers of the Affordable Care Act.

MINIMUM THRESHOLD FOR HEALTHCARE TAX AND SE TAX

Over twenty years ago, my ten-year old daughter, Kirsten, had her first big year of babysitting. She had earned about $500 for the year of 1994. When I told her that she had an obligation to file a tax return for that year and must pay approximately $70 of SE tax, she suddenly had tears in her eyes. She could not believe that she owed money to the government. I stoically advised her that if she had earned less than $400 for the year, she would owe no tax. This was no consolation as she quickly figured out that the IRS would lay claim to 70% of her final $100 earned at the end of the year.

Today, we have the same limit of $400 of net income that serves as the threshold to determine if a taxpayer is exempt from self-employment tax. This limit goes back to the early 1950s. Obviously, this amount should be adjusted for inflation after more than sixty years on the books. The 20/20 Tax would increase this limit to $2,000 and would apply the same limit to all income subject to the healthcare tax.

Chapter 6.11

THE REST OF THE MYRIAD

Progress begins with the belief that what is necessary is possible.
—Norman Cousins, American Journalist

At this point of the book, I have described approximately sixty major changes that the 20/20 Tax would make to our current income tax code. Not to alarm you, but there are more than two hundred additional changes that are left to be described. Most of these can only be found in Appendix A of this book with little, if any, detailed explanation. However, I will briefly describe in this chapter a handful of the low-dollar proposed changes that affect millions of American taxpayers and have not yet been explained in earlier chapters.

REPEAL THE DEDUCTION OF EMPLOYEE BUSINESS EXPENSES

An issue that comes up for many taxpayers is how to deduct their employee business expenses. For some tax returns, this area of the filing process will consume more time for the return preparer (and for the client) than all other deductions reported on one's tax return. The most frequent items in this category are auto expense (mileage, depreciation, etc.), business meals, entertainment and sports tickets, homeoffice expense, association fees, union dues, uniforms, work clothing, and career education. Many of these expenses that are directly related to one's employment are often reimbursed by the employer and thus not deductible. Those expenses not reimbursed will normally require detailed written documentation, which is difficult for many taxpayers to produce. Thus, good citizens often end up with potential deductions that can easily be challenged by the government. Furthermore, even those who maintain excellent documentation are subject to the 2% limitation rule, which means that only job expenses and miscellaneous deductions in excess of 2% of one's adjusted gross income (AGI) can be deducted. Then to add insult to injury, the deductible expenses exceeding 2% of one's AGI are subject to the alternative minimum tax (AMT). It's not uncommon for the AMT to wipe out all remaining tax benefits of a taxpayer's unreimbursed job expenses.

The bottom-line result is that employees are much better off to get their employer to reimburse job expenses rather than expecting to receive a savings on their tax returns for out-of-pocket expenses. With this in mind, the 20/20 Tax has eliminated employee job expenses as a deductible item or as a source for any tax credits. Once this law change becomes effective, most employers are more likely to reimburse those employee expenses that are truly "ordinary and necessary" to the active conduct of their business. More importantly, taxpayers will not be attempting to deduct the exaggerated business mileage, the unreasonable business meals, or the gray-area entertainment tickets. One further benefit of eliminating the deduction of employee business expenses is that it greatly simplifies the preparation of many tax returns while denying sizeable tax benefits for only a miniscule percentage of taxpayers.

REPEAL DEDUCTION OF OTHER MISCELLANEOUS ITEMIZED DEDUCTIONS

For some of the same reasons, the 20/20 Tax would repeal the itemized deduction of tax preparation fees and other miscellaneous deductions, such as safe deposit boxes and investment advisory fees. The 2% rule and the AMT already effectively eliminate the tax benefit of these deductions for most taxpayers. And the deduction of professional fees has often been questioned as a justifiable tax benefit to taxpayers. Most tax reform proposals, with simplification in mind, advocate the elimination of all miscellaneous itemized deductions, as does the 20/20 Tax.

REVISE THE AUTOMOBILE ENERGY CREDITS

Ever since 1993, our tax law has provided tax incentives for the purchase of certain energy-efficient automobiles. The example of the earliest subsidy that most of us remember is that of the $2,000 federal credit offered to taxpayers for the purchase of a new hybrid vehicle. This tax credit was praised by some as a catalyst of energy efficiency in the auto world but also loathed by many as needless spending by our lawmakers in Washington. Most of us consider energy efficiency as a worthy goal, but at the same time we must answer the question of whether or not we are getting our money's worth from energy-related subsidies. In other words, is this tax incentive just another form of corporate welfare to help the auto companies, or has our country actually seen a net benefit from this tax expenditure?

In the case of the $2,000 tax credit for the early hybrid vehicles, I would have to argue that our government's forgone revenue came back to benefit all of us, even for those of us who have never purchased a hybrid vehicle. Hybrid technology has clearly reduced oil consumption, lowering the price at the pump for everyone and providing cleaner air in most of our cities. The world's largest manufacturer of hybrid vehicles, Toyota Motor Company, has sold more than seven million of their hybrid models over the last eighteen years. Would this kind of success have occurred if it were not for the consumer tax incentives offered by most states as well as the governments of the United States, Japan, and certain other developed nations? It is quite possible that the Prius would have survived without the tax incentives, but I also believe it's just as likely that without any government assistance, the Prius could have been another model facing extinction. At the very least, the tax credits going to hybrid auto buyers helped to stimulate sales to the point that today most of the world's major auto manufacturers are offering their own hybrid models just to meet their competition.

In recent years, much of the environmental auto attention has turned to the electric vehicles (EVs). The totally electric vehicles and plug-in hybrids (which have large battery-storage capability combined with small gasoline engines) currently entitle their buyers to a federal tax credit of $7,500. Has this higher tax credit been successful at promoting the sales of such vehicles? EVs are still relatively new on the scene, but after five years of sales, the 2014 volume of EVs and plug-in hybrids sold was well under 1.0% of total US auto sales (including light trucks and SUVs). Some have argued that a $7,500 tax credit is not enough incentive to move these vehicles, and the White House has advocated an increase of the credit to $10,000.

I believe that our government is already paying too much to motivate buyers to purchase an EV. If $7,500 does not induce a person to buy a $90,000 Tesla, then I don't think a $10,000 tax credit will close the deal. Most people purchase a vehicle that best fits their needs and lifestyle, and today's electric vehicles and plug-in hybrids may not be the right answer for most consumers, at any price.

The 20/20 Tax would deemphasize the importance of battery-powered electric vehicles as compared to other technologies. The emphasis really should be on miles per gallon (mpg) or the equivalent of mpg in alternative fuel sources, such as hydrogen or natural gas, and of course, clean air needs to be a major consideration. Thus, the 20/20 Tax would establish a limited credit of $2,000 for those vehicles that average 80–99 mpg, and a $3,000 credit for those vehicles that average at least 100 mpg, regardless of the technology involved. The above criteria were arrived at by considering that the CAFE standards require auto manufacturers to attain an average fleet standard of 54.5 mpg by the year 2025. Already there are a small number of manufacturers offering vehicles that average the equivalent of more than 100 mpg, mostly smaller lightweight vehicles. It is no easy task for manufacturers to reach this standard, and in the years ahead, it will be a major accomplishment to produce several larger models getting the equivalent of 80–100 mpg.

It is my opinion that our country will achieve more by incentivizing millions of future auto purchases with credits of $2,000–$3,000 rather than trying to induce a smaller number of car buyers with extremely high incentives of $7,500 to $10,000. Many states are offering their own incentives for EV purchases, and in my state of Colorado, the $6,500 state credit when combined with the $7,500 federal credit seems like an overstated subsidy for those who decide to purchase a $30,000 all-electric Nissan Leaf or comparable vehicle. I don't think that most Americans are interested in having their government pay for nearly half the price of a vehicle they or their neighbors might purchase. The majority of car buyers would find it more prudent to receive a 5–10% government incentive for making the "right choice" for the environment while buying a vehicle that fulfills their personal needs with respect to size, safety, range, and desired features like all-wheel drive. The battery-operated cars of today offer limited range, options, and equipment, and may experience very low resale value or utilitarian value in five to seven years. Is our government wisely spending billions of dollars to promote electric vehicles when other technologies like hydrogen fuel-cell vehicles may eventually win the battle of consumer choice?

Obviously, there needs to be an overall dollar limit on the tax credits allowed for the car-buying public. This limit should be comparable to our current federal law.

TIME TO COLLECT THE "NANNY TAX"

One of the darker secrets of our income tax system is the issue sometimes referred to as the "nanny tax." Our tax law requires the issuance of a W-2 form to each "household employee" who is paid more than $1,900 during calendar year 2014. The problem with this tax provision is determining who is a household employee. It is safe to say that almost all childcare providers (nannies) who come to the house of the parent(s) to care for their child (children) are considered to be household employees under the tax code. Since childcare providers are typically supervised by the parents, and the provider is utilizing the parents' home and using the parents' furnishings and supplies, there is no premise to deny employee status and the requirement to issue a W-2.

A W-2 should be issued to each household employee and filed with the IRS by February 28 of the following year if 2014 compensation exceeds $1,900. This requires that 15.3% of the employee's compensation must be paid in FICA taxes, either totally paid by the taxpayer, or 7.65% paid by the employee with employer matching of 7.65%. Then there is federal unemployment tax (FUTA) to be paid, and most states require the payment of state unemployment tax (SUTA) along with the related payroll tax forms, which can cost as much as $1,200 per year if prepared by an independent tax preparer. Is it any surprise that the compliance rate in our country is less than 10% for the tax reporting of household employees? The complexity and burden of payroll tax reporting, not to mention the additional expense, has caused millions of American citizens to ignore this area of our tax law.

Unfortunately, the rules for household employees apply to several occupations other than nannies. Many taxpayers employ "cleaning ladies," yard workers, window washers, and other help who may be defined as household employees subject to employer tax reporting rules. Many of these hired helpers may be considered independent contractors and not employees, provided they are not supervised by the home owner (taxpayer) and assuming they provide their own equipment and tools (i.e., vacuum, lawn mower, etc.). All too often there is a fine line between an employee and an independent contractor, sometimes leading to tax assessments upon audit.

Faced with the dilemma of almost total noncompliance for household employees, our government needs new legislation to cope with an untenable situation. The 20/20 Tax proposes the following code changes to attain higher compliance for the reporting of income paid to household employees:

1. Totally eliminate the federal unemployment tax for all household employees and legislatively encourage all fifty states to eliminate their state unemployment taxes for such employees. The reporting requirements for this minor tax is often more costly for taxpayers than the unemployment tax that is collected. If unemployment taxes were eliminated, taxpayers would find it much easier to report the income of their household employees. The federal and state

governments would be much better off to focus on collecting only the FICA and income tax due.

2. Provide a free government website that would easily process the W-2 forms and other necessary paperwork for household employees on an annual basis with minimal input from the taxpayer. This would minimize the excessive tax return processing costs that make household-employee reporting very tempting for most taxpayers to ignore.

3. Permanently establish a threshold of $2,000 for the annual requirement to issue a W-2 to each household employee. This amount should not be adjusted annually for inflation but only changed upon future congressional action. A stable amount would improve taxpayer compliance rates.

4. For taxpayers who find it difficult to determine employee status or to prepare timely W-2 forms for employees, they should be given the option of reporting amounts paid to all household employees and independent contractors by filing proposed Form 1099-H for each "household worker" paid at least $1,000 during the taxable year. Household workers would be defined as those unincorporated workers who provide their services to a nonbusiness individual taxpayer. The filing of all appropriate Forms 1099-H (a new form) under this provision would result in a waiver of any requirement to report workers as household employees, and thus relieve taxpayers of payroll tax filing requirements.

Please refer to Appendix A for a summary of the rest of the myriad.

Proposed tax forms on the following pages.

In Chapter 5.5, I revealed the first page of the new tax return for the 20/20 Tax. By now you may be curious to see what page two of the tax forms may look like for the 20/20 Tax. The following pages show the author's draft of pages one and two of the new Form 1040. In Appendix B you will also find the Form EIC, which most taxpayers will need for the preparation of their 20/20 tax returns.

FORM 1040   **2020**   **PAGE ONE**

M D Y

Taxpayer Name _____   Date of Birth __/__/__   SSN _____
Spouse Name _____   Date of Birth __/__/__   SSN _____
Address _____
City, State, Zip _____

Filing Status   1 ___ Single   4 ___ Head of household (SSN of qualifying person) _____
                 2 ___ Married filing jointly   5 ___ Qualifying widow(er) with dependent child
                 3 ___ Married filing separately
                 Enter separate-filing spouse's SSN above and full name here _____

Personal Credits: 6a _____ Yourself. 6b _____ Spouse
6c Dependents – Names (First)   (Last)   Birth Date M/D/Y   SSN   Relationship

_____
_____

6d Total eligible for Personal Credit between the ages of 18 and 65 (include taxpayer and spouse under 65) _____
6e Total eligible for Personal Credit age 65 and over (include taxpayer and spouse if over 65) _____
NOTE: Dependent children under the age of 18 are only eligible for the Child Tax Credit on Line 62 of taxpayer's return.
           All children under 18 filing their own tax returns may claim the Personal Tax Credit but not the Child Tax Credit.

Ordinary	7	Wages, salaries, etc. Attach W-2(s) (To include employer-provided health insurance)	7	_____
Income	8	Alimony received 8b Payor's SSN _____	8	_____
	9	Business income or (loss). Attach Schedule C	9	_____
	10	Short-term and other gains or (losses). Attach Form 4797	10	_____
	11	IRA, 401(k), 403(b) and 457 distributions 11a _____ Taxable amount	11b	_____
	12	Pensions and annuities 12a _____ Taxable amount	12b	_____
	13	Rental real estate, royalties, partnerships, S Corporations, trusts, etc. Attach Schedule E	13	_____
	14	Partnership self-employment income (Should not be included in line 13)	14	_____
	15	Farm income or (loss). Attach Schedule F	15	_____
	16	Unemployment compensation	16	_____
	17	Other income. List type 17a (SE Income) _____ 17b (Non SE) _____	17	_____
	18	Total Ordinary Income—Combine the amounts on lines 7 through 17.	18	_____

Exclusionary	19	Interest - Attach Schedule B	19 _____	
Income	20	Dividends - Attach Schedule B	20 _____	
	21	Long-term capital gains - Attach Schedule D	21 _____	
	22	Social Security benefits	22 _____	
	23	Disability benefits	23 _____	
	24	Workers' compensation	24 _____	
	25	Total Exclusionary Income (Add lines 19 through 24) 25a _____ (X 50%)	25b	_____
	26	Total Combined Income (Add lines 18 and 25b)	26	_____

Deductions	27	Moving expenses-Attach Form 3903	27 _____	
	28	Self-employed SEP and qualified retirement plans	28 _____	
	29	Alimony paid b. Recipients SSN _____	29a _____	
	30	Total deductions (Add lines 27 through 29)	30	_____
	31	Taxable Income (line 26 minus line 30)	31	_____

		Single & H of H	Married Filing Jointly	Married Filing Separate	
Tax Calculation:					
	32	Tax at 10% rate $0–30,000	$0–50,000	$0–25,000	32 _____
	33	Tax at 20% rate $30,001–120,000	$50,000–200,000	$25,001–100,000	33 _____
	34	Tax at 30% rate $120,001+	$200,001+	$100,001+	34 _____
	35a	**Income Tax Before Credits (Add lines 32 thru 34)**			**35a** _____
	35b	**Income Tax Before Credits With Indexing Added (Sch. D) 35b _____ (35a+35b)35c**			**35c** _____

NOTE: Lines 35b and 35c only apply if taxable income exceeds $300,000 (Single); $500,000 (MFJ); and $250,000 (MFS).

FORM 1040   2020   PAGE TWO

Income Tax	36 Income tax before credits (Amount from line 35a or 35c if applicable, page 1)	36 _____
	37 Cash donations _____ less: 1% X line 31 _____	37 _____
Payments	38 Noncash donations: _____ less: 1% X line 31 _____ Attach Form 8283.	38 _____
Eligible for	39 Home mortgage interest and points from your Forms 1098	39 _____
20% Credits	40 Home mortgage interest and points not on Forms 1098. Attach Schedule A.	40 _____
to Reduce	41 Other deductible interest. Attach Schedule A (see instructions).	41 _____
Income Tax	42 Medical and dental expenses (in excess of 10% of line 31). Attach Schedule A.	42 _____
	43 State and local taxes (in excess of 10% of line 31). Attach Schedule A.	43 _____
	44 Total payments eligible for 20% credits (Add lines 37 through 43)	44 _____
	45 Nonrefundable 20% credits (line 44 X 20%)	45 _____
Other Credits	46 Personal credits: _____ @ $500 each, age 18-64; _____ @ $1,000 each, age 65 +.	46 _____
to Reduce	47 Residential energy credits. Attach Form 5695.	47 _____
Income Tax	48 Alternative motor vehicle credit. Attach Form 8910.	48 _____
	49 Credit for child and dependent care expense x 20% (up to $1,000 1 child; $2,000 if 2+)	49 _____
	50 Other credits from: a _____ 8801; b _____ add $1,000 if Head of Household (a+b)	50 _____
	51 Foreign tax credit. Attach Form 1116	51 _____
	52 Adoption credit ($10,000 limit). Attach Form 8839.	52 _____
	53 General business credits: Attach Form 3800.	53 _____
	54 Total nonrefundable credits (lines 45–53, but not to exceed line 36)	54 _____
	55 Income tax after nonrefundable credits (line 36 minus line 54)	55 _____
Other	56 Self-employment tax: 10.0% X (line 9 _____ plus lines 14, 15, 17a_____)	56 _____
Taxes	57 Unreported FICA tax from Form: a _____ 4137; b _____ 8919	57 _____
	58 Additional tax on IRA's, qualified plans. Attach Form 5329.	58 _____
	59 Household employment taxes from Schedule H.	59 _____
	60 Healthcare tax: 2.5% X (line 31, less lines 7 and 11b, less 50% of line 22)	60 _____
	61 Total tax before refundable credits (Add lines 55–60)	61 _____
Refundable	62 Child tax credits: _____ at $1,000 each (only for dependents under age 18)	62 _____
Credits	63 Uniform health insurance credit (UHIC premiums _____ X 20%)	63 _____
to Reduce	64 Earned income credit. Attach Schedule EIC.	64 _____
All Taxes	65 Higher education credit. Attach Schedule HEC.	65 _____
	66 Net premium tax credit (Form 8962). Also, Small employer ins. credit (Form 8941)	66 _____
	67 IRA savings credit—Credit IRA up to $5,000 per taxpayer (X 20%)	67 _____
	68 Total refundable credits (Add lines 62 through 67)	68 _____
	69 Total tax (refund) after refundable credits (line 61 minus line 68)	69 _____
Payments	70 Federal income tax withheld from Forms W-2 and 1099 70 _____	
	71 2020 estimated tax payments and amounts applied from 2019 return 71 _____	
	72 Amount paid with request for extension to file 72 _____	
	73 Excess social security and tier 1 RRTA tax withheld 73 _____	
	74 Credit for capital-gain tax paid by mutual funds 74 _____	
	75 Total payments (Add lines 70 through 74)	75 _____
Refund	76 If line 75 is more than line 69, the difference is the amount overpaid	76 _____
	77 Amount of line 76 you want refunded to you.	77 _____
	If Form 8888 is attached, check here ___ Routing # _____ Account # _____	
Amount	78 Amount of line 76 you want applied to your 2021 estimated tax 78. _____	
Owed	79 Amount you owe. Subtract line 75 from line 69.	79 _____
	80 Estimated tax penalty (see instructions) 80 _____	
Third-Party	Do you want to allow another person to discuss this return with the IRS? Yes ___ No ___	
Designee	If yes, Designee's name: _____ PTIN _____	

Sign Your signature _____ Date _____
Here Spouse's signature _____ Date _____

Paid Preparer Print/Type Preparer's name_____ Date _____
Use Only _____ PTIN _____
Preparer's Signature _____

Chapter 7

CORPORATE INCOME TAX AND OTHER FEDERAL TAXES

The primary emphasis of this book is on the individual income tax system of our country. Together with FICA taxes, the income tax on individuals raises about 80% of our nation's annual federal revenue through taxes that are primarily based on the wages and earnings of private citizens, their investments, and their closely-held businesses. This share of the federal revenue pie has expanded over the last thirty years while the burden of most other federal taxes has been shrinking. Let's take a look at why this has happened and what, if anything, should be done to change the course of events for some of our more significant federal taxes.

Chapter 7.1

CORPORATE INCOME TAX

The US corporate income tax was adopted four years before the Sixteenth Amendment approved the personal income tax. This 1909 legislation called for a 1% excise tax on corporate income over $5,000, and it was cunningly supported by President William Howard Taft in a failed political attempt to prevent the personal income tax. As with most of our nation's taxes, the federal corporate income tax rate has risen over time, reaching a peak of 53.0% during World War II. In the last half century, the rate has been as high as 52.8% during the late 1960s with the Vietnam War era, later to drop gradually in the 1970s to a rate of 46% (1979). The Tax Reform Act of 1986 then dramatically lowered the top corporate rate from 46% to 34%. This rate was nudged back up to 35% by Congress under President Clinton in 1993, which is where it stands today.

In the 1950s and 1960s, the federal corporate income tax revenue was approximately 4.0% of GDP. However, in the last twenty-five years, the average has dropped to slightly less than 2.0% of GDP. This drop in corporate tax revenue as a percentage of GDP is only partially due to the reduction in the corporate tax rate. Much of the decrease is also due to a gradual erosion of the corporate tax base, partly caused by a trend in Congress to enact new tax breaks for businesses without offsetting the added tax breaks with the closure of existing loopholes. Such offsets are often promised by our lawmakers in Washington but in fact are rarely carried out in the legislative process. A second and larger factor contributing to lower the tax base has been the growing transfer of corporate profits outside the United States to other countries with lower tax rates (i.e., Ireland with a top corporate rate of 12.5%.)[1] Finally, the US corporate income tax base has been further diluted by the widespread use of S-corporations, partnerships, and limited liability companies, which became the preferred forms of doing business for small- and medium-sized businesses after the Tax Reform Act of 1986. These pass-through entities serve to avoid the corporate-level tax and only result in the taxation of business profits for the entity owners at their individual tax rates. This avoids the double taxation that results when large corporations pay dividends to their shareholders, which is a severe handicap for big business.

Of the three contributing factors that lower the corporate tax base as described above, the largest enabling issue of the twenty-first century has been that of corporate offshore profits. An interesting study was provided in Martin Sullivan's book *Corporate Tax Reform*, in which the author compared the effective tax rates of America's twenty most profitable, publicly-traded corporations for the years of 1997–1999 to the comparable effective rates for years 2005–2007.[2] Based on company annual reports, the effective tax rates (including state taxes) had a group average of 35.8% for the years 1997–1999, whereas the same group average dropped to 30.3% for the years 2005–2007.[3] According to the author of the book, this decline in effective tax rates had little to do with congressional tax breaks but "primarily is attributable to U.S. corporations doing more business outside the United States, a steady decline in foreign tax rates, and the increasing ability of tax managers to shift a disproportionate share of profits to tax havens like Ireland, Switzerland, Bermuda, and the Cayman Islands."[4]

The Organisation for Economic Co-operation and Development (OECD) released a report in June 2014 recommending various tax reform measures to strengthen the US economy. According to the report, business investment is often discouraged by high US marginal tax rates.[5] The report recommended the reduction of the marginal corporate income tax rates while broadening the tax base. It urged the

United States to take steps "to prevent base erosion and profit shifting."[6] The OECD is constructing a set of standards to curb such abuses.

"Another consequence of the current international tax rules is that multinational firms avoid paying taxes by using a host of legal provisions to narrow their tax base and shift their profits to low-tax foreign jurisdictions," said the report. It continued as follows:

> The magnitude of these operations is so large that some multinational firms pay very low taxes, despite being highly profitable. In the current context of fiscal constraints and severe loss of trust in institutions, it is important that these firms pay their fair share of taxes. Taxes unpaid by multinational firms transfer the tax burden to everybody else, hence imposing distortions on other sectors. Reforms to combat base erosion and profit shifting (BEPS) would go a long way towards achieving this goal and towards supporting overall tax reform by leveling the playing field. In this regard continued U.S. leadership on the BEPS project is crucial for ensuring that such reforms are consistent and coordinated across countries.[7]

A more recent report was issued by the Tax Foundation in September 2014, which released its 2014 International Tax Competitiveness Index to rank the tax policies of the thirty-four countries in the OECD. This index ranks the United States at thirty-second overall, trailed only by France and Portugal.[8] The Tax Foundation report stated "The largest factors behind the United States' score are that the U.S. had the highest corporate (income) tax rate in the developed world and that it is one of the six remaining countries in the OECD with a worldwide system of taxation."[9]

Before describing the problems (and merits) of our worldwide system of taxation, let me further expound on the position of the United States having the highest corporate income tax rate in the developed world.

It is no secret in the business world that this has put US companies at a major disadvantage relative to foreign competitors. Between 1997 and 2013, thirty-one of the thirty-four OECD countries reduced their corporate tax rates to attract jobs and capital.[10] The only three countries not lowering their corporate tax rates during this period were Chile, Norway, and the United States, with Norway joining the rest of the countries in early 2014 by lowering its corporate tax rate to 27%. The following table 7.1-1 shows the United States with the highest marginal tax rate compared to the other economies of the OECD.

Table 7.1-1 2014 Corporate Tax Rates
(National and Local) for OECD [11]

Country	Rate	Country	Rate
Australia	30.0%	Japan	37.0%
Austria	25.0%	Korea Republic	24.2%
Belgium	33.9%	Luxembourg	29.2%
Canada	26.3%	Mexico	30.0%
Chile	20.0%	Netherlands	25.0%
Czech Republic	19.0%	New Zealand	28.0%
Denmark	24.5%	Norway	27.0%
Estonia	21.0%	Poland	19.0%
Finland	20.0%	Portugal	31.5%
France	34.4%	Slovak Republic	22.0%
Germany	30.2%	Slovenia	17.0%
Greece	26.0%	Spain	30.0%
Hungary	19.0%	Sweden	22.0%
Iceland	20.0%	Switzerland	21.1%
Ireland	12.5%	Turkey	20.0%
Israel	26.5%	United Kingdom	21.0%
Italy	27.5%	United States	39.1%

Despite the fact that the United States indisputably has the highest marginal corporate tax rate in the world, there is a widespread belief that most US corporations pay little or no corporate income tax. This perception was further heightened in July 2013 when the Government

Accountability Office released a study concluding that the effective US corporate tax rate (after all deductions and credits) was only 12.6%. However, the GAO report was very misleading as described by Andrew Lyon, an international tax expert at PricewaterhouseCoopers. He wrote in the October 2013 Tax Notes that GAO did not count all corporate taxes paid.[12] Furthermore, the GAO research only examined data for one year, 2010, when corporate taxes fell to their lowest level in many years due to the stimulus write-offs and net operating losses following the severe 2007–2009 recession. Mr. Lyon extended the analysis to a more representative period of 2004–2010, to include all taxes paid worldwide (including foreign, state, and local taxes), and he concluded that "The effective tax rate based on worldwide current tax payments for all U.S. corporations exceeded 35% for the 2004–2010 period."[13]

There is no question that US corporate income tax rates must be lowered to allow American multinationals to compete with foreign companies, but now let's consider the other major impediment to competition as cited by the Tax Foundation in its report of the 2014 International Tax Competitiveness Index.

THE US WORLDWIDE TAX SYSTEM

Based on the premise of a worldwide tax system, the United States maintains the right to tax all income of American corporations (and our citizens) no matter where the income is earned. In our worldwide system, double taxation is avoided by allowing our corporate and individual taxpayers a foreign tax credit, which normally reduces US income taxes by the income taxes paid to foreign governments. So, if an American company earns $100,000 of profit in a foreign country having a 25 percent tax rate, it pays $25,000 of foreign tax. Since the US corporate tax rate is 35%, the American company would, in theory, pay the IRS $35,000 less the $25,000 foreign tax paid, for a net US tax of $10,000. This way the American corporation theoretically pays the same amount of tax whether the income is earned in the States or abroad. However, if this simple example was the full story, it would be extremely difficult for American companies to compete with those companies domiciled in countries with tax rates well below 35%.

An important aspect of US international tax law is the concept of deferral, which allows American companies to avoid paying US tax on foreign income until such profits are passed on as dividends by the offshore subsidiary to its US parent company. In reality, this payment of dividends rarely happens, and most foreign subsidiaries serve to shelter foreign profits indefinitely from US taxes. Thus, in our earlier example of the net US tax of $10,000, this amount can easily avoid the grasp of the US Treasury by the company not repatriating dividends to its US parent company. As of this writing, US corporations have accumulated approximately $2 trillion of foreign earnings in other countries, mostly with the intention of avoiding the US corporate income tax. The strong tax incentive to keep accumulated earnings offshore has had a negative impact on the US economy and job growth. For this reason, many economists would like to see a change from the worldwide system of taxation that has existed for several decades.

CONSIDER A TERRITORIAL TAX SYSTEM

The likely alternative to our worldwide system would be one of the territorial systems adopted by most OECD countries. The basic theory of a territorial system is for a country to only tax business profits generated within its own borders. If the United States were to adopt this alternative approach, our country would no longer tax US multinationals on their foreign profits, and there would be no need for the deferral concept. With a territorial system, foreign profits would only be subjected to the tax rate and rules of the country where the profits are earned, and there would be no additional tax for bringing such earnings back to the US parent company. The obvious advantage to the territorial system is that it puts US international companies on a level playing field with the competing businesses of most developed foreign countries. Another clear advantage is that it eliminates the lock-out effect that discourages US multinationals from repatriating foreign profits back to the United States. The downside of a territorial system is that US companies may be biased toward foreign investments over domestic opportunities due to the lower rates of other countries. However, this issue, which has been mostly neutralized by the deferral concept, could be more effectively ameliorated by a lowering of corporate tax rates to a level close to the average of other OECD countries (25.3% as of February 2014: from table 7.1-1).

After many years of discussion, almost all factions agree that the United States should adopt a territorial system for taxing its international companies. Business lobbyists have advocated this approach for years, as have most economists, labor leaders, and several politicians on both sides of the aisle. However, the roadblock lies in choosing the specific rules and regulations of the territorial system to be adopted. Since the current US international tax system is deceptively favorable to corporations, the elimination of foreign profits from the US income tax could actually result in a tax increase for American multinationals. According to the economist, Martin Sullivan, "American corporations do not want a territorial system that raises their taxes. What they want is a territorial system like the one adopted in the United Kingdom (2009). This would cut their taxes."[14]

Why would a territorial system like the United Kingdom's reduce tax revenue as compared to other territorial systems that would increase tax revenue? The answer lies mostly in the accounting methods legislatively allowed under any given system, especially the rules for matching of foreign expenses with foreign income. Two very reputable proposals for territorial taxation were put forth in 2005 by nonpartisan groups including the Joint Committee on Taxation (JCT). Both of these 2005 proposals called for strict adherence to the "matching principle," which means that all expenses for research, etc. that should be matched and deducted against foreign profit do not get deducted against US income, which is normally taxed at higher rates than foreign income. American multinationals considered the 2005 territorial tax proposals to be a tax increase due to the resulting inability to deduct foreign expenses against their US income.

MAJOR CORPORATE TAX CHANGES PROPOSED

It would take hundreds of pages to fully describe all the business and corporate tax positions of the 20/20 Tax. In Appendix A of this book, you will find many proposed changes (in summary form) that broaden the base of US corporate taxable income. Most of these 20/20 Tax changes emulate the corporate tax changes presented in the proposed Tax Reform Act of 2014 as drafted by the House Ways and Means Committee in February 2014, which is arguably the most comprehensive and thoroughly researched tax reform proposal put forth by Congress in the last twenty years. The committee, chaired by Congressman David Camp, R-MI, proposed a gradual reduction of the corporate tax rate to 25%. This is the same eventual corporate tax rate that is advocated by the 20/20 Tax. While the Ways and Means Committee proposal calls for a gradual decrease in the top corporate rate for the years 2015 (33%), 2016 (31%), 2017 (29%), 2018 (27%), and 2019– (25%), the 20/20 Tax proposes an initial rate adjustment of 30% for years 2016–2020, and the final adopted rate of 25% for 2021 and later years. By lowering the corporate tax rate to 25%, both proposals would diminish the number of corporate "inversions," which are essentially the movement of US corporations to foreign countries in pursuit of lower corporate tax rates.

At this time, you may be asking how can the corporate tax rate be lowered from 35% to 25% without a large decrease in government revenue. This question can be partly answered by reading Titles III and IV of the Discussion Draft prepared by the House for the proposed Act of 2014. A summary of the contents of the Discussion Draft can be found in Appendix A of this book. Titles III and IV of the proposed 2014 Act contain 184 sections that change or repeal various business and corporate provisions in our tax code. Surprisingly, most of the corporate revenue impact of the 2014 proposed legislation can be found in the analysis of just 15 of the 184 sections, which are summarized as follows:

> Warning: The following summary is difficult to comprehend for readers
> who do not have an advanced degree in accounting, economics, or tax law.
> Please focus on the top five sections (3001–3122) and the revenue column.

Table 7.1-2

JCT Estimates of Revenue Increases (Decreases) [15]

2014–2023 (in billions)

Sec. 3001.	Reduce corporate tax rate to 25%	$(680.3)
Sec. 3104.	Reform of accelerated cost recovery system (depreciation)	269.5
Sec. 3108.	Amortization of research and experimental expenditures	192.6
Sec. 3110.	Amortization of certain advertising expenses	169.0
Sec. 3122	Repeal of deduction for domestic production activities	115.8
Sec. 4001.	Deduction for dividends received by domestic corporations from certain foreign corporations	(212.0)
Sec. 4002.	Limitation on losses for specified 10% owned foreign corps	*
Sec. 4003.	Treatment of deferred foreign income upon transition to participation exemption system of taxation	170.4
Sec. 4101.	Repeal of section 902 indirect foreign tax credits; determination of section 960 credit on current year basis	*
Sec. 4102.	Foreign tax credit limitation applied by allocating only directly allocable deductions to foreign source income	*
Sec. 4103.	Passive income expanded to include other mobile income	**
Sec. 4201.	Subpart F income to only include low-taxed foreign income	**
Sec. 4202.	Foreign base company sales income	**

Sec. 4203.	Inflation adjustment for foreign base company income	**
Sec. 4211.	Foreign intangible income subject to taxation at reduced rate; intangible income treated as subpart F income	<u>115.6</u>

Net effect of the revenue changes from the above 15 sections $<u>140.6</u>

* The revenue effects of sections 4002, 4101, and 4102 are included in the JCT estimate provided for section 4001 of the Discussion Draft.

** The revenue effects of sections 4103, 4201, 4202, and 4203 are included in the JCT estimate provided for section 4211 of the Discussion Draft.

As can be seen in the foregoing summary of major revenue estimates of the 2014 Act, there are plenty of base-broadening provisions to offset the revenue loss caused by the lowering of the corporate tax rate to 25%. In fact, if we consider the JCT revenue estimates of all 184 sections proposed in Titles III and IV (the business and corporate provisions) of the Discussion Draft, the estimated net revenue gain to the Treasury is approximately $534 billion for the ten years of 2014–2023.

This all sounds good for the first ten years after tax reform. However, some critics are concerned about what would happen to our federal budget more than ten years after the adoption of the House bill of 2014. One distinguished group, known as Fix the Debt Campaign (chaired by Michael Bloomberg, Judd Gregg, and Edward Rendell), has raised the legitimate concern that the House proposal generates much of its revenue in the first ten years "from timing shifts and temporary revenue provisions to offset permanent rate reductions; given this, we are concerned the (2014 Tax Reform) draft would add to the deficit over the long-term."[16] This is certainly a valid concern when one considers the up-front revenue benefit that would come from Sections 3104, 3108, and 3110 of the act. These sections deal with the depreciation of fixed assets and the amortization of significant expenses (i.e., research, advertising). There is not much doubt that these three sections of the 2014 Act would generate far more tax revenue in the first ten years than in years eleven through twenty. This is because these sections essentially delay or stretch out business deductions (depreciation and amortization) without reducing such write-offs in the long run. Thus, companies eventually get the same amount of deductions but only in later years.

There is a similar concern with the "temporary revenue provision" of Section 4003 of the 2014 Act, which encourages the repatriation of offshore earnings to their US parent companies. The cash portion of these earnings would be taxed at a special rate of 8.75%, while any remaining earnings would be taxed at a special rate of 3.5%. "According to JCT, the provision would increase revenues by $170.4 billion over (years) 2014–2023, $126.5 billion of which would be attributable directly to the one-time tax on accumulated E & P (earnings and profits), with the remainder attributable to indirect revenue effects."[17] Thus, the $126.5 billion is not revenue that would continue to flow to the Treasury after 2023.

The following table 7.1-3, compiled by Fix the Debt Campaign, shows the overall revenue impact of the proposed 2014 Act.

Table 7.1-3
Budgetary Impact of Tax Reform Act of 2014[18]

	2014–2018	2014–2023
Individual Reform		
Reduce rates to 10%, 25% & 35%, limit certain tax preferences to 25% bracket, phase out 10% rate	-$232 billion	-$544 billion
Tax capital gains/dividends with 40% exclusion	$15 billion	$45 billion
Consolidate, reform, and extend personal exemptions, standard deduction, CTC, and EITC	$18 billion	-$16 billion
Modify various itemized deductions	$309 billion	$858 billion
Require 401(k) contributions above half of current limit be placed in Roth-style accounts	$56 billion	$144 billion
Reform education tax preferences	$27 billion	$19 billion
Enact other changes	$76 billion	$237 billion
Reform Alternative Minimum Tax	-$443 billion	-$1,332 billion
Subtotal, Individual Reforms*	**-$174 billion**	**-$589 billion**

	2014–2018	2014–2023
Business Reforms		
Reduce corporate rate to 25% and repeal AMT	-$234 billion	-$791 billion
Reform accelerated depreciation schedules	$59 billion	$270 billion
Modify net operating loss deduction	$30 billion	$71 billion
Amortize R & E and advertising expenses	$152 billion	$362 billion
Phase out domestic production deduction	$44 billion	$116 billion
Repeal LIFO accounting rules	$6 billion	$79 billion
Reform international tax system	$20 billion	$68 billion
Enact other changes+	$103 billion	$359 billion
Subtotal, Business Reforms*	**$180 billion**	**$534 billion**
Excise Taxes		
Impose .035% tax on large banks	$30 billion	$86 billion
Repeal medical device tax and other changes	-$12 billion	-$28 billion
Subtotal, Excise Taxes	**$18 billion**	**$58 billion**
Total Budgetary Impact	**$24 billion**	**$3 billion**

*For pass-throughs, the rate reductions are captured in individual reforms while base-broadening is captured in business reforms.

+Other corporate tax changes include revenue from tax-exempt entities and tax administration and compliance.

EXPLANATION FOR S-CORPORATIONS AND PARTNER-SHIPS TAXED AT HIGHER MAXIMUM RATE

Some may question the fact that major corporations will have a maximum rate of 25% while S-corporations, partnerships, and LLC business entities will often be subject to a rate of 30% (plus another 2.5% for the proposed healthcare tax). The reason this rate differential can be easily justified is the issue of double taxation, which is required of all C-corporations upon the eventual distributions of earnings or even the sale of stock of a company with considerable retained earnings. This second level of taxation at a rate of 10.0–21.25% (albeit deferred to a later date) puts the C-corporation tax obligation on a fairly even playing field with most pass-through entities (S-corporations, etc.). Also, it should be pointed out that pass-through entities typically benefit from the lower individual tax rates of 10% and 20% on the first $120,0000 of income (singles) or $200,000 of income (marrieds).

THE DEDUCTION OF BUSINESS INTEREST EXPENSE

The 20/20 Tax adopts most of the business and corporate provisions found in the House's proposed Tax Reform Act of 2014. However, one of the major differences adopted by the 20/20 Tax is the limited deduction for all business interest expense. If you recall the discussion in chapter 6.9, only half of all interest income will be taxable for individuals under the 20/20 Tax. This 50% exclusion concept comes with an important corollary, and that is the provision that only half of all business and investment interest expense will be deductible. The foundation for this principle is that borrowed money is almost always repaid with lower valued dollars as a result of inflation. And if we tax only half of interest income, then we should only allow the deduction of 50% of interest expense. For business and investment interest expense with an average rate in excess of 8% for a taxpayer entity, only a 4% inflation factor would be eliminated from the taxpayer's deduction.

At first blush, one may assume that the tax revenue gained on the 50% interest expense limitation would be offset by the tax revenue lost from the 50% exclusion of interest income. However, this assumption is far from accurate for a number of reasons. First, the 20/20 Tax would tax interest income and allow interest expense deductions at 100% for banks and other financial institutions that participate in most business and investment interest loans. Likewise, the interest income paid on customer deposits in the normal course of business would be treated as 100% deductible expense for financial institutions. Second, the interest rate "spread" between what banks are charging customers and what banks pay depositors is considerable. It's not unusual for financial institutions to charge their average borrower more than three times the "cost of funds" to the lender. Finally, the amount of corporate bond financing would be greatly reduced in favor of equity financing by large corporations being faced with the limited 50% deduction of interest expense, saving the Treasury billions of dollars annually. The reduction of corporate bond financing would have the added side benefit of financially strengthening many of our large corporations that would be more inclined to finance their long-term operations with shareholder equity as opposed to debt financing.

The amount of tax revenue generated from the 50% interest expense limitation would be enormous. For 2011, the Treasury reported total corporation interest deductions of $860 billion,[19] which includes finance and insurance company interest deductions of $265 billion.[20] These amounts do not include other significant business and investment interest deductions for partnerships and sole proprietors, nor does it include individuals claiming investment interest as an itemized deduction. If we were to count just the net corporate interest deduction amounts stated above ($860 billion less $265 billion attributed to finance and insurance companies) and multiply that by roughly half of the proposed corporate tax rate of 25%, the resulting annual tax revenue increase would be approximately $74 billion. And this is based on the one year of 2011 when rates were at a relative low point. The most important factor to consider is that this tax revenue would not be "from timing shifts and temporary revenue provisions," but rather it would be an ongoing tax revenue source that would significantly offset the loss of revenue upon the US corporate tax rate reduction from 35% to a globally competitive rate of 25%.

As with most major tax changes, the 50% interest expense limitation would have to be phased in over several years to allow an adjustment period for certain major industries. The 20/20 Tax would apply the new 50% interest limit to all new business borrowing incurred after 2015. However, the interest on any prior business debt incurred before 2016 would still be 100% deductible for the years 2016 through 2020, and it would be 75% deductible for the years of 2021 through 2025. After 2025, all business and investment interest expense would be only 50% deductible. This phase-in of the 50% interest limitation would help to allow our tax code the ability to generate sufficient revenue at a 25% corporate rate long after the first ten years following tax reform.

The concept of limiting the deduction for business and investment interest is not a new idea. It has been used by several OECD countries in various forms. In 2011, proposed legislation was put forth by Senators Ron Wyden (D-OR) and Dan Coats (R-IN) that would have cut the value of inflation out of the interest deduction as part of their comprehensive tax reform package. Republican Senator Rob Portman (OH) put forth a similar proposal in 2012, as did the White House in the President's Framework for Business Tax Reform (February 2012). The time has come to embrace the concept of interest deduction limitations.

Chapter 7.2

ESTATE TAX REFORM

I believe in a graduated income tax on big fortunes, and in another tax which is far more easily collected and far more effective–a graduated inheritance tax on big fortunes, properly safeguarded against evasion and increasing rapidly in amount with the size of the estate.
—Theodore Roosevelt

These words, spoken in 1910 after his serving as one of our most popular presidents, have taken on many interpretations over the years. As early as 1906, Roosevelt had advocated an inheritance tax "to put a constantly increasing burden on the inheritance of those swollen fortunes, which is certainly of no benefit to this country to perpetuate." Historians believe that Roosevelt, who grew up in a wealthy family, was primarily targeting families like the Rockefellers, railroad barons, and multimillionaires who came out of the gilded age with what appeared to be perpetual fortunes able to survive many generations. It was not until 1916 and the presidency of Woodrow Wilson that our country first passed a permanent estate tax. In the beginning, the new estate tax affected only the very upper class, but by the end of World War II, it had become a tax borne even by the middle class and especially by the upper-middle class (not at all what Teddy Roosevelt had in mind).

Today our estate tax has once again become a tax that primarily affects multimillionaires. And yet, there is no other tax on the books that attracts more media attention and publicity while raising such a minor amount of revenue. In recent years, the unified estate and gift tax has raised less than $50 billion of tax collections per year, roughly 1.6% of our nation's total federal revenue. Some of my clients have asked the question, "Why do we even have an estate tax?" Certainly, it is not doing much to balance the federal budget. Often known as the "death tax", it is not even popular with the middle class who fear that someday it may apply to their family wealth at the end of life.

As of this writing, the federal estate tax is essentially a flat tax on taxable estates greater than $5.34 million (the lifetime exclusion). To determine a decedent's taxable estate, there are multiple deductions that can be used to reduce the sum of the market value of one's assets owned at the date of death. The most significant tax savings comes from the unlimited marital deduction, available upon a transfer of assets to the surviving spouse. This is used by most married couples to totally eliminate the taxable estate of the first spouse to die. Then, assuming no taxable gifts or bequests have been made by the deceased spouse, the surviving spouse is entitled to the predeceased spouse's lifetime exclusion, as well as his or her own lifetime exclusion, meaning the surviving spouse in 2014 can avoid the death tax on $10.68 million of taxable estate assets. There are several other deductions that can be used, of which one of the most significant is the charitable deduction that can be utilized to eliminate as much as 100% of one's taxable estate. The multiple deductions and exclusions are the good news of the estate tax. The bad news is that any remaining taxable estate is subject to a flat 40% federal estate tax rate, and then several states have their own estate or inheritance tax with rates as high as 16%. Thus, the estates of some wealthy taxpayers can be faced with paying taxes of approximately 50% of the last several million dollars' worth of assets left to one's heirs.

Over the last twenty years the federal estate tax has imposed top rates as high as 55%, and for only a few of those years the rate has dipped as low as 35%. Because it taxes their accumulated wealth at a high rate, it tends to put the fear of God into most high-net-worth taxpayers. The fact that the government has the power to confiscate half or more of one's wealth upon death is enough to motivate most wealthy taxpayers to seek complex estate planning advice to avoid such catastrophic financial results. Auspiciously, those wealthy families with less than $100 million of net assets and multiple compatible family members can usually manage to pay little or no estate taxes without large charitable donations, provided they seek tax advice early and often. For those very successful families with more than $100 million of net worth, there is often a large amount of philanthropy involved to avoid estate taxes. However, this "charitable giving" may largely consist of bequests to the family's private foundation to be controlled by family members of present and future generations.

The point I wish to make is that the estate tax in its present form is the most avoidable tax on the books. It is probable that most estate tax is paid by those who have not taken the time to adequately get their affairs in order. Our estate tax is not "properly safeguarded against evasion" or avoidance as Theodore Roosevelt had envisioned. But rather it is a very porous maze of rules and regulations that has produced an infinity of tax breaks and loopholes. No other federal tax law offers such ample opportunity to avoid paying tax as a statutory right. If we are to keep this tax alive, it must be thoroughly reformed to justify its future existence.

As the estate tax currently exists, arguably its primary benefit to our nation has been the stimulus it provides for contributions to many good charities and tax-exempt organizations. Studies have shown that the estate tax in recent years has spurred far more benefit in the way of donations to our universities, museums, hospitals, medical research, and other charitable causes than it has been able to produce revenue for the US Treasury. This should not necessarily be considered a negative result since the philanthropic funding of many worthy institutions has saved taxpayers an immeasurable amount of money for such important benefits to society. Understandably, these causes would not be produced as efficiently if provided and funded by government agencies. The attribute of promoting charitable contributions may be one of the best reasons to retain the estate tax, but it should not be the primary reason.

Every tax needs to stand on its own merits, and the estate tax is no exception. To justify the existence of any tax, it must be fair to all parties to whom it applies, and it must provide sufficient revenue to warrant the time, effort, expense, and personal sacrifice incurred by the government and its taxpayers. Our current estate tax completely fails to meet these criteria. It is not fair to all applicable parties, but rather it acts as a trap for the unwary and those who have not prepared financially for death. Nor does it provide sufficient government revenue to warrant the time, expense, or personal sacrifice it demands of the taxpayers. Because of this tax, families are often pressured into premature decisions regarding gifting, inheritance, donations, and business succession. Many families have been torn apart by the decisions that can be forced upon parents prior to having the right answers. For a tax that raises so little revenue, many have asked if the high price of its economic and emotional impact on families can be justified.

To correct the inadequacies of the estate tax, the 20/20 Tax calls for the following major changes:

1. *Valuation discounts.* Our tax code should eliminate minority discounts and other valuation discounts upon the transfer of a business or investment interest from one family member to another. These discounts, usually ranging from 20% to 50%, have been routinely accepted by the courts, and even by the IRS, for decades. Taxpayer advocates argue that a noncontrolling interest should never have a per share value as high as that of the controlling interest. Thus, when a father and sole shareholder gifts 10% of a $10 million company to a son, the value of the gift, after say a 40% discount, would be reported on a gift tax return at $600,000 and not $1 million. A typical strategy for estate planners is to continue lifetime gifting for the father until he owns less than a 50% interest in his company at death. This allows the father's estate to claim a valuation (minority) discount on the remaining interest at his death. If done properly, this type of estate planning could result in the family transfer of a $10 million company at an estate/gift tax value

of only $5–$8 million, depending on the size of the discounts that can be justified. Many years ago, the IRS fought these discounts on family transfers, but Congress and the courts have not supported the IRS position. In recent years, there have been many bills in Congress to curb the use of valuation discounts on family transfers, but most tax experts believe it will take comprehensive tax reform combined with a lowering of tax rates to eliminate these valuation discounts. The 20/20 Tax calls for the end of family valuation discounts for the main purpose of lowering tax rates.

2. *GRATs, GRITs, and GRUTs.* Estate planning attorneys love the use of trusts. They utilize a large variety of trusts to fit almost any situation. The tax savings from some of these legal entities can be mind-boggling. Among the more popular trusts used for tax and estate planning are the grantor retained annuity trust (GRAT), the grantor retained income trust (GRIT), and the grantor retained unitrust (GRUT). Each of these trusts is established with the purpose of moving invested assets to the next generation(s) at discounted values well below their true fair market value. The parents who establish these trusts will normally retain most if not all of the income from the trust assets for the parents' lifetime, but the terms of such trust documents dictate that the assets in trust have already been essentially gifted to one's heirs at a deeply discounted value long before death. Thus, any such trust assets, if property arranged and documented, are not included in the taxable estate of the grantor who established the trust. The 20/20 Tax would eliminate the estate tax benefit of GRATs, GRITs, and GRUTs by preventing the up-front gift status of such "gifted" trust assets and include the full value of the trust assets in the decedent's estate.

3. *CRATs and CRUTs.* Trusts that are similar to GRATs and GRUTs are those often used for charitable gifting, which are the charitable retained annuity trust (CRAT) and the charitable retained unitrust (CRUT). Both of these planning devices have the intended purpose of transferring investments to a worthy charity but only after the transferor (grantor of the trust) is able to collect most, if not all, of

the income from the trust assets for life. One significant tax benefit of such trusts is the immediate charitable deduction of the present value of the trust assets at the time the trust is started, usually several years before the donor passes away. Both the CRAT and the CRUT are established by taxpayers with a charitable purpose in mind, but in many cases the tax savings to the grantor (taxpayer) is almost as great as the value of the transfer to the designated charity. The 20/20 Tax would take the bloom off the rose by eliminating the up-front charitable deduction for the present value of such future gifts in trust.

4. *IDGTs*. Possibly the most effective estate planning tool of all is the intentionally defective grantor trust (IDGT). Some tax experts refer to the IDGT tax concept as "estate planning on steroids." Basically, an IDGT is a trust that is recognized for estate and gift tax purposes, but when properly drafted, it is "defective" and not recognized for income tax purposes. The family that establishes an IDGT can realize major tax savings in as many as five different ways. First, the assets to be transferred (typically a family business or rental property) will usually be eligible for valuation discounts. Second, there will often be an installment sale of the business interest or rental property to the defective grantor trust, but the sale to one's own grantor trust creates no taxable gain. Third, since there is a sale to the trust, there is no taxable gift transfer to recognize on such sale despite the fact that sons or daughters, as beneficiaries of the trust, will receive all future benefits of the transferred property. Fourth, the income and appreciation of the asset(s) transferred will likewise go to the beneficiaries of the trust, thus avoiding the grantor's taxable estate. And fifth, the final icing on the cake is that the grantor who established the trust gets to pay all the income tax on the taxable earnings going to the trust because the trust is a "defective" grantor trust. By paying the income tax on the annual earnings of the trust assets, the grantor (parent) is accomplishing a further transfer of wealth to the trust beneficiaries free of any estate or gift tax. Thus, one's children are relieved of their duty to pay

income tax on the trust earnings, and their parents' taxable estates are lowered by the payment of such income taxes.

The IDGT concept turns our estate and gift tax system into a sham. This approach to avoiding estate and gift taxes, as well as income taxes, has been used by thousands of American families to legally avoid millions of dollars of estate and gift taxes per family. It may be the single biggest reason why families with total assets of $50 to $100 million often pay no federal estate tax upon the death of the second spouse to die. To close this giant complex loophole, the 20/20 Tax would treat the transfer of assets to a grantor trust that has nongrantor beneficiaries, as a sale subject to income tax. At the same time, if the amount paid for trust assets is less than full consideration, a gift tax would apply on the difference between the fair market value and the selling price. In addition, the 20/20 Tax would no longer allow the avoidance of estate and gift tax on the income tax paid by the grantor of a trust having beneficiaries entitled to the income of such trust. By eliminating most of the tax benefits of the IDGT approach, the 20/20 Tax would broaden the taxable base of the estate and gift tax, thus allowing the reduction of rates for all transfer taxes.

5. *The unlimited marital deduction.* Prior to the Tax Reform Act of 1976, our federal tax code allowed an estate tax marital deduction of no more than 50% of the adjusted gross estate (defined as the gross estate minus certain allowable deductions other than charitable contributions). The Tax Reform Act of 1976 expanded the amount by providing an estate tax marital deduction equal to the greater of $250,000 or one half of the adjusted gross estate for property passing to a decedent's spouse. The 1976 Act also provided a *gift tax* marital deduction for the first $100,000 of spousal gifts and a 50% deduction for gifts in excess of $200,000. Approximately five years later, the Economic Recovery Tax Act of 1981 eliminated the ceiling on the estate and gift tax marital deduction for estates of decedents dying, and gifts made, after 1981. Thus, ever since 1982, an unlimited amount of property transfers between spouses

has been allowed free of any estate or gift tax. It is important to note that in 1982 the estate tax lifetime exclusion was $300,000, scheduled to increase gradually each year to $600,000 by 1987. This compares to a lifetime exclusion of $5.34 million in 2014, obviously much greater than that of the mid-1980s.

The 20/20 Tax would revert to the pre-1976 concept of providing an estate tax marital deduction of 50% of the adjusted gross estate for property passing to a decedent's surviving spouse. When combined with a revised lifetime exclusion of $5 million, this would mean that an adjusted gross estate of $20 million, leaving $10 million to the surviving spouse, would end up with a taxable estate of $5 million, arrived at as follows:

Adjusted gross estate	$20,000,000
Less: Lifetime exclusion	- 5,000,000
Marital deduction (50% x $20,000,000)	-10,000,000
Net taxable estate	$ 5,000,000

It is the author's opinion that with the lifetime exclusion set at $5 million or more, there is no longer adequate reason for an unlimited marital deduction as there was in 1982 when this provision was adopted. In recent years, the unlimited marital deduction has often led to problematic decisions as well as restrictions on the flow of capital in order to avoid or defer estate taxes. As a nation, we would be better served by having a lower marital deduction and lower estate tax rates.

6. *Unlimited charitable deduction.* When the estate tax was passed in 1916, it did not include a provision for charitable deductions. However, in 1917 when the highest income tax rate soared, Congress approved the income tax deduction for charitable donations (limited to 15% of a taxpayer's income). At the same time, the estate tax was amended to approve an *unlimited* charitable deduction for determining one's taxable estate. Ever since 1917, the estate tax has had no limit on the amount of a decedent's charitable deductions, allowing the wealthiest of Americans to leave most if not all of

their assets to charitable causes upon death while often paying zero federal estate tax. This strategy, as declared by Warren Buffet as part of his own estate planning, provides a mixed blessing for our country. On the one hand, most of us admire Mr. Buffett for his commitment to the Giving Pledge, which he has ardently promoted, calling for current and future billionaires to commit at least half of their wealth to philanthropy. On the other hand, one must ask the question if it's right for some of our wealthiest citizens to totally dodge the estate tax by giving most of their wealth to "favorite causes" as Mr. Buffet has stated he plans to do. Keep in mind that some wealthy individuals' favorite causes may not always be deemed as worthy as the Buffett or Bill Gates causes (mostly education and world health).

The 20/20 Tax takes the position that the estate tax charitable deduction should be limited to 50% of an adjusted gross estate. Given this lower limit, it is important to note that Warren Buffett and his wife could still arrange their affairs to leave approximately 90% of their wealth to charitable causes even assuming today's 40% estate tax rate. Here's a summary explanation of how this could happen:

Total gross estate of couple	$60 billion
Marital deduction at first death	- 30 billion
Charitable deduction at first death	- 30 billion
Taxable estate of first to die	$ 0
Total gross estate of surviving spouse	$30 billion
Charitable deduction at second death	- 15 billion
Taxable estate of second to die	$15 billion
Estate tax on taxable estate at 40%	$ 6 billion

I ask that you be the judge of whether the Buffets or any other billionaires should pay zero estate tax to the federal government if they give it all away to charities upon death. Many believe that the above 10% tax outcome would be preferable to having the extremely wealthy pay zero estate tax by generously funding their favorite charities after death.

Finally, there is little doubt that adopting a 50% limit on charitable bequests would motivate philanthropic giving of the very wealthy during the donor's life rather than at one's death. This would partially offset the impact of the 50% limit and further reduce the taxable estate as well as the income tax of the donor. Such incentive would be a positive philanthropic effect of the 50% charitable deduction limitation, but its potential for abuse would be restrained by a 20/20 Tax provision that pulls all donations within three years of death back into the donor's taxable estate where they could still be deducted subject to the 50% limit.

7. *Lower estate tax rates.* Until now, most of this chapter has been devoted to closing loopholes and raising estate taxes. Now it's time to share the more alluring side of my reform message. As I stated earlier, the estate tax, given its abrupt 40% flat rate (plus another 12–16% rate for several states), is enough to develop a strong defensive instinct among most wealthy taxpayers. As a result, many of the well-to-do take on extreme planning measures to disperse the wealth they have worked so hard to accumulate. Highly successful taxpayers usually indulge in a complex assortment of trusts as described earlier. Then they are inclined to make large gifts to their children, often complicating the lives and career incentives of their offspring. It is not unusual to see family conflicts due to one child getting more than another (or the same as another) or battles over two or more siblings each wanting the keys to the family business. Much of this family strife and complexity could be avoided or largely deferred if wealthy parents did not have the current estate tax gun-to-the-head dilemma of having to act sooner rather than later. All too often, decisions are made and wealth is transferred before the next generation is able to handle the fruits of their parents' financial success. It is my opinion that many family estate conflicts could be minimized if our tax code eliminated the above described

estate tax loopholes and lowered the estate tax rates to those in the following schedule.

If the Taxable Estate is:		Tax	Maximum Bracket Amount	
Over	But not over	Rate	Total Tax	Eff. rate
-0-	$5,000,000*	0%	-0-	0%
$5,000,000	10,000,000	10%	$500,000	5%
10,000,000	30,000,000	20%	4,500,000	15%
30,000,000	-----	30%	------	-----

*Taxable estates would be entitled to full portability of the $5 million lifetime exclusion. This means, if the estate of the first spouse to die could not take advantage of the full $5 million at the 0 percent bracket, the unused portion of the 0 percent bracket would be portable (carry over) to the estate of the surviving spouse (similar to current law). The portability feature would not apply to the higher brackets of 10%, 20%, or 30%.

The above estate tax rate schedule obviously provides a totally different result than our current 40% flat rate. At first glance, one might conclude that this revised set of lower rates would result in a loss of revenue to the Treasury. In reality, the federal estate tax collections would increase dramatically upon the adoption of the 20/20 estate tax provisions. The main reason this result would occur is because the elimination of all the tax breaks listed earlier would significantly broaden the base of most taxable estates. There would also be a mentality shift among taxpayers willing to accept the inevitability of estate taxes at a 10% or 20% rate for most taxable estates. The rich would be less inclined to gift away their wealth prematurely, if at all, as many would find it more desirable to give the IRS its 10–20% pound of flesh rather than relinquish lifetime control of hard-earned assets to their children.

Despite the proposed 50% limitation for estate charitable deductions, there should be a net philanthropic benefit to the charities of our country. This would take place because estates valued between $30 million and $100 million would no longer find it feasible to "zero out" their taxable estates as we often see today by using a shrewd combination of gifting, valuation discounts, IDGT trusts, and other evasive planning devices. At a deduction rate of 30%, there would be ample incentive to make charitable bequests for those parents who feel they have already given their kids enough.

It is important to note that the 20/20 Tax would provide no deduction or tax credit for estate tax or inheritance tax paid to any state or local government. It is the author's opinion that it's counterproductive for states to assess death taxes, and there has been a growing trend of states, including California, that have wisely eliminated or avoided transfer taxes upon the demise of their residents.

For many years, the United States has had one of the five highest estate tax rates of any country in the world. A maximum rate of 30% would bring our country closer to (but still above) the average estate tax rate of all other OECD countries. The estate tax proposals of the 20/20 Tax would end the deceptive mockery of our current Federal estate tax system.

Chapter 7.3

THE EXCISE TAX ON GASOLINE

The Federal excise tax for gasoline was initially imposed in 1932 as part of the Revenue Act of 1932. The original rate was only one-cent per gallon, and the resulting tax revenue flowed to the General Fund of the Treasury to reduce the deficits of the Depression years. It was not until 1940 that we started to see lasting increases in the gasoline tax, the first two hikes being for national defense needs. The tax went to 1.5 cents per gallon on July 1, 1940 and later to 2.0 cents per gallon on November 1, 1951, with all such revenue directed to the General Fund. [21]

With the launch of President Eisenhower's Interstate Highway System, the Federal excise tax on gasoline took on the new character of a user tax or "user fee". The Highway Revenue Act of 1956 adopted an increase in the gasoline tax rate from 2.0 cents to 3.0 cents per gallon, but more significantly, 100% of the federal gasoline tax receipts went to finance the Highway Trust Fund and not the General Fund. The new tax rate of 3.0 cents per gallon was authorized to run for sixteen years (1956–1972). However, in 1959 the levy was raised again to 4.0 cents per gallon, and this rate was retained until 1983. [22]

With the Interstate Highway System yet to be completed, and after many years of high inflation, Congress voted to raise the gasoline tax from 4.0 cents to 9.0 cents per gallon effective April 1, 1983. Included in the five-cent increase was one cent allocated to a separate Mass Transit Account for mass transit purposes of various cities, thus somewhat undermining the user fee theory. However, proponents of the mass transit appropriation argued that highway users benefit from mass transit improvements because of the reduced congestion on our roads and highways.

Seven years later, the Omnibus Budget Reconciliation Act of 1990 increased the fuels tax by another 5.1 cents per gallon to 14.1 cents. Of the 5.1 cent increase, only 2.0 cents went for our nation's highways, while an additional 0.5 cents was dedicated to the Mass Transit Account, 2.5 cents per gallon was deposited in the General Fund for deficit reduction, and 0.1 cents went to the Leaking Underground Storage Tank Trust Fund (LUST).[23] Thus, the conventional view of the user fee concept of the federal gasoline tax largely came to an end with the 1990 Act.

The federal gasoline tax experienced its last rate increase in 1993 when Congress increased the rate from 14.1 cents to 18.4 cents per gallon. The entire 4.3-cent additional tax was allocated to the General Fund, resulting in a total of 6.8 cents per gallon dedicated to deficit reduction, and this lasted until October 1, 1997. With the Taxpayer Relief Act of 1997, there was a provision to restore the General Fund portion of the gasoline tax to the Highway Trust Fund. The resulting allocation provided 15.44 cents to the Highway Account, 2.86 cents to the Mass Transit Account, and 0.1 cents to the LUST Fund.[24] This reallocation from the General Fund may have satisfied some of the user-fee proponents but certainly not all. The increased tax on motor fuels had become unpopular with voters, having risen 360% from 1983 to 1993. Thus, Congress has not been able to further increase the gasoline excise tax above the 1993 rate of 18.4 cents per gallon despite repeated attempts over the last twenty years.

The unusually low gas prices of 2014–2015 have given rise to renewed efforts in Washington to raise the federal gasoline tax. Not only Democrats but many Republican leaders have acknowledged that the gas tax may be the single best source to finance our nation's crumbling highway and bridge infrastructure and to replenish the Highway Trust Fund, which is nearly depleted. In June 2014, Senators Chris Murphy, D-CN, and Bob Corker, R-TN, cosponsored a bipartisan plan to raise federal gasoline and diesel taxes. Their plan would increase the motor fuels tax by six cents per gallon for each of the next two years and then index this excise tax to keep pace with inflation. The bipartisan proposal, which increases the tax by almost 65%, would not be enough to fully adjust for inflation of the last twenty-two years (which has caused average prices to nearly double since 1993), but it would be a giant step in the right direction. The 2014 average price of a gallon of gas has more than doubled since 1993 when gas averaged $1.09 per gallon, and thus the proposal of Senators Murphy and Corker is not out of line with fuel prices and the other costs related to operating a motor vehicle on our nation's roads and highways.

The 20/20 Tax proposes increases similar to the Murphy-Corker plan but with three years of six-cent increases from 2016 through 2018 and no indexing thereafter. It is thought that the concept of indexing would be a tough sale with Congress as well as the public since there has been little if any precedent for tax increases tied to inflation the way exemptions, tax brackets, and certain credits and deductions have been indexed in the income tax code. Also, having three straight years of six-cent increases should provide a reasonable replenishment of the Highway Trust Fund and allow Congress to avoid this thorny issue for many years to come. With Americans buying more fuel-efficient vehicles and driving fewer miles per capita, we will need this higher fuel tax rate to collect sufficient revenue to maintain our nation's roads and bridges during the coming decade. Given the promising future of alternative energy vehicles, we will eventually have to find a new way to assess user fees for our roads and highways, but that necessity is probably at least another ten years away.

You might be asking, just how much would a six-cent-per-gallon tax increase cost the typical driver? Since the average new car sold in 2014 attains approximately twenty-four miles per gallon, and since the average vehicle travels approximately twelve thousand miles per year, it would be fair to conclude that the typical vehicle bought in recent years would consume about five hundred gallons per year and thus would incur approximately $30 of additional annual cost due to a six-cent-per-gallon increase. Assuming, the six-cent increases occurred for three years, the eventual additional annual cost per vehicle would be approximately $90 per year. This is a small cost relative to the annual total operating costs of $5,000–$7,500 for most motor vehicles.

In recent years, the federal spending on our transportation infrastructure has been about $50 billion per year while many experts believe this amount needs to be increased by approximately 50% in the near future. Currently, the federal gasoline tax raises about $34 billion annually, resulting in roughly $16 billion per year that must come from the Treasury's General Fund. An increase of eighteen cents per gallon would provide about $33 billion more per year for our Highway Trust Fund, resulting in total annual funding of $67 billion.

It was a mistake in the 1990s to utilize the gasoline tax user fee for deficit reduction purposes, but it is a bigger mistake to let the General Fund subsidize American motorists as it has for most of the last ten years. The best chance for increasing the federal gasoline tax is by including it as part of a comprehensive tax reform bill, which is one reason why the 20/20 Tax includes this important proposal.

Chapter 8

THE FEDERAL DEFICIT AND OPTIONAL REVENUE RAISERS

As stated in earlier chapters, the 20/20 Tax is designed to be revenue-neutral in its initial year as well as in the first five years of its implementation. Politics being what it is, almost all major tax reform of the last seventy years has been accomplished with the goal of revenue neutrality (although some significant legislation has lowered the individual income tax while raising other federal taxes). To expect the passage of comprehensive tax reform to provide a large overall increase or decrease in our nation's tax collections is unrealistic given today's balance of power in Washington. Yes, there will be some winners and some losers with respect to how tax reform impacts certain taxpayers, but that is always the case with true tax reform by its very definition. If major federal tax legislation is going to happen in the next few years, it will have to happen based on a set of proposals that minimizes any large tax increases or significant tax savings among the various classes, groups, or organizations in our society. The exceptions to this rule should primarily impact those parties who unjustly benefit from the crass loopholes or misguided welfare imbedded in our current tax laws, or they should provide relief for those who suffer unjust treatment due to inept or outdated tax code sections.

Before going further, it is important to point out that my method of determining the revenue-neutral outcome of the 20/20 Tax can best be described as trial and error. I started this quest for neutrality by testing most of my own clients' 2011–2013 tax returns to see what combination of 20/20 Tax brackets, tax rates, credits, deductions, exclusions, and other tax benefits would result in the majority of my clients paying approximately the same income tax as what they paid in the years 2011 through 2013 under our current system. As you might guess, the numerous adjustments proposed in the 20/20 Tax have resulted in no clients having exactly the same results under the 20/20 Tax as they actually experienced on their 2013 tax returns. However, I was able to refine the 20/20 Tax to the point that most of my 2013 test returns were within a range of tax increases as high as 12% and tax decreases of as much as 15%. Overall, the returns showing lower taxes outweighed those with higher taxes by about a 3:2 ratio, an outcome that I had hoped to attain, knowing that any shortfall could be made up with the additional corporate and other taxes as described in chapter 7.

As most readers will remember, there were significant fiscal cliff tax increases for wealthy taxpayers beginning in 2013. These increases primarily affected taxpayers with incomes over $250,000. The 20/20 Tax, with much of its theory defined in 2011–2012, has strived to attain future tax levels for the wealthy that average about halfway between the results of the 2011–2012 tax law and those of the higher fiscal cliff tax code of 2013 and 2014.

Recognizing the importance of revenue-neutral tax reform in its early years, our country may want to embrace a new tax system that has a high probability of gradually increasing our future tax revenues over those of our current system. With the large deficits of recent years, we can ill-afford to go backward in tax revenues as a lower percent of our gross domestic product (GDP). For many years, our Treasury collections have typically averaged 17–18% of our nation's GDP, which is the range likely to occur for the fiscal years ending in 2015 and 2016 using our current tax laws.

Most economic theory supports the position that a more streamlined tax system with fewer loopholes, lower rates, less return-preparation time, more incentive for American companies to produce onshore, and the removal of barriers to the flow of capital will help to improve our economy and lead to higher tax collections. These are the attributes the 20/20 Tax brings to the table, and although nobody can accurately quantify the exact economic benefit to be derived from this new tax system, most economists should agree that our economy will see widespread improvement as a result of the 20/20 Tax. Probably within five to ten years of adopting the 20/20 Tax we will see our nation's tax collections move into the range of 19–20% of GDP as a result of higher household incomes and more taxpayers moving up into the 20% or 30% tax brackets of the new system. These higher 20% or 30% brackets will usually be lower than the marginal tax rates currently being experienced, but the overall tax revenue will no longer be diluted by all of today's inefficient tax breaks.

In his 2012 campaign, Mitt Romney argued that in the years ahead our country will need to collect taxes of approximately 20% of its GDP in order to meet our government obligations on a sustainable basis without making drastic cuts in spending. I am willing to accept Mr. Romney's 20% prediction, but in order to achieve this target and avoid raising the 20/20 Tax rates, some optional revenue raisers should be considered by Congress if it is necessary to gradually increase our tax revenue by 2–3% of GDP beyond the initial revenue-neutral years of the 20/20 Tax. These possible alternative revenue sources are described on the following pages.

Chapter 8.1

REVISE THE ANNUAL INFLATION ADJUSTMENTS (INDEXING)

You may have observed that almost nowhere in this book has there been mention of the annual inflation indexing for tax bracket tables, credits, deductions, or other elements of the tax code. This was not an oversight; rather, I intended by design to address indexing primarily in this chapter. For more than forty years, there has been a growing list of tax code provisions to index various items in our tax law based on the increase in the Consumer Price Index. For example, one year of 2.5% inflation would raise one's personal exemption from $4,000 up to $4,100 as a result of indexing.

The concept of inflation adjustments was essentially ignored for the first sixty years of our federal income tax. Indexing was initially adopted by the Employee Retirement Income Security Act of 1974 (ERISA), which provided inflation adjustments of certain dollar limitations applicable to retirement plans. On a broader scale, the Economic Recovery Tax Act of 1981 (ERTA) brought inflation-indexing to several additional tax code provisions, most notably the tax rate brackets. Every year since 1985, we have had automatic adjustments to the tax rate schedules to adjust for inflation and to prevent bracket creep.

Indexing was a political triumph for Ronald Reagan and lawmakers from both sides of the aisle who passed the 1981 Act, and for good reason. The years leading up to ERTA '81 mostly saw annual inflation increases of 6–12%, and taxpayers were watching their taxes soar due to inflation and higher tax rates, even if they had no real increases in income. The concept of inflation-indexing was the right answer at the right time.

Today, the Internal Revenue Code has over one hundred inflation-driven adjustments to make every year, and the list grows almost every time Congress passes tax legislation. As a result, we have a more complicated tax system that changes annually even without new legislation being passed. One might ask if we have created a cure that is worse than the cold.

The 20/20 Tax would systemically eliminate almost half of the automatic inflation adjustments due to the streamlining of our tax code, which would result in fewer rates, credits, deductions, etc. to index. Thus, if the standard deduction is eliminated by the 20/20 Tax, the related indexing requirement would go away as well. The only targeted elimination of indexing endorsed by the 20/20 Tax would be for those provisions contained in our estate and gift tax code that Congress just started to index in recent years.

Inflation in the twenty-first century has been greatly reduced from what our country experienced in the 1970s and 1980s. The annual US rate of inflation for the last ten years has been mostly in the range of 1–3%, and these relatively low rates are expected to continue for the foreseeable future. Given this anticipated price stability, Congress should consider as part of comprehensive tax reform changing the inflation-indexing to a process that is done every two years rather than every year. This biannual approach would avoid the constant complexity of indexing annually, and it would save the Treasury millions of dollars due to the reduction in labor and software development, not to mention the additional billions of dollar in tax revenue raised by a two-year lag for indexing. This revised method would be similar in nature to most state and local residential property tax assessments, which are based on valuations updated every other year rather than every year.

As a final thought for inflation-indexing, I wish to offer one more proposed revenue raiser for consideration. Rather than having mandatory inflation adjustments every year (or every two years), there should be a required congressional vote at the end of each year or two years to determine if the inflation adjustments should be utilized for the upcoming one to two year(s). This approach would allow Congress to impose a tax increase across-the-board at the end of any year or two-year session in which spending exceeds the congressional budget by having the ability to override the automatic inflation adjustments. Congress would then be in a position to make expedient decisions on a regular basis regarding the need for additional government revenue. It is my guess that Congress would rarely override the inflation adjustments that taxpayers have become so accustomed to, but at least our lawmakers would have one more budget tool to compensate for runaway spending. This would also help to avoid the constant tampering with our tax laws to raise additional revenues.

Chapter 8.2

CONSIDER A CARBON TAX

In recent years, there has been considerable attention given to the harmful effects of carbon dioxide (CO_2) emissions. In the years 2005 to 2010, one common proposal for curbing carbon emissions was the theoretical system of "cap and trade." Using this approach, a governmental body would establish a goal for total emissions and then somehow allocate or even auction a limited number of permission units that represents the target goal for total emissions. There would then be a market for these permission units, which could be bought, sold, or traded at the market price. In theory, this system would serve as a tax on polluting activities and help to curb CO_2 emissions. Despite the initial interest in this theoretical concept, we have yet to see a successful cap-and-trade system implemented in any country. The very notion of this concept seems to be a regulatory nightmare.

A more practical approach to controlling carbon emissions is possibly the adoption of a carbon tax with the goal of reducing the emissions of greenhouse gases. Climate change and worldwide air pollution has long been a cause of the Democratic Party, but it is also becoming a growing concern among Republicans, although many refuse to admit to this. It is important to note that the Debt Reduction Task Force of the Bipartisan Policy Center considered various options to promote public policy goals. The task force concluded that "Of the alternatives considered, a tax on carbon dioxide (CO_2) emissions from fossil fuel combustion received the greatest—though not unanimous—support."[1]

Their report went on to state, "The specific option that the task force examined would have introduced a tax of $23 per ton of CO_2 emissions in 2018, increasing at 5.8 percent annually … Staff projections estimate that this option would have raised about $1.1 trillion in cumulative revenue by 2025, while resulting in CO_2 emissions of 10 percent below 2005 levels in that year."[2] If these projections are correct, a carbon tax of this magnitude could be a game changer in achieving what is becoming one of our national priorities. It should be considered in the quest to lower tax rates and achieve a balanced budget.

Chapter 8.3

CONSIDER A FINANCIAL TRANSACTION TAX

In 1972, the Nobel-prize-winning US economist James Tobin proposed a new tax concept known as the financial-transaction tax (FTT). This tax would be a small decimal levy on the sales and trading of stocks, bonds, and other financial instruments. Tobin saw the tax as a method to reduce financial market volatility as well as a progressive revenue source that would have little effect on the wallets of the middle class.

Often referred to as the Tobin tax, this concept has gained little traction until recent years. Sweden tried its own version of the FTT but gave up on it when it found the tax pushed financial trading to other countries. In 2012, the EU entertained a strong push by Germany and France to adopt a transaction tax for the entire EU. These two dominant countries were strongly opposed by the UK and Sweden among other European nations, but eventually they gained the support of nine more EU countries willing to try the new tax. One common theme among the eleven approving nations is that the FTT would serve as a means to make banks, financial markets, and frequent traders pay for the financial meltdown of the Great Recession. Thus, the transaction tax also became known as the Robin Hood tax. Critics, however, contend that the FTT would hurt investors much more than banks and financial institutions.

With EU approval, the "band of eleven" has forged ahead with plans to put their transaction tax into effect beginning January 2016. They have agreed to a levy of 0.1% for stocks and bonds while derivatives would be taxed at a rate of 0.01%. However, as of the end of 2014, the finance ministers from the eleven countries had failed to reach agreement on many key issues, making the 2016 start date appear unlikely.

As of this writing, the White House has expressed little interest in the FTT, however, this could change if the entire EU and major Asian countries were to adopt it. The populist appeal, ease of collection, and large revenue potential make the Tobin tax a possible option that should be considered by the United States if most of the developed world chooses to go in that direction. It may take a common cause like a United Nations resolution requiring large international expenditures to unite the world's leaders in the pursuit of this tax concept.

Chapter 8.4

SOME ADVOCATE A WEALTH TAX

A tax that has been tried and tested in Europe over the last 125 years is the wealth tax, which started in Prussia in the late 1800s and later was adopted by Sweden in the early 1900s. Both the Germans and Swedes dropped or suspended their wealth taxes by the early twenty-first century. However, the tax reached a more refined level in France (starting in the 1980s), where it still exists today. Similar taxes have been used in other European countries with mixed results. Some have joined the ranks of Germany and Sweden and said "enough." The wealth tax is essentially an estate tax on the living. In its purest form, the tax is based on the current value of all the taxpayer's assets less the total of one's debts or liabilities. It is usually designed only for wealthy taxpayers, often those having a net worth of more than one million euros (roughly $1,100,000). Of the European countries that have adopted a wealth tax, most are taxing real estate at a much higher rate than stocks, bonds, or bank deposits. Exemptions for personal residences, closely held businesses, family farms, and other assets are quite common. The rates are often as low as 0.1% per year on bank deposits, but sometimes will exceed 3% on real estate, especially for some of the very wealthy who usually incur the higher graduated rates of their country.

The wealth tax has the potential to be a source of high tax collections, but in reality, most European countries obtain tax revenues of less than 0.5% of their GDP from this unpopular tax. The numerous exemptions allowed and the typically low tax rates result in relatively modest collections. Also, the wealth tax is often subject to a high occurrence of tax fraud, and there is difficultly with enforcement due to the subjective nature of asset valuations and the failure of taxpayers to report all taxable assets.

In the United States, we have not utilized a federal wealth tax, although many states, cities, and counties have employed property taxes that are similar in nature but usually limited to only real estate values. Also, a few states like Florida have what they call an intangibles tax, which is based on the value of one's stocks, bonds, and other financial instruments. These taxes are relatively easy to enforce and comply with as compared to a true wealth tax, which would require many of our successful citizens to file an annual net worth statement with appraisals to support certain asset values.

Some economists see the wealth tax as a potential solution to the worldwide problem of economic inequality between the haves and the have-nots. The argument behind this theory is that we must tax capital in a new and different way than just taxing income from capital gains, which typically does not get taxed until the year of sale, if ever. The wealth tax provides the ability to tax unrealized gains (i.e., appreciation) on capital investments that often are not liquidated for years, and under our current tax laws will usually escape any tax at death due to the stepped-up basis rules. It is clearly a tax on capital and wealth accumulation, one that has incurred the wrath of most conservatives.

For those who embrace the concept of economic redistribution, the notion of a wealth tax can be an appealing concept. At graduated rates of 1% to 5% per year, it would have the potential to gradually erode or reduce the growth of large fortunes. In theory, the revenue raised from such a tax could be targeted to the needs of the lower and middle classes of our society, including education and healthcare. The taxable base for this type of tax in the United States may be as much as $50 trillion. If applying a 2% effective rate, then we are talking about the potential to raise (or redistribute) $1 trillion per year. This may sound okay to the majority of those who are exempt from the tax, say those with a net worth of less than $1 million, but if you have a net asset value above that threshold, would you be in favor of giving up 1% or more of your wealth each and every year? This is a dilemma faced by many Europeans, and since this tax concept has not been widely accepted on the continent, I think it would face a steep uphill battle in our country. An American wealth tax is considered an undesirable possibility by this author.

Chapter 9

HOW DO WE GET THERE?

Every noble work is at first impossible.
—Thomas Carlyle, Scottish Philosopher and Writer

After reading the forgoing chapters, if you have concluded that our nation unequivocally needs comprehensive tax reform, then you are probably asking how our country can accomplish this seemingly impossible task. After all, we have been listening to most of our politicians proclaim the need for major tax reform since at least the beginning of this century, and some were even calling for reform another ten years before that. Not only have our lawmakers preached this gospel for much of the last fifteen to twenty-five years, but it has been hard to read the news in recent years without seeing multiple articles every month advocating the need for a complete overhaul of our federal tax system. Almost nobody cares to defend the current tax laws, and yet our two major political parties have not been able to agree to a new improved tax code to guide us through the first part of the twenty-first century.

Tax reform is a fragile proposition that almost always requires the proper alignment of players and political agendas in the governing bodies of the House of Representatives, the Senate, and mostly of the White House. If any of these three bodies is out of sync with the other two, tax reform doesn't stand a chance. In fact, it is quite difficult just to get a major tax bill out of committee from either legislative body to be voted upon by all members of the House or Senate. The power of special interest groups manifests itself in the strongest way with proposed tax legislation, and any attempt to lessen or eliminate tax breaks that have been imbedded in the system will invariably bring lobbyists out of the woodwork to defend the status quo and often to make fierce threats of reprisals against lawmakers who oppose existing tax incentives and loopholes.

If one were to analyze the legislative process of the Tax Reform Act of 1986, it would be evident that this monumental project, which took over two years in the halls of Congress and was strongly supported by a Republican White House, actually established its roots with the reform efforts of certain liberal Democrats in the 1960s like Harvard Law Professor Stanley Surrey. By the early 1980s, the movement was largely propelled by two former professional athletes, Senator Bill Bradley (D-NJ) and Congressman Jack Kemp (R-NY). Eventually the task fell into the hands of two very capable Treasury Secretaries, Donald Regan and later, James Baker who worked tirelessly with then House Ways and Means Chairman Dan Rostenkowski (D-IL) and Senate Finance Chairman Bob Packwood (R-OR) as well as their tax-writing committees. In the end, this landmark legislation was truly an anomaly that was fortunate to have materialized. In order for comprehensive tax reform to happen again three decades later, it may take an act of divine intervention.

On the positive side, let's take a look at the key players involved in today's tax reform movement. The chairman of the House Ways and Means Committee has historically been the primary mover in Washington for the drafting of new tax legislation. For the years 2011–2014, this position was very ably held by David Camp (R-MI). Having served in Congress for twenty-four years, Mr. Camp dedicated much of his last two terms to the pursuit of bipartisan comprehensive tax reform. Before retiring at the end of 2014, Chairman Camp and his committee produced an exhaustive report of approximately one thousand pages as a proposal for sweeping tax reform. Camp's proposal, called the Tax Reform Act of 2014, was never introduced on the floor of the House, but it is recognized by many tax experts as a benchmark for future tax reform deliberations.

Beginning in 2015, Congressman Paul Ryan (R-WI) became the new chairman of the House Ways and Means Committee. Having served in Congress for more than sixteen years, Mr. Ryan is one of the GOP's most influential policy makers. He has been an energetic leader who previously served as chairman of the House Budget Committee, and in 2012 he was the running mate of Mitt Romney in a failed bid for the White House. Mr. Ryan is often known among his peers and the press as a "policy wonk" due to his astute attention to detail and understanding of the numbers. He is arguably the most qualified congressman to chair the Ways and Means Committee since Wilbur Mills (D-AR) stepped down in 1974 after eight terms at the helm. Chairman Ryan, at age forty-five, became the youngest chairman ever of this committee, and his decision against running for the presidency in 2016 should allow him considerable time for significant accomplishments in chairing the powerful Ways and Means Committee. Most of all, Paul Ryan has been a strong advocate for tax reform, and he has the mutual respect of lawmakers on both sides of the aisle. His legislative talents may be the deciding factor in accomplishing meaningful tax reform in this decade.

As for the Senate leadership, the key position for tax matters has always been the chairman of the Senate Finance Committee. This position was held by Senator Max Baucus (D-MT) from 2007 until early 2014 when Mr. Baucus accepted a presidential appointment to serve as the US ambassador to China. Up until that time, Senator Baucus had worked closely with David Camp in the pursuit of bipartisan tax reform. In February 2014, Max Baucus was replaced as chairman of the Senate Finance Committee by Senator Ron Wyden (D-OR), who has served in the US Senate since 1996 and previously served in the House of Representatives from 1981 to 1996. Mr. Wyden has a long history of actively participating in the tax reform debate and sponsoring bipartisan tax legislation. When the Democrats lost control of the Senate in the 2014 elections, it resulted in the end of Mr. Wyden's chairmanship of the Senate Finance Committee after a brief ten-month tenure. If the

Republicans lose control of the Senate in 2016, Ron Wyden would most likely return as chairman of the Finance Committee. One way or the other, Senator Wyden should be a powerful voice in tax reform proceedings.

When the 114th Congress convened in January 2015, the president pro tempore of the US Senate was Orrin Hatch, who also assumed the position of chairman of the Senate Finance Committee. Having served as Senator for Utah since 1977, Mr. Hatch is the most senior of GOP senators. Although a conservative Republican, he has a reputation for reaching across the aisle and was a longtime friend and on many occasions a political ally of the late Senator Edward Kennedy, a liberal Democrat. Senator Hatch, who turned eighty-one in March 2015, will probably complete his final term in office in 2018, and the passage of comprehensive tax reform legislation would create a great legacy that this elder statesman could be proud of. He has worked closely with his counterpart, Ron Wyden, in the Senate Finance Committee, and there is strong reason to believe that their committee is very capable of crafting a bipartisan bill with the more conservative House Ways and Means Committee.

Then there is the White House. It is no secret that comprehensive tax reform is not high on the agenda of President Obama. Unfortunately, tax reform rarely happens without support of the Oval Office, and in fact most major tax legislation of the last forty years has only transpired when the White House was leading the charge. In this case, it is not so much that the president is opposed to tax reform, but rather he is opposed to the likely outcome of the current tax reform consensus. In the first year of the Obama presidency, he strongly urged Congress to establish a commission that would provide answers to our growing deficit and make recommendations to revise our tax code. Congress eventually authorized the National Commission on Fiscal Responsibility and Reform (Simpson-Bowles), and after nineteen members, almost evenly divided politically, spent most of the year 2010 on this difficult task, the commission issued its report in December 2010.

The tax recommendations of the commission's report were not

what Mr. Obama had anticipated. As you will remember, the president articulated very clearly in his 2008 campaign that the maximum tax rate for the wealthy needed to be increased to 39.6%, and that married couples with incomes over $250,000 (and singles over $200,000) should all pay higher taxes. The commission came to a different conclusion on tax rates, and its most likely scenario called for a maximum rate of 28% while broadening the taxable base and eliminating most tax breaks and loopholes. One month earlier, the Debt Reduction Task Force had reached a similar conclusion that the maximum individual rate should be 27% (later changed to 28%). Even Ron Wyden who has cosponsored and been the primary mover of the Bipartisan Tax Fairness and Simplification Act of 2011 has called for just three income tax rates of 15, 25 and 35% which means dropping the current higher rates of 28, 33 and 39.6%.

Most tax reformers strongly believe that tax rates must be lowered if reform is to happen, and yet President Obama has steadfastly advocated a maximum individual rate of 39.6% for the last seven years. At this point in his political career, it is hard to imagine him changing his position. One only needs to consider that it took the administration four years of lobbying Congress before getting his 39.6% rate passed. Thus, the chance of gaining White House support for comprehensive tax reform in 2015–2016 appears to be slim and none, especially with 2016 being a presidential election year when major tax legislation almost never happens. President Obama might project a strong effort for a major 2015 corporate tax bill, but the odds are against passing corporate tax reform without comprehensive individual tax reform.

It is very likely that the greatest progress we will see toward comprehensive tax reform prior to 2017 will be the drafting of a major legislative report by Paul Ryan's Ways and Means Committee to expand and refine the proposal presented in 2014 by David Camp. A similar project may be forthcoming from Orrin Hatch and the Senate Finance Committee to present the Senate's version of tax reform. It would be significant progress to have a major tax bill get out of committee and put before the entire House or Senate for vote in 2015–2016, but again the 2016 election year may obviously preclude this from happening. Nevertheless, if one or both committees are able to produce their own comprehensive draft report(s) on tax reform, it will give the presidential candidates a strong point of reference from which to debate during the nominating process. This policy awareness during the presidential campaigns could set the stage for a major overhaul of our tax system during the 115th Congress (2017–2018). I believe it is very important that the American public start right away to let each of their presidential candidates know that comprehensive tax reform needs to be a high priority to be dealt with in the first year of the next administration. For political reasons, most of our country's significant tax reform of the last hundred years has taken place during the first two years in office of our newly elected presidents (1986 was an exception to this rule). Our candidates all need to acknowledge that our current tax system is not acceptable, and they must spend whatever political capital is necessary to change this broken model as soon as possible.

There are many political observers who believe that no matter which candidate wins the White House in November 2016, there is only a remote possibility that we will see the monumental tax legislation that our country so desperately needs. This negative thinking is fueled by our experience of the past where special interests and misguided public perception have repeatedly blocked tax reform. And even if tax reform happens, its results may be no better than the 1986 Tax Reform Act, which most tax experts will agree was only a half-a-loaf victory, leaving our tax laws more complicated than ever.

The fact that our federal tax code has been held hostage by our political system for more than one hundred years is enough to make me believe that we must find a better way to rewrite our nation's tax laws. Despite my great respect for the current and immediate-past chairmen of the two tax writing committees of Congress, I think that our country should give serious consideration to reforming our tax system by authorizing a non-politician commission of economists and tax specialists to rewrite the federal tax system. I wrote about this concept in chapter 3, "The Norwegian Experience," where I described the 1988–1992 historical events of Norway transcending its political system to adopt entirely new tax rules that have led to arguably one of the fairest and most efficient and understandable tax codes in the developed world. This accomplishment happened largely because a group of dedicated experts knew the subject matter and did not have to answer to any special-interest groups.

As stated by my good friend, Norwegian associate professor emeritus in tax law, Arthur J. Brudvik, the current highly respected tax laws of Norway would not have happened had his country not taken this legislative task out of the hands of politicians. According to Arthur, their chosen tax writing committee was composed of ten unelected appointees who were all highly qualified economists, tax lawyers, and tax professors who held no political office. The political leadership and the rest of the cabinet were not involved before they got the finished report, which was presented on October 12, 1989 after almost eighteen months of deliberations and report writing. The committee's finished tax report was then highly publicized and much discussed in the media. On the basis of this report, the Ministry of Finance proposed and published the detailed rules and regulations needed to implement the proposed tax laws. Upon receiving comments and reactions to the published rules and regulations, the ministry sent its final proposed rules and regulations to the parliament in April 1991 where they were approved with little change later that year. The new tax rules went into effect on January 1, 1992.

I think the time has come for our country to delegate the structuring of our next tax code to some of our best economists and tax minds and not to our politicians. We need to accept the fact that our senators and members of Congress are not tax experts, and most of them have only a few hours each month (if that) to analyze complicated tax laws and the resulting impact on our economy and the lives of the American people. Despite their access to some very good staff members, our lawmakers are subject to information overload, not to mention partisan politics and the influence of special interest groups. We must recognize that our elected representatives in Washington are mere mortals who have their limitations. Unfortunately, most of them have to spend a high percentage of their time campaigning and fundraising while political survival is almost always a high priority. Regrettably, the congressional promotion of righteous tax legislation can often be political suicide. Thus, it is my opinion that the task of comprehensive tax reform is too much for our congressional system to handle. If we attempt to reform our nation's tax laws by using the same process we have used for the last hundred years, then I think we should expect a similar outcome. In other words, that is how we got to where we are today.

The tax commission concept that I am advocating is somewhat similar to the 2010 Simpson-Bowles Commission that many of us thought was going to result in an "up or down" vote by Congress to determine a new tax system and a set of budgetary constraints for our country. However, the Simpson-Bowles Commission was quite different from my proposal in that most of its nineteen members were politicians, including six sitting US Senators and six sitting members of the US House of Representatives. Is it any wonder that this group of mostly elected officials could not reach a super-majority decision (75%) as required for an ultimate congressional vote? The 20/20 Tax highly recommends a commission of only unelected experts to achieve a fitting result for Congress to vote on.

Realizing that the wheels of government (and justice) turn slowly, I do not expect an act of Congress to immediately authorize the concept of a Norwegian-type tax commission of specialist appointees. It will take a leap of faith for the political leaders of our country to allow this novel approach to happen, and ultimately Congress will have to accept the notion of giving up part of its power to tax, one of the greatest powers that our lawmakers have. Obviously, Congress would still have to establish the targeted goals, guidelines, and budget constraints for the commission to work toward achieving. This concept may take time to jell with our nation's leaders, but I suggest that if Congress is unable to deliver a sound bipartisan comprehensive tax bill to our next president and the American people by the fourth quarter of 2017, then we should pass the baton to a well-organized commission of ten to twelve nonpolitician tax experts, including economists, tax attorneys and accountants, and tax professors. An assembly of such experts would be much more likely than Congress to adopt most of the concepts recommended in this book. If this were to happen, I believe the United States would have a world-class tax system by the year 2020, if not before.

Chapter 10

A FINAL SYNOPSIS OF
THE 20/20 TAX

When I decided to write this book I thought it might take one year of giving up my weekends and evenings to accomplish the task of explaining my thoughts on tax reform. Never did I expect to still be writing after more than three years of diligent research and the recording of my observations. Now it is time to conclude my efforts and to let the readers of this book reach their own conclusions about the future of our country's tax system.

As a courtesy to those who may wish to have a *CliffsNotes* version of the 20/20 Tax, the following are what I consider to be the ten most important concepts that I hope the readers of this book will come away with:

1. *Our progressive individual income tax can be fixed and should be turned into an efficient and coherent system* capable of generating as much as half of our nation's total tax collections. There is not a compelling reason for it to be supplemented or replaced by a value-added tax (VAT), a national sales tax, or any other regressive tax as often suggested in recent years by some politicians, economists, and political pundits, provided we take the right steps to reconstruct what we have.

2. *Comprehensive tax reform will require a concerted bipartisan effort by the two chambers of Congress working together with the White House* and the Treasury to craft legislation that resolves and corrects key differences, unnecessary complexities, and the fairness concerns of both major parties. This book has involved a great effort to identify many of the unacceptable concepts imbedded in our current tax code, but the scope of our nation's pending tax reform must be expanded far beyond the reach of this treatise. It is imperative that our national leaders address the deficiencies of the corporate income tax, estate tax, and even the motor fuels excise tax (all touched on lightly in chapter 7) at the same time they reform the individual income tax. The political leverage will be much greater if this battle is fought on all fronts at the same time, and not on a piecemeal basis. To be very candid, tax reform must be an extremely high priority of the 114th and 115th Congresses (2015–2018) as well as the next president of the United States, or we won't see it happen for several years. It is very unlikely that major tax reform will occur before the end of 2016.

3. *If tax reform is to have a chance, there must be a political consensus to attain revenue neutrality.* We live in a country where approximately half of all taxpayers want to see their taxes go down, and most of the other half want to see taxes go up (just not theirs). It is important to note that revenue-neutral tax reform means something different depending on who you talk to. This term gives most taxpayers the idea that their taxes will stay about the same assuming they earn a similar amount of income. Unfortunately, the end result of major tax reform is that there are always winners and losers. The probable winners tend to sit back and hope for reform to happen (if they are even aware of the resulting benefits), and the potential losers figure it out quickly and assert all possible pressure to address such concerns with their congressional representatives. The 20/20 Tax has tried to minimize the number of losers and the magnitude of their losses, but the inevitable cannot be denied. There will be losers, and almost any attempt to increase the overall revenue of our country in the

initial years of tax reform will magnify the size of their losses and spell defeat for the entire movement. To reduce this possibility, the 20/20 Tax attempts to slightly lower the average individual taxes of most Americans while marginally raising the average taxes on corporations, estates, and motorists in order to achieve the overall goal of revenue neutrality.

4. *Our current tax system is so incoherent that the calculation process must be replaced with a new framework to make the preparation of tax returns a more understandable procedure.* The 20/20 Tax replaces the existing labyrinth of itemized deductions, standard deductions, exemptions, phase-outs, gross income, adjusted gross income, alternative minimum tax, and other confusing terms with a more streamlined approach that will save hundreds of millions of hours for American taxpayers and their return preparers. This new framework will include the following logical and user-friendly concepts:

    a) *There will be a 50% exclusion for most forms of investment and retirement income,* meaning that half of all interest (including muni-bonds), dividends, Social Security benefits, and capital gains will not be included in taxable income. There is an exception that indexes capital gains and dividends for the upper 1% of income earners who receive over half of all US capital gains.

    b) *A series of 20% credits replaces the current maze of credits, exclusions, itemized deductions, and other deductions.* This concept will avoid our current upside-down subsidy system whereby high income taxpayers are rewarded for their deductions and exclusions at a much higher tax-saving rate than low income taxpayers. One prime example of the new 20% credit concept is that all health-insurance premiums paid by employers and taxpayers (and not subsidized by the government) would be eligible for a 20% tax credit. However, employer-provided health insurance would no longer be excluded from taxable income which has given a distinct advantage to high income earners.

c)   *All personal and dependent exemptions would be replaced by $500 personal tax credits (nonrefundable) for each taxpayer under the age of sixty-five and for their qualified dependents age eighteen and over. Taxpayers ages sixty-five and over would each be entitled to $1,000 personal tax credits. All taxpayers would be entitled to a $1,000 fully refundable child tax credit for each dependent child claimed under the age of eighteen.* This child tax credit would offset one's federal taxes or be refunded if the taxpayer has zero tax reported on his and/or her income tax return. There would be no phase-out of any of these tax credits as we often see under current law.

d)   *A revised and simplified earned-income credit (EIC) would apply to all taxpayers with salaries, wages, and self-employment income,* and this new EIC would replace the current standard deduction while supplementing the income of families with children. The credit would be a maximum of $4,400 for singles and $6,600 for married couples, depending on income and the number of the taxpayers' children (under the age of eighteen) claimed as dependents. The new EIC would be one of only two credits in the 20/20 Tax subject to a phase-out rule, and this phase-out would only apply to taxpayers with taxable incomes above $200,000 (singles) and $300,000 for married couples.

e)   *There are just three simple rates with the 20/20 Tax, and those are 10%, 20%, and 30%.* There is no bubble rate as in the 1986 Act, and there is no phase out of the lower rate brackets.

f)   *The alternative minimum tax (AMT) will be completely gone on the first day of the 20/20 Tax,* hopefully to never return to the American tax scene.

5.   *Taxes should not reduce the incentive to work, save, invest, or be married.* All of these are virtuous deeds that are often discouraged by our tax laws. As a general rule, high tax rates often have a negative effect on each of these activities. The lowering of tax rates can help to stimulate the economy and promote the above activities, but the downward movement of such rates must be accompanied by the closing of loopholes, unnecessary deductions, and other tax

incentives in order to broaden the tax base enough to maintain financial support for our government's necessary services. As this book points out, our tax laws are rife with marriage penalties that must be minimized if we wish to help preserve this important institution of our society. The 20/20 Tax works toward this goal.

6. *Most taxes should be based on our citizens' ability to pay, and this is especially true of an income tax.* That is the reason our country adopted a graduated-rate income tax system in 1913 and has adhered to this model ever since. Our federal income tax is one of the few taxes that can claim to be a progressive tax, and it serves as a healthy balance to the many regressive taxes in our country, such as payroll taxes, property taxes, and sales taxes, which are less complex and easier to collect. As much as I admire the profound quote of Leonardo da Vinci that "simplicity is the ultimate sophistication," I do believe we have to accept the role of certain complexities in any tax system if we wish to achieve fairness and economic progress. Thus, I prefer to describe the 20/20 Tax as a rational and understandable tax rather than a simple tax. Despite the awful condition of today's Internal Revenue Code, we need to remember that fairness, ability to pay, and economic results should almost always trump simplicity.

7. *America is part of a global economy, and our tax rates must be globally competitive.* In recent years, other countries have lowered their tax rates, especially for their corporate income tax, and this has put American businesses at a competitive disadvantage. Gradually, we are losing American ownership of some of our international companies that are taking tax revenues and many high paid jobs with them to other countries that dangle the carrot of low tax rates. The 20/20 Tax would lower our corporate income tax rate from 35% to 25% just as recommended in David Camp's House Ways and Means report titled the 2014 Tax Reform Act. Several other steps are proposed in chapter 7.1 and Appendix A in order to broaden the corporate tax base, resulting in more tax revenue raised despite the lower tax rate.

8. *Inflation must be considered as part of the taxable earnings computation in any just and fair income tax system.* The developed world has lived for many years with the factor of inflation, and it is important that we not ignore this economic phenomenon in the structure of our tax laws. It would be a great injustice to subject inflationary gains to taxation upon the sale of investment assets as if inflation was not a false profit. The 20/20 Tax attempts to recognize this issue in a pragmatic way by allowing a 50% exclusion for most taxpayers' capital gains while requiring inflation-indexing in lieu of the 50% exclusion for only the top 1% of income earners who harvest a majority of all capital gains. Along the same lines, interest income and business interest expense are both given recognition on a 50% basis as well, so that interest income is only half-taxable and interest expense is only half-deductible. A near perfect measurement of inflation could be painstakingly applied in these situations, but I am reminded of the words earlier quoted from the late Randolph E. Paul who wrote that "A perfectionist is a dangerous man in the tax world, which is full of things that need to be done only as well as they can be done."[1] Suffice to say that I think for most situations the 50% approach is the prudent answer to the inflation issue.

9. *The one significant tax rate increase that I have called for is that of the excise tax on gasoline and motor vehicle fuels.* In chapter 7.3, I have proposed that the federal rate of 18.4 cents per gallon be nearly doubled over three years by adding six cents per year to the rate. This total increase would cost the typical motor vehicle owner about $90 per year, and it would provide more than $30 billion per year of additional funding to our Highway Trust Fund. With our country having gone without a gasoline tax rate increase for the last twenty-two years (1993), I can think of no more appropriate way to finance the revival of our highway infrastructure.

10. *The mission of comprehensive tax reform is an overwhelming task that is possibly beyond the reach of our Congress.* I am convinced that we have excellent leadership in the tax legislation committees of the House and the Senate, but in order to achieve true tax reform

that America can be proud of, I believe that Congress will need to appoint a commission of tax experts who are not elected to public office and who can present a bipartisan tax plan to Congress for congressional approval. The members of this commission need to be free of political pressure and not connected to any special-interest groups, and they need to commit a great amount of time and judicious thought to this monumental undertaking.

It is my sincere belief that if the concepts and rules of the 20/20 Tax were adopted as explained in this book, it would reduce the preparation time of most tax returns by 50% or more. I also believe that nearly half of those taxpayers who use a professional tax return preparer would be inclined to prepare their own tax returns.

In conclusion, I wish to point out that the income rate brackets, tax credit amounts, and other quantitative decisions used to formulate the 20/20 Tax in this book may need to be adjusted slightly (none more than 10%) in order to reach the desired goal of revenue neutrality. This type of statistical adjustment is a job usually delegated to some of the sharpest mathematical minds at the US Treasury and the staff of the Joint Committee on Taxation (JCT). In my quest for revenue neutrality, I have been limited to the data base of my firm's clients, which is unlikely to provide a sufficient representation of all American taxpayers. Nevertheless, I would encourage any of my readers to compare the results of their 2014 income tax returns to the revised tax rules found in this book. For those willing to manually recompute their tax returns using my proposal, please find the three necessary 20/20 Tax forms provided in Appendix B. As a final warning, however, don't be surprised if your taxes are higher using the 20/20 Tax. This was the result on my personal tax return, and I estimate that would be the outcome for 30–40% of all US taxpayers. That means we'll just have to revise our tax planning if the 20/20 Tax comes to pass.

APPENDIX A

Appendix A

SUMMARY ANALYSIS OF 20/20 TAX PROPOSAL AS COMPARED TO HOUSE WAYS AND MEANS COMMITTEE TAX REFORM ACT OF 2014

Bold print represents position of the 20/20 Tax not in agreement with House Proposal as provided in non-bold print.

A = Agree with House Proposal

D = Disagree with House Proposal

A/D

Title I – Tax Reform for Individuals

　Subtitle A – Individual Income Tax Rate Reform.

　　Secs. 1001-1003. Simplification of individual income tax **D** rates the current seven tax brackets would be consolidated and simplified into three brackets: 10%, 25%, and 35%; deduction for adjusted net capital gain; conforming amendments related to simplification of individual income tax.

Chapter 5.1 Social Security benefits would be subject to a 50% exclusion, and there would no longer be a 15% to 100% phased exclusion.

Chapters 5.2 and 6.2 Capital gains and dividends would be eligible for a 50% exclusion, except that inflation indexing would apply to taxable income in excess of $300,000 (single) and $500,000 (married).

Chapter 5.5 Simplification of individual income tax rates— the current seven tax brackets would be consolidated and simplified into three brackets: 10%, 20%, and 30%.

Subtitle B – Simplification of Tax Benefits for Families.

Sec. 1101. Increases the standard deduction for taxpayers **D**
across all filing statuses: $22,000 for married individuals
filing a joint return and $11,000 for all other taxpayers.

**Chapters 5.7 and 6.7 Repeal of the standard deduction to be
replaced by a fully revised earned-income credit up to $4,400
(single) and $6,600 (married) with children, and up to $800
(single) and $1,200 (married) if no children.**

Sec. 1102. Increase and expansion of child tax credit: $1,500 **D**
would be allowed for qualifying children and a reduced
credit of $500 would be allowed for non-child dependents.

**Chapters 5.7 and 6.7 Replacement of the child tax credit. A
fully refundable child tax credit of $1,000 would be allowed
for all dependent children under the age of eighteen.**

Sec. 1103. Modification of earned income tax credit: **D**
taxpayers with a qualifying child, the maximum credit
amount would be $200 for joint filers ($100 for other filers);
all taxpayers with one qualifying child, the maximum credit
would be $2,400; taxpayers with more than one qualifying
child, the maximum credit would be $4,000 in the case of a
joint return and $3,000 for single and others.

**Chapters 5.7 and 6.7 Revised earned-income credit would
provide taxpayers without a child up to $1,200 for joint filers
and $800 (single or head of household). Taxpayers with
children would have a maximum EIC of $6,600 (married—
three children) or $4,400 (single with two children). The
limits for married filing separately are half as much as
married filing jointly.**

Sec. 1104. Repeal of deduction for personal exemptions. **A**

**Chapters 5.7 and 6.7 Personal exemptions would be replaced
by a revised earned-income credit and by new personal
credits of $500 for ages eighteen to sixty-four and $1,000 for
ages sixty-five and over. Taxpayers under the age of**

eighteen would also be entitled to a personal credit of $500 on their own tax returns (if required).

Chapter 6.9 Municipal bond interest and all other interest income would be subject to a 50% exclusion. All municipal bonds issued prior to the date of enactment would be entitled to tax-exempt status per current law.

Subtitle C – Simplification of Education Incentives.
Sec. 1201. American Opportunity Tax Credit (AOTC) - four   **D**
existing higher education tax benefits (AOTC, Hope
Scholarship Credit (HSC), lifetime learning credit (LLC),
and the tuition deduction would be consolidated into a
permanent, reformed AOTC.

Chapter 5.6 Repeal of the American Opportunity credit.

Chapter 5.6 Creation of the higher education credit (HEC)— it would replace all three credits: American Opportunity credit, Hope Scholarship credit, lifetime learning credit and the tuition deduction with one fully refundable credit (HEC). The HEC would equal 20% of the first $10,000 of qualified tuition and fees paid per calendar year. The HEC could be claimed up to ten years for each taxpayer/dependent earning ten or more semester hours of credit per year.

Sec. 1202. Expansion of Pell Grant exclusion from gross   **A**
income - all Pell Grants would be excluded from income
regardless of how they are used.
Sec. 1203. Repeal of exclusion of income from United States   **A**
savings bonds used to pay higher education tuition and fees.
Sec. 1204. Repeal of deduction for interest on education   **A**
loans.
Sec. 1205. Repeal of deduction for qualified tuition and   **A**
related expenses.
Sec. 1206. No new contributions to Coverdell education   **A**
savings accounts after 2014 but allow tax-free rollovers from
Coverdell accounts into section 529 plans.
Sec. 1207. Repeal of exclusion for discharge of student loan   **A**
indebtedness.
Sec. 1208. Repeal of exclusion for qualified tuition   **A**
reduction.

Sec. 1209. Repeal of exclusion for education assistance programs.   A

Sec. 1210. Repeal of exception to 10% penalty for higher education expenses.   D

The 20/20 Tax would retain the exception to 10% penalty on higher education expenses paid with early retirement payments.

Subtitle D – Repeal of Certain Credits for Individuals.

Sec. 1301. Repeal of dependent care credit.   D

The 20/20 Tax would apply child and dependent care credit to 20% of the first $5,000 of expense for one qualifying person and the first $10,000 of expense for two or more persons.

Sec. 1302. Repeal of credit for adoption expenses.   D

The 20/20 Tax would retain current nonrefundable adoption credit but be limited to $10,000 of qualified expense.

Sec. 1303. Repeal of credit for nonbusiness energy property.   A

Sec. 1304. Repeal of credit for residential energy efficient property. (REEP)   D

The 20/20 Tax would retain 2014 credit limits for REEP, but credit rate would be 20% for all such property.

Sec. 1305. Repeal of credit for qualified electric vehicles.   A

Sec. 1306. Repeal of alternative motor vehicle credit.   A/D

Chapter 6.11 Revise the automobile energy credit—establish a credit of $2,000 for those vehicles that average equivalent of 80–99 mpg, and a $3,000 credit for those vehicles that average equivalent of at least 100 mpg, regardless of the technology involved, provided certain low emission standards are met.

Sec. 1307. Repeal of alternative fuel vehicle refueling   A property credit. (AFVRP)

Sec. 1308. Repeal of credit for new qualified plug-in electric drive motor vehicles. **A**

Sec. 1309. Repeal of credit for health insurance costs of eligible individuals. **A**

Chapter 5.1 Repeal of exclusion for employer sponsored health insurance—eliminate the income exclusion for all employer-provided healthcare benefits and replace with a 20% refundable tax credit for health insurance provided by employers as well as for self-paid health insurance.

Sec. 1310. Repeal of first-time homebuyer credit. **A**

Subtitle E – Deductions, Exclusions, and Certain Other Provisions.

Sec. 1401. Exclusion of gain from sale of a principal residence - a taxpayer would have to own and use a home as the taxpayer's principal residence for five out of the previous eight years to qualify for the exclusion and a taxpayer would only be able to use the exclusion once every five years. **D**

Chapter 5.1 Exclusion of gain from sale of a principal residence—Allow the exclusion of as much as $50,000 (married) or $25,000 (single) for each full year of ownership and occupancy up to a maximum of $500,000 (married) and $250,000 (single) after more than ten years of ownership.

Sec. 1402. Mortgage interest - a taxpayer may continue to claim an itemized deduction for interest on acquisition indebtedness, but the $1 million limitation would be reduced to $500,000 in four annual increments. **D**

Chapter 6.5 Home mortgage and other interest deductions: the itemized deduction for mortgage interest would be replaced by a 20% nonrefundable mortgage interest credit that could apply to a primary residence and one secondary residence. Additionally, the mortgage limit for married couples filing jointly would remain at $1,000,000, but single and other taxpayers would see a revised limit of $500,000.

Sec. 1403. Charitable contribution – numerous changes **D** would be made: extension of time to file, AGI limitations, 2% floor, value deducted limited to adjusted basis, qualified conservation contributions, college athletic event seating rights, and income from intellectual property.

Chapter 6.6 Repeal the current charitable deduction and adopt a 20% nonrefundable tax credit for cash donations that exceed 1% of taxable income and for property donations that exceed 1% of taxable income.

Sec. 1404. Denial of deduction for expenses attributable to the trade or business of being an employee.   A

Chapter 6.11 Repeal the deduction of employee business expenses.

Sec. 1405. Repeal of deduction for taxes not paid or accrued in a trade or business.   D

Chapter 6.4 Creation of a 20% nonrefundable credit for state and local income, property, and sales taxes that exceed a threshold floor of 10% of one's taxable income.

Sec. 1406. Repeal of deduction for personal casualty losses.   A
Sec. 1407. Limitation on wagering losses - all deductions for   A
expenses incurred in wagering transactions would be limited to wagering winnings.
Sec. 1408. Repeal of deduction for tax preparation expenses.   A
Sec. 1409. Repeal of deduction for medical expenses.   A

Chapter 6.1 Repeal the current deduction for medical expenses and adopt a 20% nonrefundable healthcare credit that would apply to those medical and healthcare costs that exceed 10% of one's taxable income. This 10% threshold would apply to all taxpayers, including those over the age of sixty-five who currently must exceed only 7.5% of their adjusted gross income in order to deduct medical expenses. Health insurance would not be included in this calculation since it is eligible for the uniform health-insurance credit (UHIC).

Sec. 1410. Repeal of disqualification of expenses for over-   A the -counter drugs under certain accounts and arrangements.

Sec. 1411. Repeal of deduction for alimony payments and corresponding inclusion in gross income. **D**

Sec. 1412. Repeal of deduction for moving expenses. **D**

Sec. 1413. Termination of deduction and exclusions for contributions to medical savings accounts. **A**

Chapter 6.1 Creation of a uniform health-insurance credit (UHIC)—the 20/20 Tax would continue the HSA concept but would no longer allow taxpayers a deduction or exclusion for the annual contributions. Employer and employee contributions to HSAs would be entitled to the 20% UHIC tax credit.

Sec. 1414. Repeal of 2% floor on miscellaneous itemized deductions. **A**

Chapter 6.11 Elimination of all miscellaneous itemized deductions.

Sec. 1415. Repeal of overall limitation on itemized deductions **A**

Sec. 1416. Deduction for amortizable bond premium allowed in determining adjusted gross income. **A**

Sec. 1417. Repeal of exclusion, etc., for employee Achievement awards. **A**

Sec. 1418. Clarification of special rule for certain govern- **A** mental plans - the special rule would be extended to accident or health plans established in connection with a public retirement system or established by State or political subdivision.

Sec. 1419. Limitation on exclusion for employer- provided **A** housing would be limited to $50,000 ($25,000 for a married individual filing a separate return).

Sec. 1420. Fringe benefits - repeal the exclusion from **A** Income for air transportation provided as a no-additional cost service to the parent of an employee.

Sec. 1421. Repeal of exclusion of net unrealized **A** appreciation in employer securities.

Sec. 1422. Consistent basis reporting between estate and **A** person acquiring property from decedent - the basis of property acquired may not exceed the fair market value of property and the estate would be required to report the value of the property to the IRS and to the beneficiary receiving the property.

Subtitle F – Employment Tax Modifications.
Sec. 1501. Modifications of deduction for Social Security taxes in computing net earnings from self-employment - SECA taxes would be economically equivalent to FICA taxes. **D**

Chapter 6.10 Adjust the Medicare tax rate—the 20/20 Tax would eliminate the 0.9% Medicare surtax while raising the Medicare tax rate on all W-2 wages from 1.45% to 1.50%.

Chapter 6.10 Self-employment Tax—the 20/20 Tax would adopt the median rate of 10.0% (net) as the appropriate Social Security tax rate to apply to all self-employed taxpayers on their net self-employment income up to the ceiling of the OASDI wage base, allowing no related deduction for the equivalent of the employer matching.

Chapter 6.10 Healthcare Tax - the median rate of 2.5% (net) would replace the current Medicare tax rate to apply to all self-employment income and allow no related deduction.

Sec. 1502. Determination of net earnings from self-employment - the SECA tax would be clarified to apply to general and limited partners of a partnership (including LLCs) as well as to shareholders of an S corporation. **D**

Sec. 1503. Repeal of exemption from FICA taxes for certain foreign workers. **A**

Sec. 1504. Repeal of exemption from FICA taxes for certain students. **A**

Sec. 1505. Override of Treasury guidance so that all payments would be subject to income and payroll taxes (i.e., FICA, FUTA and RRTA). **A**

Sec. 1506. Certified professional employer organizations– if an employer becomes a customer of a certified PEO, the certified PEO and not the customer, would be treated as the employer and would be released from liability for employment taxes. **A**

Chapter 6.10 Employer-sponsored health insurance (ESHI)—The 20/20 Tax would subject all ESHI benefits to FICA taxes for the employer and employees just like all other W-2 wages. The employer would be entitled to a 5% credit for all ESHI benefits paid, in order to offset most if not all of the additional payroll taxes related to this provision.

Subtitle G – Pensions and Retirement.
Part 1 – Individual Retirement Plans.
Secs. 1601-1603. Elimination of income limits on **D**
contributions to Roth IRAs; No new contributions to traditional IRAs; Inflation adjustment for Roth IRA contributions.

Chapter 6.3 Retirement-plan deduction—the 20/20 Tax would set a common standard for Roth IRAs and credit IRAs (that replace traditional IRA's), which would both be phased out for single filers when modified taxable income (not modified AGI) is between $110,000 and $120,000, and joint filers would be phased out between $180,000 and $200,000.

Sec. 1604. Repeal of special rule permitting **A**
recharacterization of Roth IRA contributions as traditional IRA contributions.
Sec. 1605. Repeal of exception to 10% penalty for first home **D**
purchases.

Chapter 6.3 Rollovers from credit IRAs or traditional IRAs to Roth IRAs would no longer be permitted under any circumstance.

Part 2 – Employer-Provided Plans.
Secs. 1611-1612. Termination for new SEPs; Termination **A**
for new SIMPLE 401(k)s.
Sec. 1613. Rules related to designated Roth Contributions - **D**
employees would generally be able to contribute up to half the maximum annual elective deferral amount into a traditional account.

Chapter 6.3 Retirement-plan deduction—the 20/20 Tax would allow all employees (including those over the age of

fifty) to contribute the lesser of **$20,000 or 20% of one's W-2 income to their 401(k) plans. At the same time, an employer would be entitled to contribute as much as $40,000 total for each employee when combined with any employer and employee deposits to all defined contribution retirement plans for the participant (not to exceed 20% of one's W-2 compensation). Taxpayers would no longer be able to contribute 100% of their compensation up to the IRA maximum limit ($5,000). They would be limited to 20% of their compensation similar to the 401(k) limitations.**

Sec. 1614. Modifications of required distribution rules for pension plans - if an employee becomes a 5% owner after age 70½ but before retiring, the beginning date for RMDs would be April 1 of the following year. When the IRA owner or employee dies distributions would be required within five years.   A

Sec. 1615. Reduction in minimum age for allowable in-service distributions - all defined-benefit plans would be permitted to make in-service distributions beginning at age 59½.   A

Sec. 1616. Modification of rules governing hardship distributions - the IRS would be required within one year of the date of enactment to change its guidance to allow employees taking hardship distributions to continue making contributions.   A

Sec. 1617. Extended rollover period for the rollover of plan loan - employees whose plan terminates or who separate from employment while they have plan loans outstanding would have until the due date for filing their tax return for that year to contribute the loan balance to an IRA in order to avoid being taxed as a distribution.   A

Sec. 1618. Coordination of contribution limitations for 403(b) plans and governmental 457(b) plans - all defined contribution plans would be subject to the annual contribution limits currently applicable to 401(k) plans.   A

Chapter 5.1 Retirement-plan exclusions—if 401(k) participants and their employers each have a combined limit, it is important that 403(b) plans, 457 plans, other profit-sharing plans, and defined contribution pension plans should all have a similar combined limit per employee ($40,000).

Sec. 1619. 10% early distribution tax to governmental 457 plans.   A

Secs. 1620-1624. Inflation adjustments for qualified plan   A
benefit and contribution limitations; Inflation adjustments
for qualified plan elective deferral limitations; Inflation
adjustments for SIMPLE retirement accounts; Inflation
adjustments for catch-up contributions for certain employer
plans; Inflation adjustments for governmental and tax-
exempt organization plans (all suspended until 2024).

Subtitle H – Certain Provisions Related to Members of Indian
Tribes
Secs. 1701-1703. Indian general welfare benefits; Tribal   A
Advisory Committee; Other relief for Indian tribes.

Title II – Alternative Minimum Tax Repeal
Sec. 2001. Repeal of alternative minimum tax.   A

Chapter 5.4 Repeal of alternative minimum tax.

Title III – Business Tax Reform
Subtitle A – Tax Rates
Sec. 3001. 25% corporate tax rate - the corporate tax rate   A/D
would be a flat 25% rate beginning in 2019 gradual decrease
in the top corporate rate for the years 2015 (33%), 2016
(31%), 2017 (29%), 2018 (27%), and 2019 (25%).

**Chapter 7.1 Corporate Income Tax—the 20/20 Tax proposes
an initial rate adjustment of 30% for years 2016–2020, and
the final adopted rate of 25% for 2021 and later years.**

Subtitle B – Reform of Business-related Exclusions and
Deductions
Sec. 3101. Revision of treatment of contributions to capital -   D
the gross income of a corporation would include
contributions to its capital to the extent the amount of money
and fair market value of property contributed to the
corporation exceeds the fair market value of any stock that is
issued in exchange for such money or property.

Sec. 3102. Repeal of deduction for local and Indian tribal   A
lobbying expenses.

Sec. 3103. Expenditures for repairs in connection with casualty losses - taxpayers could elect either to claim a casualty loss for damaged property or to deduct the repair of such property, but not both.   **A**

Sec. 3104. Reform of accelerated cost recovery system - MACRS recovery periods and methods would be repealed and rules substantially similar to the ADS rules would apply using the straight-line method.   **A**

An additional depreciation deduction for inflation effects could be elected.   **D**

Sec. 3105. Repeal of amortization of pollution control facilities.   **D**

Sec. 3106. Net operating loss deduction – C corporations could deduct an NOL carryover or carryback only to the extent of 90% of the corporation's taxable income (determined without regard to the NOL deduction) conforming to the current-law AMT rule.   **A**

Sec. 3107. Circulation expenditures - taxpayers would recover the cost of circulation expenditures by capitalizing and amortizing such costs over 36 months, thus conforming to the current-law AMT rule.   **A**

Sec. 3108. Amortization of research and experimental expenditures - all R&E expenditures would be amortized over a five-year period beginning with the midpoint of the tax year in which the expenditure is paid or incurred.   **A**

Sec. 3109. Repeal of deductions for soil and water conservation expenditures and endangered species recovery expenditures. Expenditures are to be capitalized in basis of underlying property.   **D**

Sec. 3110. Amortization of certain advertising expenses - 50% of certain advertising expenses would be currently deductible and 50% would be amortized ratably over a ten-year period. **(20/20 Tax to amortize remaining 50% over five years and apply changes only to C Corporations.)**   **A/D**

Sec. 3111. Expensing certain depreciable business assets for small business - code section 179 expensing would be made permanent at the 2008-2009 levels ($250,000/year)   **A**

Sec. 3112. Repeal of election to expense certain refineries.   **A**

Sec. 3113. Repeal of deduction for energy efficient commercial buildings.   **A**

Sec. 3114. Repeal of election to expense advanced mine safety   **A** equipment.

Sec. 3115. Repeal of deduction for expenditures by farmers for fertilizer, etc. **D**

Sec. 3116. Repeal of special treatment of certain qualified film and television productions. **A**

Sec. 3117. Repeal of special rules for recoveries of damages of antitrust violations, etc. **D**

Sec. 3118. Treatment of reforestation expenditures - the election to deduct up to $10,000 for reforestation expenditures would be repealed. **A**

Sec. 3119. Extending from 15-year to 20-year amortization of goodwill and certain other intangibles. **D**

Sec. 3120. Treatment of environmental remediation costs-environmental remediation costs would be recovered ratably over 40 years beginning with the midpoint of the tax year in which the expenditures are paid or incurred. **A**

Sec. 3121. Repeal of expensing of certain disaster expenses. **A**

Sec. 3122. Phaseout and repeal of deduction for income attributable to domestic production activities. **A**

Sec. 3123. Unification of deduction for organizational expenditures - the various existing provisions for start-up and organizational expenses would be combined into a single provision applicable to all businesses. The provision would allow a taxpayer to deduct up to $10,000 in start-up and organizational costs, with a phase-out beginning at $60,000. **A**

Sec. 3124. Prevention of arbitrage of deductible interest expense and tax-exempt interest income - C corporations, including financial institutions and dealers in tax-exempt obligations, would be required to use the same interest-disallowance method. **A**

Sec. 3125. Prevention of transfer of certain losses from tax indifferent parties - the related-party loss rules would be modified to prevent losses from being shifted from a tax-indifferent party to another party in whose hands any gain or loss with respect to the property would be subject to US tax. **A**

Sec. 3126. Entertainment, etc. expenses - no deduction would be allowed for entertainment, amusement or recreation activities, facilities or membership dues relating to such activities or other social purposes. **A**

Sec. 3127. Repeal of interest limitation on corporate acquisition indebtedness. **A/D**

Chapter 7.1 Business and investment interest expense deductions would be limited to 50% of the interest paid or accrued. For interest expense in excess of 8%, only a 4% inflation factor would be eliminated from the deduction. Banks and finance companies would follow old law.

Sec. 3128. Denial of deductions and credits for expenditures A
in all illegal businesses.

Sec. 3129. Limitation on deduction for FDIC premiums - A
percentage of such assessments would be non-deductible for
institutions with total consolidated assets in excess of $10
billion.

Sec. 3130. Repeal of percentage depletion. A

Sec. 3131. Repeal of passive activity exception for working A
interests in oil and gas property.

Sec. 3132. Repeal of special rules for gain or loss on timber, A
coal, or domestic iron ore. Income is to be treated as
ordinary income rather than capital gains.

Sec. 3133. Repeal of like-kind exchanges. A

Sec. 3134. Restriction on trade or business property treated A
as similar or related in service to involuntarily converted
property in disaster areas - tangible business property that is
involuntarily converted in a Federally declared disaster area
would qualify for deferral of gain recognition only if the
depreciation class life of replacement property does not
exceed that of the converted property.

Sec. 3135. Repeal of rollover of publicly traded securities A
gain into specialized small business investment companies.

Sec. 3136. Termination of special rules for gain from certain A
small business stock.

Sec. 3137. Certain self-created property not treated as a A
capital asset - gain or loss from the disposition of a self-
created patent, invention, model or design, or secret formula
or process would be ordinary in character.

Sec. 3138. Repeal of special rule for sale or exchange of A
patents to treat as long term capital gain prior to commercial
exploitation.

Sec. 3139. Depreciation recapture on gain from disposition A
of certain depreciable realty - the recapture rules with respect
to depreciable real property are revised to limit the amount
treated as ordinary income to the lesser of: (1) the difference

between the accelerated depreciation and straight-line depreciation attributable to periods before 2015, plus the total amount of depreciation attributable to periods after 2014, or (2) the excess of the amount realized over the adjusted basis.

Sec. 3140. Common deduction conforming amendments – a number of conforming changes that are common to various sections in Subtitle B of Title III of the discussion draft would be made. **A**

Subtitle C – Reform of Business Credits

Sec. 3201. Repeal of credit for alcohol used as fuel. **A**

Sec. 3202. Repeal of credit for biodiesel and renewable diesel used as fuel. **A**

Sec. 3203. Research credit modified and made permanent- **A**
The research credit would equal: 15% of the qualified research expenses for the tax year that exceed 50% of the average qualified research expenses for the three tax years preceding the tax year for which the credit is determined, plus (2) 15% of the basic research payments for the tax year that exceed 50% of the average basic research payments for the three tax years preceding the tax year for which the credit is determined.

Sec. 3204. Modification of the Low-income housing tax **A**
credit – the credit would be modified in several ways, *Allocation of basis*: State and local housing authorities would allocate qualified basis, rather than credit amounts, *Credit period*: the credit period would be extended from 10 years to 15 years to match the current 15-year compliance period, *Credit amount*: the 4% credit would be repealed. The 9% credit for newly constructed property and substantial rehabilitations would be retained. Occupancy and other rules would be modified.

Sec. 3205. Repeal of enhanced oil recovery credit. **A**

Sec. 3206. Repeal of inflation adjustment for electricity and **A**
refined coal - 10-year phase-out of recovery credit.

Sec. 3207. Repeal of Indian employment credit. **A**

Sec. 3208. Repeal of credit for portion of employer Social **A**
Security taxes paid with respect to employee cash tips.

Sec. 3209. Repeal of credit for clinical testing expenses for **D**
certain drugs for rare diseases or conditions.

Sec. 3210. Repeal of credit for small employer pension plan **A** startup costs.

adopted a method of accounting - the IRS guidance with respect to determining whether a taxpayer has adopted a method of accounting would be codified.

Sec. 3303. Certain special rules for taxable year of inclusion - a taxpayer on the accrual method of accounting for tax purposes would be required to include an item of income no later than the tax year in which such item is included for financial statement purposes. The provision also would provide that cash and accrual method taxpayers may defer the inclusion of advance payments for certain goods and services in income for tax purposes up to one year. Also repeal of certain exceptions.   **A**

Sec. 3304. Installment sales - the interest charge rules would apply to any installment sale in excess of $150,000, provided the obligation remains outstanding at the end of the tax year, eliminating the aggregate $5 million limitation. The provision also would repeal the exceptions and special rules for sales of farm property, timeshares, and residential lots.   **D**

Secs. 3305-3306. Repeal of special rule for deferral of prepaid subscription income; Repeal of special rule for deferral of prepaid dues income of certain membership organizations.   **A**

Sec. 3307. Repeal of special rule for deferral of income for magazines, paperbacks, and records returned after close of the taxable year.   **A**

Sec. 3308. Modification of rules for long-term contracts - the completed-contract method would be limited to taxpayers with average gross receipts of $10 million or less.   **A**

Sec. 3309. Nuclear decommissioning reserve funds - the special 20% tax rate for nuclear decommissioning reserve funds would be repealed, and the tax rate generally applicable to corporations would apply.   **A**

Sec. 3310. Repeal of last-in, first-out method of inventory and reduced tax rate of reserves for small closely held entities. Under the provision, the LIFO inventory accounting method would no longer be permitted. Thus, taxpayers could use FIFO or any other method that conforms to the best accounting practice in a particular trade or business and clearly reflects income. A taxpayer would include its LIFO reserve in income over a four-year period beginning with its first tax year beginning after 2018 in the following amounts: 10 percent include in the first year (2019); 15 percent in the   **A** second year (2020); 25 percent in the third year (2021); and 50 percent in the fourth year (2022). Taxpayers could elect to begin the four-year inclusion period in an earlier tax year. Closely held entities - generally defined as having no more than 100 owners as of February 26, 2014 (using rules similar to those used for S Corporations and taking indirect ownership into account) - would be subject to a reduced 7 percent tax rate on their LIFO reserves. This provision would apply to tax years beginning after 2014. **(years beginning after 2018 for the 20/20 Tax)** **A/D**

Sec. 3311. Repeal of lower of cost or market method of inventory. **D**

Sec. 3312. Modification of rules for capitalization and inclusion in inventory costs of certain expenses - the exception to the UNICAP rules for businesses with average annual gross receipts of $10 million or less that acquire property for resale would be expanded to include all types of property, whether produced or acquired by the taxpayer and eliminate exceptions. **A**

Sec. 3313. Modification of income forecast method - the forecast period under the IFM would be extended to 20 years, with required computations based on the income earned before the close of the fifth, tenth, fifteenth and twentieth years. **A**

Sec. 3314. Repeal of income averaging for farm income. **A**

Sec. 3315. Treatment of patent or trademark infringement awards - the judicial standard for determining the treatment of patent or trade mark infringement awards would be codified. **A**

Sec. 3316. Repeal of redundant rules with respect to carrying charges. **A**

Sec. 3317. Repeal of recurring item exception for spudding of oil or gas wells. **A**

Subtitle E – Financial Instruments
Part 1 – Derivatives and Hedges

Sec. 3401. Treatment of certain derivatives - any gains or losses from marking a derivative to market would be treated as ordinary income or loss rather than 60 percent long term and 40 percent short term. **A**

Sec. 3402. Modification of certain rules related to hedges **A**

- taxpayers could rely upon (for tax purposes) an identification of a transaction as a hedge that they have made for financial accounting purposes. The provision also would modify the hedging tax rules so that the rules would apply when an insurance company acquires a debt instrument to hedge risks relating to assets that support the company's ability to honor future insurance claims.

Part 2 – Treatment of Debt Instruments

Sec. 3411. Current inclusion in income of market discount - **A** purchasers of bonds at a discount on the secondary market would be required to include the discount in taxable income over the post-purchase life of the bond, rather than only upon retirement of the bond or resale of the bond by the purchaser. Any loss that results from the retirement or resale of such a bond would be treated as an ordinary loss to the extent of previously accrued market discount. Also, limit taxable secondary market discount to greater of original yield plus 5 percentage points or Federal rate plus 10 percentage points.

Sec. 3412. Treatment of certain exchanges of debt **A** instruments - the issue price of a modified debt instrument generally would be equal to the lesser of (1) the issue price of the debt instrument before it was modified, or (2) the stated principal amount of the modified debt instrument.

Sec. 3413. Coordination with rules for inclusion not later **A** than for financial accounting purposes - fees and other amounts received by a taxpayer would not be treated as OID income to the extent they are subject to section 3303 of the discussion draft.

Sec. 3414. Rules regarding certain government debt - certain **A** clerical amendments to the current-law rules would be made to reflect that some of the rules have been superseded by subsequently enacted tax rules relating to the accrual of original issue discount. Repeal of rule that permits US obligations to be exchanged without recognition of gain or loss.

Part 3 – Certain Rules for Determining Gain and Loss

Sec. 3421. Cost basis of specified securities determined **A** without regard to identification - taxpayers who sell a portion of their holdings in substantially identical stock generally would be required to determine their taxable gain or loss on a FIFO basis.

Sec. 3422. Wash sales by related parties - losses from the disposition of stock or securities also would be disallowed if certain parties that are closely related to the taxpayer acquire substantially identical stock or securities within 30 days before or after the disposition. **D**

Sec. 3423. Nonrecognition for derivative transactions by a corporation with respect to its stock - a corporation generally would not recognize income, gains, losses, or deductions with respect to derivatives that relate to the corporation's own stock, except for certain transactions that involve the corporation acquiring its own stock and entering into a forward contract with respect to its own stock. **A**

Part 4 – Tax Favored Bonds

Secs. 3431-3432. Termination of tax exemption of interest of private activity bonds; Termination of mortgage credit certificate from PAB's. **A**

Sec. 3433. Repeal of tax exempt interest on advance refunding bonds. **D**

Sec. 3434. Repeal of tax credit bond rules. Holders and issuers would continue receiving tax credits and payments for existing bonds, but no new bonds could be issued. **A**

Subtitle F – Insurance Reforms

Sec. 3501. Exception to pro rata interest expense disallowance for corporate-owned life insurance restricted to 20% owners - the exception to the pro rata interest expense disallowance rule would not apply to officers, directors, or employees, and thus only would apply to 20% owners of the business that holds the insurance contract. **A**

Sec. 3502. Net operating losses of life insurance companies - life insurance companies would be allowed to carry net operating losses back up to two tax years or forward up to 20 tax years, in conformity with the general net operating loss carryover rules. **A**

Sec. 3503. Repeal of small life insurance company deduction. **A**

Sec. 3504. Computation of life insurance tax reserves - the current-law prescribed discount rate for life insurance reserves would be replaced with the average applicable **A**

344

Federal mid-term rate over the 60 months ending before the beginning of the calendar year for which the determination is made, plus 3.5 percentage points.

Sec. 3505. Adjustment for change in computing reserves - A
the special 10-year period for adjustments to take into account changes in computing reserves by life insurance companies would be repealed.

Sec. 3506. Modification of rules for life insurance proration A
for purposes of determining the dividends received deduction - the portion of dividends and tax-exempt interest received that is set aside for obligations to policyholders would be determined separately for the company's general account and for each separate account.

Sec. 3507. Repeal of special rule for distributions to share- A
holders from pre-1984 policyholders surplus account.

Sec. 3508. Modification of proration rules for property and A
casualty insurance companies - the fixed 15% reduction in the reserve deduction for P&C insurance companies would be replaced with a formula whereby the reserve deduction is reduced by a percentage that is equal to the ratio of the tax-exempt assets of the company to all assets of the company.

Sec. 3509. Repeal of special treatment of Blue Cross and A
Blue Shield organizations, etc.

Sec. 3510. Modification of discounting rules for property A
and casualty insurance companies - P&C insurance companies would use the corporate bond yield curve to discount the amount of unpaid losses.

Sec. 3511. Repeal of special estimated tax payments. A

Sec. 3512. Capitalization of certain policy acquisition A
expenses   - The three categories of insurance contracts would be replaced with two categories: (1) group contracts; and (2) all other specified contracts. The percentage of net premiums that would be spread over ten years would be 5% for group insurance contracts and 12% for all other specified contracts.

Secs. 3513-3514. Tax reporting for life settlement A
transactions; Clarification of tax basis of life insurance contracts - a taxpayer that purchases an interest in an existing life insurance contract with a death benefit equal to or exceeding $500,000 would be required to report (1) the purchase price, the identity of the buyer and seller, and the issuer and policy number to both the IRS and the seller, and

(2) the identity of the buyer and seller, and the issuer and policy number to the issuing insurance company. Upon the payment of any policy benefits to the buyer of a previously issued life insurance contract, the insurance company would be required to report the gross benefit payment, the identity of the buyer, and the insurance company's estimate of the buyer's basis to the IRS and to the payee.

Sec. 3515. Exception to transfer for valuable consideration   A
rules - the exception for carryover basis transfers and transfers to the person whose life is insured would not apply if the acquirer of the life insurance contract has no substantial relationship with the insured apart from the acquirer's interest in the contract.

Subtitle G – Pass-Thru and Certain Other Entities
Part 1 – S Corporations

Sec. 3601. Reduced recognition period for built-in gains   A
made permanent - the temporary five-year period would be made permanent.

Sec. 3602. Modifications to S corporation passive   A
investment income rules - the passive-income threshold would be increased from 25% to 60%. The provision also would repeal the current-law provision terminating the S corporation election for excessive passive income.

Sec. 3603. Expansion of qualifying beneficiaries of an   A
electing small business trust - a nonresident alien individual could be a potential current beneficiary of an ESBT.

Sec. 3604. Charitable contribution deduction for electing   A
small business trusts - the charitable contribution rules applicable to individuals, rather than to trusts, would apply to ESBTs.

Sec. 3605. Permanent rule regarding basis adjustment to   A
stock of S corporations making charitable contributions of property - the pre-2014 basis-adjustment rule would be made permanent. Thus, an S corporation shareholder would reduce the basis in his S corporation stock by his pro rata share of the adjusted basis of the contributed property.

Sec. 3606. Extension of time for making S corporation   A
elections - the election process would be simplified by permitting a small business corporation to elect on its income tax return to be treated as an S corporation for the tax year to which the return relates, provided that the return

is filed not later than the applicable due date (with extensions).

Sec. 3607. Relocation of C corporation definition – the definition would be moved to Code section 7701, which provides generally applicable definitions. A

Part 2 – Partnerships

Sec. 3611. Repeal of rules relating to guaranteed payments end liquidating distributions. A

Sec. 3612-3614. Mandatory adjustments to basis of partnership property in case of transfer of partnership interests; Mandatory adjustments to basis of undistributed partnership property; corresponding adjustments to basis of properties held by partnership where partnership basis adjusted. A

Sec. 3615. Charitable contributions and foreign taxes taken into account in determining limitation on allowance of partner's share of loss - a partner would be required to take into account charitable contributions and foreign taxes paid by a partnership in calculating the limitation on the partner's share of losses, conforming the partnership rules to the S corporation rules and thus preventing a partner from deducting losses in excess of basis. A

Sec. 3616. Revisions related to unrealized receivables and inventory items - any distribution of an inventory item would be treated as a sale or exchange between the partner and the partnership, eliminating the requirement that inventory be substantially appreciated in value to trigger gain recognition. A

Sec. 3617. Repeal of time limitation on taxing pre-contribution gain. Gain or loss would be recognized at time of distribution by partnership. A

Sec. 3618. Partnership interests created by gift - the rule would be clarified to provide that a person is treated as a partner in a partnership in which capital is a material income-producing factor whether such interest was obtained by purchase or gift and regardless of whether such interest was acquired from a family member. A

Sec. 3619. Repeal of technical termination. Thus, the partnership would continue even if 50 percent of total capital or profit interests are sold or exchanged. A

Sec. 3620. Publicly traded partnership exception restricted to A mining and natural resources partnerships - the special exceptions for publicly traded partnerships would be repealed other than for partnerships with 90% of their income from activities relating to mining and natural resources.

Sec. 3621. Ordinary income treatment in the case of partnership interests held in connection with performance of services - certain partnership interests held in connection with the performance of services would be subject to a rule that characterizes a portion of any capital gains as ordinary income.

A/D

Chapter 5.2—The 20/20 Tax would not allow capital gain treatment for "carried interest" which must be defined broadly.

Sec. 3622. Partnership audits and adjustments - the current TEFRA and Electing Large Partnership rules would be repealed, and the partnership audit rules would be streamlined into a single set of rules for auditing partnerships and their partners at the partnership level.

A

Part 3 – REITs and RICs

Sec. 3631. Prevention of tax-free spinoffs involving REITs- the 2001 IRS ruling would be overturned, so that REITs could not satisfy the active trade or business requirement for tax-free spin-off transactions.

A

Sec. 3632. Extension of period for prevention of REIT election following revocation or termination - the five-year waiting period for electing to be treated as a REIT following the termination or revocation of a prior REIT election would be extended to ten years.

A

Sec. 3633. Certain short-life property not treated as real property for purposes of REIT provisions - the term "real property" would not include tangible property with a class life of less than 27.5 years for purposes of the REIT income and asset tests.

D

Sec. 3634. Repeal of expired special rules for timber held by REITs; timber not included in term "real property" with regards to REIT rules.

A

Sec. 3635. Limitation on fixed percentage rent and interest

D

exceptions for REIT income tests - rents from real property and interest would not include amounts that are based on a fixed percentage of receipts or sales to the extent that such amounts are received or accrued from a single tenant that is a C corporation and the amounts received or accrued from such tenant constitute more than 25% of the total amount received or accrued by the REIT that is based on a fixed percentage of receipts or sales.

Secs. 3636-3637. Repeal of preferential dividend rule for publicly offered REITs; Authority for alternative remedies to address certain REIT distribution failures.   A

Sec. 3638. Limitations on designation of dividends by REITs   A
- the aggregate amount of dividends that could be designated by a REIT as qualified dividends or capital gain dividends would not be permitted to exceed the dividends actually paid by the REIT.

Sec. 3639. Non-REIT earnings and profits required to be   A
distributed by REIT in cash only, not property or stock.

Sec. 3640. Debt instruments of publicly offered REITs and   A
mortgages treated as real estate assets. Income from debt instruments would be treated as qualified income for 95% income test, but not 75% income test. No more than 25% of REIT assets can be debt instruments.

Sec. 3641. Asset and income test clarification regarding   A
ancillary personal property – certain ancillary personal property that is leased with real property would be treated as real property for purposes of the 75% asset test.

Sec. 3642. Hedging provisions - the current-law treatment of   A
REIT hedges would be extended to include income from hedges of previously acquired hedges that a REIT entered to manage risk associated with liabilities or property that have been extinguished or disposed.

Sec. 3643. Modification of REIT earnings and profits   A
calculation to avoid duplicate taxation - current REIT earnings and profits for any tax year would not be reduced by any amount that is not allowable in computing taxable income for the tax year and was not allowable in computing its taxable income for any prior tax year.

Sec. 3644. Reduction in percentage limitation on assets of   A
REIT which may be taxable REIT subsidiaries - the 25% Taxable REIT subsidiaries (TRS) stock limitation would be reduced back to 20%.

Sec. 3645. Treatment of certain services provided by taxable A
REIT subsidiaries - TRSs would be permitted to operate
foreclosed real property without causing income from the
property to fail to satisfy the REIT income tests. In addition,
TRSs would be permitted to develop and market REIT real
property, but only on arms-length transactions, without
subjecting the REIT to 100% excise tax rule.

Sec. 3646. Study relating to taxable REIT subsidiaries - the A
Treasury Department would be required to conduct a
biannual study, and submit a report to the Ways and Means
Committee and Senate Finance Committee regarding
number of TRSs and taxes paid by TRSs.

Sec. 3647. C corporation election to become, or transfer A
assets to, a RIC or REIT - the current-law entity-level tax on
built-in gains would be imposed at the time the C
corporation elects to become a REIT or RIC or transfers
assets to the REIT or RIC in a carryover basis transaction,
without regard to when the gain otherwise would be
recognized by the REIT or RIC.

Sec. 3648. Interests in RICs and REITs not excluded from A
definition of United States real property interests with regard
to FIRPTA exception.

Sec. 3649. Dividends derived from RICs and REITs A
ineligible for deduction for United States source portion of
dividends from certain foreign corporations - the deduction
for dividends received from a foreign subsidiary would not
apply to dividends that are attributable to dividends received
by the foreign subsidiary from a RIC or REIT.

Part 4 – Personal Holding Companies

Sec. 3661. Exclusion of dividends from controlled foreign A
corporations from the definition of personal holding
company income for purposes of the personal holding
company rules - dividends received from a foreign
subsidiary would not be subject to the additional 20% tax.

Subtitle H – Taxation of Foreign Persons

Sec. 3701. Prevention of avoidance of tax through A
reinsurance with non-taxed affiliates - US insurance
companies would not be permitted to deduct reinsurance
premiums paid to a related company that is not subject to US
taxation on the premiums, unless the related company elects

to treat the premium income as effectively connected to a US trade or business.

Sec. 3702. Taxation of passenger cruise gross income of foreign corporations and nonresident alien individuals - the income of foreign taxpayers that is derived from the operation of passenger cruise ships within US territorial waters would be subject to US tax, without regard to whether the country in which the taxpayer is a resident grants an equivalent exemption to US taxpayers. **A**

Sec. 3703. Restriction on insurance business exception to passive foreign investment company rules - the PFIC exception for insurance companies would be amended to apply only if (1) the PFIC would be taxed as an insurance company were it a US corporation, (2) more than 50% of the PFIC's gross receipts for the tax year consist of premiums, and (3) loss and loss adjustment expenses, unearned premiums, and certain reserves constitute more than 35% of the PFIC's total assets. **A**

Sec. 3704. Modification of limitation on earnings stripping- the threshold for excess interest expense would be reduced to 40% of adjusted taxable income. In addition, corporations would no longer be permitted to carry forward any excess limitation. **A**

Sec. 3705. Limitation on treaty benefits for certain deductible payments - if a payment of FDAP income is deductible in the United States and the payment is made by an entity that is controlled by a foreign parent to another entity in a tax treaty jurisdiction that is controlled by the same foreign parent, then the statutory 30% withholding tax on such income would not be reduced by any treaty unless the withholding tax would be reduced by a treaty if the payment were made directly to the foreign parent. **A**

Subtitle I – Provisions Related to Compensation

Part 1 – Executive Compensation

Sec. 3801. Nonqualified deferred compensation - an employee would be taxed on compensation as soon as there is no substantial risk of forfeiture with regard to that compensation. **A**

Sec. 3802. Modification of limitation on excessive employee remuneration - the exceptions to the $1 million deduction limitation for commissions and performance-based **D** compensation would be repealed and definition of covered employee revised.

Part 2 – Worker Classification

Subtitle J – Zones and Short-Term Regional Benefits

Title IV – Participation Exemption System for the Taxation of Foreign Income

Subtitle A – Establishment of Exemption System

transition to participation exemption system of taxation - US shareholders owning at least 10% of a foreign subsidiary would include in income for their last tax year beginning before 2015 their pro rata share of the post-1986 historical E&P of the foreign subsidiary to the extent such E&P has not been previously subject to US tax. Portion of E&P consisting of cash taxed at 8.75% and remaining E& P taxed at 3.5%

Sec. 4004. Look-thru rule for related controlled foreign   A
corporations made permanent in regards to passive income received by one foreign subsidiary from related foreign subsidy not included in US income.

Subtitle B – Modifications Related to Foreign Tax Credit System

Sec. 4101. Repeal of section 902 indirect foreign tax credits,   A
which allows deduction for foreign taxes paid or accrued with respect to dividends (related to Sec. 4001).

Sec. 4102. Foreign tax credit limitation applied by allocating   A
only directly allocable deductions to foreign source income.

Sec. 4103. Passive category income expanded to include   A
other mobile income.

Sec. 4104. Source of income from sales of inventory   A
determined solely on basis of production activities - income from the sale of inventory property produced within and sold outside the United States (or vice versa) would be allocated and apportioned between sources within and outside the United States solely on the basis of the production activities with respect to the inventory which is currently based up to 50%.

Subtitle C – Rules Related to Passive and Mobile Income
Part 1 – Modification of Subpart F Provisions

Sec. 4201. Subpart F income to only include low-taxed   A
foreign   income - the 90% threshold for treating foreign income as subpart F income would be increased to 100% for foreign personal holding company income.

Sec. 4202. Foreign base company sales income - FBCSI no   A
longer would include income earned by a foreign subsidiary that is incorporated in a country that has a comprehensive income tax treaty with the United States, or to income that has been taxed at 12.5% or greater.

353

available research - the exception from the UBIT rules for fundamental research would be limited to income derived from the research made available to the public.

Sec. 5005. Parity of charitable contribution limitation between trusts and corporations – charitable contributions for purposes of determining UBIT would be limited to 10% of the unrelated business taxable income whether the contributing entity is organized as a corporation or a trust. **A**

Sec. 5006. Increased specific deduction - the $1,000 deduction would be increased to $10,000. **A**

Sec. 5007. Repeal of exclusion of gain or loss from disposition of distressed property. **A**

Sec. 5008. Modification of UBIT exception for qualified sponsorship payments - First, if the use or acknowledgement refers to any of the business sponsor's product lines, the payment would not be a qualified sponsorship payment. Second, if a tax-exempt organization receives more than $25,000 of qualified sponsorship payments for any one event, such a contribution would be subject to UBIT. **A**

Subtitle B – Penalties

Sec. 5101. Increase in information return penalties – the penalties for failure to file various returns, disclosures, or public documents on organizations and managers would be increased (double their current amounts). **D**

Sec. 5102. Manager-level accuracy-related penalty on underpayment of unrelated business income tax - a 5% penalty (with $20,000 limit) would apply to managers of a tax-exempt organization when an accuracy-related penalty is applied to the organization for any substantial understatement of UBIT. Also, a 10% penalty ($40,000 limit) would apply if understatement due to reportable or listed transactions. **D**

Subtitle C – Excise Taxes

Sec. 5201. Modification of intermediate sanctions – the excise tax on excess-benefit transaction would be expanded to apply not only to public charities, but also to labor, agricultural, and horticultural organizations and business leagues, chambers of commerce, real-estate boards, and boards of trade. Excise tax of 10% would be imposed on **A** organization when excise tax is imposed on disqualified person.

Sec. 5202. Modification of taxes on self-dealing- an excise   **A**
tax of 2.5% would be imposed on a private foundation when the self-dealing tax is imposed on a disqualified person.

Sec. 5203. Excise tax on failure of public charities to   **D**
distribute contributions from donor advised fund within 5 years of receipt.

Sec. 5204. Simplification of excise tax on private foundation   **A**
investment income - the excise tax rate on net investment income would be reduced to 1%.

Sec. 5205. Repeal of exception for private operating   **A**
foundation failure to distribute income.

Sec. 5206. Excise tax based on investment income of private   **A**
colleges and universities - certain private colleges and universities would be subject to a 1% excise tax on net investment income.

Subtitle D – Requirements for Organizations Exempt from Tax

Sec. 5301. Repeal of tax-exempt status for professional   **A**
sports leagues.

Sec. 5302. Repeal of exemption from tax for certain   **A**
insurance companies and co-op health insurance issuers.

Sec. 5303. In-State requirement for workmen's   **A**
compensation insurance organizations - an exempt workmen's compensation insurance organization would be exempt from tax only if it provides no insurance coverage other than workmen's compensation insurance required by State law, or coverage incidental to such insurance.

Sec. 5304. Repeal of Type II and Type III supporting   **A**
organizations. Thus organizations that support public charities must be operated, supervised or controlled by public supported organization (Type I) to qualify for tax exempt status.

Title VI – Tax Administration and Compliance

Subtitle A – IRS Investigation-Related Reforms

Sec. 6001. Organizations required to notify Secretary of   **A**
intent to operate as 501(c)(4) (social welfare organization) within 60 days of formation. Current 501(c)(4) organizations

are required to file Form 1024 or 990 within 180 days to qualify for tax exempt status.

Sec. 6002. Declaratory judgments for 501(c)(4)   **A**
organizations - declaratory judgment relief would be extended to controversies involving the initial or continuing qualification of section 501(c)(4) social-welfare organizations.

Sec. 6003. Restriction on donation reporting for certain   **D**
501(c)(4) organizations - a social welfare organization exempt under Code section 501(c)(4) would be required to include on Schedule B only information concerning a donor who both (1) contributes $5,000 or more during the current tax year and (2) is either an officer or director of the organization or one of the five highest compensated employees of the organization for the current or any preceding tax year.

Sec. 6004. Mandatory electronic filing for annual returns of   **A**
exempt organizations.

Sec. 6005. Commissioner's duties would be expanded to   **A**
ensure that IRS employees are familiar with and act in accord with certain taxpayer rights.

Sec. 6006. Termination of employment of IRS employees   **A**
for taking official actions for political purposes.

Sec. 6007. Release of information by Federal employees   **A**
regarding the status of certain investigations may be lawfully disclosed.

Sec. 6008. Review of IRS examination selection procedures   **A**
- the Comptroller General would be directed to undertake an initial review of each IRS operating division and would be directed to report to Congress and the Treasury Secretary the results of the initial review d any recommendations.

Sec. 6009. IRS employees prohibited from using personal   **A**
e-mail accounts for official business.

Sec. 6010. Moratorium on IRS conferences. IRS precluded   **D**
from holding conference until TIGTA submits report to Congress.

Sec. 6011. Applicable standard for determinations of   **A**
whether an organization is operated exclusively for the promotion of social welfare - the IRS would be required to apply the standards and definitions in effect on January 1, 2010, to determine whether an organization is operated

exclusively for the promotion of social welfare for purposes of Code section 501(c)(4).

Subtitle B – Taxpayer Protection and Service Reforms
    Sec. 6101. Extension of IRS authority to require truncated Social Security numbers on Form W-2.   **A**

    Sec. 6102. Free electronic filing - the IRS would be directed to continue working cooperatively with the private-sector technology industry to maintain a program that provides free individual income tax preparation and individual income tax electronic filing services to lower-income and elderly taxpayers.   **A**

    Sec. 6103. Pre-populated returns prohibited.   **D**

    Sec. 6104. Form 1040SR for seniors - the IRS would be required to develop a simple tax return to be known as Form 1040SR, which would be as similar as practicable to the current Form 1040EZ.   **D**

    Sec. 6105. Increased refund and credit threshold for Joint Committee on Taxation review of C corporation return - the threshold for JCT review of refunds or credits with respect to returns filed by C corporations would be increased to $5 million.   **A**

Subtitle C – Tax Return Due Date Simplification
    Secs. 6201-6203. Due dates for returns of partnerships, S corporations, and C corporations; Partnerships and S Corporations would be required to file by March 15 (or 2 1/2 months after close of tax year) and C Corporations by April 15 (or 3 1/2 months after close of tax year) all with 6 month extensions.   **A/D**

The 20/20 Tax would make April 15 the initial due date for all three business entity forms, and September 15 (5 month extensions) would be the extended due date for all three.

Subtitle D – Compliance Reforms
    Sec. 6301. Penalty for failure to file - the minimum penalty for failure to file a tax return would be increased to $400.   **A**

    Sec. 6302. Penalty for failure to file correct information returns and provide payee statements would be increased (substantially at all levels).   **D**

    Sec. 6303. Clarification of 6-year statute of limitations in   **A** case of overstatement of basis - the six-year statute of limitations would apply to a return on which the taxpayer claims an adjusted basis for any property that is more than 125% of the correct adjusted basis.

Sec. 6304. Reform of rules related to qualified tax collection contracts - the IRS would be required to use qualified tax collection contracts to collect certain inactive tax receivables.   A

Sec. 6305. 100% continuous levy on payments to Medicare providers and suppliers - the Treasury Department would be authorized to levy up to 100% of a payment to a Medicare provider to collect unpaid taxes.   A

Sec. 6306. Treatment of refundable credits for purposes of certain penalties - the penalty for underpayment of tax would take into account the full amount of refundable credits.   A

Title VII – Excise Taxes

Sec. 7001. Repeal of medical device excise tax.   A

Sec. 7002. Modifications relating to oil spill liability trust fund - the excise tax would continue to be imposed at a rate of 9 cents per barrel for 2018 through 2023. Definition of "crude oil" and "petroleum products" broadened.   A

Sec. 7003. Modification relating to inland waterways trust fund financing rate - the excise tax rate would be increased to 26 cents per gallon on fuel used in powering commercial cargo vessels on inland or intra-coastal waterways.   A

Sec. 7004. Excise tax on systemically important financial institutions - every SIFI would be required to pay a quarterly excise tax of 0.035% of the SIFI's total consolidated assets in excess of $500 billion, subsequently indexed for increases in GDP.   A

Sec. 7005. Clarification of orphan drug exception to annual fee on branded prescription pharmaceutical manufacturers and importers - eligibility for the orphan drug exemption would be expanded to include any drug or biological product that is approved or licensed by the FDA for marketing solely for one or more rare diseases or conditions, regardless of whether the section 45C credit was ever allowed.   A

Title VIII – Deadwood and Technical Provisions

Subtitle A – Repeal of Deadwood
Secs. 8001-8084. Repeal of Deadwood. Repeal of any   A
provisions relating to past tax years involving situations that
were narrowly defined and unlikely to recur.

Subtitle B – Conforming Amendments Related to Multiple
Sections
Sec. 8101. Conforming amendments related to multiple   A
sections of this discussion draft.

A list of other 20/20 Tax significant changes found in chapters 5 through 7 is as follows:

Chapter 5.1—Eliminate the $5,500 catch-up contribution for all employee retirement plans.

Chapter 5.1—Eliminate the $50,000 exclusion for employee group-term life insurance.

Chapter 5.1—Eliminate the percentage depletion allowance.

Chapter 5.5—The head-of-household rates are eliminated and replaced by a $1,000 nonrefundable credit.

Chapter 6.3—The traditional IRA would be replaced with a credit IRA to provide a refundable credit of 20% on as much as $5,000 annual contribution.

Chapter 6.5—Interest expense on the home equity loan of $100,000 would no longer be deductible unless it is part of the original acquisition indebtedness.

Chapter 6.5—Student loan interest would no longer be deductible.

Chapter 6.6—Noncash contributions would no longer avoid gain on the unrealized appreciation unless the donated property is utilized by the charity for at least three years.

Chapter 6.8—Assets transferred at death will inherit a carryover basis from the decedent and not a stepped-up basis. The estate of each decedent will be entitled to a $1

million exemption from carryover basis as well as a $250,000 exemption for the appreciated value of a personal residence.

Chapter 6.10—The 3.8% net investment income tax would be replaced by a new 2.5% healthcare tax.

Chapter 6.10—A new 2.5% healthcare tax will apply to all taxable income except that which is subject to FICA and SE tax, including W-2 income, IRA and 401(k) type distributions, and Social Security income. Taxpayers with less than $2,000 of such income are exempt from the 2.5% healthcare tax.

Chapter 6.11—The rules for the nanny tax would be modified to promote more compliance and eliminate the FUTA.

Chapter 7.2—The estate tax would no longer allow valuation discounts for transfers to family members.

Chapter 7.2—The use of various trusts to avoid estate tax would be minimized.

Chapter 7.2—The unlimited marital deduction for the estate tax would be reduced to 50% of the adjusted gross estate.

Chapter 7.2—The unlimited charitable deduction for the estate tax would be reduced to 50% of the adjusted gross estate.

Chapter 7.2—Estate tax rates would be lowered to 10% on the first $10,000,000 of taxable estates, 20% on the next $20,000,000; and 30% on taxable estates in excess of $30,000,000. The first $5,000,000 of a taxable estate would be exempt similar to 2011 law.

Chapter 7.3—The excise tax for gasoline would be increased 6.0 cents per gallon for each of three years from 2016 through 2018.

NOTE: The Appendix A pages include most but not all changes of the 20/20 Tax described in Chapters 5 through 7.

APPENDIX B

M D Y

Taxpayer Name _____	Date of Birth __/__/__	SSN _____
Spouse Name _____	Date of Birth __/__/__	SSN _____
Address _____
City, State, Zip _____

Filing Status　　1 ___ Single　　　　　　　　　4 ___ Head of household (SSN of qualifying person) _____
　　　　　　　　2 ___ Married filing jointly　　　5 ___ Qualifying widow(er) with dependent child
　　　　　　　　3 ___ Married filing separately
　　　　　　　　Enter separate-filing spouse's SSN above and full name here _____

Personal Credits: 6a _____ Yourself. 6b _____ Spouse
6c Dependents – <u>Names (First)</u>　　　　<u>(Last)</u>　　　<u>Birth Date M/D/Y</u>　　　<u>SSN</u>　　　<u>Relationship</u>

6d Total eligible for Personal Credit between the ages of 18 and 65 (include taxpayer and spouse under 65) _____
6e Total eligible for Personal Credit age 65 and over (include taxpayer and spouse if over 65) _____
NOTE:　Dependent children under the age of 18 are only eligible for the Child Tax Credit on Line 62 of taxpayer's return.
　　　　All children under 18 filing their own tax returns may claim the Personal Tax Credit but not the Child Tax Credit.

Ordinary	7	Wages, salaries, etc. Attach W-2(s) (To include employer-provided health insurance)	7 _____
Income	8	Alimony received 8b Payor's SSN _____	8 _____
	9	Business income or (loss). Attach Schedule C	9 _____
	10	Short-term and other gains or (losses). Attach Form 4797	10 _____
	11	IRA, 401(k), 403(b) and 457 distributions 11a _____　Taxable amount	11b _____
	12	Pensions and annuities　　　　12a _____　Taxable amount	12b _____
	13	Rental real estate, royalties, partnerships, S Corporations, trusts, etc. Attach Schedule E	13 _____
	14	Partnership self-employment income (Should not be included in line 13)	14 _____
	15	Farm income or (loss). Attach Schedule F	15 _____
	16	Unemployment compensation	16 _____
	17	Other income. List type 17a (SE Income)_____ 17b (Non SE) _____	17 _____
	18	Total Ordinary Income—Combine the amounts on lines 7 through 17.	18 _____

Exclusionary	19	Interest - Attach Schedule B	19 _____
Income	20	Dividends - Attach Schedule B	20 _____
	21	Long-term capital gains - Attach Schedule D	21 _____
	22	Social Security benefits	22 _____
	23	Disability benefits	23 _____
	24	Workers' compensation	24 _____
	25	Total Exclusionary Income (Add lines 19 through 24)　25a _____ (X 50%)	25b _____
	26	Total Combined Income (Add lines 18 and 25b)	26 _____

Deductions	27	Moving expenses-Attach Form 3903　27 _____	
	28	Self-employed SEP and qualified retirement plans　28 _____	
	29	Alimony paid b. Recipients SSN _____　29a _____	
	30	Total deductions (Add lines 27 through 29)	30 _____
	31	Taxable Income (line 26 minus line 30)	31 _____

Tax Calculation:		Single & H of H	Married Filing Jointly	Married Filing Separate	
	32	Tax at 10% rate	$0–30,000	$0–50,000	$0–25,000	32 _____
	33	Tax at 20% rate	$30,001–120,000	$50,000–200,000	$25,001–100,000	33 _____
	34	Tax at 30% rate	$120,001+	$200,001+	$100,001+	34 _____

35a Income Tax Before Credits (Add lines 32 thru 34)　　　　　　　**35a** _____
35b Income Tax Before Credits With Indexing Added (Sch. D) 35b _____　**(35a+35b)35c** _____
NOTE: Lines 35b and 35c only apply if taxable income exceeds $300,000 (Single); $500,000 (MFJ); and $250,000 (MFS).

Income Tax	36	Income tax before credits (Amount from line 35a or 35c if applicable, page 1)	36 _____
	37	Cash donations _____ less: 1% X line 31 _____	37 _____
Payments	38	Noncash donations: _____ less: 1% X line 31 _____ Attach Form 8283.	38 _____
Eligible for	39	Home mortgage interest and points from your Forms 1098	39 _____
20% Credits	40	Home mortgage interest and points not on Forms 1098. Attach Schedule A.	40 _____
to Reduce	41	Other deductible interest. Attach Schedule A (see instructions).	41 _____
Income Tax	42	Medical and dental expenses (in excess of 10% of line 31). Attach Schedule A.	42 _____
	43	State and local taxes (in excess of 10% of line 31). Attach Schedule A.	43 _____
	44	Total payments eligible for 20% credits (Add lines 37 through 43)	44 _____
	45	Nonrefundable 20% credits (line 44 X 20%)	45 _____
Other Credits	46	Personal credits: _____ @ $500 each, age 18-64; _____ @ $1,000 each, age 65 +.	46 _____
to Reduce	47	Residential energy credits. Attach Form 5695.	47 _____
Income Tax	48	Alternative motor vehicle credit. Attach Form 8910.	48 _____
	49	Credit for child and dependent care expense x 20% (up to $1,000 1 child; $2,000 if 2+)	49 _____
	50	Other credits from: a _____ 8801; b _____ add $1,000 if Head of Household (a+b)	50 _____
	51	Foreign tax credit. Attach Form 1116	51 _____
	52	Adoption credit ($10,000 limit). Attach Form 8839.	52 _____
	53	General business credits: Attach Form 3800.	53 _____
	54	Total nonrefundable credits (lines 45–53, but not to exceed line 36)	54 _____
	55	Income tax after nonrefundable credits (line 36 minus line 54 _____)	55 _____
Other	56	Self-employment tax: 10.0% X (line 9 _____ plus lines 14, 15, 17a_____)	56 _____
Taxes	57	Unreported FICA tax from Form: a _____ 4137; b _____ 8919	57 _____
	58	Additional tax on IRA's, qualified plans. Attach Form 5329.	58 _____
	59	Household employment taxes from Schedule H.	59 _____
	60	Healthcare tax: 2.5% X (line 31, less lines 7 and 11b, less 50% of line 22)	60 _____
	61	Total tax before refundable credits (Add lines 55–60)	61 _____
Refundable	62	Child tax credits: _____ at $1,000 each (only for dependents under age 18)	62 _____
Credits	63	Uniform health insurance credit (UHIC premiums _____ X 20%)	63 _____
to Reduce	64	Earned income credit. Attach Schedule EIC.	64 _____
All Taxes	65	Higher education credit. Attach Schedule HEC.	65 _____
	66	Net premium tax credit (Form 8962). Also, Small employer ins. credit (Form 8941)	66 _____
	67	IRA savings credit—Credit IRA up to $5,000 per taxpayer (X 20%)	67 _____
	68	Total refundable credits (Add lines 62 through 67)	68 _____
	69	Total tax (refund) after refundable credits (line 61 minus line 68)	69 _____
Payments	70	Federal income tax withheld from Forms W-2 and 1099 _____ 70 _____	
	71	2020 estimated tax payments and amounts applied from 2019 return 71 _____	
	72	Amount paid with request for extension to file _____ 72 _____	
	73	Excess social security and tier 1 RRTA tax withheld _____ 73 _____	
	74	Credit for capital-gain tax paid by mutual funds _____ 74 _____	
	75	Total payments (Add lines 70 through 74)	75 _____
Refund	76	If line 75 is more than line 69, the difference is the amount overpaid	76 _____
	77	Amount of line 76 you want refunded to you.	77 _____
		If Form 8888 is attached, check here ___ Routing # _____ Account # _____	
Amount	78	Amount of line 76 you want applied to your 2021 estimated tax 78. _____	
Owed	79	Amount you owe. Subtract line 75 from line 69.	79 _____
	80	Estimated tax penalty (see instructions) _____ 80 _____	
Third-Party		Do you want to allow another person to discuss this return with the IRS? Yes ___ No ___	
Designee		If yes, Designee's name: _____ PTIN _____	

Sign	Your signature _____	Date _____
Here	Spouse's signature _____	Date _____

Paid Preparer	Print/Type Preparer's name _____	Date _____
Use Only	_____	PTIN _____
	Preparer's Signature _____	

Schedule EIC   **Earned Income Credit**

Name as shown on return _____   **Social Security Number** _____

Part 1   Filing Status and Dependents

Single or Head of household (HOH)—use Part 3 to determine credit
Married Filing Jointly (MFJ)—use Part 4 to determine credit
Married Filing Separately (MFS)—use Part 5 to determine credit
Qualifying Child (Dependent child must qualify for Child Tax Credit as shown on line 62 of Form 1040)

Part 2   Qualified Earned Income

1	Wages, salaries, etc. on line 7 of Form 1040	1 _____
2	Business income or (loss) on line 9 of Form 1040	2 _____
3	Partnership self-employment income or (loss) on line 14 of Form 1040	3 _____
4	Farm income or (loss) on line 15 or other SE income on line 17a of Form 1040	4 _____
5	Total earned income (lines 1–4)	5 _____
6	Enter lesser of line 5 or $20,000 (Single, HOH); $30,000 (MFJ); or $15,000 (MFS)	6 _____

Part 3   Earned Income Credit for Taxpayers Filing Single or Head of household

7	Multiply line 6 times 4% (.04)	7 _____
8	If you have a qualified child as described in Part 1, multiply line 6 x 9% (.09).	8 _____
9	If you have two or more qualified children as described in Part 1, enter amount on line 8.	9 _____
10	**Preliminary earned-income credit** (total of lines 7, 8, and 9)	10 _____
11	Enter amount from line 31 of Form 1040.	11 _____
	Is line 11 less than $200,000? **If yes, STOP. Enter line 10 on 1040, line 64.**	- 200,000
	If line 11 is greater than $200,000, you are subject to phase-out amounts below:	
12	Subtract $200,000 from line 11 above.	12 _____
13	Multiply line 12 x 2.0% (.02).	13 _____
14	Subtract line 13 from line 10, but not less than zero. **Enter this amount on 1040, line 64**	14 _____

Part 4   Earned Income Credit for Taxpayers Married Filing Jointly

15	Multiply line 6 times 4% (.04)	15 _____
16	If you have a qualified child as described in Part 1, multiply line 6 x 6% (.06).	16 _____
17	If you have a second qualified child as described in Part 1, enter amount on line 16	17 _____
18	If you have three or more qualified children as described in Part 1, enter amount on line 16	18 _____
19	**Preliminary earned income credit** (total of lines 15, 16, 17, and 18)	19 _____
20	Enter amount from line 31 of 1040.	20 _____
	Is line 20 less than $300,000? **If yes, STOP. Enter line 19 on 1040, line 64.**	- 300,000
	If line 20 is greater than $300,000, you are subject to phase-out amounts below:	
21	Subtract $300,000 from line 20 above.	21 _____
22	Multiply line 21 x 2.0% (.02).	22 _____
23	Subtract line 22 from line 19, but not less than zero. **Enter this amount on 1040, line 64**	23 _____

Part 5   Earned Income Credit for Taxpayers Married Filing Separately

24	Multiply line 6 times 4% (.04)	24 _____
25	If you have a qualified child as described in Part 1, multiply line 6 x 9% (.09).	25 _____
26	If you have two or more qualified children as described in Part 1, enter amount on line 25.	26 _____
27	**Preliminary earned income credit** (total of lines 24, 25, and 26)	27 _____
28	Enter amount from line 31 of Form 1040.	28 _____
	Is line 28 less than $150,000? **If yes, STOP. Enter line 27 on 1040, line 64.**	- 150,000
	If line 28 is greater than $150,000, you are subject to phase-out amounts below:	
29	Subtract $150,000 from line 28 above.	29 _____
30	Multiply line 29 x 2.0% (.02).	30 _____
31	Subtract line 30 from line 27, but not less than zero. **Enter this amount on 1040, line 64**	31 _____

NOTES

Chapter 2

1   John Bell Henneman, 1971. *Royal taxation in fourteenth century France: the development of war financing, 1322-1356.* http://alltitles.ebrary.com/Doc?id=11017675

2   Jay Starkman, *The Sex of a Hippopotamus, a Unique History of Taxes and Accounting* (Atlanta: Twinset Inc., 2008), 116.

3   Ibid., 117

4   Ibid., 151-152

5   Ibid., 155

6   Ibid., 156–157

7   Ibid., 159

8   Roy G. Blakey and Gladys C. Blakey, *The Federal Income Tax*, (The Law Book Exchange, Ltd. Clark, New Jersey 2006). 68

9   Jay Starkman, *The Sex of a Hippopotamus, a Unique History of Taxes and Accounting* (Atlanta: Twinset Inc., 2008), 161

10 Randolph E. Paul, *Taxation for Prosperity* (Indianapolis: the Bobbs-Merrill Company, 1947), 22.

11 Bascom N. Timmons, *Garner of Texas–A Personal History* (New York: Harper & Brothers, 1948), 85.

12 Jay Starkman, *The Sex of a Hippopotamus, a Unique History of Taxes and Accounting* (Atlanta: Twinset Inc., 2008), 164-165.

13 Ibid., 164.

14 Ibid., 164.

15 Richard J. Caroll, *The President as Economist: Scoring Economic Performance from Harry Truman to Barack Obama* (Santa Barbara, CA, ABC-CLIO, LLC 2012), 136

16 Allen J. Matuso, *Nixon's Economy: Booms, Busts Dollars and Votes*, (University Press of Kansas, USA 1998), 165

17 John L. Palmer and Isabel Sawhill, *The Reagan Experiment, An Examination of Economic and Social Policies Under the Reagan Administration* (The Urban Institute, Washington, DC 1982), 109

18 Richard Worth, *Social Security Act*, (Marshall Cavendish Corporation, Tarrytown, NY 2011), 32

19 *Social Security in the 21st Century*, edited by Eric R. Kingston, James H. Schulz, (Oxford University Press, New York 1997), 28

20 Martin L. Gross, *National Suicide: How Washington is Destroying the American Dream from A to Z* (Berkley Books, New York 2009)

21 James Pratt and William Kulsrud, *Individual Taxation 2013* (South-Western Cengage Learning, New York 2013) 1-19

22 Budget of the United States Government for Fiscal Years 2009 and 2014.

Chapter 4

1   Michael J. Graetz, *100 Million Unnecessary Returns* (New Haven, CT; Yale University Press, 2008), 65–66.

2   Ibid., 66.

3   *The Economist*, November 19, 2009, 75.

4   *OECD Consumption Tax Trends 2014: VAT/GST and excise rates, trends and policy issues* (Paris: OECD Publishing).

5   Martin A. Sullivan, *Corporate Tax Reform* (New York: Apress, 2011), 129.

6   Ibid., 133.

7   Ibid., 135.

8   Ibid.

9   Bruce Bartlett, *The Benefit and the Burden* (New York: Simon & Schuster, 2012), 179.

10 Jay Starkman, *The Sex of a Hippopotamus, a Unique History of Taxes and Accounting* (Atlanta: Twinset Inc., 2008), 165.

11 Ibid., 395.

12 Ibid., 165.

13 Ibid.

14 *The Moment of Truth: Report of the National Commission on Fiscal Responsibility and Reform*, co-chaired by former Sen. Alan Simpson and former White House Chief of Staff Erskine Bowles (December 2010), 28.

15 Ibid.

16 Ibid.

17 Ibid., 29.

18 Ibid., 30.

19 Ibid., 31.

20 The Debt Reduction Task Force, former Senator Pete Domenici and Dr. Alice Rivlin, Co-Chairs; "*Restoring America's Future*, Bipartisan Policy Center (November 2010) Appendix A: 126.

21 Ibid.

22 Ibid., 127.

23 *Domenici-Rivlin Debt Reduction Task Force Plan 2.0*, former Senator Pete Domenici and Dr. Alice Rivlin, Co-chairs; Bipartisan Policy Center, 2012), 7–8.

Chapter 5

1 *2014 U.S. Master Tax Guide* (Chicago: CCH, 2013), 30.

2 Ibid., 495–503.

3 Ibid., 503.

4 Ibid., 503–507.

5 See further discussion in chapter 5.4 about the earned-income credit and the child tax credit.

6 *The Moment of Truth: Report of the National Commission on Fiscal Responsibility and Reform*, Alan Simpson and Erskine Bowles, Co-Chairs (December 2010), 31.

7 Randolph E. Paul, *Taxation for Prosperity* (Indianapolis: the Bobbs-Merrill Company, 1947), 301.

8 Jay Starkman, *The Sex of a Hippopotamus*, a Unique History of Taxes and Accounting (Atlanta: Twinset Inc., 2008), 394.

9 IRS Publication 17, pg. 12.

10 Jennifer DePaul, *The Bond Buyer, CRS: Tax Expenditures Too Popular to Easily Cut* (March 28, 2012), 3.

11 Report of the 1979 Advisory Council on Social Security, Committee on Ways and Means Print No. WMCP 96-45, P. 75, January 02, 1980.

12 Theodore J. Sarenski, CPA, "Strategies for the Social Security Safety Net," *The Tax Adviser*, December 2011.

13 Leonard E. Burman and Joel Slemrod, *Taxes in America* (New York: Oxford University Press, 2013), 153.

14 Julie Appleby, "Big Changes Ahead for Those Who Buy Their Own Insurance," *Kaiser Health News* (June 28, 2013).

15 *2014 U.S. Master Tax Guide* (Chicago: CCH, 2013), 393.

16 Ibid., 607.

17 Ibid.

18 *Estimates of Federal Tax Expenditures For Fiscal Years 2010–2014*, Joint Committee on Taxation (December 15, 2010).

19 *Estimates of Federal Tax Expenditures For Fiscal Years 2005–2009*, Joint Committee on Taxation (January 12, 2005).

20 *The Moment of Truth: Report of the National Commission on Fiscal Responsibility and Reform* (December 2010), 31.

21 The Debt Reduction Task Force, Senator Pete Domenici and Dr. Alice Rivlin, Co-Chairs; "*Restoring America's Future*, Bipartisan Policy Center, pg. 37.

22 Section 415(c) of the Internal Revenue Code, *U.S. Master Tax Guide 2014* (Chicago: CCH, 2013), 702.

23 Ibid., 282.

24 Ibid.

25 Randolph E. Paul, *Taxation for Prosperity* (Indianapolis: the Bobbs-Merrill Company, 1947), 305.

26 Ibid.

27 Ibid., 305–306.

28 Ibid., 306.

29 Ibid., 304.

30 Ibid., 307.

31 Code Section 263(c), *2014 U.S. Master Tax Guide*, 383.

32 Martin A. Sullivan, *Corporate Tax Reform* (New York: Apress, 2011), 70.

33 Ibid.

34 Internal Revenue Code Sec. 1222 (3).

35 Bruce Bartlett, *The Benefit and the Burden*, (New York: Simon & Schuster 2012), 133.

36 Ibid., 134.

37 Ibid.

38 Ibid., 135.

39 Ibid.

40 Ibid.

41 *Present Law and Background Information Related to the Taxation of Capital Gains: Prepared by the Staff of the Joint Budget Committee on Taxation* (September 14, 2012), 19–23.

42 Tax Foundation Special Report, Arthur P. Hall, *50 Years of the Federal Capital Gains Tax Burden* (March 1995 #45), 7.

43 Ibid.

44 Cato Institute Policy Analysis No. 242: *The ABC's of the Capital Gains Tax*, Stephen Moore & John Silvia (October 4, 1995).

45 Ibid.

46 Alan S. Blinder, "The Level and Distribution of Economic Well-Being," in *The American Economy in Transition*, ed. Martin Feldstein (Chicago: University of Chicago Press, 1980), 48.

47 Cato Institute Policy Analysis No. 242: *The ABC's of the Capital Gains Tax*, Stephen Moore & John Silvia (October 4, 1995), Statement before the Republican member of the Joint Economic Committee (June 22, 1993), 24.

48 Ibid., 3.

49 Ibid.

50 The Debt Reduction Task Force, Senator Pete Domenici and Dr. Alice Rivlin, Co-Chairs; "*Restoring America's Future*, Bipartisan Policy Center, pg. 30.

51 Randolph E. Paul, *Taxation for Prosperity* (Indianapolis, The Bobbs-Merrill Company, 1947), 272.

52 OECD, Table II.4, *Overall 2011 statutory tax rates on dividend income and computations by Ernst & Young LLP*, pg. 10.

53 Ernst & Young LLP, *The 2011 Global Executive, 2011 and computations by Ernst & Young LLP*, pg. 13.

54 Extrapolated from Budget of the United States Government, Fiscal Year 2012, Historical Tables: table 17.3; http://wwwwhitehouse.gov/omb/budget/historicals.

55 IRS Statistics of Income, Individual Income Tax Returns (2009), table 1.

56 Martin R. Sullivan, *Corporate Tax Reform* (New York: Apress, 2011), 33.

57 Code Section 1(h)(11), *2014 U.S. Master Tax Guide* (Chicago: CCH, 2013), 289.

58 Tax Report, "Carried Interest in the Cross Hairs," *Wall Street Journal*, August 6, 2011, editorial page.

59 Joshua Green, "The MBA Candidate Meets the Mad-As-Hell Electorate," *Bloomberg Businessweek*, January 25, 2012, 18.

60 Ibid.

61 Richard Rubin, "Carried Interest Tax Increase Measure Introduced by Levin," *Bloomberg Businessweek*, February 16, 2012.

62 "Carried Interest: A Very Big Wolf in Sheep's Clothing," *Huff Post* Business, September 20, 2011.

63 Ibid.

64 Suzanne Luttman and Roxanne Spindle, "An evaluation of the revenue and equity effects of converting exemptions and itemized deductions to a single nonrefundable credit," *Journal of the American Taxation Association* 16.2, Fall 1994, 43.

65 Ibid.

66 Ibid.

67 Jeffrey H. Birnbaum and Alan S. Murray, *Showdown at Gucci Gulch* (New York: Vintage Books, a Division of Random House, 1988), 6.

68 Suzanne Luttman and Roxanne Spindle, "An evaluation of the revenue and equity effects of converting exemptions and itemized deductions to a single nonrefundable credit," *Journal of the American Taxation Association* 16.2, Fall 1994, 43.

69 Ibid.

70 Ibid., 43, Canadian Department of Finance (1986).

71 Alan Simpson and Erskine Bowles, cochairs, *The Moment of Truth: Report of the National Commission on Fiscal Responsibility and Reform* (December 2010), 31.

72 Debt Reduction Task Force, Senator Pete Domenici and Dr. Alice Rivlin, Co-Chairs, *Restoring America's Future* (November 2010), 33–34.

73 Alan Simpson and Erskine Bowles, cochairs, *The Moment of Truth: Report of the National Commission on Fiscal Responsibility and Reform* (December 2010), 31.

74 Statistics of Income—2012, Individual Income Tax Returns, IRS Pub. 1304 (Rev. 08-2014), table 1.2, pg. 30.

75 Ibid.

76 Ibid.

77 Ibid.

78 From table 1 of the *Distribution of Major Tax Expenditures in the Individual Income Tax System*, Congressional Budget Office (May 2013), 6.

79 Roger Colinvoux, Brian Galle, Eugene Steuerle, *Evaluating the Charitable Deductions and Proposed Reforms*, Urban Institute and Tax Policy Center (June 2012), 12.

80 Rob Reich and Christopher Wimer, Stanford University, *Charitable Giving and the Great Recession* (October 2012), pg. 2, figure 2.

81 Ibid.

82 Ibid.

83 Constance J. Crawford and Corine L. Crawford, "The Inequity in the Current Tax System: Does the Alternative Minimum Tax Create Additional Problems in the System?" *Journal of Business & Economics Research*, February 2007, 10.

84 Leonard E. Burman, William G. Gale, and Jeffrey Rohaly, "Policy Watch, The Expanding Reach of the Individual Alternative Minimum Tax," *Journal of Economic Perspectives* 17, no. 2, (Spring 2003): 180.

85 Leonard E. Burman and Joel Slemrod, *Taxes in America* (New York: Oxford Univ. Press, 2013), 42–43.

86 Ibid., 42.

87 Ibid., 43.

88 Constance J. Crawford and Corine L. Crawford, "The Inequity in the Current Tax System: Does the Alternative Minimum Tax Create Additional Problems in the System?" *Journal of Business & Economics Research*, February 2007, 10.

89 Urban-Brookings Tax Policy Center, table T12-0168, Aggregate AMT Projections and Recent History, 1970–2022.

90 Ibid.

91 Derived from table 1 of *The Distribution of Major Tax Expenditures in the Individual Income Tax System*, Congressional Budget Office, May 2013, pg. 6.

92 Leonard E. Burman, William G. Gale, and Jeffrey Rohaly, "Policy Watch, The Expanding Reach of the Individual Alternative Minimum Tax," *Journal of Economic Perspectives* 17, no. 2 (Spring 2003): 184.

93 Joel Slemrod and Jon Bakija, *Taxing Ourselves*, fourth edition (Cambridge, MA: the MIT Press, 2008), 173.

94 *Individual Income Tax Returns 2010, Publication 1304 (Rev. 08-2012)*, Department of the Treasury, Internal Revenue Service, 25.

95 Thomas Piketty and Emmanuel Saez, *How Progressive Is the U.S. Federal Tax System? A Historical and International Perspective*, Working Paper 12404 National Bureau of Economic Research, Cambridge, MA (July 2006), 5.

96 *Individual Income Tax Returns 2011, Publication 1304 (Rev. 08-2013)*, Department of the Treasury, Internal Revenue Service, 24.

97 Ibid.

98 Piketty and Saez, *How Progressive Is the U.S. Federal Tax System? A Historical and International Perspective*, 3.

99 Bruce Bartlett, *The Benefit and the Burden* (New York: Simon & Schuster, 2012), 5.

100 Piketty and Saez, *How Progressive Is the U.S. Federal Tax System? A Historical and International Perspective*, table 2 with Average Income (2) added from table 1, 25–26.

101 Emily Y. Lin and Patricia K. Tong, "Marriage and Taxes: What Can We Learn from Tax Returns Filed by Cohabiting Couples?" *National Tax Journal*, 65(4), December 2012, 815.

102 Ibid., 816.

103 Lily L. Batchelder, Fred T. Goldberg, Jr. and Peter R. Orszag, "Efficiency and Tax Incentives: The Case for Refundable Tax Credits," *Stanford Law Review* 59, no. 1 (2006): 35.

104 Congressional Budget Office (CBO) Refundable Tax Credits (January 2013) Appendix table A-1.

105 IRC. Sec. 24(d)(1)(1998).

106 Congressional Budget Office (CBO) Refundable Tax Credits (January 2013), 7.

107 Ibid., table 2, pg. 10.

108 Lily L. Batchelder, Fred T. Goldberg, Jr. and Peter R. Orszag, "Efficiency and Tax Incentives: The Case for Refundable Tax Credits," *Stanford Law Review* 59, no. 1 (2006): 27.

109 Ibid., 57.

110 Ibid., 47.

111 Congressional Budget Office (CBO) Refundable Tax Credits (January 2013), 46.

112 *2014 U.S. Master Tax Guide* (Chicago, CCH, 2013), 497–498.

113 Ibid., 497.

114 Ibid., 420.

115 American Institute of Certified Public Accountants, Written Testimony for the Record, Senate Finance Committee Hearing on Education Tax Incentives and Tax Reform (July 25, 2012), pg. 1.

116 Congressional Budget Office (CBO) Refundable Tax Credits (January 2013), Appendix table A-1.

117 Ibid.

118 Jason Furman, *Center on Budget and Policy Priorities: Tax Reform and Poverty* (April 10, 2006), 1.

119 Ibid.

120 Bartlett, *The Benefit and the Burden*, 91.

121 Ibid., 90.

122 Jason Furman, *Center on Budget and Policy Priorities: Tax Reform and Poverty* (April 10, 2006), 2.

123 Congressional Budget Office (CBO) Refundable Tax Credits (January 2013), figure 3, pg. 8.

124 Slemrod and Bakija, *Taxing Ourselves*, 44.

125 *2014 U.S. Master Tax Guide*, 503–505.

126 Ibid., 504.

127 Ibid.

128 Bartlett, *The Benefit and the Burden*, 91.

129 Steven Goldsmith, Spotlight on Poverty and Opportunity, "Reform the EIC to better Serve our Nation's Low Income Workers," (November 2012), 1.

130 Internal Revenue Service, Issue Number: IR-2013-9 (January 25, 2013), "On EIC Awareness Day," 2.

131 Report of the President's Advisory Panel on Federal Tax Reform (November 2005), 228.

132 The Debt Reduction Task Force, Senator Pete Domenici and Dr. Alice Rivlin, Co-Chairs; "*Restoring America's Future*, Bipartisan Policy Center (November 2010), 35.

133 Ibid., 35.

134 Ibid., 43.

135 Domenici-Rivlin Debt Reduction Task Force Plan 2.0, Senator Pete Domenici and Dr. Alice Rivlin, Bi-Partisan Policy Center (2012), 7.

136 Alan Simpson and Erskine Bowles, cochairs, *The Moment of Truth: Report of the National Commission on Fiscal Responsibility and Reform* (December 2010), 31.

137 A refundable tax credit allows one to receive the tax reduction even if the taxpayer does not have an income-tax liability.

138 *2014 U.S. Master Tax Guide* (Chicago: CCH, 2013), 500.

139 Ibid.

140 Ibid.

141 Ibid., 500–501.

Chapter 6

1 Sec. 3(3) of the Congressional Budget and Impoundment Control Act of 1974, P.L. 93-344 (codified at 2 U.S.C. §622(3) (2006).

2 Derived from table 1 of The Distribution of Major Tax Expenditures in the Individual Income Tax System, Congressional Budget Office (May 2013), 6.

3 The Distribution of Major Tax Expenditures in the Individual Income Tax System, Congressional Budget Office (May 2013), 4.

4 Jonathan Gruber, *The Tax Exclusion for Employer-Sponsored Health Insurance*, Working Paper 15766 National Bureau of Economic Research, Cambridge, MA (February 2010).

5 The Distribution of Major Tax Expenditures in the Individual Income Tax System, Congressional Budget Office (May 2013), 15.

6 (Left blank for sentence deletion)

7 Bruce Bartlett, *The Benefit and the Burden* (New York: Simon and Schuster, 2012), 93.

8 *2014 U.S. Master Tax Guide* (Chicago: CCH, 2013), 718.

9 Internal Revenue Code, Section 415(b) (2) (A) as amended in 2001.

10 *2014 U.S. Master Tax Guide*, 719.

11 Ibid., 740.

12 Ibid., 702.

13 Ibid., 702.

14 *The RIA Complete Analysis of the '81 Economic Recovery Tax Act* (New York: the Research Institute of America, 1981), 180.

15 Ibid.

16 *2014 U.S. Master Tax Guide*, 725–726.

17 Ibid., 726.

18 Victoria L. Bryant and Jon Gober, "Accumulation and Distribution of Individual Retirement Arrangements, 2010," *Statistics of Income Bulletin*, Fall 2013, Washington, DC, 6.

19 Ibid., 5.

20 *2014 U.S. Master Tax Guide*, 730.

21 "The Impact of Repealing State and Local Tax Deductability," Kim Rueben, Tax Analysts Special Report (August 15, 2005), 498.

22 Ibid.

23 Jeffrey H. Birnbaum and Alan S. Murray, *Showdown at Gucci Gulch* (New York: Vintage Books, a Division of Random House, 1988), 202.

24 The Committee for a Responsible Federal Budget, *The Tax Break-Down: The State and Local Tax Deduction* (August 20, 2013), 5.

25 The Debt Reduction Task Force, former Senator Pete Domenici and Dr. Alice Rivlin, Co-chairs; *"Restoring America's Future*, Bipartisan Policy Center (November 2010) Appendix A: 126.

26 *A Bipartisan Path Forward to Securing America's Future, Moment of Truth Project*, co-chaired by Erskine Bowles and former Senator Alan Simpson (April 2013), 34.

27 From table 1 of the Distribution of Major Tax Expenditures in the Individual Income Tax System, Congressional Budget Office (May 2013), 4.

28 Leonard E. Burman and Joel Slemrod, *Taxes in America* (New York: Oxford Univ. Press, 2013), 42–43.

29 The Committee for a Responsible Federal Budget, T*he Tax Break-Down: The State and Local Tax Deduction* (August 20, 2013), 1.

30 Ibid., 2.

31 "The Impact of Repealing State and Local Tax Deductability," Kim Rueben, Tax Analysts Special Report (August 15, 2005), 501.

32 *Tax Foundation* report cited in 24/7Wallst.com, pg. 1.

33 Ibid., 2–8.

34 *The Distribution of Major Tax Expenditures in the Individual Income Tax System*, Congressional Budget Office (May 2013), 4.

35 Urban-Brookings Tax Policy Center, table T12-0168, Aggregate AMT Projections and Recent History, 1970–2022.

36 *The RIA Complete Analysis of the Revenue Act and Pension Protection Act of 1987* (New York: the Research Institute of America, Inc., 1987), 1.

37 Ibid.

38 Ibid., 3.

39 Bruce Katz, "Cut to Invest, Reform the Mortgage Interest Deduction to Invest in Innovation and Advanced Industries," Brookings (November, 2012), 2.

40 "Setting the Record Straight on the Mortgage Interest Deduction," NAHB (July 25, 2013), 1–2.

41 Stephen J. Entin and Michael Schuyler, PhD, "Fiscal Fact, Case Study #1: Mortgage Interest Deduction for Owner-Occupied Housing," Tax Foundation (July 29, 2013), 1.

42 "Setting the Record Straight on the Mortgage Interest Deduction," NAHB (July 25, 2013), 1.

43 Bruce Katz, "Cut to Invest," 2.

44 Ibid.

45 *The RIA Complete Analysis of the '86 Tax Reform Act*, 2nd printing (New York: the Research Institute of America, 1986, 1.

46 Ibid., 2.

47 Ibid., 3.

48 Bruce Katz, "Cut to Invest," 2.

49 "Estimates of Federal Tax Expenditures for Fiscal Years 2010–2014," http://www.jct.gov/publications.html?func=startdown&id=3718.

50 Testimony of Dr. Robert Dietz, on Behalf of the National Association of Homebuilders, Before the United States Senate Committee on Finance, *Hearing on Tax Reform Options: Incentives for Homeownership* (October 6, 2011), 8.

51 "Setting the Record Straight on the Mortgage Interest Deduction," NAHB (July 25, 2013), 2.

52 Alan Simpson and Erskine Bowles, cochairs, *The Moment of Truth: Report of the National Commission on Fiscal Responsibility and Reform* (December 2010), 31.

53 Domenici-Rivlin *Debt Reduction Task Force Plan 2.0*, former Senator Pete Domenici and Dr. Alice Rivlin, Co-chairs; Bipartisan Policy Center (2012), 7–8.

54 Home Equity Loans, Car Sales Shrink: Mac Gordon, copyright Wards Auto, a division of Penton (republished under license) (December 2008), 35.

55 *Options to Improve Tax Compliance and Reform Tax Expenditures*, prepared by the Staff of the Joint Committee on Taxation (January 27, 2005), 53.

56 Ibid., 425.

57 "Setting the Record Straight on the Mortgage Interest Deduction," NAHB (July 25, 2013), 2.

58 *Estimates of Federal Tax Expenditures for Fiscal Years 2012–2017*, prepared for the House Committee on Ways and Means and the Senate Committee on Finance by the Staff of the Joint Committee on Taxation (February 1, 2013), 47.

59 Professor Ellen P. Aprill, Loyola Law School L.A., Legal Studies Paper No. 2006-13 (2001), *Churches, Politics, and the Charitable Contribution Deduction*, 849.

60 War Revenue Act of 1917, chapter 63, Sec. 1201(2) (1917), 330.

61 Roger Colinvaux, Brian Galle, and Eugene Steuerle, *Evaluating the Charitable Deduction and Proposed Reforms*, Urban Institute Tax Policy and Charities (June 2012), 5.

62 Ibid.

63 Ibid., 6.

64 Joint Committee on Taxation, *Estimates of Federal Tax Expenditures for Fiscal Years 2010–2014*, December 15, 2010.

65 Alan Simpson and Erskine Bowles, cochairs, *The Moment of Truth: Report of the National Commission on Fiscal Responsibility and Reform* (December 2010), 31.

66 Ibid.

67 Domenici-Rivlin Debt Reduction Task Force Plan 2.0, 7–8.

68 Joseph J. Cordes, "Re-Thinking the Deduction for Charitable Contributions: Evaluating the Effects of Deficit-Reduction Proposals," *National Tax Journal*, December 2011, 1011.

69 Rob Reich and Christopher Wimer, Stanford University, *Charitable Giving and the Great Recession* (October 2012), pg. 2, figure 2.

70 *Report of the President's Advisory Panel on Federal Tax Reform* (November 2005), 228.

71 The Debt Reduction Task Force, Senator Pete Domenici and Dr. Alice Rivlin, Co-Chairs; "Restoring America's Future," Bi-Partisan Policy Center, 35.

72 Revenue Act of 1921, Publication L. No. 67-98, Sec. 202, 42 Stat. 227-229/

73 Hearings on President's 1963 Tax Message before the House Committee on Ways and Means, 88th Congress, 1st Sess. 24 (1963) as cited by Marvin E. Blum, Notes, Carryover Basis: The Case for Repeal; 57 Texas L. Review 204, 1978–1979.

74 I.R.C. Section 1023 (a)(1) as legislated by the Tax Reform Act of 1976.

75 H.R. Rep. No. 1380, 94th Congress, 2nd Session 36–37 (1976), pg. 3390–91 as cited by Marvin E. Blum (see note 78).

76 Ibid., 3391.

77 Ibid.

78 Marvin E. Blum, Notes, "Carryover Basis: The Case for Repeal," 57 *Texas L. Review*, 204, 1978–1979, 206.

79 *2001 Tax Legislation: Law, Explanation and Analysis; Economic Growth and Tax Relief Reconciliation Act of 2001* (Chicago: CCH Incorporated, 2001), 116.

80 Ibid., 117.

81 Michael Graetz, from page 6 of an essay adapted and updated from the Lloyd Leva Plaine Distinguished Lecture, delivered at the University of Miami's Heckerling Estate Planning Institute on January 11, 2011 and from *Death by a Thousand Cuts: The Fight Over Taxing Inherited Wealth* (Princeton, NJ: Princeton University Press, 2005), co-authored with Ian Shapiro.

82 Ibid., 6.

83 Derived from table 1 of *The Distribution of Major Tax Expenditures in the Individual Income Tax System*, Congressional Budget Office (May 2013), 6.

84 Moment of Truth Project, Co-Chaired by Senator Alan Simpson and Erskine Bowles, *A Bipartisan Path Forward to Securing America's Future* (April 2013), 34.

85 Jay Starkman, *The Sex of a Hippopotamus, a Unique History of Taxes and Accounting* (Atlanta: Twinset Inc., 2008), 156–157.

86 Ibid., 157.

87 *South Carolina v. Baker*, 485 US 505 (1988) as cited in Jay Starkman's book (pgs. 161 and 394).

88 *Pollock v. Farmers' Loan & Trust Co.*, 157 U.S. 249 (Argued March 1895) as cited in Jay Starkman's book (pgs. 156 and 352).

89 Jeffrey H. Birnbaum and Alan S. Murray, *Showdown at Gucci Gulch* (New York: Vintage Books, 1988), 53–54.

90 Ibid.

91 Ibid., 53.

92 Randolph E. Paul, *Taxation for Prosperity* (Indianapolis: the Bobbs-Merrill Company, 1947), 350.

93 Martin A. Sullivan, *Corporate Tax Reform* (New York: Apress, 2011), 138.

94 Jennifer DePaul, "CRS: Tax Expenditures Too Popular to Easily Cut," The Bond Buyer (March 28, 2012), 3.

95 Ibid.

96 Statement of Alan Greenspan, Chairman, Board of Governors of the Federal Reserve System, before the Special Committee on Aging, United States Senate (March 27, 2000), 8.

97 Code Sec. 105(a), *2014 U.S. Master Tax Guide*, 752.

98 Social Security Online Trust Fund Data, Office of the Chief Actuary, Social Security and Medicare Tax Rates (2011), 1.

99 Ibid., 1–2.

100 Ibid., 1.

101 The 1965 Amendments established under Title XVIII of the Social Security Act.

102 Internal Revenue Code Section 3101(b)(2); Prop. Reg. 31.3102-4? From *U.S. Master Tax Guide*, 2014, 97th Edition, 868.

103 2014 U.S. Master Tax Guide, 125.

104 Ibid.

105 Social Security Online Trust Fund Data, Office of the Chief Actuary, Social Security and Medicare Tax Rates (2011), 2.

Chapter 7

1   Data based on Table II.1–Corporate income tax rates: basic/non-targeted from OECD Tax Database, accessed February 2014, http://www.oecd.org/tax/tax-policy/tax-database.htm#C_CorporateCaptial.

2   Martin A. Sullivan, *Corporate Tax Reform* (New York: Apress, 2011), 22.

3   Ibid.

4   Ibid.

5   Economic Survey of the United States, Organisation for Economic Co-operation and Development (OECD), June 2, 2014, 13–14.

6   Ibid.

7   Ibid.

8   Kyle Pommerleau and Andrew Lundeen, "2014 International Tax Competitiveness Index," Tax Foundation, 2.

9   Ibid.

10 "U.S. Corporations Pay 35%," cited Tax Foundation, *Wall Street Journal*, editorial page, October 26, 2013.

11   Data based on Table II.1–Corporate income tax rates: basic/non-targeted from OECD Tax Database, accessed February 2014, http://www.oecd.org/tax/tax-policy/tax-database.htm#C_CorporateCaptial.

12   "U.S. Corporations Pay 35%," *Wall Street Journal* editorial page, October 26, 2013.

13   Ibid.

14   Sullivan, *Corporate Tax Reform*, 83–84.

15   Table 7.1-2 was compiled from Title III and IV of Discussion Draft of the House Ways and Means Committee for the Tax Reform Act of 2014.

16   Fix The Debt, The Tax Reform Act of 2014 Discussion Draft, Overview of the Draft (April 2014), 2.

17   Tax Reform Act of 2014 Discussion Draft, House Ways and Means Committee (February 2014), 144.

18   Fix The Debt, The Tax Reform Act of 2014 Discussion Draft, Overview of the Draft (April 2014), 3.

19   2011 Statistic of Income, Corporation Income Tax Returns, Department of the Treasury, Internal Revenue Service, Commissioner John A. Koskinen (June 2014), 35 and 200.

20   Ibid., 87.

21   James M. Bickley, "The Federal Excise Tax on Gasoline and the Highway Trust Fund: A Short History," Congressional Research Service (September 7, 2012), 1–3.

22   Ibid., 3–5.

23   Ibid., 5–6.

24   Ibid., 7.

Chapter 8

1   The Debt Reduction Task Force, former Senator Pete Domenici and Dr. Alice Rivlin, Co-chairs, "*Restoring America's Future*, Bi-Partisan Policy Center (November 2010), 41.

2   Ibid.

Chapter 10

1   Randolph E. Paul, *Taxation for Prosperity* (Indianapolis: the Bobbs-Merrill Company, 1947), 272.

GLOSSARY OF TERMS

401(k) Plan

401(k) plans are the most common of all tax-advantaged retirement plans. They allow an employee the option of receiving a certain amount of his or her compensation in cash that is taxable or having it contributed pre-tax to his/her retirement plan. These plans are classified as one of many defined contribution plans that by law provide each participant an individual account but no guaranteed amount of benefits. An employee's deferrals to all 401(k) plans are subject to annual limits. Employers often match their employees' contributions with as much as a 100% matching contribution.

403(b) Plan

A retirement plan offered by public schools and certain tax-exempt organizations. An individual's 403(b) annuity can be obtained only under an employer's tax-sheltered annuity plan. Generally, these annuities are funded by elective deferrals made under salary reduction agreements and non-elective employer contributions.

457 Plan

A qualified, deferred compensation plan established by state and local governments and tax-exempt governments and tax-exempt employers. Eligible employees are allowed to make salary deferral contributions to the 457 plan. Earnings grow on a tax-deferred basis and contributions are not taxed until the assets are distributed from the plan.

Accelerated Depreciation

One of several methods by which a company, for financial accounting or tax purposes, depreciates a fixed asset in such a way that the amount of depreciation taken is higher during the earlier years of an asset's life.

Acquisition Indebtedness

A financial obligation incurred through the construction, improvement, or purchase of a primary or secondary residence. A home mortgage is an example of an acquisition debt. The Internal Revenue Code provides certain tax advantages for *home acquisition debt*. Taxpayers can deduct the interest paid for mortgages that qualify as home acquisition debt.

Additional Child Tax Credit

A refundable credit for taxpayers with three or more qualified children who cannot claim the full nonrefundable child tax credit, because it exceeds their total tax liability. This credit allows the unclaimed amount of the child tax credit to be refundable if the taxpayer meets the requirements.

Adjusted Gross Income (AGI)

The amount of income that is subject to taxation after any above-the-line deductions. The taxpayer then subtracts any personal exemptions and the standard or itemized deductions from the AGI amount to arrive at the amount of taxable income.

Adoption Credit

A tax credit for taxpayers that incur qualifying expenses related to the adoption of a child. Qualifying expenses include adoption fees, court costs, attorney fees, etc. The credit has varied from being a refundable or nonrefundable credit, depending on the year.

Affordable Care Act (ACA)

A federal statute signed into law in March 2010 as a part of the healthcare reform agenda of the Obama administration. Signed under the title of The Patient Protection and Affordable Care Act, the law included multiple provisions that would take effect over a matter of years, including the expansion of Medicaid eligibility, the establishment of health-insurance exchanges, and prohibiting health insurers from denying coverage due to pre-existing conditions.

Alternative Minimum Tax (AMT)
Income tax imposed on individuals, corporations, estates and trusts at a nearly flat rate on an adjusted amount of taxable income, determined by adding and subtracting certain adjustments and preferences to regular taxable income. Originally enacted in 1969, it was intended to limit tax shelters of wealthy taxpayers. It has been modified several times, most significantly by the 1986 Tax Reform Act.

American Taxpayer Relief Act of 2012 (ATRA)
This act was passed by Congress on January 1, 2013. It prevented many of the tax increases that were scheduled to go into effect in 2013. At the same time, it raised the highest tax rate to 39.6% and lowered deductions for many high-income individuals.

Amortization
The deduction for cost or basis of an intangible asset over the asset's useful life. Examples of amortizable intangibles include patents, copyrights, or leasehold interests. Amortization also is the paying off of debt, such as a mortgage, with a fixed repayment schedule in regular installments over a period of time.

AMT Credit
A credit to be applied against future AMT owed. AMT is obtained by two types of adjustments and preferences—deferral and exclusion items. The credit applies only to the deferral items.

AMT Patch
Because the alternative minimum tax (AMT) is not automatically updated for inflation, and more middle-class taxpayers were getting hit

with the AMT each year, Congress passes an annual "patch" to address this problem.

Average Effective Tax Rate
The actual rate at which a taxpayer pays taxes on income accounting for all taxes and offsets. The rate is calculated by dividing the total of all taxes paid, less offsets, by the total taxable income.

Base Erosion and Profit Shifting (BEPS)
Tax planning strategies that exploit gaps and mismatches in tax rules to make profits disappear for tax purposes or to shift profits to locations where there is little or no real activity but the foreign taxes are low, resulting in little or no overall corporate tax being paid.

Border-Tax Adjustment
A tariff-like penalty on imported goods that excludes exported goods in order to encourage exports while maintaining competitiveness among domestically produced goods. Many view border-tax adjustments as subsidies for exports.

Bracket Creep
A situation where inflation pushes income into higher tax brackets. The result is an increase in income taxes but no increase in real purchasing power.

Broaden the Tax Base
Generally, it means to tax more income. This is generally achieved by eliminating or minimizing deductions, exclusions, and credits while often lowering the rates at which the income is taxed.

Bush Tax Cuts
A series of temporary income tax relief measures enacted under President George W. Bush in 2001 and 2003. The tax cuts lowered federal income tax rates for everyone, decreased the marriage penalty, lowered capital gains tax rates, lowered the tax rate on dividend income, increased the

child tax credit from $500 to $1,000 per child, eliminated the phase-out on personal exemptions for higher-income taxpayers, eliminated the phase-out on itemized deductions, and for one year eliminated the estate tax.

Business Accounts Receivable
Money owed to a business and shown as a current asset on a company's balance sheet.

Cadillac Insurance Plans
The term *Cadillac plan* dates back to the 1970s and resurfaced during the health reform debates of the 1990s, before finally gaining new focus as part of the Obama administration's recent efforts to cut health costs. Named for the signature American luxury car, Cadillac or "gold-plated" health plans have the highest premiums and typically offer the most generous level of benefits. These plans may also have less restrictions or wider provider networks and wide menus of covered health services to choose from. Beginning in 2018, Obamacare heavily taxes Cadillac plans.

Cafeteria Plans
As opposed to a traditional, one-size-fits-all plan, a cafeteria plan allows employees to choose from various different types of benefits to create a customized plan of benefits, pursuant to Section 125 of the tax code.

Capital Asset
Generally, it includes property not held for sale in the normal course of business. Capital assets can include most assets but generally does not include inventory of supplies or property held for sale.

Capital Gains and Losses
The amount that a capital asset's value increases or decreases from the original purchase price, and which is recognized for tax purposes upon sale of such asset.

Carried Interest

Carried interest, also known as a "profits interest," is generally a right to receive a percentage of profits or gains from a partnership or LLC without any obligation to contribute capital to the entity. It is often awarded to the general partner, managing member, investment manager, or other service provider of the partnership or LLC.

Carryover Basis

Carryover basis occurs when a property transfer also results in a transfer of the transferor's basis in the property. The transferor's basis in the property "carries over" to the transferee.

Charitable Deductions

Allows taxpayers to deduct their contributions to qualifying charities of cash and property within certain limitations. These deductions must be reported on Schedule A of the 1040.

Charitable Remainder Annuity Trust (CRAT)

Allows a donor to place a major gift of cash or property into a trust. The trust then pays a fixed amount of income each year to the donor or the donor's specified beneficiary. When the donor dies, the remainder of the trust is transferred to the charity.

Charitable Remainder Unitrust (CRUT)

A charitable remainder unitrust is a trust from which a *fixed percentage* (which is not less than 5 percent) of the net fair market value of its assets, *valued annually,* is to be paid, not less often than annually, to one or more persons who is living at the time of the creation of the trust for a term of years no less than twenty years or for the life of the individual.

Child and Dependent Care Tax Credit (CDCTC)

A nonrefundable tax credit that helps working taxpayers pay expenses for the care of children, adult dependents, or an incapacitated spouse.

Child Care Credit

A nonrefundable credit designed to help working taxpayers recoup some of their unreimbursed childcare expenses (replaced by CDCTC above).

Child Tax Credit (CTC)

A credit given to taxpayers for each dependent child that is under the age of seventeen at the end of the tax year. The child tax credit is a nonrefundable credit that reduces the taxpayer's liability on a dollar-for-dollar basis. The child tax credit is intended to provide an extra measure of tax relief for taxpayers with qualifying dependents. For years before 2018, a portion of the CTC is a refundable credit for all taxpayers (known as the additional child tax credit). The 20/20 Tax would revise the CTC to be a fully refundable credit of $1,000 per child for all US citizen taxpayers' dependent children under the age of eighteen.

Consumer Price Index (CPI)

An index of the variation in prices paid over time by typical consumers for retail goods and services, including residential rentals.

Congressional Budget Office (CBO)

A nonpartisan staff responsible for providing unbiased data and economic analysis for Congress to utilize when considering budgetary and tax legislative decisions.

Consumption Tax

Tax levied on the value of goods and services purchased through consumer spending.

Corporate Income Tax

A tax on the income of a given corporation that generally involves a different rate structure and rules as compared to an individual. The rationale for taxing corporations lies in the fact that they are legal entities considered persons under the law. Given this rationale, corporations are taxed on their income, much like individuals.

Deduction

A deduction is generally an expense that reduces the amount of income subject to taxation.

Deferred Gains

The amount of gain that escapes current taxation and is deferred until a later date.

Deficit

A shortage, especially the amount by which a sum of money falls short of what is required; a debt. A status of financial health in which expenditures exceed revenue. A term often used to describe our nation's expenditures in excess of revenues for a single year or as a cumulative total.

Defined Benefit Plan (DB Plan)

A DB pension plan provides benefits to participants in retirement based on a formula reflecting compensation and years of service for each participant.

Defined Contribution Plan (DC Plan)

Retirement plan that sets aside a certain amount or percentage of compensation into individual accounts for each participant's benefit with restrictions on when and how the employee can withdraw the funds without penalties. The benefits that are eventually paid are not predetermined or guaranteed.

Dependent

Person who relies on someone else for support and qualifies as a taxpayer's dependent. A dependent is an individual, such as a qualifying child, whom a taxpayer can claim on his or her federal and some state income tax returns in order to lower one's income taxes.

Depletion

An accounting method that allocates the cost of extracting natural resources. The calculation is necessary for purposes of a tax deduction that allows a company to deduct the calculated amount of non-renewable resources depleted from the earth.

Depreciation
The amount of scheduled deduction for a fixed asset allowed by the tax code for loss of value because of obsolescence, wear, etc.

Dividends
A distribution of a portion of a company's earnings, decided by the board of directors, to a class of its shareholders. The dividend is most often quoted in terms of the dollar amount each share receives (dividends per share). It can also be quoted in terms of a percent of the current market price, referred to as dividend yield.

Double Taxation of Dividends
A concept of our tax law that causes the same earnings to be subjected to taxation twice. A corporation's income is taxed initially at the corporate level, and then the shareholders and investors are taxed on the distributions of such corporate income that they receive from the company.

Earned Income Credit (EIC)
A tax credit for lower-income taxpayers who meet the work requirements for a given tax year. This credit is refundable for taxpayers that meet the eligibility requirements and have earned income below certain limits while working. The EIC is greatly expanded for the 20/20 Tax.

Economic Growth and Tax Relief Reconciliation Act of 2001 (EGTRRA)
A US tax law, effective for tax years beginning in 2002, that made some of the most important changes to retirement plans along with lowering income tax rates significantly. Considered the largest tax cut since 1981, this $1.35 trillion tax reduction (over 10 years) lowered income taxes for all income groups.

Economic Income
A term that describes all income and benefits going to an individual, including nontaxable benefits like health insurance.

Education Credits
Credits to reimburse taxpayers for qualified tuition and related expenses paid for taxpayers or their dependents.

Effective Tax Rate (ETR)
The effective tax rate is the amount of taxes paid in ratio to AGI. This measure is a more useful indicator of the tax rates actually paid because it is calculated before exemptions, credits, and deductions have taken place, but it does not factor in exclusions such as municipal bond interest.

Employer-Sponsored Health Insurance (ESHI)
This is a health-insurance plan that an employer offers for the benefit of his or her employees at no cost or a relatively low cost to the employees.

Employment Retirement Income Security Act (ERISA)
ERISA is a 1974 federal law that sets standards of protection and benefit limits for individuals in most voluntarily established, private-sector retirement plans.

Estate Tax
A tax levied on an estate of a decedent if the value of the estate exceeds an exclusion limit set by law.

Excise Tax
Excise taxes are taxes paid when purchases are made on a specific good, such as gasoline or alcohol. Excise taxes are often included in the price of the product. There are also excise taxes on activities, such as on wagering or on highway usage by trucks.

Exclusion

Income that is excluded from taxable income, such as life-insurance death-benefit proceeds, child support, welfare, and municipal-bond interest.

Fair Tax

A tax proposal that proposes to replace federal income and payroll taxes with a federal retail sales tax.

Fairness

A tax policy concept rooted in the idea that a system of taxation should not overly burden any particular group. The goal of fairness is to achieve a system of taxation that does not favor one group over another.

Fiscal Year (FY) or Federal Fiscal Year

A fiscal year or financial year is a period used for calculating annual financial statements in businesses and other organizations that may or may not use the calendar year. The federal fiscal year ends every September 30.

FICA Tax (Federal Insurance Contributions Act)

A tax imposed on both employees and employers to fund Social Security and Medicare programs. Employers are required to withhold Social Security and Medicare taxes from wages paid to an employee and match the tax withheld.

Filing Status

The category a taxpayer uses to determine filing requirements, the standard deduction, eligibility for certain credits and deductions, etc. The five filing statuses are: single, married filing jointly, married filing separately, head of household, and qualifying widow(er) with dependent child.

First-Time Homebuyer Credit

A refundable credit for qualified first-time homebuyers that originated as part of the American Recovery and Reinvestment Act of 2009. For the first year, the credit was to be repaid, interest-free, over fifteen years. The credit was available for homes purchased between 2008 and 2011.

Fixed Assets
A long-term tangible piece of property that a firm owns and uses in the production of its income and which is not likely to be converted quickly into cash. Buildings, real estate, equipment, and furniture are good examples of fixed assets.

Flat Tax
A proposed alternate to our current progressive taxation system that would tax all levels of income at the same tax rate regardless of how much income the individual taxpayer earns.

Foreign Tax Credit
A nonrefundable credit that is allowed for taxes paid to a foreign jurisdiction to avoid double taxation by the United States.

Gift Tax
A federal tax applied to an individual giving something of value to other persons in excess of annual and lifetime exclusions. For a transfer to be considered a gift, the receiving party cannot pay the giver full value for the gift but may pay an amount less than its full value. The tax applies whether the donor intends the transfer to be a gift or not.

Graduated Tax
A system of taxation that increases the tax rate as the income of the taxpayer increases. Also known as a progressive tax.

Grantor Retained Annuity Trust (GRAT)
An irrevocable trust that is created for a certain term or period of time. Assets are placed under the trust, and an annuity is paid out every year to the person establishing the trust. When the trust expires, the beneficiary receives the assets tax-free.

Grantor Retained Income Trust (GRIT)

An irrevocable trust whereby the grantor transfers assets but retains the income from or the use of these assets for a stipulated period of time. At the end of the time, the remaining value of the trust will be passed to the beneficiary.

Grantor Retained Unitrust (GRUT)

An irrevocable trust into which a grantor makes a one-time transfer of property, and in which the grantor retains the right to receive a variable amount of principal and interest (based on a fixed percentage) at least annually for a specified term of years. At the end of the retained interest period or upon the death of the grantor, whichever is earlier, the property remaining in the trust passes to the remainder beneficiaries or it remains in trust for their benefit.

Gross Domestic Product (GDP)

The total value of goods produced and services provided in a country during one year. GDP is commonly used as an indicator of the economic health of a country as well as to gauge a country's standard of living.

Gross Income

The amount initially used when calculating income tax for all taxpayers. It includes all taxable forms of income from whatever source derived. This amount is not limited to money received as payment in the traditional sense; it can also include goods and services received (barter) as well as gain from illegal activities.

Group-Term Life Insurance

Insurance coverage offered to a group of people, usually employees of a particular company. The coverage provides a benefit to the group members' chosen beneficiaries in the event the covered employee dies during the defined covered period.

Head of household

Head of household is a filing status for an individual. To use the head-of-household filing status, a taxpayer must be unmarried or considered unmarried at the end of the year, have paid more than half the cost of keeping up a home for the tax year, and have a qualifying person or dependent who lived with the head of household in the home for more than half of the tax year.

Health Savings Account (HSA)

An account created for individuals who are covered under high-deductible health plans (HDHPs) to save for medical expenses that HDHPs do not cover. Contributions are made into the account by the individual or the individual's employer and are limited to a maximum amount each year. The contributions are invested over time and can be used (tax-free) to pay for qualified medical expenses, which include most medical care, such as dental, vision, and over-the-counter drugs.

Higher Education Credit (HEC)

This 20/20 Tax proposal would replace all current education credits and deductions with a 20% credit on the first $10,000 of tuition and fees per year to partially reimburse qualified tuition and related expenses for taxpayers and their dependents.

Income

Generally, it includes the amount of money or value received for labor, sale of goods, services, property, or from financial investments.

Income from Personal Property

Gains on the sale of property that generally includes any movable asset other than real property. This could also be rental income from personal property.

Indexing (also Inflation Indexing)

In general, indexing ties taxes, tax rates, wages, and other terms to an index that adjusts in response to inflation. This can avoid driving a taxpayer's income into a higher income bracket due to inflation. It can also be used to measure the amount of gain upon the sale of assets.

Indirect Tax

The increased amount that consumers pay for goods due to unseen taxes levied further up in the supply chain that are shifted to the consumer via a higher retail price.

Individual Retirement Account (IRA)

A retirement savings account that allows individuals to direct pretax income, up to specific annual limits, toward investments that can grow tax-deferred. No income on investments is taxed until distributions are made, at which time the original principal is also taxed on traditional IRAs. See also, Roth IRA.

Intentionally Defective Grantor Trust (IDGT)

An estate-planning tool used to freeze or reduce certain assets of an individual for estate tax purposes but not for income tax purposes. The intentionally defective trust is created as a grantor trust with a purposeful flaw that ensures that the transferor continues to pay income taxes on the earnings of the trust assets, as income tax laws will not recognize that assets have been transferred away from the transferor.

Individual Taxpayer

An individual that is obligated to pay various taxes.

Inflationary Gain

The amount of a gain attributed solely to the increase in value or income created by inflation.

Inheritance Tax

A tax imposed by some states on individuals or entities that inherit assets from a deceased person. The rate can vary depending on the value of the property and/or the relationship to the decedent.

Insurance Premiums (Health or Medical)

Agreed-upon fees paid for coverage of medical benefits for a defined period. Premiums can be paid by employers, unions, employees, or shared by both the insured individual and the plan sponsor.

Intangible Drilling and Development Costs (IDCs)

Costs incurred in drilling, testing, completing, and reworking oil and gas wells, such as labor, core analysis, fracturing, drill stem testing, engineering, fuel, geologists' expenses; also abandonment losses, management fees, delay rentals, and similar expenses.

Itemized Deductions

A deduction from AGI that includes specific deductions allowed for money spent on certain goods and services throughout the taxable year. The most common itemized deductions are state and local taxes, home mortgage interest, and charitable contributions.

JGTRRA (Jobs and Growth Tax Relief Reconciliation Act of 2003)

A US tax law passed by Congress and signed by President George W. Bush in May 2003 that lowered the maximum individual income tax rate on corporate dividends and long-term capital gains to a maximum of 15%. The act was intended to amplify the effects of the Economic Growth and Tax Relief Reconciliation Act of 2001.

JCT (Joint Committee on Taxation)

A Committee of the US Congress established under the Internal Revenue Code at 26 U.S.C. § 8001 to assist Congress in tax legislation. The Joint Committee is composed of ten members: five senators from the Senate Finance Committee and five representatives from the House Ways and Means Committee.

Kiddie Tax

A tax that can be imposed on individuals under twenty-four years old whose net unearned income (primarily interest and dividends) exceeds an annually determined threshold. The income earned beyond this threshold is taxed at their parent's/guardian's tax rate.

Low-Income Housing Tax Credit (LIHTC)

The low-income housing tax credit is a dollar-for-dollar nonrefundable tax credit in the United States for affordable housing investments. It was created under the Tax Reform Act of 1986 that gives incentives for the utilization of private equity in the development of affordable housing aimed at low-income Americans. The LIHTC Program is an indirect federal subsidy used to finance the development of affordable rental housing for low-income households.

Limited Liability Company (LLC)

An entity structure that minimizes the personal liability of its members (owners) in regards to the entity's debts or other liabilities. Limited liability companies (LLCs) are essentially a hybrid entity that combines the characteristics of a corporation and a partnership or sole proprietorship. While the limited liability feature is similar to that of a corporation, the availability of flow-through taxation to the members of a LLC is a feature of partnerships.

Lock-In Effect

This occurs when investors are unable or unwilling to shift invested funds or liquidate assets because of the tax effect of realizing capital gains.

Long-Term Capital Gain

The amount of gain on a capital asset held for more than one year.

Loophole

An ambiguity or technicality in the tax code that allows a person or business to avoid the scope of a law or restriction without directly violating the law, resulting in lower taxes for the taxpayer.

Marginal Tax Rate (MTR)

A marginal tax rate refers to the tax rate an individual would pay on one additional dollar of income when given a progressive tax system.

Marriage Bonus (Penalty)

A couple has a marriage bonus (penalty) if they owe less (more) income tax by filing a joint return than the married couple would pay if they were unmarried and each filed as a single or head-of-household filer.

Medicaid

Medicaid is a social healthcare program for families and individuals with low income and limited resources. Medicaid is the largest source of funding for medical and health-related services for people with low income in the United States. It is a means-tested program that is jointly funded by the state and federal governments and managed by the states, with each state currently having broad leeway to determine who is eligible for its implementation of the program.

Medicare Tax

A tax deducted from employee wages and matched by the employer used to pay for the Medicare program. This amount is normally 1.45% of all wages and salaries reported on the W-2 form.

Modified Adjusted Gross Income (MAGI)

The amount of a taxpayer's income used to determine certain exclusions, deductions, and credits allowed. This is calculated by taking the individual's adjusted gross income and adding back certain items such as municipal bond interest, foreign income, foreign-housing deductions, student-loan deductions, IRA-contribution deductions, and deductions for higher-education costs. The MAGI rules are different for various exclusions, deductions, and credits.

Mortgage Interest Credit

A credit for mortgage interest paid by the taxpayer to assist lower-income taxpayers with home ownership. The credit is available for first-time homebuyers that meet the income requirements in the area where they live. In order to claim the credit the taxpayer must obtain a Mortgage Credit Certificate (MCC). The mortgage interest deduction is reduced by the amount of the credit received by the taxpayer. The 20/20 Tax would substantially revise the tax credit for mortgage interest, replacing the home mortgage interest deduction with a 20% credit.

Municipal Bonds

Tax-exempt debt securities issued by states, cities, counties, or other municipalities to finance various capital expenditures and public infrastructure projects. The interest from such bonds is generally tax-free.

Nanny Tax

A federal tax that must be paid by people who hire household help (a babysitter, maid, gardener, etc.) and pay them a total of more than a specified threshold amount during the tax year. The reason the tax code charges the nanny tax is because an ongoing household helper is considered to be the taxpayer's employee. As such, the taxpayer becomes an employer and must pay Social Security, Medicare, and federal unemployment taxes on the wages paid to that employee.

National Sales Tax

A national sales tax, sometimes known as the "fair tax," is a tax on most consumer goods and services purchased. A taxpayer is said to be able to opt out of the tax simply by not purchasing goods or services.

Net Investment Income Tax (NIIT)

An additional tax imposed by section 1411 of the Internal Revenue Code starting in 2013 that applies to certain net investment income (interest, dividends, capital gains, rents, etc.) of individuals, estates, and trusts that have income above the statutory threshold amounts.

Non-Filer

A person or corporation who does *not file* a tax return by the required date. A non-filer may be subject to interest, late fees, and other penalties.

Nonrefundable Credits

A tax credit that reduces the amount of tax owed down to zero. Any nonrefundable credit amount in excess of income tax owed before credits is lost by the taxpayer.

OASDI (Old Age, Survivors, and Disability Insurance)

The official name for Social Security in the United States. The OASDI is a comprehensive federal benefits program that provides benefits to retirees, disabled people, and their survivors. The program was ushered in through the Social Security Act, signed by President Franklin D. Roosevelt on August 14, 1935, when the US economy was in the depths of the Depression.

Organisation for Economic Co-operation and Development (OECD)

A group of thirty-four free world countries that meet to promote trade and economic goals. See list of countries in table 7.1-1 of chapter 7.1.

Omnibus Budget Reconciliation Act of 1990 (OBRA90)

The Omnibus Budget Reconciliation Act of 1990 is a US statute enacted pursuant to the budget reconciliation process to reduce the United States federal budget deficit. The act included the Budget Enforcement Act of 1990 that established the pay-as-you-go or PAYGO process for discretionary spending and taxes. The act increased individual income tax rates.

Omnibus Budget Reconciliation Act of 1993 (OBRA93)

The Omnibus Budget Reconciliation Act of 1993 was a federal law that was enacted by the 103rd United States Congress and signed into law by President Bill Clinton. It has also been referred to, unofficially, as the Deficit Reduction Act of 1993. Part XIII dealt with taxes and is also called the Revenue Reconciliation Act of 1993. The act created new and higher marginal tax rates for the wealthy and removed the Medicare tax cap.

Ordinary Course of Business

The usual transactions, customs, and practices of a particular business.

Ordinary Income

Generally, ordinary income is characterized as income other than excluded income, capital gains, and certain other types of income that have their own designated tax rates. It can consist of income from wages, salaries, tips, commissions, bonuses, and other types of compensation from employment, interest, some dividends, or net income from a sole proprietorship, partnership or LLC. The IRS usually considers rents and royalties, pensions, annuities, retirement income, and gambling winnings as ordinary income. The 20/20 Tax would revise the definition of ordinary income by redefining all interest, dividends, long-term capital gains, and Social Security benefits as exclusionary income.

Pay-As-You-Go System (PAYGO)

PAYGO is a budget rule requiring that any tax cuts or entitlement and other mandatory spending increases must be paid for by a tax increase or a cut in mandatory spending as part of OBRA90.

Payroll Tax

Payroll tax includes at least three different kinds of taxes. The first is a tax that employers are required to withhold from employees' wages, also known as withholding tax, which consists of advance payments of income taxes and FICA contributions. The second is a tax that is the employer's contribution of FICA on behalf of the employee. The third is unemployment taxes and other state and local taxes that the employee usually does not have to share or match employers' contributions.

Percentage Depletion Allowance

A tax deduction provided as an incentive to develop domestic natural resources that assigns a set percentage of depletion to the gross income derived from extracting fossil fuels, minerals, or other nonrenewable resources from the earth. The rationale for this is that these producers deserve a depletion allowance because the natural resources they are extracting are not infinite and thus depreciable just like any other asset that has a useful life.

Personal Exemption Phase-Out (PEP)
Taxpayers whose AGI exceeds a certain threshold must reduce personal exemptions they would otherwise be entitled to. It reduces personal exemptions proportionally as a taxpayer's income increases.

Personal Exemptions
The dollar amount of deduction allowed for an individual taxpayer and for each person he or she claims as a dependent on his or her tax return.

Phase-Out of Itemized Deductions (Pease)
A limitation on itemized deductions, otherwise known as Pease, named after the congressman who created it. The phase-out reduces most itemized deductions by a percentage of the amount by which AGI exceeds a certain threshold, up to a maximum reduction of 80%.

Phase-Out Tax
It gradually reduces the amount of a tax credit or deduction a taxpayer is eligible to receive as the taxpayer's income approaches the income limit to qualify for the credit or deduction. It also reduces a taxpayer's ability to contribute to a retirement account as the taxpayer's income approaches the limit.

Progressive Tax
A system of taxation that takes a larger percentage from the income of high-income earners than it does from low-income earners. In the United States, taxpayers are taxed according to numeric brackets based on their taxable income. Any income the taxpayer makes that exceeds the bracketed threshold is taxed at the next higher bracketed rate(s).

Property Tax
A tax assessed by a local government on real estate or personal property, usually based on the value of the property (including related land) owned.

Qualified Dividends

Ordinary dividends that meet specific criteria, defined in the Internal Revenue code, to be taxed at the lower long-term capital gains tax rate rather than at the higher ordinary income tax rate.

Qualified Retirement Plan

A type of retirement plan established by an employer for the benefit of the company's employees. Qualified retirement plans give employers a tax deduction for the contributions they make for their employees, and employees are not taxed until the benefits are received. Qualified plans that allow employees to defer a portion of their salaries into the plan also reduce employees' present income tax liability by reducing taxable income.

Refund

If the amount of taxes owed is less than the amount of taxes paid through withholding, estimated taxes, or refundable credits, the taxpayer receives a refund at the end of the taxable year.

Refundable Credits

This type of credit allows a taxpayer to receive the benefit of a credit even when the value of the credit exceeds the pre-credit tax liability.

Regressive Tax

As opposed to a progressive tax, a regressive tax takes a larger percentage of income from low-income taxpayers than from high-income taxpayers.

Residential Energy Credit

Tax credit provided to residents that make energy improvements to their homes to promote effective energy usage. Certain products purchased by the home owner can qualify them for the credit, as can certain updates or modifications to existing systems. The amount of the credit varies, depending on the way that the home owner improves his or her home.

Retirement Savings Contribution Credit

A credit targeted at lower-income taxpayers to help with retirement savings credit for certain contributions to a qualified employer plan or IRA. The 20/20 Tax would replace this with the credit IRA available to most middle-class taxpayers.

Revenue Neutral

A tax concept that allows the Treasury to receive the same amount of money regardless of changes in tax laws. For every reduction in taxes, the taxes are raised elsewhere to achieve a balance in revenue.

Roth IRA

An individual retirement account allowing a person to set aside after-tax income up to a specified amount each year. Both earnings on the account and withdrawals (generally after age fifty-nine and a half) are tax-free.

Self-Employment Tax

A tax paid by a self-employed individual to equalize what a W-2 earner and his employer would pay for Medicare and Social Security taxes.

Self-Employed Contributions Act (SECA)

The act that imposed tax on small business owners to cover their Social Security, Medicare, and old-age, survivors, and disability insurance.

SEP-IRA

A simplified employee pension (SEP) plan that provides business owners with a simplified method to contribute toward their employees' retirement as well as their own retirement savings. Contributions are made to an individual retirement account (IRA) set up for each plan participant (a SEP-IRA). A SEP-IRA account is a traditional IRA and follows the same investment, distribution, and rollover rules as traditional IRAs.

SIMPLE IRA

A SIMPLE IRA plan provides small employers with a simplified method to contribute reduced amount (less than SEP plan) toward their employees' and their own retirement savings. Employees may choose to make salary reduction contributions, and the employer is required to make either matching or nonelective contributions. Contributions are made to an individual retirement account (IRA) set up for each employee (a SIMPLE IRA). A SIMPLE IRA plan account is an IRA that follows the same investment, distribution, and rollover rules as traditional IRAs.

SSDI (Social Security Disability Insurance)

Social Security disability insurance pays benefits to taxpayers and certain members of the taxpayer's family if the taxpayer has worked long enough, paid Social Security taxes, and has a medical condition preventing him or her from working for at least twelve months or ending in death.

Standard Deduction

The base amount that taxpayers are allowed to subtract from their adjusted gross income (AGI) in lieu of itemized deductions to reduce their taxable income.

Stealth Tax

A term often used to describe the personal exemption phase-out (PEP) and the phase-out of itemized deductions (Pease).

Taxable Income

The amount of income that is used to calculate an individual's or a company's income tax due. Taxable income is generally described as gross income or adjusted gross income minus any deductions, exemptions, or other adjustments that are allowable in that tax year.

Tax Burden

The amount of income tax that needs to be paid by an individual or business.

Tax Credit

An item that reduces the amount of preliminary tax owed by a taxpayer as opposed to a tax deduction that merely reduces a taxpayer's taxable income. Since a tax credit does not depend on the taxpayer's tax rate, the amount of the credit is usually of equal value to all taxpayers regardless of income level.

Tax Earmark
A type of tax whose revenues are reserved for a specific purpose and cannot be used for anything else.

Tax Expenditure
Generally, it is the amount of revenue that the Treasury forgoes through exclusions, exemptions, deductions, or credits in the tax code.

Tax-Filing Threshold
The minimum amount of gross income an individual of a certain age and an applicable filing status (e.g., single, married filing jointly, head of household) must make to be required to file a tax return.

Tax Liability
The total amount of tax that an individual or entity is legally obligated to pay to the federal government or state government as the result of the occurrence of a taxable event or income for a certain period.

Tax Rate
The percentage at which a taxpayer's income is taxed. The rate varies based on many factors, such as type of income, amount of income, taxpayer status, etc.

TRA86 (Tax Reform Act of 1986)
The US Congress passed the Tax Reform Act of 1986 to simplify the income tax code, broaden the tax base, and eliminate many tax shelters and other preferences. The top tax rate was lowered while the bottom rate was raised.

TRA97 (Taxpayer Relief Act of 1997)

The Taxpayer Relief Act of 1997 reduced several federal taxes in the United States by introducing a child tax credit and lowering marginal long-term capital gains rate.

Unemployment Insurance

A source of income for workers who have lost their jobs through no fault of their own. Unemployment is paid to workers by state governments from a fund of unemployment taxes collected from employers.

Upside-Down Subsidy

The progressive US tax system has marginal tax rates that get higher as income increases. This results in exclusions, exemptions, or deductions being more valuable for taxpayers in higher tax brackets than for those who have lower tax rates. This means that certain deductions that are meant to help all taxpayers, end up providing more tax benefits for those who need the benefit(s) less. Thus, they are referred to as upside-down subsidies.

Value-Added Tax (VAT)

A consumption tax levied on goods or services at every stage that value (or profit) is added. The amount of tax is based on the cost of the product or service less any costs of materials, labor, and profit already taxed.

W-2

The federal form that an employer must send to an employee and the IRS at the end of the year that reports an employee's annual wages and the amount of taxes withheld from his or her paycheck.

W-2 Income

Gross salary without contributions to pre-tax plans, tax-deferred retirement deductions, health plans, insurance payments, dependent care and medical expense reimbursements, parking fee deductions, etc. This is the income shown in box 1 of the Form W-2.

BIBLIOGRAPHY

Appleby, Julie. "Big Changes Ahead for Those Who Buy Their Own Insurance." *Kaiser Health News* (June 28, 2013).

Aprill, Professor Ellen P. *Churches, Politics, and the Charitable Contribution Deduction.* Loyola Law School L.A., Legal Studies Paper No. 2006-13 (2001).

Batchelder, Lily L., Fred T. Goldberg, Jr. and Peter R. Orszag. "Efficiency and Tax Incentives: The Case for Refundable Tax Credits." *Stanford Law Review* 59, no. 1 (2006).

Bartlett, Bruce. *The Benefit and the Burden.* New York: Simon & Schuster, 2012.

Bickley, James M. *The Federal Excise Tax on Gasoline and the Highway Trust Fund: A Short History.* Congressional Research Service (September 7, 2012).

A Bipartisan Path Forward to Securing America's Future, Moment of Truth Project. Cochaired by Erskine Bowles and former senator Alan Simpson (April 2013).

Birnbaum, Jeffrey H. and Alan S. Murray. *Showdown at Gucci Gulch.* New York: Vintage Books, a Division of Random House, 1988.

Blakey, Roy G. and Gladys C. Blakey, *The Federal Income Tax,* Clark, New Jersey, The Law Book Exchange, Ltd., 2006

Blinder, Alan S., Martin Feldstein. "The Level and Distribution of Economic Well-Being," *The American Economy in Transition*, ed. Chicago: University of Chicago Press, 1980.

Blum, Marvin E. "Carryover Basis: The Case for Repeal." Notes; 57 *Texas Law Review*, 1978–1979.

Bryant, Victoria L. and Jon Gober. "Accumulation and Distribution of Individual Retirement Arrangements, 2010." *Statistics of Income Bulletin*. Washington, DC (Fall 2013).

Burman, Leonard E., William G. Gale, and Jeffrey Rohaly. "Policy Watch, The Expanding Reach of the Individual Alternative Minimum Tax." *Journal of Economic Perspectives* 17, no. 2 (Spring 2003).

Burman, Leonard E. and Joel Slemrod. *Taxes in America*. New York: Oxford University Press, 2013.

"Carried Interest in the Cross Hairs." Tax Report. *Wall Street Journal*, editorial page (August 6, 2011).

"Carried Interest: A Very Big Wolf in Sheep's Clothing." *Huff Post Business* (September 20, 2011).

Caroll, Richard J. *The President as Economist: Scoring Economic Performance from Harry Truman to Barack Obama* (Santa Barbara, CA, ABC-CLIO, LLC 2012

Colinvoux, Roger, Brian Galle, Eugene Steuerle. "Evaluating the Charitable Deductions and Proposed Reforms." Urban Institute and Tax Policy Center (June 2012).

"The Distribution of Major Tax Expenditures in the Individual Income Tax System." Congressional Budget Office (May 2013).

Cordes, Joseph J. "Re-thinking the Deduction for Charitable Contributions: Evaluating the Effects of Deficit-Reduction Proposals." *National Tax Journal* (December 2011).

Crawford, Constance J. and Corine L. Crawford. "The Inequity in the Current Tax System: Does the Alternative Minimum Tax Create Additional Problems in the System?" *Journal of Business & Economics Research* (February 2007).

Decisions of the United States Supreme Court in Corporation Tax Cases and Income Tax Cases: with Dissenting Opinions, U.S. Government Printing Office, 1912

DePaul, Jennifer. "Tax Expenditures Too Popular to Easily Cut." The Bond Buyer. CRS (March 28, 2012).

Dietz, Dr. Robert, Testimony of. "Hearing on Tax Reform Options: Incentives for Homeownership" on Behalf of the National Association of Homebuilders, Before the United States Senate Committee on Finance (October 6, 2011).

Domenici-Rivlin Debt Reduction Task Force Plan 2.0. former Senator Pete Domenici and Dr. Alice Rivlin, cochairs; Bipartisan Policy Center (2012).

Economic Survey of the United States. Organisation for Economic Co-operation and Development (OECD) (June 2, 2014).

Education Tax Incentives and Tax Reform. Senate Finance Committee Hearing Written Testimony for the Record. *American Institute of Certified Public Accountants* (July 25, 2012).

Entin, Stephen J., and Michael Schuyler, PhD. "Fiscal Fact, Case Study #1: Mortgage Interest Deduction for Owner-Occupied Housing." Tax Foundation (July 29, 2013).

Ernst & Young LLP. The 2011 Global Executive, computations by Ernst & Young LLP: 13.

Estimates of Federal Tax Expenditures for Fiscal Years 2010–2014. Joint Committee on Taxation (December 15, 2010).

Estimates of Federal Tax Expenditures for Fiscal Years 2005–2009. Joint Committee on Taxation (January 12, 2005).

Estimates of Federal Tax Expenditures for Fiscal Years 2010–2014. http://www.jct.gov/publications.html?func=startdown&id=3718.

Estimates of Federal Tax Expenditures for Fiscal Years 2012–2017. Prepared for the House Committee on Ways and Means and the Senate Committee on Finance, by the Staff of the Joint Committee on Taxation (February 1, 2013).

Fix The Debt. The Tax Reform Act of 2014 Discussion Draft. Overview of the Draft. House Ways and Means Committee (April 2014).

Furman, Jason. "Tax Reform and Poverty." Center on Budget and Policy Priorities (April 10, 2006).

Goldsmith, Steven. "Reform the EIC to better Serve our Nation's Low Income Workers." Spotlight on Poverty and Opportunity (November 2012).

Gordon, Mac. "Home Equity Loans, Car Sales Shrink" copyright Wards Auto, a division of Penton (republished under license) (December 2008).

Graetz, Michael J. *100 Million Unnecessary Returns*. New Haven, CT: Yale University Press, 2008.

Graetz, Michael. From page 6 of an essay adapted and updated from the Lloyd Leva Plaine Distinguished Lecture, delivered at the University of Miami's Heckerling Estate Planning Institute on January 11, 2011, and from *Death by a Thousand Cuts: The Fight Over Taxing Inherited Wealth*, Princeton, NJ: Princeton University Press, co-authored with Ian Shapiro, 2005.

Green, Joshua. "The MBA Candidate Meets the Mad-As-Hell Electorate," *Bloomberg Businessweek* (January 25, 2012).

Greenspan, Statement of Chairman Alan. Board of Governors of the Federal Reserve System, before the Special Committee on Aging. United States Senate (March 27, 2000).

Gross, Martin L. *National Suicide: How Washington is Destroying the American Dream from A to Z* (Berkley Books, New York 2009)

Gruber, Jonathan. *The Tax Exclusion for Employer-Sponsored Health Insurance*. Working Paper 15766. National Bureau of Economic Research. Cambridge, MA (February 2010).

H.R. Rep. No. 1380, 94th Congress, 2nd Session 36-37 (1976), pg. 3390-91 as cited by Marvin E. Blum in *Carryover Basis: The Case for Repeal*.

Hall, Arthur P. *50 Years of the Federal Capital Gains Tax Burden* Tax Foundation Special Report #45 (March 1995).

Hearings on president's 1963 Tax Message before the House Committee on Ways and Means, 88th Congress, 1st Sess. 24 (1963) as cited by Marvin E. Blum, Notes, *Carryover Basis: The Case for Repeal*; 57 *Texas L. Review* 204, 1978–1979.

Henneman, John Bell. 1971. *Royal taxation in fourteenth century France: the development of war financing, 1322-1356*. http://alltitles.ebrary.com/Doc?id=11017675

Historical Tables: table 17.3. Extrapolated from Budget of the United States Government, Fiscal Year 2012. http://wwwwhitehouse.gov/omb/budget/historicals.

Individual Income Tax Returns 2009, Publication 1304. Rev. 08-2011. Department of the Treasury, Internal Revenue Service.

Individual Income Tax Returns 2010, Publication 1304. Rev. 08-2012. Department of the Treasury, Internal Revenue Service.

Individual Income Tax Returns 2011, Publication 1304. Rev. 08-2013. Department of the Treasury, Internal Revenue Service.

Individual Income Tax Returns 2012, Publication 1304. Rev. 08-2014. Department of the Treasury, Internal Revenue Service.

Internal Revenue Code Section 3101(b)(2); Prop. Reg. 31.3102-4. From *U.S. Master Tax Guide, 2014*, 97th edition.

Internal Revenue Code, Section 415(b) (2) (A) as amended in 2001.

Internal Revenue Code Section 1023 (a)(1) as legislated by the Tax Reform Act of 1976.

Internal Revenue Code Sec. 24(d)(1)(1998).

Internal Revenue Code Sec. 1222 (3).

Internal Revenue Service, Issue Number: IR-2013-9. "On EIC Awareness Day" (January 25, 2013).

Internal Revenue Service Publication 17 (2014).

Katz, Bruce. "Cut to Invest, Reform the Mortgage Interest Deduction to Invest in Innovation and Advanced Industries." Brookings (November, 2012).

Lin, Emily Y. and Patricia K. Tong. "Marriage and Taxes: What Can We Learn from Tax Returns Filed by Cohabiting Couples?" *National Tax Journal* 65, no. 4 (December 2012).

Luttman, Suzanne and Roxanne Spindle. "An evaluation of the revenue and equity effects of converting exemptions and itemized deductions to a single nonrefundable credit," *Journal of the American Taxation Association* 16.2 (Fall 1994).

Matuso, Allen, J.. *Nixon's Economy: Booms, Busts Dollars and Votes*, (University Press of Kansas, USA 1998)

The Moment of Truth: Report of the National Commission on Fiscal Responsibility and Reform. Cochaired by former Sen. Alan Simpson and former White House Chief of Staff, Erskine Bowles (December 2010).

Moore, Stephen and John Silvia. "The ABC's of the Capital Gains Tax." Cato Institute Policy Analysis No. 242. Statement before the Republican members of the Joint Economic Committee (October 4, 1995).

OECD Consumption Tax Trends 2014. "VAT/GST and excise rates, trends and policy issues." Paris: OECD Publishing.

OECD. Table II.4. Overall 2011 statutory tax rates on dividend income and computations by Ernst & Young LLP.

Data based on Table II.1–Corporate income tax rates: basic/non-targeted from OECD Tax Database. Accessed February 2014. http://www.oecd.org/tax/tax-policy/tax-database.htm#C_Corporate-Captial.

"Options to Improve Tax Compliance and Reform Tax Expenditures." Prepared by the Staff of the Joint Committee on Taxation (January 27, 2005).

Palmer, John L., Isabel Sawhill, *The Reagan Experiment, An Examination of Economic and Social Policies Under the Reagan Administration* (The Urban Institute, Washington, DC 1982)

Paul, Randolph E., *Taxation for Prosperity*. Indianapolis: the Bobbs-Merrill Company, 1947.

Piketty, Thomas and Emmanuel Saez. *How Progressive Is the U.S. Federal Tax System, A Historical and International Perspective*. Working Paper 12404 National Bureau of Economic Research. Cambridge, MA, July 2006.

Pollock v. Farmers' Loan & Trust Co., 157 U.S. 249 (Argued March 1895) as cited in Jay Starkman's book.

Pommerleau, Kyle, and Andrew Lundeen. "2014 International Tax Competitiveness Index." Tax Foundation.

Pratt, James, William Kulsrud, *Individual Taxation 2013* (South-Western Cengage Learning, New York 2013)

"Present Law and Background Information Related to the Taxation of Capital Gains." Prepared by the Staff of the Joint Budget Committee on Taxation (September 14, 2012).

"Refundable Tax Credits." Congressional Budget Office. Appendix table A-1, pg. 7, table 2, figure 3 (January 2013).

Reich, Rob and Christopher Wimer. "Charitable Giving and the Great Recession." Stanford University. figure 2 (October 2012).

Report of the 1979 Advisory Council on Social Security. Committee on Ways and Means Print No. WMCP 96-45 (January 02, 1980).

Report of the President's Advisory Panel on Federal Tax Reform (November 2005).

"Restoring America's Future" The Debt Reduction Task Force, former Senator Pete Domenici and Dr. Alice Rivlin, cochairs. Bipartisan Policy Center (November 2010).

Revenue Act of 1921, Publication L. No. 67-98, Sec. 202, 42 Stat. 227-229.

The RIA Complete Analysis of the '81 Economic Recovery Tax Act. New York: the Research Institute of America, 1981.

The RIA Complete Analysis of the '86 Tax Reform Act (2nd printing). New York: the Research Institute of America, 1986.

The RIA Complete Analysis of the Revenue Act and Pension Protection Act of 1987. New York: the Research Institute of America, Inc., 1987.

Rueben, Kim. "The Impact of Repealing State and Local Tax Deductability." Tax Analysts Special Report (August 15, 2005).

Rubin, Richard. "Carried Interest Tax Increase Measure Introduced by Levin." *Bloomberg Businessweek* (February 16, 2012).

Sarenski, Theodore J., CPA. "Strategies for the Social Security Safety Net." *The Tax Adviser* (December 2011).

Section 415(c) of the Internal Revenue Code, *U.S. Master Tax Guide 2014.* CCH.

"Setting the Record Straight on the Mortgage Interest Deduction." NAHB (July 25, 2013).

Slemrod, Joel and Jon Bakija. *Taxing Ourselves,* Fourth Edition. Cambridge, MA: the MIT Press, 2008.

Social Security in the 21st Century, edited by Eric R. Kingston, James H. Schulz, (Oxford University Press, New York 1997)

Social Security Online Trust Fund Data. Office of the Chief Actuary. Social Security and Medicare Tax Rates (2011).

South Carolina v. Baker. 485 US 505. 1988. As cited in Jay Starkman's book.

Starkman, Jay. *The Sex of a Hippopotamus, a Unique History of Taxes and Accounting.* Atlanta: Twinset Inc., 2008.

Sullivan, Martin A. *Corporate Tax Reform.* New York: Apress, 2011.

"The Tax Break-Down. The State and Local Tax Deduction." The Committee for a Responsible Federal Budget (August 20, 2013).

"Tax Foundation" report cited in 24/7Wallst.com. April 2, 2014.

Tax Reform Act of 2014 Discussion Draft, February 2014. House Ways and Means Committee.

Timmons, Bascom N. *Garner of Texas—A Personal History.* New York: Harper & Brothers, 1948.

The 1965 Amendments established under Title XVIII of the Social Security Act.

2001 Tax Legislation: Law, Explanation and Analysis; Economic Growth and Tax Relief Reconciliation Act of 2001. Chicago: CCH Incorporated, 2001.

2011 Statistics of Income, Corporation Income Tax Returns, Department of the Treasury, Internal Revenue Service. Commissioner John A. Koskinen (June 2014).

2014 U.S. Master Tax Guide. Chicago: CCH, 2013.

Urban-Brookings Tax Policy Center, table T12-0168, Aggregate AMT Projections and Recent History, 1970–2022.

"U.S. Corporations Pay 35%," cited Tax Foundation. *Wall Street Journal*, editorial page (October 26, 2013).

War Revenue Act of 1917, chapter 63, Sec. 1201(2). 1917.

Worth, Richard, *Social Security Act*, (Marshall Cavendish Corporation, Tarrytown, NY 2011)

INDEX

B

Baker, Howard, 31
Baker, James, 308
Bartlett, Bruce, 172
base erosion and profit shifting (BEPS), 265
basic framework (framework), 1-3, 30, 35, 37, 39
Baucus, Max, 309
Bipartisan Policy Center (BPC), 31, 34, 67, 95, 105, 195, 204, 220, 229, 300
  BPC Tax Reform Plan, 31
  Housing Commission, 195
Bipartisan Tax Fairness and Simplification Act of 2011, 95, *311*
Birnbaum, Jeffrey H., 373, 377, 380
Blinder, Alan, 65
Bloomberg, Michael, 272
Boortz, Neal, 25
Bowles, Erskine, 26, 30-31, 51-52, 67, 78-79, 95-96, 105, 118, 142-43, 173-74, 184, 196, 204-5, 212, 214, 229, 310, 314
  Simpson-Bowles Commission, 31, 51, 78-79, 105, 142, 173, 204, 214, 229, 314
  Simpson-Bowles tax reform plan, 31, 96
bracket creep, 297
Bradley, Bill, 64, 77, 79, 308
Bradley-Gephardt Fair Tax Act (Bradley-Gephardt), 77
brief history of our federal taxes, 7, 9, 11
British parliament, 7
broaden the tax base, 41, 320
Brookings Institution, 191-92, 199

Brudvik, Arthur Johann (Arthur), 12, 313
Bryan, William Jennings, 7
Budgetary Impact of Tax Reform Act of 2014 (table 7.1-3), 273
Buffet, Warren, 286
Burman, Leonard, 85
Bush, George H. W., 10, 66, 137, 236
Bush, George W., 10, 102-3
Bush, George W. administration, 102
Bush tax cuts, 104
business interest expense, 275, 321
Byrd (senator), 223

C

Cadillac insurance, 162
Cadillac tax, 162-63, 251
cafeteria plan, 47, 161
Camp, David, 270, 308-9, 311, 320
Canada (Canadian), 70, 78, 227
cap and trade, 300
capital asset, 58, 338
capital gains and dividends, 29, 32, 59, 61, 63, 65, 67, 69, 71, 73, 75, 93, 167-71, 318, 325
capital gains and losses, 58-59
capital gains on assets transferred at death, 155, 223-25, 227, 229
  constructive realization, 226
  estate tax, 26, 200, 221-28, 230, 278-89, 304, 317, 361
  Merchants Loan and Trust Co. v. Smietanka, 59
  Revenue Act of 1921, *221*
capital gains on noncash contributions, 213-14
capital gains rates, 13, 68, 93, 114
carbon tax, 300-301
Carlyle, Thomas, 307
carried interest, 72-75, 348